Vatican II Renewal

Path to the Future of the Church

to Bob & Valerie,

God's Blessings,

Fr. Joe Eagan, SJ.

Pray for Francis & Renewal

Joseph F. Eagan, S.J.

Pope Francis Washing Feet

ISBN: 148417254X
ISBN-13: 978-1484172544

Imprimi potest. Thomas Lawler, S.J., Wisconsin Provincial

Contents

Part IV: A World Church

Part V: A Church for the Future

This book is gratefully dedicated
to brother Jesuit
Francis, Bishop of Rome,
Spirit-called to renew the Church

and

In gratitude to valued friends,
St. Patrick's Young Couples Group *
St. Anselm's Renew Group*
St. Anselm Book Group II
St. Patrick's Laurence Garces Group
Arrupe Social Justice Group
See Acknowledgements

Acknowledgments

This book is the happy result of the prodding and support of wonderful people to whom I am immensely grateful, more than these few words can convey.

Without the five-year-prodding of my esteemed luncheon partner, Ray Colman, this book would not have seen the light of day. Over veal and red wine, we discussed theology, the Church, liturgy, politics, the Giants and 49'ers and the world in general, with the oft-repeated refrain "You must revise and upgrade *Restoration and Renewal!* Further prodding came from members of my two parish book-discussion groups who chose, as their year's book to read and discuss, *Restoration and Renewal.* At each session I jotted down their insightful critiques and suggestions which were greatly helpful once I started to write this book. With appreciation I here recognize each member whose insights, spirited discussions, and delightful companionship made our bi-weekly gatherings so enriching.

St. Patrick's Young Couples Group, together for ten years: Ray Colman, Cristine Dewey, Dr. Pat and Jennifer Finley, Joan Foley, Debbie Bellings-Kee, Andrew and Deanna La Greca, Ken and Jeanne Lombardi, John and Ruth Lynch, Bill and Jennifer Ryan. They interpreted for me the Catholic Church through their experience as marriage partners, young fathers and mothers, and business-work persons.

St. Anselm's Renew group of mainly retired persons whose 14 years together were ones of stimulating discussions, rich sharing and companionship: Jody Becker, Dr. Jack and Maureen Bennett, Tom Bertelsen, Vivian Felton, Judge Gene and Jeanne Lynch, Mack and Jeanne Miller, Bob and Joan Rorick, Mary Ruane, Margy Sheehy, John and Maria

Weiser. Their backgrounds in business, family and devoted Catholic life, and wide-ranging reading made their suggestions immeasurably helpful to me.

I owe much to so many persons of talent and experience who generously supported me during the two-years writing: Two especially, Maureen Bennett (wide-ranging reader, active in many causes) and John Weiser (lawyer, business executive, author), both esteemed friends, painstakingly read each chapter as I sent it to them and made excellent suggestions. Archbishop Rembert Weakland, former superior general of the worldwide Benedictine communities and retired archbishop of Milwaukee, shared his gracious and wise advice from his many years' pastoral and administrative experience. Dr. Hamilton Hess, patristics scholar and colleague, for his careful reading and critique. Walter Stohrer, wise philosophy professor and valued friend, for generously reading my manuscript and making insightful comments. Fellow Jesuits, scholars and friends, James Bretzke, Boston College moral theologian, Marquette University theology professors Thomas Hughson, John Laurence, Thomas Sweetser and David Schultenover, author and editor of *Theological Studies,* provided ready advice and encouragement.

I thank the following "Roman experts" who so generously gave me lengthy interviews on the workings and state of the church and insight into the "climate" of the Vatican: Cardinal Walter Kasper, theologian, former member of the Roman Curia and head of the Pontifical Council for Promoting Christian Unity; James Puglisi, ecumenism expert and Director of Rome's *Centro pro Unione*; Michael Gallagher, dean of Rome's Gregorian University; Robert Taft, prolific author, Orthodox scholar-expert and professor in the Gregorian's Russicum; Keith Pecklers, liturgist, author, Gregorian professor; Norm Tanner, Vatican II expert and author; Stephen Lopes, secretary in the Congregation of the Doctrine of the Faith; Peter Gumpert, Postulator for the Cause of the Saints; Terrence Kennedy, moral theologian, professor of the Alphonsiana University.

I am also grateful to the following who graciously helped me in a variety of ways: Tom Fox, Publisher and long-time editor of *National Catholic Reporter,* for his advice, inspiration and friendship over many years; Tom Bertelsen whose vision and generosity made possible the services of a graduate research student; John Allen, Rome correspondent for the *National Catholic Reporter,* prolific author and expert on today's Catholic Church, for sharing with me his "reading" of the Vatican and the Church today; Dr. Diana and Dr. Francis Parnell, most gracious friends who opened their home to me on my trips back to California to confer with Maureen and John mentioned above and with members of my book-discussion groups, and who read portions of the manuscript and offered expert insights; my two past Jesuit superiors James Gladstone and Patrick Burns and present "boss" Jonathon Haschka for their constant understanding and support, so important and appreciated; finally, thanks to my fellow retired-Jesuit brothers here at Camillus for encouraging while enduring me during the long days of writing.

Special words of thanks to graduate student Erin Zion, my research assistant, for her ever-prompt, professional work so generously and effectively carried out; she voluntarily read each chapter, making valuable suggestions that often reflected her experience as a young doctoral student and practicing Catholic in today's youth culture. And to Tyler Nass, computer expert, for his patience and valuable assistance, always graciously and generously given; without his skill in the final stages of publishing, this book would not have seen the light of day.

To all the above, my profound thanks.

Abbreviations

These 11 Vatican II documents treated throughout this book are identified by the following two letters in parentheses, the first two words of the original Latin text. A few other often-used abbreviations are also given.

AA *Apostolicam Actuositatem*: Decree on the Apostolate of the Laity

CD *Christus Dominus:* Decree on the Pastoral Office of Bishops in the Church

AG *Ad Gentes*: Decree on the Church's Missionary Activity

DH *Dignitatis Humanae*: Declaration on Religious Freedom

DV *Dei Verbum*: Dogmatic Constitution on Divine Revelation

GS *Gaudium et Spes*: Pastoral Constitution on the Church in the Modern World

LG *Lumen Gentium*: Dogmatic Constitution on the Church

NA *Nostra Aetate*: Declaration on the Relationship of the Church to the Non-Christian Religions

PC *Perfectae Caritatis*: Decree on the Appropriate Renewal of Religious Life

SC   *Sacrosanctum Concilium*: Constitution on the Sacred Liturgy

UR   *Unitatis Redintegratio*: Decree on Ecumenism

Other Abbreviations:

BEM Baptism, Eucharist and Ministry (Faith and Order Commission)

CDF Congregation for the Doctrine of the Faith (Roman Curia)

WCC World Council of Churches (Geneva, Switzerland)

Introduction

I recommend that the footnotes at the end of each chapter be read as part of the text. Many provide an interesting window onto the cotemporary Catholic Church with information and often refreshingly frank quotations from bishops, theologians and scholars on important church problems and needs today.

Four historic events within a period of six months occurred at the end of 2012 and the early months of 2013 that have much significance for the Catholic Church and bring a promise of hope to weary and disheartened Catholics.

The 50th anniversary celebration of the Second Vatican Council brought universal interest in that event of October 11, 1962, when approximately 2400 bishops from all over the Catholic world met in Rome for the Second Vatican Council in answer to Pope John XXIII's stirring call to update and renew the Catholic Church and recover the broken unity of the separated Christian churches. His metaphor of "opening the windows to let in fresh air" captured the bishops' imagination and that of Catholics and other Christians raising hopes worldwide of a church more in touch with the times. Convinced they were guided by the Holy Spirit, during four years of multiple speeches, debate and often sharp disagreements over competing visions of the church, the bishops presented one billion Catholics with an almost breath-taking program for church renewal and an exciting way to be church in the 21st century. In the United States, this anniversary inspired a deluge of articles and timely books[1] by scholars calling attention to the council's achievements and providing Catholics unfamiliar with the council appreciation of its rich teaching and grand vision of renewal.

Then on Feb. 11, 2013, Pope Benedict XVI shocked the world with his announcement of resignation as spiritual leader of 1.3 billion Catholics to take effect Feb. 28. His humble, prayerful and courageous act elicited universal praise and admiration. Papal scholars recognized that his resignation makes possible a new understanding of the papal office and its exercise: the papacy is an office in the church that the pope holds as successor of Peter and not a personal possession of power and pomp; the consequent distinction between the pope as rock of unity and of communion and the multiple roles that have accrued to popes through centuries including that of administration; the emphasis on the pope as bishop of Rome, therefore a fellow bishop and member of the apostolic college, thus strengthening the principle of collegiality so championed by the Second Vatican Council.

Practical consequences of Benedict's act are the freedom of future popes to resign; a demystifying of the papacy and a de-sacralization of the growing cult of the pope over the past 150 years; a blunting of the often-heard criticism of the pope as the last absolute monarch; a new context for lessening the over-centralization of authority in Rome decried by so many bishops; and the possibility of national bishops' conferences exercising some papal administrative roles such as choosing bishops and holding regional synods.

Benedict's humble act may be viewed as his final teaching, an important magisterial moment in the life of the church, his gift and legacy as pope.

Following Benedict's resignation, 113 Cardinal electors met in Rome to choose the next pope. This period before the conclave election of the *sede vacante* (empty seat of the pope's chair, symbol of authority) gave the Cardinals chances to know each other, assess their qualities to be pope, and discuss the needs of the worldwide Catholic

Church. It also provided them the opportunity to speak candidly and publicly about pressing church problems.[2] Consensus soon emerged that governance of the church and reform of the Roman Curia were major concerns that must be addressed in the light of recent problems in the Vatican.[3] During this period some archbishops and bishops, priests and papal scholars felt free to speak publicly of specific issues they felt the future pope should address.[4] Leading up to the conclave, the Catholic Church received unusual publicity in the press and TV, generally favorable and giving much interesting information. Front runners to be pope were publicized and even given betting odds. Pope watchers quoted the wise saying: "Enter the conclave pope, come out a Cardinal!"

The evening of March 13 white smoke rose above St. Peter's basilica announcing an election. On the fifth ballot the Cardinals chose the Jesuit archbishop of Buenas Aires, Argentina, Cardinal Jorge Bergoglio as the 265th successor of St. Peter, chosen rock of his church by Jesus. He took the name Francis to honor the humble, poor St. Francis of Assisi. Theologian Leonardo Boff of Brazil, captured the significance of the new pope's choice: "Francis isn't just a name; it's a plan for a church that is poor, simple, gospel-centered and devoid of power. It is a church that walks the way together with the lost and least … with communities of brothers and sisters."[5]

With his words and actions and personal warmth, Francis captured the affection of the thousands filling St. Peter's huge piazza and millions watching TV across the world. His first act of asking the vast crowd to pray for and bless him was rich in meaning and theological significance: the pope is a humble servant of the church, one with his people in need of God's help. This simple act recognized the priesthood of the people of God and of their gifts for the mission of the church. Francis was careful to refer to himself as bishop of Rome, bearer of an office of service rather than pope as personal possessor of power and pomp.

His homily at his inauguration Mass again emphasized his Petrine ministry as one of humble service to "protect all of God's people and embrace with tender affection the whole of humanity, especially the poorest, the weakest, the least important, those whom Matthew lists in the final judgment in love: the hungry, the thirsty, the stranger, the sick and those in prison." He said he realized his new ministry included "a certain power," the same power Jesus confirmed on Peter, a power of service. "Let us never forget that *authentic* power is service and that the pope too when exercising power must enter more fully into that service which has its radiant culmination in the cross."

Francis concluded his homily on a note of hope. "to protect creation, to protect every man and woman, to look upon them with tenderness and love, to open a horizon of hope ... to bring the warmth of hope." [6]

The events of those 30 days in February and March have changed the church, released a new energy, and brought joy and hope to a church whose challenges remain great and scandals yet real!

The cover design seeks to capture this energy: green ... springtime ... new life ... joy and hope ... renewal ... humble service ... the poor ... Pope Francis, bishop, washing feet!

This Book

This book is about the Second Vatican Council and the contemporary Catholic Church. My goal in writing is to present the renewal/reform program mandated by this Spirit-inspired ecumenical council of the Catholic Church as the sure way to address the church's pressing problems and urgent needs and the path to her promising future. This necessarily involves treating in depth the council's theological teaching and practical achievements and discussing honestly and respectfully the church's current crises and urgent challenges. My hope is that today's church capitalize on her rich tradition and attractive goodness, her strengths and many values, in this way to regain her lost credibility and retain her members.

This means today's church, leaders and people alike, seriously listen to the prophetic voices of those Catholic men and women and priests who in their call for renewal and change represent what the council called the *sense of the faithful* and recognize and act upon those *signs of the times* within the church and in the world through which the Holy Spirit speaks today. The conviction that pervades these pages is that the full implementation of Vatican II in the life of the church is able to invigorate the Catholic Church, restore hope to Catholics, inspire young persons, and challenge some at least who have walked away to reconsider and perhaps return.

At the outset I wish to make clear that while treating crises and challenges in the church today and recognizing the complex issues involved, I attempt to present with appreciation, fairness and respect the values that both liberal and traditional Catholics hold dear and seek to protect. For both are motivated by love for the church. I also wish to acknowledge that despite the priest abuse tragedy and the failure of so many American bishops, we should not overlook bishops' pastoral dedication, their many personal gifts and impressive accomplishments: commitment to Catholic social teaching, to the poor and to the dignity of human life in all its manifestations, and the variety and quality of their pastoral letters.

The Catholic Church Today

Despite its rich spiritual heritage and the enormous good the Catholic Church does, a growing chorus today describes the church, especially in Europe and America, as being in crisis. The emeritus archbishop of San Francisco, John R. Quinn, stated "We are at a critical point in the life of the Church. He compared it "to the magnitude of the crisis of the **Reformation**," an astonishing statement.[7]

The immediate cause of this crisis was the widening revelation of priests who sexually abused minors and the double failure of many bishops to care for the victims of abuse they are called to shepherd and their concealment viewed as preserving the institutional church's reputation. The result has been much anger on the part of Catholics in the United States, Europe and beyond, their exodus from the church in increasing numbers,[8] and a massive loss of credibility in the church's leadership. This crisis has triggered unprecedented calls for change on the part of loyal and deeply concerned Catholics and by church leaders, bishops and archbishops, who speak out for reform.[9]

Before the tragedy of abuse and bishops' concealment broke on Catholics, serious problems were becoming apparent. Many cite the following crises-problems.

- The loss of the Eucharist, the center of Catholic life, for its members because of the alarming shortage of priests in many areas throughout the world.
- The unfortunate dismissal of the church as irrelevant by educated young and older Catholics.[10]
- The large number of Catholics who leave the church, many to join other churches.
- The alienation from the church of scores of Catholic women, often the most highly educated and motivated, and the loss of their gifts for the life of the church.
- The serious loss of confidence in church leadership despite competent, caring individual bishops.

In a candid letter to his archbishop, one practicing Catholic layman expressed reasons for his loss of confidence.

The church is in a crisis because all power and decision-making are concentrated in a self-perpetuating clerical hierarchy. The hope of shared responsibility by lay and clergy so elegantly articulated in Vatican II has never come to fruition. ... As a result educated Roman Catholics both young and old are leaving. Parishes are closing due to lack of attendance and shortage of priests. ... The institutional church lacks both transparency and accountability. ... I say this [out] of concern for the future of the church.

A significant crisis-problem is the painful polarization within the Catholic Church in the United States and elsewhere between those committed to Vatican II's renewal and those desiring restoration of a more traditional church alleged to have existed in a golden age before the council. Twenty years after the council, Vatican II began to be challenged, re-interpreted and in some cases rejected, what Bishop Kevin Dowling termed a "dismantling of the renewal of the Second Vatican Council." [11]

Today, three interdependent interpretations exemplify this reaction to Vatican II.

- *Restoration* is the effort to recover and restore traditional values, teachings, discipline and practices of the period before Vatican II alleged to have been lost or distorted since the council. The term 'restoration' was first used by then Cardinal Joseph Ratzinger in an interview given to an Italian journalist. The Cardinal felt that Vatican II was not correctly understood which led to errors and excesses in theology and Catholic practice and was "disastrous for the church" resulting in a "progressive process of decadence." Those particularly guilty were progressive theologians, priests, sisters, lay Catholics, even some bishops. His solution was a two-fold return to the council's "true spirit." He defined restoration as "the search for a new balance after all the exaggerations of an indiscriminate opening to the world." [12]

- The *reform of the reform* is the expression used to describe the new translation of the Mass introduced in Advent 2011 as a *reform* that replaced Pope Paul VI's Roman Missal which was the original *reform* of the Latin Mass used for three centuries. This expression has also come to be applied to the current *reform* movement to re-interpret the renewal/reform of the Second Vatican Council.
- The *hermeneutic* (interpretation) *of continuity* stresses that Vatican II is in full continuity to Catholic tradition and seeks to de-emphasize the renewal/reform of the council. The opposite *hermeneutic of discontinuity with rupture* is the pejorative characterization of the council used by conservatives to justify the restoration and the reform of the reform.

However, Benedict XVI, in his Christmas 2005 talk to the Roman Curia, proposed a *hermeneutic of continuity and reform* that Vatican II did in fact involve significant new theological insights and elements of change and reform while remaining in substantial continuity with the tradition of the church.[13]

In announcing the Second Vatican Council, John XXIII prayed for an outpouring of the Holy Spirit. It clearly happened during the four years of the council. For an evaluation of the renewal in the Catholic Church today, see chapter one, Council of Change, concluding section, "Vatican II Renewal in the Church Today," and chapter four, Momentous Change, Liturgy/Sacraments, for "Evaluation of the Renewal of the Liturgy since the Council."

Reform

I rely on criteria proposed by the Dominican theologian-ecclesiologist Yves Congar in his classic *True and False Reform in the Church,* a work that influenced the bishops at Vatican II.[14]

Following the principle, *ecclesia semper reformanda,* the church always in need of reform, Congar distinguishes between the "concrete life of the church" and "practices and state of affairs" of the community of the faithful including her ordained hierarchy, which are open to reform, and the church's "essential structures," bishops and pope, the sacramental system, revealed Word of God, which as fundamental are not subject to change. Based on this distinction, true reform, he cautions,

- is motivated by love of the church and by pastoral concern for the needs of the entire church, members and church leaders;
- is carried out respectfully in communion with the church's teaching and governing offices;
- is patient with delay by church leaders out of respect for the complexity of reform-change and the historical consequences of hasty, imprudent change;[15] and
- is in full accord with the tradition of the church which is not static but develops dynamically.

The Catholic Church is currently experiencing a profound purification from which a new humility and fresh life may emerge. Meeting the challenge of reform is a hoped-for response to the 'enormous opportunity' and 'special moment' the Spirit may be offering the church at this period in her journey with her new leader, Pope Francis. Past crises in the church were often grace-filled periods that led to renewed health and growth. This reform longed for by her lay members, priests and many bishops is a huge challenge to the Catholic Church today.

Accordingly, in the spirit of Congar's conditions for true reform and inspired by the renewal mandated by the Second Vatican Council, this book raises these issues. What are the serious implications of the Vatican II renewal for the church today? What is the proper emphasis between authority centralized in the Vatican and exercised by the local churches of the Catholic world? Does the church need to achieve a balance between a prophetic church of pastoral service and practical Gospel love and a church accused of overly emphasizing authority and obedience? What is the appropriate relationship between an internal looking church and one actively involved in the needs of the world today? Does the Catholic Church need conversion, letting go of historical accretions and embracing the risk of change and reform in her governance practices so that Gospel values may shine through more clearly? Are both church leaders and members seriously responding to John XXIII's 'signs of the times' through which the Spirit speaks to the church and to the council's emphasis on the 'sense of the faithful'? What difficult decisions and changes are necessary for the church to be more transparently the sacrament of Christ to its own members and the world at large? Is change possible today?

Change

In a second career as associate pastor in a large urban parish, I came to know men and women who valued their Catholic faith and deeply loved the church. In three book-discussion groups on spirituality and the contemporary church over a period of 14 years,[16] I experienced their strongly-felt concerns. In addition to the crises-problems just listed, they felt that many church leaders do not seriously listen to the Catholic people or accept the consequences of the Spirit present in every baptized member of the church, that "we who are the church have no voice in the decisions affecting us," and that the church is not sufficiently meeting the spiritual needs of its members. With concern they ask "What is the future of our church?" "Will or can the church change?"

A major theme of this book is the urgency of reform-change in today's church. Some may object that change is not a major need of the Catholic Church today. Many good Catholics rightly point to the strengths and values of the church (see chapter 17): Eucharist and sacraments, parish life, dedicated priests and deacons, religious men and women, the church's worldwide care for the sick, the poor, and the hungry and being in the forefront of the fight to protect human rights, the sacredness of human life, and the family. Others caution against the potential disruptions and uncertainty of too abrupt change.

Yet the slow pace of the Vatican II renewal and the crises and problems noted above have resulted in a growing number of calls for change from priests in Europe and the United States and by some bishops speaking out.[17] Change is also the subject of articles in Catholic magazines, journals and newspapers, and is discussed in books by scholars.

The failure of church leaders to respond to Catholics' desire for change is a cause of their discouragement and loss of confidence today. It is important that church leaders understand the depth of this experience among many Catholics and their priests today. As one retired archbishop acknowledged "Church leaders must begin to listen to the reasons for the discontent that exists among Catholics and take them seriously."

Change is understandably difficult for those exercising authority. The Holy Father and the world's bishops in collegial communion with him bear the awesome responsibility of governing the church in a way that preserves Christ's teaching, the rich Catholic Tradition, and the unity of the worldwide Catholic Church, and of maintaining needed discipline. From the lessons of centuries, church leaders know that not all change is constructive.

This book advocates changes that many today agree are necessary and urgent (chapters 15 and 16) but some of which are not yet acceptable to church leaders. I attempt to treat such issues respectfully and while adhering to the church's magisterium,

Overview

This Introduction situates the Second Vatican Council in today's Catholic Church: her crises and challenges, her need for reform-change, and the hope for her future under the leadership of Francis I. The first two chapters establish the foundation for the entire book. The first presents the totally unexpected event of Vatican II, describes the most important debates between the progressive and conservative bishops over competing visions of the church that cast light on much of the polarization in the church today, and explains the seven most important documents of Vatican II that contain the council's vision for a renewed Catholic Church. Chapter two treats how the church functions in its governance structure aided by its professional theologians. This involves explaining the magisterium or teaching office of the church and clarifying the critical role of theologians and of "doing theology" better to understand church teaching and the development of doctrine that makes change and renewal possible.

Chapters three through seven show how the Second Vatican Council enriched the understanding of the Catholic Church both as divine mystery and people of God, transformed the way Catholics worship and approach God in three key sacraments, and sought to renew the essential role of bishops and the pope in serving the church. Chapter eight celebrates the gifts that religious communities of women and men bring to the church.

Chapter nine is devoted to the very reason for the church's existence: her exciting mission of bringing the good news of Jesus Christ and his salvation to the world. In its evangelizing mission this involves inculturating the Gospel message and planting the church in new cultures that lack a Christian presence. Chapter 10 treats the rich array of helps the church provides its members to develop their own spirituality and discusses the diversity of world spiritualities.

Chapters 11-14 explain the enormous influence of Vatican II on four great but often not-well-known or appreciated resources the Catholic Church offers her members and the world: the contemporary Christian ecumenical movement, the extensive Catholic social teaching, Latin American liberation theology and the theologies it influenced, and development within Catholic moral theology today.

The final four chapters examine the future of the church as one of hope. Chapters 15 and 16 discuss as major grace-filled opportunities 12 urgent challenges the Catholic Church faces; chapter 17 describes the church's many strengths and core-values coming from her rich 2000-year tradition; the final chapter 18 concludes on a note of hope. It describes the legacy of Vatican II as the path to the church's future, considers five challenges before the church universal, proposes four pastoral programs for the church in the United States, and reflects on the risk of change and the church's future as full of hope.

Each chapter features questions for discussion and further study and a list of several books chosen for their current interest, important information, and ease of reading. A more-detailed bibliography arranged according to the book's five parts precedes a glossary of technical terms identified in bold in each of the chapters. Where appropriate, chapters include an evaluation of the status of Vatican II's renewal in the church today with a view to her future. This often involves discussing tensions between the opposing visions of the church by progressives and conservatives and their efforts to achieve the right balance for the good of the church. These differences came to the fore again and again during the Second Vatican Council, are present today, and will likely continue for years to come since the urgently needed Vatican II renewal/reform of the church is an unfinished work still in progress.

Readership

In 1994, as a result of the growing polarization in the church concerning the council's program of renewal along with ignorance and lack of interest in Vatican II, I wrote *Restoration and Renewal: the Church in the Third Millennium*[18] that grew out of 20 years' teaching theology of the church to undergraduate and graduate students at the University of San Francisco. From discussions in and out of class, I came to appreciate their search for meaning and spirituality and their genuine interest in the church. I soon realized that for them Vatican II had little significance. They had not experienced the pre-Vatican II Church and the need for change. They lacked knowledge of the council, its documents, accomplishments and importance for the church. This too is the case for many Catholics not yet 50 years of age.

Accordingly, I write this present book with the following persons in mind.

- The thousands of faithful Catholics who are dispirited, impatient for renewal and who long for change but see little chance of it occurring; who seek a voice in the church but who have none, for the women and men who are the treasure of the church and her hope for the future.
- Those Catholics, young and older, who lack knowledge of the council or who, confused by the changes it inaugurated, are unaware of the theological and historical reasons for the renewal and the resulting changes.
- The many young people today, spiritual but not religious, who in their search for meaning and spirituality might be surprised and encouraged by how much the renewed Vatican II church offers them.

- And especially for all those who accept the vision of Vatican II and its renewal as gospel, great good news.19

The following groups will find this book helpful and highly informative.

- Parish study and discussion groups who wish to understand the contemporary church and its Vatican II renewal and to participate in the New Evangelization and benefit by the Year of Faith.
- Senior high and college/university students as informative class text or supplementary reading.
- Our sisters and brothers in other Christian churches and in the great world religions who may find this work informative and helpful in understanding the Catholic Church and their Catholic friends.

Despite depressing news and yet unmet urgent needs, there are abundant reasons for Catholics to be optimistic and hopeful for the church they love: the recent election of the first pope from Latin America, a man with broad pastoral experience, a love and care for the poor, and an example of humility and openness;[20] the gift of the Second Vatican Council whose renewal is far advanced in the church; highly educated and concerned Catholic women and men exercising their baptismal gifts in mission, politics, health care and church ministry;[21] the church's rich heritage and impressive strengths along with her remarkable ability to renew and reform herself; above all, the Holy Spirit alive in the church inspiring leaders and members alike.

In this spirit, I write this present book out of a deep love and admiration for the Catholic Church. My constant endeavor in seeking to present frankly and faithfully her limitations and sinfulness, yet her many strengths and values, is that the church better serve her members in imitation of her Lord, fulfill her mission of evangelizing the world, and thus become a shining *Light to the Nations,* the title of Vatican II's key document, *Constitution on the Church.*

I also offer this book in gratitude for the Catholic Church, my spiritual home, and in hope and optimism for her future. For today's Vatican II Catholic Church in her best moments is alive with the Spirit. Her unresolved issues, inner tensions, and painful divisions are the vital signs of a living organism that grows and develops as it adapts to changing environments. She is a church of modern holiness; a heroic church of martyrs in its struggle for justice and human rights; a genuinely respected church in her consistent voice for moral values, human rights and the dignity of each human person, for her commitment to the poor, and for her recent Popes - Blessed John XXIII, Paul VI, John Paul I, Blessed John Paul II and Benedict XVI and their leadership on the world stage. For these and more, the church is indeed good news for her members, for other Christians, and for the world. She seeks, despite sinfulness and contemporary problems, to be the sacrament or sign to the world of the risen Christ and his salvation. Her deepest reality is mystery. To know more fully this human-divine church is an enriching, exciting experience.

I hope these pages provide such an experience and give confident hope of a positive future for the Catholic Church under the leadership of Pope Francis.

Further Reading

LaBelle, Jeffrey, S.J., and Dan Kendall, S.J. *Being Catholic in a Changing World.* Mahwah, NJ: Paulist Press, 2009. This very readable book discusses key issues of Catholics in society today. Some questions posed are "Can I disagree with the church and still remain a good Catholic?" and "What does it mean to be a Catholic in the post 9/11 world?'

Lakeland, Paul. *Catholicism at the Crossroads: How the Laity Can Save the Church.* New York: Continuum, 2007. This challenging book by a noted author and theology professor is for "adult Catholics who want an adult church that can sustain adult faith." With frankness and honesty he deals with major problems in the Church and suggests "Ten Steps toward a More Adult Church."

Meme, Kevin and Jeffrey J. Guhen. *Youth and Catholic in America.* Mahwah, NJ: Paulist Press, 2010. This book is a collection of essays by a talented group of 18 young adult Catholic men and women who write with brutal honesty of their struggles and joys of being Catholic today. It is a fascinating window to what the future of the Catholic Church will look like.

Steinfels, Peter. *A People Adrift, the Crisis of the Roman Catholic Church in America.* New York: Simon and Schuster, 2003. This carefully researched and readable book attributes the Church's multiple crises to the abuse scandal, polarization in the Church, and current problems involving liturgy, Catholic education, sexuality and church leadership.

Footnotes

1   Massimo Faggioli, *Vatican II: the Battle for Meaning.* (Mahwah, NJ: Paulist Press, 2012; Richard R. Gaillardetz and Catherine E. Clifford, *Keys to the Council, Unlocking the Teaching of Vatican II* (Collegeville, MN: Liturgical Press, 2011); Greg Tobin, *The Good Pope John XXIII and Vatican II: The Making of a Saint and the Remaking of the Church* (New York: Harper One, 2012); William Madges and Michael J. Daley, *Vatican II: Fifty Personal Stories* (Maryknoll, NY: Orbis Books, 2012); Margaret Lavin, *Vatican II: Fifty Years of Evolution and Revolution in the Catholic Church,* (St. Paul's Publications, 2012).

2   England's Cardinal Cormac Murphy O'Connor stated "there is no doubt that today there needs to be reform in the church, especially of governance." Cardinal Cristoph Schonborn of Vienna spoke of "reform in the administration of the Vatican" and "the heads of curial offices."

3   "Vati-leaks" that revealed corruption in Vatican finances, infighting among curial officials, and the Vatican handling of priest abusers and of bishops who failed to act and were not brought to account.

4   Bishop Thomas Burns identified "freedom to discuss key ministerial concerns currently prohibited and issues affecting marriage; re-examining ethical questions, developing a simpler and humbler church model, one less hierarchical and more collegial, stripped of status and elitism; promoting Vatican II's principle

of subsidiarity; improving relations between the Holy See and dioceses." *The Tablet*, March 2, 2013, 4. *The Tablet* editorialized that "the papacy is over-centralized and the principle of collegiality, one of the most important ideas to emerge from the Second Vatican Council, has been neglected . . . the voices of the laity be heard, not least women." Feb. 23, 2013, p 2.

5   Thomas C. Fox, "Leonardo Boff: Major Pope Francis Supporter," *National Catholic Reporter,* Mar. 16, 2013.

6   http:/en.radiovaticana.va/print_page.asp?c=674758.

7   April 13, 2010 address at the Federation of Priests' Councils in Houston. Talks given at a March, 2003 conference, *Governance, Accountability and the Future of the Catholic Church,* confirmed the magnitude of the crisis. John McGreevy viewed the fallout from the sexual abuse scandal as having "no parallel in the [American] church's history." Gerard Manion feared the scandal might lead "to the demise of Catholic Ireland." John Bean spoke of "betrayals of trust and abuses of power" and called "the lack of truthfulness the modern church's besetting sin."

8   In Austria alone the daily *Der Standard* reported that 201,705 Catholics left the Catholic Church in the five-year period 2004-08 with 53,216 leaving in 2009 and 87,000 just in 2010. In Germany 180,000 Catholics "out of deep disgust at the sex abuse scandals," left the church in 2010, an increase of 40% over 2009, according to a poll by the German Catholic weekly, *Christ und Welt.* Many are "committed Catholics ... seriously concerned about the church. They have despaired of it and lost hope." One person, referring to bishops' handling of the priest abuse scandal, said "The church is on parole."

9   Cardinal Cristoph Schonborn, the Archbishop of Vienna, stated that the Roman Curia "was urgently in need of reform adding that the church needs to reconsider its position on re-remarried divorcees (*The Tablet*, 8 May 2010): 30. Diarmuid Martin, Archbishop of Dublin, re-iterated the need for church reform and said that "the narrow culture of clericalism has to be eliminated." Bishop Kevin Dowling of Rustenburg, South Africa, emphasized that " if the church and its leadership professes to follow the Gospel and the principles of Catholic social teaching, its internal life, its methods of governing and its use of authority will

be scrutinized on the basis of what we profess." As one aspect of governance he believes "we should have a church ... where the leadership recognizes and empowers decision-making at the appropriate levels in the local church." *The National Catholic Reporter,* Vol. 46, No 20, 1, 9-10.

10 Referring to the church as "irrelevant to people," Bishop Kieran Conroy of Ireland said "the church is intolerant, demanding, exclusive. I think it has to re-present itself instead of simply blaming everything on the ills of society ... to become a little more tolerant, accessible, welcoming, compassionate." *The Tablet,* (July 10, 2010): 38.

11 Bishop Dowling described the "carefully-planned dismantling of the theology, ecclesiology, pastoral vision of ... Vatican II in order to restore a previous, or more controllable model of church through an increasingly centralized power structure ... which now controls every aspect in the life of the church through a network of Vatican Congregations by Cardinals who ensure strict compliance with what is decreed to be orthodox." Bishop Kevin Dowling, "Catholic Social Teaching Finds Church Leadership Lacking" [talk given June 1, 2010, Cape Town, South Africa, reported in] *National Catholic Reporter,* July 8, 2010.

12 Joseph Ratzinger with Vittorio Messori, *The Ratzinger Report: An Exclusive Interview on the State of the Church* (San Francisco: Ignatius Press 1985), 37-38. According to Arbuckle "Restorationism is ... the movement within the church towards the uncritical re-affirmation of pre-Vatican II structures and attitudes in reaction to the stress resulting from the theological and cultural turmoil generated by the changes of the council and the modern world at large." Gerald Arbuckle, *Refounding the Church,* (London: G. Chapman, 1993), 3-4.

13 For an analysis of these interpretations of Vatican II, see Joseph Komonchak, "Novelty in Continuity: Pope Benedict's Interpretation of Vatican II," *America,* Feb. 12, 2009.

14 Congar published *True and False Reform* in 1950 during the ferment for reform in France. In 1952 the Vatican Holy Office forbade its reprinting and translation into other languages. Pope John XXIII, who had read the book, invited Congar to attend Vatican II as a theological expert. He was a major influence in the

council's *Constitution on the Church* and *The Decree on Ecumenism.* In recognition of his contribution to the council, John Paul II made him a cardinal. Yves Congar, *True and False Reform in the Church* (Collegeville, MN: Liturgical Press, 2011)

15   Congar cautioned church "overseers" not to overly test the patience of Catholics! "We must ask overseers to be aware of the pressure on peoples' demands which threaten to explode some day because they have been held in check for too long." Congar, *op.cit.,* 289.

16   The three groups consisted of young married couples in their late twenties and early thirties; retired business and professional men and women; and those still active. All are university-educated, practicing Catholics. See Acknowledgements.

17   In 2011, 500 Austrian priests signed a statement *Call to Disobedience* calling for "massive church reform" of compulsory celibacy, women priests, laity allowed to preach, communion for divorced and remarried Catholics. Msgr. Schuler, founder of the group, *The Priests' Initiative,* said the word disobedience was a deliberate expression of "clear grievances and years of frustration." Four hundred priests signed a somewhat similar petition in Ireland. In an interview before his death, Cardinal Carlo Martini, former archbishop of Milan, Italy, stated "the church has to travel a radical journey of change."

18   Joseph F. Eagan, *Restoration and Renewal, the Church in the Third Millennium* (Kansas City, MO: Sheed and Ward, 1995). Reviewers' comments: "Three decades after the event, Vatican Council II is still the center of the Church's pastoral life and academic concerns. Fr. Eagan captures, with utmost honesty, both these aspects. His views are not always comfortable, but they are insightful and challenging." "An extraordinarily fine book, outstanding in its breadth, easy readability and balance." The Catholic Press Association awarded it first place for theology books published in the United States in 1995.

19   Cardinal Avery Dulles, the recently-deceased eminent ecclesiologist, called the church's efforts to incarnate Vatican II's theological insights into its life a "reshaping of Catholicism."

20 "With his experience as pastor, with a new view of things from below, he will be able to reform the [Roman] Curia, decentralize the administration [of the Vatican], and give the church a new and credible face." Leonardo Boff.

21 "Vatican II changed everything for ordinary Catholics by making clear ... that we all are equal in baptism, that baptism is our entry into mission ... [and to] truly own our church." Paul Lakeland, Catholicism at the Crossroads, How the Laity Can Save the Church (New York: Continuum, 2007), 5.

Chapter 1:
Vatican II, Council of Change

"…a major turning point in the history of Catholicism."[1]

"…conversion experience for the Roman Catholic Church."[2]

" …an event of the utmost importance in the almost two thousand year history of the church" and "the beginning of a new era in the life of the church.' John Paul II

"…the church's first official actualization as a world church."[3]

These comments capture the immense importance of the Second Vatican Council that brought 2400 Catholic bishops to Rome from 1962-1965. These bishops and archbishops, colorful Eastern Patriarchs and Cardinals from five continents and most countries of the world, were men of diverse cultures and contrasting experiences of being Catholic. During four years of intense debate, often over opposing understandings of the church, they gave one billion Catholics an exciting vision of a renewed church ready for the twenty-first century.

Vatican II has rightly been called the greatest event in the Catholic Church since the Protestant Reformation almost 500 years ago. In working out a program for the renewal and reform of the church in 16 documents, the bishops took the formidable risk of changing the 'unchangeable' church of the **Counter Reformation** period in the Catholic Church.[4] This chapter explains the seven most important of those documents that best express the bishops' overarching vision and program of renewal.

Better to understand and appreciate the precedent-breaking event of Vatican II, we first identify an ecumenical council and meet the extraordinary pope who stunned the Catholic world by calling this 21st Ecumenical Council of the Catholic Church.

An ecumenical or universal council is a meeting of all Catholic bishops and archbishops throughout the world convoked by the pope.[5] Councils were summoned to meet crises in the church, generally of a doctrinal or teaching nature, to clarify and express Christian teaching or to condemn a major error or **heresy** in Christian belief. The first ecumenical council in 325 in the city of Nicaea near Constantinople (modern Istanbul, Turkey) condemned Arianism, the heresy that Jesus is not equal to the Father in the trinity of persons and therefore not God. The second council in Constantinople in 381 formulated the teaching on the trinity of persons in one God expressed in the Nicene-Constantinopolitan creed recited during each Sunday Mass. A council can deal also with disciplinary matters as in the Counter-Reformation **Council of Trent**, named after the northern Italian city of Trent where it was held from 1545-1563. Here the bishops reformed church life and corrected abuses in addition to clarifying Catholic teaching challenged by Martin Luther and John Calvin and condemning some of their teachings. However, Vatican II was totally different.

The council was the inspiration of the beloved, elderly Pope John XXIII. Without his optimistic vision of the world and of the church and his humble trust in the Holy Spirit guiding the church, Vatican II would never have occurred. In calling the council and entrusting it to the bishops of the world, he took an enormous risk of change!

John XXIII

Angelo Roncalli, Cardinal Archbishop of Venice, was a grandfatherly man of 79 deliberately elected pope so that, as it was facetiously said, he would not " rock the boat" (the barque of Peter, the church) by being pope for a long period! John XXIII was a man unashamed of his peasant origin, a humble man blessed with a sense of humor and the common touch, a wise man of broad vision owing to his sense of history and his experience as **nuncio** (ambassador) in countries as diverse as Bulgaria and Turkey after World War I and France after World War II; above all, he was a prayerful, saintly man.

And so it was that this elderly pope of youthful spirit revealed that "by means of an impulse of Divine Providence [we] felt the urgency of the duty to call our sons together" and "... welcoming as from above the intimate voice of the Spirit we consider that the times now were right to offer to the Catholic Church and to the world the gift of a new ecumenical council." His optimistic intention was to apply the gospel of Christ to the great problems of the world by a renewed Catholic Church that more faithfully reflected Jesus' good news.[6]

In his official document of December 25, 1961 convening the council, John looked toward the modern world. He optimistically felt that "humanity is on the edge of a new era." He looked also at the division within the Christian churches and hoped that the council would provide both "doctrinal clarity and mutual charity" to inspire unity with our "separated brothers. To refer to Protestants and Orthodox as "our separated brothers" was a positive first for a pope. John closed his words with a beautiful prayer that the council would be for all Christians a new outpouring of the Spirit on earth. "Renew Your wonders in our time, as though for a new Pentecost, and grant that the holy Church ... may increase the reign of the Divine Savior, the reign of truth and justice, the reign of love and peace. Amen."[7]

John's positive, optimistic, world-embracing vision shone even more in the stirring address he gave to the 2540 bishops assembled in St. Peter's basilica in Vatican City for the opening session of Vatican II on October 11, 1962. Rarely has a pope publicly spoken like this!

In the daily exercise of our pastoral office, we sometimes have to listen, much to our regret, to voices of persons who, though burning with zeal, are not endowed with too much sense of discretion or measure. In these modern times they can see nothing but prevarication and ruin. ... We feel we must disagree with those prophets of gloom, who are always forecasting disaster, as though the end of the world were at hand. In the present order of things, Divine providence is leading us to a new order of human relations which, by men's own efforts and even beyond their very expectations, are directed toward the fulfillment of God's superior and inscrutable designs. And everything, even human differences, leads to the greater good of the church.

[The Church] must ever look to the present, to the new conditions and new forms of life introduced into the modern world which have opened new avenues to the Catholic apostolate.[8]

The "prophets of gloom" to whom John refers are members of the **Vatican (Roman) Curia** who opposed the ecumenical council and constantly put obstacles in its way.

Two phrases stand out in John's opening remarks: "signs of the times" and "*aggiornamento.*" John had a strong conviction that God spoke to the Church and people of good will everywhere through the events and movements in history which were "signs" pointing to God's activity and concerns. *Aggiornamento*, updating, from *giorno*, today, expressed his desire to modernize the church to be a more effective voice in the modern world. It became a pervasive theme during the four years of the council.

A New Kind of Council and the Great Debate

Vatican Council II differed dramatically from the previous 20 ecumenical councils in many ways. First, in sheer numbers. Trent at best had 200 members; Vatican I some 700 whereas 2540 bishops attended the opening session of Vatican II. Vatican II was representative of the whole Catholic world. With his ecumenical sensitivity, John invited Orthodox and Protestant churches to send observers who attended all the sessions. Although they did not vote, the many informal conversations between the bishops and these observers added a rich dimension to the council. Journalist and radio and television figures followed the council closely, publicizing its debates and rousing the interest and expectations of the Christian world. Bishops brought theologians as their *periti* or experts to advise them; their predominantly historical approach encouraged change. Rather than condemn heresies or alleged aberrations in the church, the council's goal was positive and pastoral. Its subject was the church itself, its inner nature and mission. Vatican II is pre-eminently the council on the Catholic Church.

In announcing the council Pope John had prayed that it would be a new Pentecost for the Catholic Church. The totally unexpected happened. The timeless unchangeable Catholic Church was about to experience the Spirit's strong wind of change!

Convinced that the Holy Spirit was indeed guiding them and their work to renew and update the church, the council bishops gave Catholics a stunning new vision for their church. The Italian *aggiornamento,* updating, captured the bishops' spirit and became the driving force as they began their work. The French *resourcement,* returning to the sources of the faith, especially to the **Fathers of the Church,** provided the bishops with theological insights and practices from the early church.

As the bishops set to work in the Fall of 1962, a split soon developed between traditional bishops resistant to change who understood the

5

church according to the Council of Trent and its Counter-Reformation theology and progressive bishops who took Pope John's *aggiornamento* seriously and desired the church to change in its worship, its disciplinary practices, and even in some of its doctrinal formulations. This was seen by the traditionalists as disloyalty to the great tradition of the church and an embarrassing admission that the church could change and in fact needed to change.

The debate that was to last through all four sessions of the council was between competing visions of the church. Both groups sensed they were fighting for the soul, the very future of the Catholic Church. It was an exciting time, reported daily in the press.

The progressives' critique of the pre-Vatican II Counter-Reformation church was dramatically expressed by Bishop DeSmedt from Brugges, Belgium, who had the audacity to criticize the traditionalists' first draft *On the Church* as being *triumphalistic* (a superiority attitude), *clericalistic* (bishops and priests dominating the laity in all phases of church life) and *legalistic,* (too law-centered, thus failing to emphasize the larger "law of love" that is the gospel of Jesus).

Underlying the competing positions of traditionalists and progressives were three basic issues: the church's relation to the modern world of democracy, pluralism, freedom and the primacy of conscience; a monarchic view of papal authority or a servant model of collegiality, co-responsibility and shared decision-making; an historical method applied to doctrinal questions and the fact of development of church teaching that opened the way for change in structures of government and sacramental practice.

Between the first and second sessions, John XXIII died on June 3, 1963, after a long, painful illness and final agony which he offered to God for the success of the council. With typical humor and peacefulness, he told his doctors "Don't be too worried. My bags are packed and I'm ready to go." Cardinal Giovanni-Battista Montini of Milan was elected to succeed John XXIII and took the name Paul VI. A brilliant, cautious progressive with much Vatican experience under Pope Pius XII, Paul VI successfully steered the council through the next three years.

The "Great Debate'" of Vatican II between the majority progressive bishops and the minority traditional bishops came to a head in the second session in 1963 and spilled over into the third in 1964. In retrospect this debate makes fascinating reading as famous cardinals and bishops argue their convictions with force and emotion, disagreeing and sometimes verbally attacking their 'esteemed confreres."[9] Our treatment relies on *What Happened at Vatican II* by John O'Malley.[10]

The debate, crucial to the nature and functioning of the Church, was over "the relationship of the bishops or episcopal hierarchy to the papacy. What kind of authority did the bishops have over the church at large when they acted collectively, that is *collegially*? How was that authority exercised in relationship to the pope?" (O'Malley, 7)

O'Malley identifies three practical factors underlying the above issue: The circumstances in which *change* is appropriate; the relationship in the Church of *center* to *periphery*, that is, how authority is distributed between the papacy including the congregations … of the Vatican Curia and the rest of the church; and the style or model of *exercising authority*. (O'Malley, 8)

This debate carried high stakes for the church since it involved "the fundamental issue of how the church is to operate in the future: continue its highly centralized mode of operation with its top-down style of management … [or achieve] broader consultation and sharing of responsibility." (O'Malley, 193) The principle of **collegiality**, rigorously resisted by the traditionalists fearful of diminishing the authority of the pope, was thus at the heart of the debate.

Two turning points in the debate came in the second session in 1963. In two key votes on Oct. 30, the bishops affirmed the principle of collegiality: "The body or College of Bishops in its evangelizing, sanctifying and governing task is successor to the original College of the Apostles and, always in communion with the Roman pontiff, enjoys full and supreme power over the universal church" 2,148 yes votes, 336 no, and clarified the power of bishops in relation to the pope: "the power of the College of Bishops ... belongs to it by divine ordinance and therefore not by papal delegation," 2,138 yes, 408 no. (O'Malley, 184)

On November 8, called by Michael Novak "The Most Dramatic Day" dealing with Cardinal Ottaviani's **Holy Office**, Cardinal Frings expressed amazement at Cardinal Browne's remarks against collegiality and severely criticized the Roman Curia and especially the procedures of the Holy Office as being "out of harmony with modern times" and "a source of harm to the faithful and of scandal to those outside the church." Cardinal Ottaviani rose to "protest most vigorously against the condemnation of the Holy Office" and to argue against the collegiality of bishops. Then in a powerful talk Archbishop D'Souza of India said the Roman Curia "must be thoroughly reformed"; concerning collegiality of bishops he asked rhetorically: "We twentieth-century bishops ... are we really incapable of deciding what is good for the churches entrusted to our care?"[11]

We have treated this debate at length to recapture the exciting dynamics of the council as intelligent, dedicated churchmen debated complex issues of great importance for the church; to indicate that Vatican II was in fact a deliberate break with the church's dominant pre-Vatican II theology and practice; and, most significant, to emphasize that the issues at the heart of the debate are very much alive in the church today. Their practical consequences are responsible for some of the church's crises and challenges today, including the restoration movement's gradual dismantling of the Second Vatican council's renewal of the church. I shall point these out in succeeding chapters.

The Council's 16 Documents[12]

The council's final documents are the result of a complete revision of the original traditional drafts produced by the Vatican Curia and their Roman theologians, of seemingly endless "interventions" by the bishops, of extensive work in multiple drafting- commissions, of chapter-by-chapter and even article-by article discussions and votes by the entire council, and through it all of considerable compromise by both traditionalists and progressives to assure a consensus vote on each document. Nine documents are decrees, three are declarations, and four are termed *constitutions* to signify their importance and close relationship to the nature of the church. Of the constitutions, those on the church and divine revelation are called *dogmatic* to stress their doctrinal content, and one, the *Church in the Modern World,* is termed *pastoral* to highlight how the church cares for the needs of people and of the world. Because of critical debates, the first session produced no documents.

It must be admitted that these documents often make difficult reading, since they are technical, lengthy, repetitious, full of scriptural references, "churchy," and attempt to say almost everything about each topic. Perhaps it could not be otherwise since they break such new ground and are the work of bishops representing different world backgrounds and concerns, divergent theological positions, and varied experiences of Catholic life. To achieve consensus, they include compromise statements between the progressive and the traditionalist bishops each seeking to preserve important values. Nonetheless, they reward careful reading for they represent a remarkable achievement of the intense four year interaction of 2400 bishops

The Seven Most Influential Council Documents

Each of these seven documents, achieved after long and arduous debate in the council, are dramatic examples of the bishops, acting under the inspiration of the Holy Spirit, boldly and confidently taking the risk of major change!

Dogmatic Constitution on the Church, LG, *Lumen Gentium*, *Light of Nations*, Nov. 21, 1964.

To appreciate why this document has been considered "the centerpiece of the council" or "perhaps the greatest achievement of the council," we need to understand how the church viewed herself before the council. Prior to the Protestant Reformation, the Catholic Church gave little explicit theological thought to her own nature as church. Since the office of pope and bishop were attacked by Luther, Calvin and other reformers, the Catholic Church became defensive and focused on her hierarchical and institutional aspects, emphasizing the authority of pope, bishops and clergy. For the next four hundred years this theology of church dominated Roman Catholic thinking, climaxing in the definition of Vatican Council I in 1870 on the primacy and infallibility of the pope.

Nineteenth century movements in and outside the church caused Catholic theologians to challenge this predominantly juridical and institutional understanding of the church. Bible scholarship challenged church assumptions about the origin of ecclesial institutions, drew attention to the role of Jesus and the Spirit in the life of the church, and made untenable an absolute identification of the Catholic Church with the kingdom of God. The recovery of the teaching of the great bishop-theologians of the fourth to seventh centuries and the writings of the French theologians[13] representing the ***nouvelle theologique (new theology)*** called attention to the historical character of the church as a developing and changing reality. The liturgical movement recovered the understanding of the church as the primordial sacrament of Christ (Karl Rahner's *ur sacrament)* and shifted the focus from the universal church to the local worshipping community. The ecumenical movement begun by Anglicans in 1910 gradually caused the Roman Catholic Church to reconsider its negative assessment of other Christian churches and even of other religions. The philosophical shift from classical metaphysics to post-Kantian critical philosophies led to more emphasis on experience and historical existence and changed the method of theological reflection.

Thus was born a "new" ecclesiology or theology of the church as mystery, as the pilgrim people of God, as sacrament of the risen Christ and of our salvation. It was new in the sense that it recovered older understandings "lost" in the growth and centralization of papal power through the centuries and in Rome's defensive reaction to Protestantism at the time of the Council of Trent and after. This newer ecclesiology embraced by the progressive bishops and their theologians clashed with the classical Roman theology centered on the hierarchy and the church as institution and perfect society.

These two theologies of the church have been popularly visualized as a pyramid with pope, bishops, priests on top and the non-ordained lay Christians below and as a large circle made up of all the baptized with the hierarchy in the center serving rather than dominating the people. The confrontation of these ecclesiologies resulted in a long battle over this document lasting into the third session of the council: the sharply-criticized first draft of the church document was sent back for a complete re-writing; the second draft received 4000 amendments; a thoroughly revised third draft was voted on chapter-by-chapter with the third chapter on "The Hierarchical Structure of the Church" voted on article by article. Finally on November 21, 1964, The *Dogmatic Constitution on the Church* of eight chapters[14] was approved by a vote of 2151 positive, 5 negative.

We have described the three-year genesis of *Lumen Gentium* to emphasize its profound importance for the church today and its clear break with its past. Catholics now have the official teaching of the Roman Catholic Church on its own nature. The other council documents depend on and further develop *LG*'s teaching. With this newer understanding of itself, the church established a theological basis of her program of renewal and embarked on an exciting new direction.

The Constitution's Theological Insights for Renewal

- The church in its deepest nature is a participation in the communitarian life of the Trinity of persons in one God. She is Christ-centered as the visible sacrament or sign of Christ on earth and is Spirit-filled with the Holy Spirit as the life of the church, the source of its gifts and the principle of its inner unity. Presenting the deepest reality of church as divine mystery is a much-needed corrective to the exaggerated emphasis on its institutional aspects that so many find repugnant today.
- The church is a communion of *local* churches each with its own bishop. Each diocese is not simply a sub-division of the universal church. Recovery of the importance of the local church counters present over-centralization of power and authority and decision-making in Rome. This understanding of church as communion is a promising model for the hoped-for union of the separated Christian churches.
- The principle of collegiality is *the* major emphasis of Vatican II and perhaps its greatest achievement. This restored the proper role and relationship of bishops to the pope after centuries of what some have termed "papalolatry"
- In describing the church as the *People of God*, the council stressed that the Catholic Church is primarily a community of

persons, thus shifting the emphasis from her institutional aspect and giving a powerful vote of confidence in Catholic lay men and women.

- *Lumen Gentium* emphasized the *dignity, equality, and mission of the baptized non-ordained* in the church. By their baptism, the too-often second class laity have a genuine ministry in the church and are called by God to holiness and to the fullness of Christian life and love.
- The Catholic Church is not *exclusively identical* with the church founded by Christ and the Holy Spirit or with the kingdom of God. This makes possible a new relationship with other Christians and members of the world religions and all people of good will.
- Because exaggerated devotion to Mary tended to overshadow the role of Christ, bishops refused to have a special document on Mary as originally desired. Instead, by inserting a chapter on Mary in *LG,* the bishops articulated a theology of Mary that emphasized her role in the mystery of salvation and in the life of the church. Vatican II's title for Mary is "Mother of the Church."

The Constitution on the Sacred Liturgy, SC, Sacrosanctum Concilium, the Most Holy Council, Dec. 4, 1963

By approving this constitution in a landslide vote 2,147 for, 4 against, "the council set in motion a programmatic reshaping of virtually every aspect of Roman Catholic liturgy unlike anything attempted before."[15]

This constitution, more than all the other documents, brought home immediately and concretely to Catholics the changes made by the council. Since the Council of Trent and before, Catholic **liturgy** or worship, especially the Sunday Mass or Eucharist, was fixed, **rubrical**, clergy-oriented, and often unintelligible. That is, worship was unchanging, stressed external ritual actions, was what priests with their back to the people did "up there" while the people were passive viewers, and was in Latin. To the joy of most Catholics and the consternation of some, the bishops at Vatican II changed all this.

It was significant that the bishops chose liturgy as the first document to be debated. For liturgy, the public worship of the whole church, laity and clergy alike, expresses the very nature of the church and her mission, embodies what Catholics believe, and is where the "work of our salvation takes place."

Thus, in calling for a complete revision of the church's liturgical rites, her sacraments and especially the Mass, the bishops provided Catholics with a new experience of worshipping together in their own language. Lay men and women read Scripture passages for the first time and became Eucharistic ministers. Catholics received the consecrated bread in their hands and drank the consecrated wine from the cup. A wider variety of Scripture readings were introduced; the Word of God in the Bible became central in preaching homilies rather than the traditional sermons, and in the spirituality of Catholics. A welcome sense of community developed.

The following four principles guided the bishops' renewal of the liturgy

- *Full active participation* by everyone is the right and duty of every Christian by their baptism and demanded by the very nature of liturgy. This is the primary goal of renewing and restoring the liturgy to the people of God.
- *Adaption of worship* to local circumstances, especially important in missionary countries.
- *Authority of local bishops* and of *national bishops' conferences* to make decisions adapting liturgy to local circumstances and cultures, rather than the Vatican Congregation of Rites regulating each aspect of worship from afar.

- *Aggiornamento* or bringing worship in line with the contemporary spiritual needs, education and maturity of Catholics.

However, these principles, especially the first and third, are being compromised today. A dramatic recent example, to be treated in chapter 4, is the new translation of the Mass for English-speaking countries, Advent 2011. Chapters 4, 5 and 6 are devoted to liturgical and sacramental renewal.

The *Pastoral Constitution on the Church in the Modern World. GS, Gaudium et Spes, Joy and Hope*, Dec. 7, 1965.[16]

"The joys and hopes, the grief and anguish of the people of our times, especially those who are poor or afflicted, are the joys and hopes, the grief and anguish of the followers of Christ as well."

These famous opening words of GS identifying Catholics with the peoples of the world capture the goal and spirit of this last and longest document of Vatican II: that the renewal of the Catholic Church is intimately involved with her relation to the world of today. The title of the constitution is significant: *pastoral,* the church takes seriously her desire to serve and better the world and in so doing to present the truths of the Christian message in a way that speaks to contemporary women and men and *in,* the church exists in the world and fully involves herself in the life of the human family, their needs and problems. In many ways GS sums up and completes the spirit of the other Vatican II documents. These dealt with the *internal* life of the Church; GS looks *outward,* to the world in order to bring the church's saving message of Christ to it.

The Pastoral Constitution is an extraordinary document, a first in many ways. It is addressed not exclusively to Catholics but to the "whole of humanity." It is a new way of looking at the world, from past hostility to respect, from conflict to dialogue, from condemnation to collaboration, from trying to dominate to serving. In recognizing for the first time the goodness present in the world, the Catholic Church officially admitted it has something to learn from the world. No other document reveals so dramatically the contrast between the defensive, siege mentality of the pre-Vatican II church and the council's renewed church. In its new consciousness and vision, GS re-defined the church's mission and what it means to be a Catholic Christian. In committing the church to be a moral force in the world for the dignity of each person, for human rights, for justice and peace, it challenges Catholics to become involved in the great issues facing the human family today. A purely individualistic religious life is no longer sufficient.

Gaudium et Spes is a document for our times. It points the way for further church renewal today.

Major Themes of GS

Numbers in parentheses refer to paragraphs in GS and subsequent documents.

- *The Church's Role* is to be "a leaven and kind of soul for human society to be renewed in Christ and transformed into God's family." (40)
- *The Vocation of Christians* is to work for a just social order in the political community as "a leaven and kind of soul for human society to be renewed in Christ. (74)
- *A Common Good Morality*: "profound and rapid changes make it particularly urgent that no one ... content himself with a merely individualistic morality." (30)
- *The Social Order* "By its very nature private property has a social dimension based on the law of the common distribution of earthly

goods.' (71) "… the right of freely founding unions" and "the right to strike.' (68) "Created goods should be in abundance for all. (69)

- *Christian Anthropology* or theology of the human person. GS based the dignity of the human person on man's call to communion with God" (10) and on Jesus Christ, the "focal point and goal of man [as well as] of all of human history (10) and the ultimate key to understanding the human condition." (38) The rich theological treatment of humanity in the introduction and first four chapters of GS is an answer to the criticism that an overly optimistic treatment of the world lacked theological justification.
- *Dialogue.* The bishops chose dialogue as the pre-eminent way the Catholic Church hopes to relate to the world.
- *Human Solidarity* across ethnic, racial, religious and socio-economic differences is the responsibility of all peoples to work together for a more just and humane world.
- *Dignity* of conscience, of marriage, of human culture, of the human person is a pervasive theme of the constitution.
- *Change.* In its relation to the world, GS recognizes the reality and value of change, using words like development, progress and evolution.
- *Signs of the Times.* The contrast between great wealth and poverty (4), women's initiatives (9), and humanity's longings (9) are signs pointing to the Spirit's activity in the world.[17]
- *Culture.* GS offered a new appreciation for human culture, recognizing "a plurality of cultures" in the world and the need to adapt the gospel as the new way of evangelization."(44)
- *New Methodology.* Previous church documents began with the truths of faith, a deductive approach. GS began with "the world which is the theater of man's history." (2) This inductive approach takes seriously the concrete experience of women and men and the events of history, the "signs of the times" emphasized by John XXIII.

Two issues overshadowed the council bishops: birth control occasioned by the "pill' created by Catholic Dr. John Rock and the threat of nuclear destruction. Debate on both was intense resulting in compromise statements to preserve each sides' strong values but which left the door open for future renewal. (47-52)

- *Marriage and the Family.* Chapter one of part II is an inspiring, profound treatment of the holiness of marriage, of married love and its fruitfulness. By praising the spouses' love and partnership and by refusing to rank the purposes of marriage as in the past, the council implicitly rejected procreation as primary and the spouses' mutual love as secondary. The bishops encouraged personal conscience-responsibility in stating "the married couple themselves must in the last analysis judge before God" the size of their family.
- *War, the Arms Race, Peace* (78-82). The bishops condemned war, indiscriminate destruction of cities and the arms race; approved conscientious objection; gave begrudging acceptance to nuclear weapons as deterrence and urged peace-making affirming that "peace is more than absence of war.'

Influence of GS in the Life of the Church

- Three important pastoral letters by the United States bishops: *Challenge to Peace (1983), Economic Justice for All (1986), Century of Social Teaching (1990)* were inspired by GS opening the Catholic Church to become involved in the problems of society. (See chapter 12)
- Latin American liberation theology rose thanks to GS' emphasis on solidarity with the poor, building a just world, and ideas of

freedom and liberation. (Chapter 3, Socio-economic life, 63-72 and Chapter 4, The Political Community, 73-76)

- American religious priests and sisters began moving in great numbers from their traditional work in schools, hospitals and education to live with the poor and to labor for social justice and human rights, particularly in Latin America;
- Dioceses throughout the world formed Peace and Justice Commissions while the Vatican established the Pontifical Council for Justice and Peace.
- In his social encyclicals and world travels Pope John Paul II constantly emphasized justice, human rights, peace among nations and the plight of the oppressed poor of the world. Pope Benedict XVI spoke out often and eloquently for the dignity of the human person and for justice. His 2010 encyclical, *Truth in Charity, is* a strong statement of Catholic social teaching in the context of the global economy. In his speeches Pope Francis emphasizes social justice and "a poor church for the poor."
- Lay Catholics, both young and old, generously give time and effort to a variety of social works at home and abroad. Thousands of college graduates give one or more years of work for the poor within the United States and in foreign countries.

Dogmatic Constitution on Divine Revelation, DV, Dei Verbum , Word of God, Nov.18, 1965.

"... this document represents an incredible achievement; it is a genuine watershed in the history of Roman Catholicism." So speaks Scripture scholar Fr. Donald Senior.

One has only to remember how some things were before the council: the style of manual theology, the virtual absence of the Bible from Catholic devotional life, the rationalist approach to our catechisms, the muffling of the Word within our liturgical life, the ridicule directed towards Protestants because of their clinging to the Bible, the pale diet of historical minutiae and archaeological questions considered the only legitimate interest of Catholic biblical studies. Such memories help us realize the extraordinary change in consciousness that has come over Roman Catholicism since the time of the council.[18]

In the light of this pre-Vatican II situation, it is not surprising that momentous battles between traditionalists and progressives occurred throughout all four years of the council over this document. In Senior's judgment, "nothing is more fundamental and nothing so exposes one's theological worldview as this topic" of **revelation**.[19] That is, did God reveal or speak to us *exclusively* in the Bible as Protestants held or *primarily* through Tradition as Catholics emphasized against the Protestant Reformers? It took the initiatives of Pope John XXIII in 1962 and Pope Paul VI in 1963 to send the highly traditional draft back to committee for revision and then to move the more progressive statement to completion. Yet the final document is an "uneasy compromise between opposing worldviews: one, more traditional, essentialist, heavily supernatural and static; the other more historically sensitive, immanentist, dialectical and process-oriented."[20]

Theological Achievements of DV for Church Renewal

- A major achievement, ecumenically significant, DV rejected the two-source theory of revelation which stressed Tradition over Scripture which had resulted in the Bible playing a lesser role in theologizing and in the spiritual lives of Catholics. DV stated that "sacred Tradition and sacred Scripture make up a single deposit of the Word of God." (10) The Word of God thus prophetically challenges the hierarchical church and the People of God

- DV approved the historical-critical method of exegesis (12) that emphasized human authors of the Bible and the time-conditioned circumstances of their writing (11-13). Catholic scripture scholars of high quality became numerous and in dialogue with their Orthodox, Anglican and Protestant colleagues.

- DV avoided literal interpretation of the Bible and its freedom from all error on the supposition that everything is directly inspired by God. (11-12) This avoids the excesses of fundamentalism providing Catholics with clear identity in relation to evangelical Christians and confidence in dealing with Catholics who interpret the **magisterium** in a fundamentalist manner.

- A dynamic view of revelation as God's continuing personal and ongoing self-communication to humans through their experiences and in the myriad events of daily life. (2,3,6) That God through the Spirit inspires each person is the basis for needed change in the church, for church leaders to listen to lay Catholics, to respect their 'sense of the faith,' and to respond to the 'signs of the times' for the renewal of the church.

- DV encouraged that the Word of God, the church's "support and strength" and the primary source of its spirituality, be made "widely available" to Catholics (21,22). Catholics recovered the Bible in their spiritual lives and began to read and pray the Hebrew and Christian Scriptures. The result has been a deeper love of God and Jesus, practical love of others and commitment to the works of justice.

I do not devote a separate chapter to this important document; its influence, however, pervades the entire book.

Decree on Ecumenism , UR, *Unitatis Redintegratio, the Restoration of Unity,* Nov. 21, 1964.

This decree constituted another of the great "breakthroughs" of Vatican II and is directly traceable to Pope John XXIII's goal for the council of restoring unity among the separated Christian churches. The Roman Catholic Church enthusiastically entered the ecumenical movement which had been led by the predominantly Protestant World Council of Churches and its Faith and Order Department.

The magnitude of this breakthrough can only be appreciated if one contrasts the attitude of Catholics toward Protestants before and after the council. Before Vatican II Catholics were deliberately isolated from Protestants, were ignorant of their beliefs and practices, often were hostile and felt superior to them. Supporting this situation was the Catholic conviction that "we" were the only true church of Christ having real priests and a real Eucharist thanks to our theology of ordinations in the apostolic succession. Thus the expression "no salvation outside the church" was interpreted as excluding non-Catholics from the possibility of salvation since they belonged to false churches with false worship. Catholics would therefore sin by participating in Protestant worship.

Once the Catholic Church recognized the baptism of all Christians as valid and thanks to the new theology of the church of Christ extending beyond the Roman Catholic Church, Catholic theologians entered into serious theological dialogue with their Protestant counterparts and rank and file Catholics began to pray with their newly termed "separated brothers and sisters in Christ." This remarkable about-face on the part of the Catholic Church delighted most Catholics who saw it as reasonable and long overdue for they had recognized the goodness and holiness and Christian commitment of their Protestant acquaintances and friends; but it distressed other Catholics who felt the church was guilty of compromise and of becoming Protestant; for some, ecumenism became a "dirty word," ecclesially speaking! In committing the church to Christian ecumenism, the bishops dared to make a major change.

The entire chapter 11, *That All May Be One,* is devoted to this important decree so integral to the renewal of the Catholic Church.

Declaration on Religious Liberty, DH, *Dignitatis Humanae, Of Human Dignity,* Dec.7, 1965.

"The most controversial document of the whole council" is the way its major architect, the American Jesuit John Courtney Murray characterized it.[21] The council's traditional bishops claimed this was a new teaching in the Catholic Church. Their opposition was intense and forcefully argued. The declaration was passionately debated, going through six drafts before finally being approved 2308 for, 70 against, on the very last day of the Second Vatican Council.

Arguments of the Opposition

- The declaration reverses long held Catholic teaching. Pope Pius IX in his 1864 **Syllabus of Errors** clearly condemned the separation of church and state and religious freedom.
- The declaration seems to deny that there is only one religious truth as held by the Catholic Church, thus fostering indifferentism and implying one church or religion is as good as another.
- The Catholic Church would lose its privileged position in Catholic countries with the state no longer favoring the church.
- The declaration endangers the Catholic Church in arranging concordats (agreements) with secular states.

- Religious liberty tolerates false religion; error has no rights.

Counter Arguments of the Majority Progressives

- Change in Catholic teaching has indeed occurred and doctrine has developed in the long history of the Church as **John Henry Newman** showed in his classic *An Essay on the Development of Christian Dogma*[22] and John T. Noonan in his *A Church that Can and Cannot Change: the Development of Catholic Moral Teaching.*
- It is Catholic teaching that religion and faith are free acts. "The exercise of religion by its very nature consists primarily of those voluntary and free acts by which a man directs himself to God." (*DH* 3). The act of faith by its very nature is a free act. (10)
- The erring person has rights based on his/her human dignity. Murray's distinction between error which has no rights and the erring person persuaded many opposition bishops.
- Religious liberty brings the church's teaching in line with contemporary political philosophy and practice. "… more and more people are demanding … responsible freedom in their actions and not be subject to the pressure of coercion. (10)
- The theological basis of the entire declaration is the God-given sacred dignity of the human person, as expressed in its two opening Latin words, *Dignitatis Humanae.*

Immense Importance of Human Dignity for Church Renewal

- The Catholic Church formally recognizes that "the human person has a *right to religious freedom* because "in matters religious no one is to be forced to act in a manner contrary to his own beliefs." (2) The church thus repudiates its double standard "of freedom for the church when Catholics are a minority and intolerance for others when Catholics are a majority."[23]

- The council has officially approved the theological principle of *development of doctrine,* a principle with far-reaching implications for urgently needed changes that challenge the Catholic Church today.
- The council affirmed the *primacy of individual conscience,* a welcome assertion for those Catholics today who struggle with moral questions and some teachings of church authority they cannot accept in conscience.
- The bishops admitted that the Catholic Church had in the past failed in regard to religious liberty, a long over-due admission. (*DH* 12)
- The council made a strong case for the rights of the church and its members to enjoy *free exercise of religion,* especially in totalitarian states. Pope John Paul II's strong insistence on this principle in his trips to Poland inspired the Solidarity Movement.
- *DH* is an example of John XXIII's exhortation to examine the "signs of the times," to discover God and the Spirit at work in the church and the world, and of his goal of *aggiornamento* for the church.

The council's *Declaration on Religious Liberty* is a long overdue gift to the Catholic Church. Its principles and message need to be more fully carried out within the church herself!

Decree on the Church's Missionary Activity, AG, Ad Gentes, To the Nations, Dec. 7, 1965.

This document, important for the church's missionary future, experienced a rough ride in the council's debates. For one third of all the council bishops were from mission countries and were facing unprecedented difficulties in the new political and economic situations of their countries plus directives from Rome often insensitive to their life and culture.

Speaking for many African bishops, Bishop Michael Ntuyahaga of Burundi "pleaded for greater autonomy" for local bishops since "we live in ... a time of young churches which are autonomous and exist in their own right."[24] Their most profound problem was how to be Catholic and Christian without being Western and Mediterranean, the fault of much past missionary methods.

The significant renewal contribution of *Ad Gentes* is the inspiration and principles it established for the Catholic Church's missionary evangelization of bringing the good news of Jesus Christ to all peoples and planting the church where it has not existed before. Successful evangelization demands **inculturation**[25] in adapting the Christian message and life to different cultures of the world.

In its six chapters, *AG* spelled out a radical renewal of the missionary spirit and method. "The work of implanting the church" involves being "rooted in the social life of the people, ... conformed to its culture ..." having "its own priests, its own religious and laity, under the leadership of its own bishop." *(10)* "The church by its very nature is missionary." (2) Therefore evangelization is the "fundamental task" of the entire people of God (35) and is no longer exclusively the work of missionary orders and congregations of men and women. It is urgent. "There are two billion people ... who have never or barely heard the Gospel message. (10)

Thanks to *Ad Gentes*, Catholic women and men have become lay missionaries and vigorous Catholic communities in Africa, Asia, India, and Latin America celebrate joyous, meaningful worship drawing on their own rich cultures. Yet former mission churches need to become more fully autonomous.

Chapter Nine is devoted to Evangelization, Christ's "Great Commission" to the Catholic Church.

Vatican II's Legacy

Inspired by the Holy Spirit and building on the rich spiritual and intellectual tradition of the church, the bishops who gave Catholics the gift of the Second Vatican Council, formulated an exciting new direction for the church.

The Church's Nature: In calling the Catholic Church a *mystery* of the presence and activity of the risen Christ and *people of God,* the baptized who make up the body of Christ, the bishops corrected past emphasis on the hierarchy and the church as institution. By defining the church as a communion, they restored the importance of local churches and their bishops and people,[26] thus offsetting over-centralization of power in Rome and emphasizing that the life of the church occurs in each diocese and parish.

Church Life. The council recovered the ancient principle of collegiality between bishops and pope at all levels of the church as the preferred form of her life. In their renewal of Catholic worship, the bishops restored the Eucharist to the center of Catholics' spirituality. *Gaudium et Spes* opened the church to a positive relationship to the world as the theatre of God's activity and committed her to work for justice and peace to bring about the kingdom of God. The bishops invited the church to join with other Christian churches to recover the unity of the church willed by Christ, and to begin dialogue with the religions of the world, especially the Jewish people after years of hostility. They recognized the historic development of doctrine and practice that makes future change possible. The bishops acknowledged sinfulness in the church and her constant need for reform and renewal.

The Laity. The council gave new prominence to the sacrament of baptism as entrance into the body of Christ, the church, as the basis and guarantee for Christians' rights within the church and for each

Christian's call to holiness of life, to evangelize and to ministry in the church. In stressing for the first time religious freedom and the inviolability of each individual conscience, the council encouraged a more adult, mature spirituality. *Gaudium et Spes* enriched married life by proclaiming that the spouses' married love is equally the goal of sexual union as procreation.

The Holy Spirit. Vatican II emphasized that the Spirit speaks to both leaders and individual Catholics through the 'signs of the times' and in the Word of God in Scripture and in the liturgy. Catholics developed a "Spirit spirituality."

Evaluating the Council

At the Extraordinary Synod of Bishops called by Pope John Paul II in 1985 to celebrate and evaluate the council on its 20th anniversary, the bishops gave a positive assessment of Vatican II. In his report, Cardinal Godfried Danneels called the four constitutions (SC, LG, DH, GS) the Church's *Magna Charta*. He praised the post-conciliar church as "alive and living with intensity." The Synod's *Message to the People of God* called the council "a gift of God to the church and to the world," "a source of light and strength." The *Final Report* praised Vatican II as being "in continuity with the great tradition of the church" and "the greatest grace of the century."[27] We now have the Catholic Church's official positive judgment on the Second Vatican Council.

Pope John Paul II, on various occasions, called the council "an event of the utmost importance in the almost two-thousand year history of the church," "a providential event," "the beginning of a new era in the church." In 2001 he said "… the council is the great grace bestowed on the church in the twentieth century: there we find a sure compass by which to take our bearings in the century now beginning."[28] An ecumenical council is the highest authority in the Catholic Church. As such, its teaching and mandate for the church is to be respected and followed. Today's Catholic Church *is* the church of the Second Vatican Council.

Vatican II Renewal in the Church Today

In the United States, the council has been well-received by the majority of Catholics, has produced rich benefits for the people of God, and in many respects is far advanced. The majority of Catholics are pleased with the liturgical renewal. Eucharistic celebration has become first in the devotional life of Catholics with the people participating along with the priests as leaders of the community. A success story has been Catholics' new-found familiarity and appreciation of the Bible and the biblical spirituality they developed. They have discovered the Holy Spirit in their lives and in the church's life. Over 17,000 married deacons serve as ordained clergy with dedication and distinction in American parishes. The council's emphasis that the people of God *are* church has re-invigorated Catholics to grow in mature spirituality and to exercise their ministry both within and outside the church.

The universal Catholic Church has assumed leadership in the ecumenical movement through official theological national and international dialogues that have achieved remarkable agreements. Catholics have become ecumenical in thinking and outreach to their Protestant sisters and brothers. Popes Paul VI, John Paul II and Benedict XVI and most bishops give strong leadership in justice issues and a preferential option for the poor. Catholics too are increasingly committed to and active in work for justice and the poor. Religious orders and congregations have reclaimed the charism of their founders. Religious women are in the forefront of the renewal as leaders in social justice, in championing the poor, and addressing the treatment of women in the Church.

There are grounds for much hope for the future of the American church.

However, the picture is mixed. "The fundamental issue in the council – how the church was to operate in the future: continue its highly centralized mode of operation with its top-down style of management and apodictic mode of communication, or somehow attenuate them by broader consultation and sharing of responsibility," remains problematic.[29] The council's renewal has gradually been de-emphasized and in many cases rejected and replaced by a growing conservatism, resistance to change and a return to some pre-Vatican II practices.[30] Critics refer to the retrenching of the council's renewal. The following are some well-known examples.

- The Latin Tridentine Mass is viewed as a repudiation of Pope Paul VI's Mass; and the new Vatican translation of the Mass prayers violates liturgical principles of the *Constitution on the Liturgy* and replaces in a non-collegial way many years' work by ICEL, the International Commission of English in the Liturgy, commissioned by eleven bishops' conferences of the English-speaking countries which have authority over liturgy according to Vatican II. (See chapter 4)
- The council's urgent call for collegial relationships at all levels of the church but particularly between the bishops of the world and pope has been severely curtailed by the Roman Curia and by the centralization of authority and decision-making in Rome.
- The call by educated and caring Catholics for greater transparency and accountability on the part of local bishops and Rome has largely gone unheeded.
- The tragic abuse by priests and the bishops' failures in government and pastoral care for the victims is a dramatic example

of the council's recognition of the sinfulness of the church and its continuing need of reform and conversion.

The controversy in the church today concerning the proper interpretation (hermeneutic) of the council and the battle over the council's meaning has important implications for the church's renewal. Pointing to the impressive accomplishments of the council, as listed under the legacy of Vatican II above, progressives claim that the council was a distinct change, a hermeneutic of *discontinuity* from the pre-Vatican II church. Joseph Komonchak supports this hermeneutic of discontinuity as expressed in Pope John XXIII's goals for the council, "the spiritual renewal of the church, pastoral updating (aggiornamento) and the promotion of eventual reunion of Christians." He explains that

> For any of these goals to be achieved would require change in the church: spiritual renewal would demand repentance; updating would mean abandoning attitudes, habits and institutions no longer relevant and introducing ones more appropriate to the last third of the 20th century; and promoting Christian unity would mean working to overcome alienations with centuries of inertial force behind them. Something new and different appeared on the horizon. Pope John composed a prayer that the council might be a "new Pentecost!"[31]

Those who see the council as "in all important respects continuous with the Catholic past" favor a hermeneutics of *reform* and oppose those who, they contend, interpret the council as a "discontinuous rupture" with the past. This interpretation is employed to deny that the Second Vatican Council was a major change in the Catholic Church and to explain, some would say justify, the current retrenchment of the council's program of renewal. In his carefully-nuanced talk to the Roman Curia, December 22, 2005, Pope Benedict XVI proposed a 'hermeneutic of continuity and reform,' that the council did involve important elements of change and reform, but remained predominately in substantial *continuity* with the tradition of the church. "It is precisely in this combination of continuity and discontinuity at different levels that the very nature of true reform consists," he said.[32]

In seeking the "correct" interpretation of the Second Vatican Council today, a strict dichotomy between hermeneutic of continuity and discontinuity is to be avoided. Komonchak wisely observes that "a hermeneutic of discontinuity need not see rupture everywhere; and a hermeneutic of reform, it turns out, acknowledges some important discontinuities."[33]

As the Church marks the 50th anniversary of the Second Vatican Council, the battle for the meaning of Vatican II has come to the fore. The clash of interpretations of the council – Vatican II as a *rupture* in the history of Catholicism or the need to read the council in *full* continuity with the past – is a manifestation of the current polarization in the church between progressives and conservatives. As a result, the very renewal of the church is at stake today.

Three recent books treat this critically important debate. *Vatican II: Did Anything Happen* asks "Is Vatican II a pivotal event in the life of the church?" *Keys to the Council: Unlocking the Teachings of Vatican II* Identifies 20 texts from the documents of the council that have special significance in the church's life today. *Vatican II: The Battle for Meaning* poses the critical question for today's Catholic Church: Is today the end of Vatican II or the beginning of her renewal?[34]

The observation of the eminent ecclesiologist Cardinal Avery Dulles made at the time of the 1985 Extraordinary Synod of Bishops, is applicable to the reality of renewal today.

If there is disenchantment … it is … because the necessary reforms have been resisted and partly blocked. The Catholic Church has not yet succeeded in giving its laity an adequate sense of participation and co-responsibility in the mission of the Church. The urgent need today is for a further development of collegial and synodal structures so that the Church may become a free and progressive society, a sign of unity in diversity, at home in every nation and sociological group. (FN 35)

For Discussion

1. What do you see as important "signs of the times" in the world and within the Catholic Church today?
2. Why is the *Dogmatic Constitution on the Church* "the greatest achievement of the Council"?
3. What are the practical results of the *Pastoral Constitution on the Church in the Modern World* "?
4. Why is the *Declaration on Religious Liberty* a truly revolutionary change in the Catholic Church? What difference can it make for dialogue with the non-Christian religions of the world? With the Church's missionary evangelization mission?
5. Has the Second Vatican Council affected your life? What do you find positive? Negative?

Further Reading

Dennis Michael Doyle. *The Church Emerging from Vatican II: A Popular Approach to Contemporary Catholicism, Revised Edition. New London,* CT: Twenty Third Publications, 2002 An introduction to Catholic Social teaching through the Vatican II documents Constitution on the Church and Church in the Modern World using stories of contemporary theologians and activists, such as Dorothy Day and Caesar Chavez, as well as contemporary social movements to understand these two critical documents.

John W. O'Malley. *What Happened at Vatican II.* Cambridge, MA: Harvard University Press, 2010. A one-volume history of Vatican II and its four sessions, focusing not only on the documents produced but also the debates and back-stage drama surrounding the Council's workings. O'Malley keeps an eye on Vatican II in the context of its reception today, providing a larger context for the reforms of the Council.

Xavier Rynne. *Vatican Council II.* Maryknoll, NY: Orbis, 1999. "This [informative, entertaining, eminently readable] account of the Second Vatican council, first serialized in *The New Yorker*, remains the classic work on this historic event. Writing under the pseudonym Xavier Rynne, Redemptorist priest Francis X. Murphy captured the attention of the English-speaking world with his first-ever insider look at a church council in progress."

Maureen Sullivan, O.P. *101 Questions and Answers on Vatican II.* New York: Paulist Press, 2002. Introduces Vatican II through a clear, frank and pithy question-and-answer format. A wonderful quick-reference guide that helps explain and understand Vatican II, both for people who have never studied it in detail before and for people who want to find a way to explain it clearly to others.

Footnotes

1   John W. O'Malley, *Tradition and Transition: Historical Perspectives on Vatican II* (Wilmington: Michael Glazier, Inc., 1989), 24.

2   2 Franz Jozef van Beeck, *Catholic Identity after Vatican II (*Chicago: Loyola University Press, 1985) 19.

3   Karl Rahner, "Toward a Fundamental Theological Interpretation of Vatican II," *Theological Studies* 40 (Dec. 1979): 717. Rahner defines world church as "for the first time a worldwide Council with a worldwide episcopate came into existence and functioned independently."

4   In re-acting to the Protestant Reformers, the Catholic Church developed a 'ghetto-fortress' mentality against the world and too often spent its energies condemning errors and false teachings.

5   The first seven ecumenical councils covering the years 325-787 were called by the emperors of the time and were attended mainly by eastern bishops; today only these seven councils are recognized by Orthodox churches. Succeeding councils were called by the popes and were attended by western Roman Catholic bishops.

6   John XXIII, *Humanae Salutis* convoking the Council, in Walter Abbott, ed., *The Documents of Vatican II* (New York: Guild Press, 1966), 705.

7   Ibid.

8   Ibid.

9   The leaders of the two groups soon became household names thanks to international press coverage. The conservatives were led by the venerable Cardinal Alfredo Ottaviani, the most powerful man in the Roman Curia and the "watchdog of orthodoxy" as head of the much feared "**Holy Office**"; Archbishop Pericle Felici, secretary-general of the Council whose wit and Latin verses enlivened the general assembly; Archbisop Guiseppi Siri of Genoa, Italy; the Curia's Cardinal Michael Browne of Ireland. The progressives were led by the indefatigable Cardinal Josef Frings of Cologne, the charismatic Cardinal Josef Suenens of Belgium; Cardinals Franciscus Koenig of Vienna; Lienart of France, Julius Doepfner of Munich; Augustine Bea, the Jesuit scripture scholar; Albert Meyer of Chicago, Paul Leger of Montreal and Bernard Alfrink of Holland. They were aided by theologian-experts, the intellectual architects of the Council: Jesuit Karl Rahner, Dominicans Eduard Schillebeeckx of Belgium and Yves Congar of France, Joseph Ratzinger of Germany and Hans Kung of Switzerland. In the confrontations between these two groups, the progressives succeeded in sending the preliminary drafts on the church prepared by the Vatican Curia and conservative Roman theologians back to newly constituted commissions for rewriting.

10   John W. O'Malley. *What Happened at Vatican II* (Cambridge, MA: Harvard University Press, 2008), 155-58; 175-85; 189-193 for a thorough, informative day-by-day very readable treatment of the debate.

11   Michael Novak, *The Open Church, Vatican II* (New York: The Macmillan Co., 1964), 223-41.

12   1963: Constitution on the Sacred Liturgy; Decree on the Means of Social communication. 1964: Dogmatic Constitution on the Church; Decrees on the Catholic Eastern Churches and on Ecumenism. 1965: Decrees on the Pastoral Office of Bishops, On the Up-to- Date Renewal of Religious Life; On the

Training of Priests; Declarations on Christian Education and On the Relation of the Church to Non-Christian Religions; Dogmatic Constitution on Divine Revelation; Decree on the Apostolate of Lay People; Declaration on Religious Liberty; Decrees on the Church's Missionary Activity; On the Ministry and Life of Priests; Pastoral Constitution on the Church in the Modern World.

13 Henri de Lubac, Jean Danielou, Yves Congar, Louis Boyer, Marie-Dominique Chenu leaders of the new theology in France before Vatican II. They later became experts at the council.

14 1.The Mystery of the Church. 2. The People of God. 3. The Hierarchic Structure of the Church with Special Reference to the Episcopate. 4. The Laity. 5. The Call of the Whole Church to Holiness. 6. Religious.7.The Eschatological Nature of the Pilgrim Church and Her Union with the Heavenly Church. 8. The Role of the Blessed Virgin Mary, Mother of God, in the Mystery of Christ and the Church.

15 *What Happened at Vatican II, 139.*

16 After the Introduction, the Condition of Humanity in the World, GS is divided into two parts: Part I deals with the dignity of the human person, the human community, human activity, and the Church's task in its relationship to the world. Part II addresses five urgent problems: marriage and the family, proper development of culture, socio-economic life, the political community, promoting peace and the bond between nations.

17 "Never before has the human race enjoyed such an abundance of wealth, resources, and economic power, and yet a huge proportion of the world's citizens are still tormented by hunger and poverty while countless numbers suffer from total illiteracy." (4) "Women claim for themselves an equity with men, laborers seek ... to take part in regulating economic, social, political and cultural life." (9) Beneath all these demands lies a deeper and more widespread longing – person and societies thirst for a full and free life. (9)

18 Donald Senior, in Timothy O'Connell, *Vatican II and its Documents: An American Reappraisal* (Wilmington, DE: Michael Glazier, Inc., 1986), 127.

19 The Council minority bishops fought passionately for their position that there are truths in the Church's Tradition not found in Scripture. Part of their concern was papal authority concerning the dogmas of the Immaculate Conception and Assumption of Mary defined by Popes Pius IX and XI that had little or no clear scriptural warrant. See Chapter 2 in DV.

20 Senior, *op.cit.,* 127.

21 John Courtney Murray, quoted in Abbott, *Documents of Vatican II, 673.*

22 Ibid. Murray argued that "the notion of development," more than religious free-dom "was the real sticking point for those who opposed DH even to the end ... because it raised with sharp emphasis the issue that lay below the surface of the conciliar debates ... the development of doctrine." Newman, the Anglican priest and scholar, who became a Catholic and later a cardinal, was beatified by Benedict XVI in London, Sept. 19, 2010.

23 The traditional church position was that since all must embrace the true faith, the state must promote that true faith as possessed by the Catholic Church. Accordingly, other churches do not have the same rights. However, for the common good and for peace, the state may tolerate the existence of "false religions."In his talk to the Council on this issue, Cardinal Josef Beran, Archbishop of Prague, just released from prison and house arrest, said "the burning of John Hus at the Council of Constance and then the imposition of Catholicism on the population of Bohemia in the seventeenth century had done immeasurable harm to the Church."

24 *What Happened at Vatican II,* 269. During the Council a group of African Bishops begged Pope Paul VI's permission to ordain their married catechists so their people would have the Eucharist. He refused.

25 Jesuit Mateo Ricci is a prime example of inculturation. He became expert in the Chinese language and Confucian classics, adopted the dress of a mandarin, and understood that the Chinese rites did not constitute worship of ancestors as gods. The Emperor invited him to join his court and gave permission to preach Christianity and make Catholic converts.

26 "From the late Middle Ages until Vatican II the characteristic emphasis of Catholicism had been on the universal church, commonly depicted as an almost monolithic society. Vatican II, by contrast, emphasized the local churches, each under the direction of a bishop ... making responsible decisions rather than simply carrying out Roman directives." Avery Dulles, *The Reshaping of Catholicism, Current Challenges in the Theology of Church* (San Francisco: Harper and Row, 1988), 22.

27 Cardinal Josef Ratzinger gave a somewhat pessimistic answer in his interview in *The Ratzinger Report, An Exclusive Interview on the State of the Church* (San Francisco: Ignatius Press, 1986), Ch. 2, "A Council to be Rediscovered," 27-44.

28 John Paul II, Apostolic Letter *Novo Millennio Ineunte* (Jan. 6, 2001), 57: AAS 93 (2001), 308.

29 *What Happened at Vatican II, 193.*

30 "Conciliar changes such as regular synods to promote collegiality between the world bishops and Rome on matters of governance, autonomy for regional conferences of bishops charged with implementing liturgical renewal, vernacular translations, enculturation and greater participation by the laity, were slowly eroded by Vatican bureaucrats who again took control." *National Catholic Reporter,* (Sept. 18, 2009) : 8a.

31 See Joseph Komonchak, "Novelty in Continuity: Pope Benedict's Interpretation of Vatican II," *America,* Feb. 12, 2009, 11.

32 *Ibid.,* 13.

33 *Ibid.*

34 John W. O'Malley, S.J., Joseph A. Komonchak, Stephen Schloesser, Neil J. Ormerod,, *Did Anything Happen?* (2007); Richard R. Gaillardetz and Catherine E. Clifford, *Keys to the Council: Unlocking the Teaching of Vatican II (* Collegeville, MN: Liturgical Press, 2012); Massimo Faggioli, *Vatican II: The Battle for Meaning* (Mahwah, NJ: Paulist Press, 2012.
35 Avery Dulles, *op. cit., 192.*

Chapter 2:
Five Major Actors

This chapter is essential for understanding how the Catholic Church actually functions through its institutional structures and for appreciating the difficult and awesome responsibility of church leaders in dealing effectively with complex challenges of a world church embracing five continents. It provides the necessary context to the Second Vatican Council's program of renewal and the continuing tensions and opposing views present in the church today. We identify five major actors: the bishops of the world together with the pope as bishop of Rome; the magisterium or teaching office of the church by the bishops and the pope; the Roman Curia congregations that help the pope and the bishops in communion with him govern the worldwide church; the Congregation for the Doctrine of the Faith (CDR) which serves the official magisterium in its role as 'watch-dog' of doctrine and morality; and those experts known as theologians who provide by their scholarship indispensable service to the church's teaching office, though not officially part of it. The frequent tensions between these five actors who engage with both the forces of reform and change and those of stability and continuity are evidence of a healthy dynamic in the Catholic Church as she strives to respond to the needs of her members and to ensure the church's progress in the post-modern world.

On these actors effectively depends the Vatican II renewal of the Catholic Church today.

Worldwide Bishops and the Bishop of Rome

Bishops throughout the world and the pope in Rome comprise the divinely-given leadership structure of the Catholic Church for its 1.3 billion members. As successors of the 12 Apostles chosen by Jesus, the world's Catholic bishops, each within his own diocese or local church, are pastors or shepherds of their people with the three-fold responsibility of *teaching* and preserving the Christian belief, of *leading* them in worship and the sacraments and of *governing* or over-seeing their spiritual and temporal welfare. The pope, the bishop of Rome as successor of the Apostle Peter chosen by Jesus to be the rock of unity of his Church, in communion with the world's bishops, leads the "universal church with full and supreme authority." (LG 22)

We devote an entire chapter to the critically important leadership role of bishops and the pope in the Catholic Church today. (Chapter 7)

The Magisterium[1]

The term **magisterium** (Latin from *magister*, teacher) describes the official *teaching office* of the Catholic Church exercised by the pope and the bishops of the Catholic world in union with him, commonly referred to as the "**hierarchy**." The authority of the magisterium comes from Christ to guarantee that the truths of the faith be safeguarded and church order be maintained. The *ordinary* magisterium is the day-to-day teaching of the Catholic hierarchy: of the pope through encyclicals or statements clarifying doctrinal matters (*motu proprio,* by his own hand) or by individual bishops through letters and statements and by national conferences of bishops.[2] The *extraordinary* magisterium is exercised by the bishops united with the pope in an ecumenical council of the church or by the pope speaking as successor of Peter infallibly defining faith and morals. Papal infallibility has been used only twice, in1854 for the Immaculate Conception of Mary and in 1950 for her Assumption body and soul to heaven.

The magisterium is responsible for doctrine and dogma. *Doctrine* is church teaching in its many forms, both orthodox beliefs and disciplinary decrees. *Dogma* is a divinely revealed truth proclaimed as such by the infallible teaching authority of the church and is to be accepted in faith. Though doctrines can be taught infallibly by the ordinary magisterium,[3] teaching of the ordinary magisterium is subject to error and the limitations of culture and the circumstances in which the teaching was formulated. Accordingly, doctrines have changed in the church's long history. This is known as the development of doctrine, the progressive growth in the church's understanding of its faith through reflection on the Scriptures, the writings of its scholars, insights from culture, historical events and Christians' life experience, all under the guidance of the Holy Spirit. Examples of past development in church teaching are the areas of slavery, usury, racism, sexism, capital punishment, ecology and the purposes of marriage.[4]

Some confusion exists in the church today over how the magisterium arrives at its doctrinal teaching and discipline and the level of its authoritative teaching. Some too readily invoke infallibility for its teaching or invoke it to support ideological positions. Many Catholics are selective, lauding for example teaching on sexual matters but ignoring the church's social teaching, and vice versa. It is therefore important to understand the important, necessary role and function of the magisterium in the Catholic Church.

The Roman or Vatican Curia[5]

To appreciate the curia's interaction with the other four actors, it is essential to know its organization and function, its role during Vatican II and after, and its influence in the church today.

The curia in Rome is the vast bureaucracy that helps the pope conduct the day-by-day business of the worldwide Catholic Church. The heart of the curia is nine congregations, each headed by a cardinal and staffed by bishops, priests and laymen as secretaries including more recently a few women: The Doctrine of the Faith, Eastern (Oriental) Churches, Causes of Saints, Bishops, Divine Worship and the Discipline of the Sacraments, Evangelization of Peoples (Propagation or the Faith), Institutes of Consecrated Life and the Societies of Apostolic Life, The Clergy, and Seminaries and Institutes of Studies (Catholic Education). Each congregation oversees its area, sets policy and issues documents and directives. The cardinal prefect of each congregation meets regularly with the pope. The curia also contains three Tribunals, 12 Pontifical Councils of which the Laity, Promoting Christian Unity, Justice and Peace, Migrants and Itinerants, Interreligious Dialogue, and Dialogue with Non-believers are the most prominent, and numerous lesser offices. The Secretary of State, who is in charge of relations with countries having diplomatic relations with the Holy See, supervises these curial congregations and offices.

The curia serves the pope and the church with much hard work and unswerving loyalty. However, bureaucracies tend to become entrenched and out of touch - jokes abound in Rome that 'popes come and go but the curia goes on forever.' At periods throughout its long history there were frequent outcries to 'reform the curia.' At Vatican II in speech after speech, the bishops severely criticized the curia and the way it operated. They charged that the curia had become a powerful force between them and the pope. By the time of Vatican II the chain of command seemed to be pope-curia-bishops rather than the curia helping and serving the world's bishops who, as successors of the Apostles, are to govern the universal church in union with the successor of Peter.[6]

The curia will appear frequently in these pages! Its reform is discussed in Chapter 15, section 9.

The Congregation for the Doctrine of the Faith (CDF)[7]

CDF's responsibility is to assist bishops and the pope in their roles as authentic teachers by safeguarding faith and morals, clarifying doctrine, issuing documents and directives, investigating the writings and teachings primarily of theologians that it deems contrary to Catholic teaching and to the faith and inaugurating discipline. In these cases, it contacts them, asking for clarification and a statement of acceptance of Catholic teaching and of faith. After an often long period of dialogue, if the person in question is found to be in doctrinal error and refuses adequately to recant, the congregation takes disciplinary action, often the extreme step of refusing him/her the right to publish and to teach in Catholic institutions. Though this appears harsh, and indeed in some cases has been unduly so, it underscores the serious responsibility church leaders have to keep from substantial error the truths of faith revealed by God, taught by Jesus and handed down through 2000 years.

CDF is the most important of all the congregations. Documents of the other congregations or of pontifical councils that deal with faith or morals are submitted to CDF before publication. The Pontifical Biblical and the International Theological Commissions operate under its jurisdiction. CDF also handles irregularities in the celebration of the sacraments and offenses against morals. It was given authority over all facets of the recent priest abuse scandals. Cardinal Ratzinger, later Benedict XVI, headed CDF from 1981 to 2005 when he was elected pope.

The bishops at Vatican II criticized CDF for its secretive, non-democratic way of acting, for condemning and disciplining theologians without revealing their accusers, and for creating a climate of fear and intimidation in the church. In some cases, theologians' writings at variance with current church positions have not been sufficiently understood or officially discussed with them with the result that their careers have been ruined. Before Vatican II, important theologians, whose writings later had a major influence on Vatican II and who became experts at the council, were condemned and removed from their teaching posts.[8]

Theologians and "Doing Theology"

The formidable task of explaining and interpreting the church's beliefs and teaching in terms understandable in today's world and of proposing fresh interpretations and insights for further development is the domain and responsibility of theology and of specially-trained theologians, both clerical and lay. They provide an enormous service to the church: for individual bishops in their teaching-preserving responsibility, for the universal magisterium, and for individual Catholics. Theologians have been responsible for important doctrinal development. Ideally, bishops and theologians respect each other's roles. But inevitably tensions arise when theologians advance new understandings of the Christian Tradition which CDF and bishops and the pope are not yet ready or able to accept, as happened before the Second Vatican Council. This tension has always been present throughout the church's history and is acute in the Catholic Church today. We treat areas of tension in later chapters.

Without a carefully expressed theology, Catholics would not have an adult coherent understanding of the Christian faith able to meet the challenges of modern life. Theology has been necessary and at the center of the church's life throughout its long history. Indeed, in its beginning years, different theologies or ways of explaining and presenting religious truths were present in each of the four Gospel writers and in the great theologian St. Paul as they endeavored to explain the mystery of the God-man Jesus, his teaching, and the great saving actions of his crucifixion, resurrection, ascension, and sending the Spirit at Pentecost. So it should not surprise one that throughout the church's history various theologies emerged. Since we will be "doing theology" frequently throughout these pages, it will be helpful, indeed necessary, to understand what theology is and how it works.

Broadly speaking, theology, or more exactly, theologizing, is simply faith seeking understanding. It is critical, rational reflection on any religious tradition and the resulting systematic expression of that reflection. Theology thus has two elements: the *process* of reflection and the *product* of that reflection in statements of belief (creeds), in worship (cult), and in moral behavior (code).[9]

Christian theology then is the *process* of critical reflection on what Christians believe about God, Jesus Christ, the Holy Spirit, the Church, the sacraments, and so forth. Christian theology has two focal points: Scripture and Tradition. Tradition, as distinguished from various traditions, is the full Christian belief and the teaching, practices and code of behavior of the church's life. Theology's second aspect is the attempt to *express* what one believes, the *content* of Christian faith, in a way that people in any given period of history can understand and make sense of. In the 4th century the great theologian-bishops of the church wrestled with the mystery of Jesus Christ as both God and man; their resulting explanation was expressed in the **Nicene-Constantinopolitan creed** which almost all Christian churches accept and which Catholics recite every Sunday at worship. Theology is thus the science of finding adequate descriptive language to speak about the things of God.

Another way of expressing this second aspect is that theology attempts to explain the significance and meaning of these beliefs for human living today, for the questions and problems people meet in daily life. Two contemporary examples illustrate this second aspect of theology. First, the environment. By reflecting on the Christian belief of a creator God who gave us a good world as gift to use responsibly, we realize better today that a Christian has a twofold responsibility to protect planet earth and to make land and food and water available to all people. Second, liberation theology. Gustavo Gutierrez of Peru and other Latin American liberation theologians reflected on the words of Jesus in Luke 4:18, "The spirit of the Lord has been given me for he has anointed me. He has sent me to bring the good news to the poor, to proclaim liberty to captives and to the blind new sight, to set the downtrodden free, to proclaim the Lord's year of favor." These theologians applied Jesus' words to the situation of massive poverty, oppression, denial of the most basic human rights to the majority of Latin Americans. Liberation theology was born!

Accordingly, Christian theology cannot be done in the abstract divorced from the real world of human experience and growth in knowledge. Since our understanding of the Tradition has developed and deepened over the centuries and our own self-understanding and experiences of life have matured and changed, theology has undergone change or development throughout the church's history and continues to do so today.

Prior to the Second Vatican Council most Catholic theologians were priests. Since the council and thanks to departments of theology offering masters' and doctoral programs of theology at Catholic universities and colleges, the Catholic Church is now enriched with outstanding lay men and women theologians in considerably larger numbers than priests and women religious and who teach in both Catholic and secular universities and whose scholarly publications are prolific. As lay persons and as women, they often provide new insights, creativity, and freedom of expression in their theologizing, though sometimes challenging the vigilance of the magisterium.

We should note that "doing theology" is not limited to these professional theologians. Since theologizing is to ask and seek answers to serious questions about their beliefs, most persons of adult faith engage in theological reflection in their lives. A growing number of Catholics are well-versed in theology from their high school and college theology classes, from their reading of popular theologians and the many theological books now in print, and Catholic periodicals and magazines.[10]

The Vatican's International Theological Commission (ITC) recently issued an important, forward-looking document on the role of theology in the church today.[11] Noteworthy is its threefold emphasis on the role of the Catholic laity, of history, and of spiritual experience as sources of theologizing.

- "Theology should strive to discover and articulate what the Catholic faithful actually believe, the *sensus fidelium*, the understanding of the faith of the whole people of God.
- History as lived by the church and dialogue with the world are important sources for theology today. Because the Catholic laity and lay theologians live on "the interface between the Gospel and everyday life," they have a special role to play in interpreting the "signs of the times" as evidence of the Spirit's activity.
- Doing theology involves paying attention to the spiritual and religious experiences of both ordinary Catholics and the Saints and mystics.
- This threefold emphasis has special significance in the light of Catholics' concerns and urgent needs in the church today. (See Chapter 15)

For Discussion

1. What aspects of the Catholic Church described in this chapter surprise you?
2. How does one theologize or "do theology?" When have you theologized?
3. Why are theology and theologizing absolutely necessary for the Catholic Church?
4 Would you characterize yourself a progressive or traditionalist in terms of the Catholic Church? Why?

Further Reading

Darragh, Neil. *Doing Theology Ourselves: A Guide to Research and Action.* Aukland, NZ: Accent Publications, 1995. Darragh introduces the practice of theology that serves to move it away from the inaccessibility of academia and into the everyday life and experiences of the Catholic faithful. The focus of his book stresses that doing theology should be done in community rather than alone.

Dwyer, John. *Church History: Twenty Centuries of Catholic Christianity.* New York: Paulist Press, 2002. A candid and accurate picture of the church in its historical reality and ambiguity with emphasis on the role of theology in the church's life and critical judgment of past mistakes. Especially clear explanation of major theological developments in church history.

Gaillardetz, Richard R., *By What Authority? A Primer on Scripture, the Magisterium, and the Sense of the Faithful.* Collegeville, MN: Liturgical Press, 2003. Writing about the function and use of authority in the church from a post-Vatican II perspective, he explains the complex ways in which the authority of the Scriptures and Tradition, the magisterium and the sense of the faithful all play integral roles in the understanding and interpretation of doctrine and dogma.

Footnotes

1   Massimo Faggioli, *Vatican II: the Battle for Meaning.* (Mahwah, NJ: Paulist Press, 2012; Richard R. Gaillardetz and Catherine E. Clifford, *Keys to the Council, Unlocking the Teaching of Vatican II* (Collegeville, MN: Liturgical Press, 2011); Greg Tobin, *The Good Pope John XXIII and Vatican II: The Making of a Saint and the Remaking of the Church* (New York: Harper One, 2012); William Madges and Michael J. Daley, *Vatican II: Fifty Personal Stories* (Maryknoll, NY: Orbis Books, 2012); Margaret Lavin, *Vatican II: Fifty Years of Evolution and Revolution in the Catholic Church,* (St. Paul's Publications, 2012).

2   Cardinal Ratzinger de-emphasized bishops' conferences as not having theological justification for teaching. In demanding *universal* agreement of all bishop members, the practical result was their loss of authority and the cessation of letters like the United States Bishops' 1983 *Challenge for Peace* and 1986 *Economic Justice for All.*

3   The ordinary magisterium speaks infallibly when the Catholic bishops dispersed throughout the world but maintaining the bond of communion among themselves and with the pope as successor of Peter agree in teaching a doctrine of faith and morals. *Lumen Gentium*, no 25. Since Vatican II there has been development in the secondary object of infallibility, that is, truths not revealed but intimately connected with revealed truth, which can be taught infallibly by the ordinary magisterium. *Mysterium Ecclesiae,* CDF, 1973; *Catechism of the Catholic Church,* 1997, no 88. For an extensive treatment of the "significant development" of doctrine taught infallibly by the ordinary magisterium and of papal teaching "to be held definitively," see Francis Sullivan, "Development in Teaching Authority since Vatican II," *Theological Studies* 73:3 (2012) 579-589.

4   As a result of a fuller understanding of the human person and the important place of sexual love in marriage, the church stated that both procreation and sexual love are the *primary* purpose of marriage rather than the previously taught procreation as primary and the partner's sexual love secondary. See the recently beatified John Henry Newman, *An Essay on the Development of Christian Doctrine,* a scholarly book that profoundly influenced the bishops and their periti at Vatican II. See also John T Noonan "Development in Moral Doctrine," *Theological Studies* 54 (1993) 662-77, and "On the Development of Doctrine," *America* 180 (3 April 1999) 6-8, for his excellent scholarly treatment of the church's development in other areas too.

5   Richard P. McBrien, Gen. Ed. *The HarperCollins Encyclopedia of Catholicism.* San Francisco: Harper Collins, 1995, 1125-30 and 354.

6   Two recent examples in the United States of curial congregations failing to respect the authority of local bishops that was expressly acknowledged in Vatican II were the investigation, without discussion with American bishops, of religious congregations of women by the Congregation For Institutes of Consecrated Life and the imposition of a new translation of the Mass and sacramentary by the Congregation for Divine Worship over the objections of English-speaking national bishops' conferences. This lack of subsidiarity and collegiality championed by Vatican II has wounded the body of Christ by causing much resentment and serious loss of confidence and respect for church leadership.

7   CDF has an interesting pedigree. In 1546 Pope Paul III created the Holy Office to deal with the spread of 'Lutheranism' in his Papal States. In 1558 it became the Sacred Congregation of the Holy (sic) Inquisition; in 1908 the Sacred Congregation of the Holy Office and in 1968 the Sacred Congregation for the Doctrine of the Faith.

8   Marie-Dominique Chenu, Yves Congar, Hans Kung, Henri de Lubac, John Courtney Murray, Karl Rahner.

9   For this material I am indebted to Brennan Hill, Paul Knitter, and William Madges, *Faith, Religion and Theology*. (Mystic, CN: Twenty-Third Publications, 1990), 251-61.

10 To know and experience today's Church throughout these pages, it will be interesting and profitable to become acquainted with *periodicals, magazines* and *newspapers* that report ongoing events and struggles of the contemporary church. See the conclusion of the bibliography section at the end of this book for a selection of the most informative ones, with brief identifying description of each.

11 "Theology Today: Perspectives, Principles and Criteria" approved by ITC and promulgated by the Congregation for the Doctrine of the Faith, *Origins* 40 (March 15, 2012).

Chapter 3:
Mystery - Pilgrim People

"The Church is a mystery ... a reality imbued with the hidden presence of God."

(Pope Paul VI)

In light of the publicized sinfulness within the Catholic Church from the priest-abuse scandal and the bishops' cover-up and the recent revelations of financial and other abuses in the Vatican Curia over church governance, it is difficult to recognize the divine nature of the church. By calling the Catholic Church mystery, the bishops at Vatican II emphasized that the church is permeated in its deepest reality by the presence and action of Jesus Christ and his gifts of grace and salvation that make faith possible. Their naming the church mystery is also a corrective for those who focus on the church's sinfulness or alleged wealth or identify it primarily with its institutional aspects.

This chapter is the foundation for our treatment of the Catholic Church in the following chapters. It is taken from the *Constitution on the Church (LG),* called "the centerpiece" and "the greatest achievement of the council."[1]

Mystery

To comprehend the great mystery that is the church, we turn to St. Paul, the indefatigable Apostle of the Gentiles and what he wrote to his new Christians in the Greek city of Ephesus. St. Paul announced to them "God has given us the wisdom to understand fully the mystery of the plan he was pleased to decree in Christ" (Ephesians 1:9) and that he "was given the grace to preach to the Gentiles the unfathomable riches of Christ and to enlighten all men on the *mysterious design* which for ages was hidden in God, the Creator of all." (Ephesians 3:8-9) Italics added.

Paul's mysterious design is God's plan of salvation for the human family to be achieved through the church, the body of Christ. "For God so loved the world that he gave his only Son so that everyone who believes in him may not perish but may have eternal life." (John 3:16) Let us reflect on this extraordinary plan.

From all eternity, the Triune God, Father, Son, and Holy Spirit, out of boundless love and compassion, desirous that all people share their very own life in an eternity of joy and glory, and in fulfillment of the promises made to the Jewish prophets for a messiah to come, the Father sent his Son to become a human like ourselves. This enfleshment of a divine person is the astounding mystery of the **Incarnation**. The Father gave Jesus, the "Word made flesh," the great mission of revealing to the world God's loving plan. Jesus of Nazareth, the God-man, appeared in Palestine 2000 years ago, announced God's kingdom, healed people, forgave sins, and freely endured a terrible crucifixion for the sins of all peoples to bring salvation to the human family. The Father raised Jesus from the dead giving him a totally new form of risen life to be shared by all who love God in Jesus in a new creation livened by the Holy Spirit. Chirst's Church is established to bring this good news of God's salvation to the world.

After his dramatic conversion by an appearance from the risen Christ (Acts 9:1-9), St. Paul became so absorbed by "God's secret plan" (Ephesians 3:3) and "that mystery hidden for ages and generations past now revealed in and through Jesus" (Colossians 1:26-27) that it became a constant theme in his letters to the Christians in the churches he founded throughout Asia Minor, now Turkey.

Is it possible for us today to grasp and appreciate the extraordinary excitement and enthusiasm of Paul and the early Christians when they realized the enormity of God's plan for them? For Paul, God's plan is Jesus Christ; it is the mystery of Christ in us sharing his own life and salvation: "Christ in you, your hope of glory." (Colossians 1:27) To Gentile listeners and to his new Christians, Paul's preaching about Christ was gospel, great good news indeed.

The mystery of God's grand design culminates in the church. Following Vatican II's *Light of the Nations (LG),* we consider four characteristics of the Catholic Church as mystery.

The Church is the *Sacrament* of the Risen Christ

In the opening paragraph of the *Constitution on the Church, LG,* in its first chapter, "The Mystery of the Church," the bishops at the Second Vatican Council gave the church a new name – sacrament. "… the church, in Christ, is a sacrament, that is, a sign and an instrument of communion with God and of the unity of entire human race." (LG 1). Why is this so significant?[2]

A sacrament is a visible *sign* that points to a hidden reality beyond itself and as *instrument* accomplishes what it points to.

As visible sign. To persons open to a transcendental God, the entire universe becomes a sacrament of the invisible God. Some examples: ocean waves crashing white against a rocky coast speak eloquently of the power and immensity of God, a delicate orchid of God's beauty, an athlete's skills of God's creative gifts, a loving mother or grandmother of God's enduring love and acceptance. The poet Gerard Manley Hopkins captured the sacramental reality of nature in his poem *God's Grandeur* whose opening line proclaims "The world is charged with the grandeur of God."[3]

People too are sacraments of the invisible God in our midst. Malcolm Muggeridge in his brief gem of a book, *Something Beautiful for God*, saw in Mother Teresa of Calcutta the face of a loving God. At the funeral in St. Patrick's cathedral in New York of Dorothy Day who dedicated her long life to helping the extreme poor and to fighting for social justice, a street person with tears streaming down his face said "This dear lady is the closest thing to God I will ever see!" Their love and compassion are powerful sacramental signs that make real to us Jesus' compassion and love.

As instrument. The key is "in Christ." As Jesus' miracles and healing are signs on earth of God's compassion and love, so the church is the sacrament of Christ because she accomplishes today what Jesus did in his lifetime: forgives peoples' sins, heals their hurts, establishes God's kingdom of justice and peace and love, leads people to know and love God, and helps Christians in countless ways in their pilgrimage to heaven. Through the seven sacraments, Christ acts through the church's ministers whenever the church baptizes, confirms, celebrates Eucharist, reconciles sinners with God, blesses married love, ordains bishops and priests and deacons, and anoints the sick.

The almost cosmic vision of Vatican II in calling the church sacrament is its challenge not only *to be seen* as able to bring its members into union with God and to be an agent of world union and peace but actually to accomplish it. This vision challenges the church, members and leaders alike, both to manifest more fully and authentically the compassionate love and example of Jesus and to make it a reality. A critical question becomes: do people see in the lives and actions of Catholics and their leaders the humble, selfless, loving Christ?

The Church is the Body of Christ

Vatican II declared that all baptized believers are incorporated into the body of Christ, the church. St. Paul refers to this as being "in Christ Jesus," a favorite phrase he used 164 times in his letters, especially to the Galatians, first letter to the Corinthians, to the Colossians and to the Ephesians. Paul insists that through baptism Christians are so completely united to Christ that they form one body, a single supernatural organism, with Christ as their head. In his living body Christ is the source of supernatural life for each member who receives from him all the graces or gifts needed to live the Christian way of life. Since Christians form one body in Christ, they are profoundly united with each other "in Christ Jesus." A major breakthrough of Vatican II was to recognize and emphasize that the body of Christ, the church, includes all validly[4] baptized Christians: Anglicans, Orthodox, Protestants, Roman Catholics, since their baptism is incorporation (*corpus*, body) into the body of Christ, the church. That is, baptized Christians through Jesus' saving death and resurrection are united to Christ in his "mystical" body in the spiritual life, the bond uniting Christians, constituting the profound reality of the church as mystery.[5]

> Do you not know that your bodies are members of Christ?
> (1 Corinthians 6:15)
> The body is one and has many members, but all the members, many though they are, are one body; and so it is with Christ. It was in one Spirit that all of us, whether Jew or Greek, slave or free, were baptized into one body. ... You then are the body of Christ. Every one of you is a member of it. (1 Cor 12:12-13, 27).
> It is he [Christ] who gave apostles, prophets, evangelists, pastors and teachers roles of service for the faithful to build up the body of Christ, till we become one in faith and in the knowledge of God's Son, and form that perfect man who is Christ come to full stature (Ephesians 4:11-14)

A great challenge Vatican II gave the church, leaders and members, is to "grow to the full maturity of Christ the head." (Eph 4:15)

The Risen Christ is Present and Active in the Church

A third characteristic of church-as-mystery is the reality that the risen Christ is present and active in the church. Christians encounter Christ in the word of God each time they read or hear the Scriptures; they meet him in each of the seven sacraments, especially in the Eucharist in his real presence in the consecrated bread and wine.[6] Catholics also value his presence in the tabernacle symbolized by the red sanctuary lamp and come often to Catholic churches to "make a visit" and to pray. Catholics meet him in the worshipping community each Sunday "whenever two or three are gathered together in my Name, there I am in your midst." (Mt 18:20) The risen Christ promised his special presence and protection to the infant church before he visibly left this earth: "Know that I am with you always until the end of the world." (Mt 28:20)

The Church is the Realm of the Spirit Sent by Christ

"The Spirit dwells in the church and in the hearts of the faithful as in a temple … [and] guides the church into the fullness of truth and gives her a unity of fellowship and service." (*LG 4*)

God's loving plan for the church was dramatically revealed on Pentecost when the risen Christ, to fulfill his promise of the Spirit to be with his church all days to the end of time, sent his Spirit on the Apostles and on the thousands of pilgrims present in Jerusalem for the feast. Thanks to the Second Vatican Council, the Catholic Church and individual Catholics rediscovered the **Holy Spirit** in the life of the church and in their own lives. Catholics experience the Spirit each time they are strengthened in their faith and hope and are empowered to love God and their neighbor and to make difficult decisions.

Of the many gifts the Holy Spirit gives Christians, his gift of faith is pre-eminent. In today's increasingly secular world, only by a vital faith can Christians accept God's plan of salvation, believe that Jesus is divine and actually rose from the dead, is present as risen Lord in the Eucharist and the sacraments and the lives of Christians. Only by the Spirit's gift of faith can the Catholic Church be accepted as the mystery of God's love in Jesus Christ! A beautiful name Vatican II gave the Church is *community of faith.*

The Spirit's inspiration gives rise to the theological reality of the **sensus fidei** (sense of the faith), that instinctive awareness that believers have of the Catholic faith.

> The body of the faithful as a whole ... cannot err in matters of faith. Thanks to a supernatural sense of the faith which characterizes the people as a whole, it manifests this unerring quality when 'from bishops down to the last member of the laity' it shows universal agreement in matters of faith and morals. For by this sense of faith which is aroused and sustained by the Spirit of truth, God's people accept not the word of men but the very Word of God. (LG 12)

This teaching was introduced and emphasized by Vatican II and has far-reaching practical consequences for the renewal of the Catholic Church. We refer to it often in subsequent chapters.

The People of God

In giving this new name to the Catholic Church, the Vatican II bishops reached back to the Hebrew Scriptures' name for the Jewish people as the covenant people of God. This name captured the imagination and hope of Catholics. It was an exciting and long overdue official recognition that they, and not exclusively the hierarchical church of pope and bishops, *are* the church, no longer second-class citizens. It inspired Catholics to take initiative in their church. The result has been phenomenal growth in lay ministry in parishes across the United States and in the growth of lay organizations like Pax Christi, Network, Voice of the Faithful, Christian Family Life, Cursillo retreats and many others..

Referring to church as people also goes back to the earliest days of Christianity. The word church comes from the Greek *ekklesia,* a gathering or assembly of people to describe the Sunday gatherings of the new Christians in Palestine in the homes of Christians to hear the teachings and healings of Jesus read aloud, to offer prayers and petitions, and then to receive Jesus' body and blood as their spiritual food and drink. Church also means the local church in each city gathered to remember Jesus.

In Chapter 2, 9-17, LG enumerates the profound meaning of being People of God. By their baptism they share the priesthood of Christ (10); by taking part in the Eucharist sacrifice, they offer the divine victim to God (11); they share Christ's prophetic office by their witness of faith and love and their gift of "the sense of the faithful" (11); they are in communion with the faithful worldwide (13); as disciples of Christ they are sent to evangelize the world (17).

Pilgrim People

The church, the people of God, are people on a pilgrimage. This earth and this life are not their final home. They are journeyers seeking a better life in their home in heaven. They are strengthened and aided on their pilgrimage by being united in their belief in **"the communion of saints,"** with all those who have gone ahead and await them in heaven. Pilgrim Catholics proclaim in the Apostles Creed each time they pray the rosary and in the longer Nicene Creed during

Sunday eucharists: "We believe ... in the communion of saints, the resurrection of the body, and life everlasting."

This title brings out in a magnificent way the utter uniqueness and awesome mystery of the Christian Church: it is a church that bursts the bonds of time and this cosmos to encompass eternity itself; it is the heavenly church made up of those who have passed through the barrier of death to life eternal, the communion of saints.

> The Church ... will receive its perfection only in the glory of heaven when will come the time of renewal of all things (Acts 3:21). At that time, together with the human race, the universe itself ... will be perfectly re-established in Christ. (LG 9)
> Indeed we know that when the earthly tent in which we dwell is destroyed, we have a dwelling provided for us by God, a dwelling in the heavens, not made by hands, but to last forever. (2 Cor. 4:13-5.1)

In calling the church people of God, Vatican II introduced a theology of the church as communion, emphasized the baptismal vocation of the laity, and stressed for the first time their rights within the church.

The Church is a Communion

A major accomplishment of the bishops of the council was recovering the understanding of the church as a communion of local churches each with its own bishop. Vatican II declared that the fullness of the "church of Christ is truly present in all legitimate local congregations of the faithful." (LG 26) The apostle Paul addressed his Christians in Asia Minor as "the church of Corinth," "the church at Ephesus," and so forth. The importance of the local church has vast implications for the church today, as we shall indicate in later chapters.

This communion model represents the council's shift from the previous hierarchical, institution model of church.[7] *Lumen Gentium* described the Catholic Church as a fellowship of believers in Christ bonded together by common belief and shared ideals, "a community of life, love and truth established by Christ." As a eucharistic community, Catholics come together in Sunday worship to experience the presence of the risen Christ in their midst, to recall the "Christ event" of his life-death-resurrection-ascension-glorification, to renew their faith and hope in him and their love of God and of each other. Jesus Christ is the basic experience of the community; his Spirit is the community's vivifying life, giving each member gifts for building-up the community.

This vision of community has important practical implications for the renewal envisioned by the council. Three are especially important.

- Community provides *our link with Jesus Christ.* The priest sociologist Andrew Greeley notes the importance of community.

  I have encountered Jesus only through community. ... Members of the community of the faithful have strengthened, reinforced, challenged, and reassured me as I have tried ... to grow in my knowledge of Jesus as a person, in my faith in him as the Lord, and in my loving service in imitation of him as savior.[8]

- Community answers a *deep-felt need* of people today. As modern life becomes more urbanized and impersonal, people instinctively feel the need to relate to others on deeper levels and to belong. A living, loving Christian community where people truly care about each other and move out to help others is a necessary support today.

- The church as community of people of faith is *good news* in a way the institutional church alone cannot be. Christians whose lives radiate the enthusiasm and joy of the love of Christ and their neighbor are powerful examples to others, becoming "good news" for them. Mother Teresa of Calcutta is one such.

An example I personally was privileged to experience is the community of San Egidio in Rome. This group of young Christians, single and married, ages 17 to 40 or more, have taken seriously the gospel of Christ to love others especially those in need. They distribute clothes to the poor of Rome; serve a substantial hot meal daily to 500 hungry men and women, young and old; provide counseling to the mentally disturbed off the streets who otherwise have no care; tutor poor students and immigrants; and do other works of Christian love. Their spiritual energy comes from their half-hour daily community prayer based on the Scriptures and their weekly eucharist together. Other young people see their dedication to Christ's poor and their joy and love in action and ask to join the community which now numbers over 70,000 in Rome and Italy, Latin America and Africa.

The Catholic *Laity*

By devoting a special document to the laity,[9] Vatican II rescued Catholic laymen and women from their secondary status in the church. For too long they had not received the respect nor exercised the role due them. The old adage "pray, pay and obey' too often described the laity. To be sure, parishes, diocese and the universal church gladly benefitted from their experience, skills, and money. Often their reward: titles, photo-ops, and lavish dinners! But lay men and women are not allowed to participate in the decisions that most affect their lives as Catholics, for the church defines them as "the non-ordained" and only the ordained have power. The success of today's renewal of the Catholic Church depends on its well-educated and articulate, generous and concerned laywomen and men ready and able to serve and save the church when given the chance. They are the future of the Catholic Church. (Chapter 15, Section 4)

Chapter 4 of the *Constitution on the Church* is titled *The Laity*, the Church's first official recognition of their important place and of their high vocation and personal rights. It speaks of their special vocation: "to seek the kingdom of God by engaging in temporal affairs and directing them according to God's will" (31); their equality in the church (32); their apostolate "a sharing in the salvific mission of the church... through baptism and confirmation" (33); their high role as sharing in Christ's priestly and prophetic roles (34-6); and their rights. (37) Chapter 4 closes with this eloquent sentence: "Each individual layman must be a witness before the world to the resurrection and life of the Lord Jesus and a sign of the living God" (38).

Ministry, Vocation of the Laity

The word ministry means service. Christian lay ministry is the vocation or call to service which baptized Catholic women and men have from Christ. The council insisted that the primary ministry of the lay faithful is a *ministry in and to the world,* a ministry proper to them as living and working in the world. Through them, in Michael Lawler's graphic statement, "the church is incarnate in the world to be leaven-symbol of love, hope, reconciliation, forgiveness, peace, justice, transformation, grace, presence, mystery."[10] Their high vocation is to establish and build the kingdom of God in our world.

According to *Lumen Gentium,* they "share the priestly, prophetic and kingly office of Christ[11] and to the best of their ability carry on the mission of the whole Christian people in the church and in the world" (31). "The laity are ... to make the church present and fruitful in those places and circumstances where it is only through them that she can become the salt of the earth" (33);"...the laity consecrate the world itself to God." (34)

Since Vatican II more and more Catholics realize that their family lives and daily work is their Christian ministry for God's kingdom. In growing numbers they intentionally choose careers in law and politics, foreign service, healing professions, education and social work. Likewise young people are increasingly joining the Peace Corps, Jesuit Volunteers, Maryknoll Associates and similar groups from a motive of Christian ministry. In the church of the first centuries, every Christian was a witness to Christ in his daily life and an evangelizer; through them the Mediterranean world became Christian.

Another ministry that is attracting growing numbers of Catholics, especially women, young adults, and married couples, is *church ministry.* A valuable resource for the church, Catholic lay people are full-time teachers in Catholic schools, parish youth ministers, spiritual directors, retreat givers, directors of Confraternity of Christian Doctrine, members of parish pastoral teams and eucharistic ministers. In a growing number of European and North American parishes, lay people and religious women – technically considered among the laity because not-ordained – are parish administrators, ministering to the people in everything except conducting the eucharist and the sacraments. Such opportunities, expanding at a fast pace, are changing the face of the church.

Rights of Laity

Another great accomplishment of the council was to recognize and officially state the rights of Catholic lay persons.

Like all Christians the laity have the right to receive in abundance the help of the spiritual goods of the church, especially that of the

Word of God and the sacraments from their pastors. To the latter the laity should disclose their needs and desires ... By reason of the knowledge, competence or pre-eminence which they have, the laity are empowered, indeed sometimes obliged, to manifest their opinion on those things that pertain to the good of the Church. (37)

Some phrases of this remarkable statement bear repeating: "have the right to receive... the sacraments"; "should disclose their needs and desires...";"are empowered, indeed sometimes obliged ... to manifest their opinion ... [for] the good of the Church." Why have not more Catholics taken these words seriously and acted upon them? Or has the church succeeded too well in forming the laity into passive, obedient sheep?

Has the church failed to carry out her responsibility to those she has proclaimed to be the church and to have specific rights? In many countries, Catholics participate in the Eucharist and sacraments only rarely. Entire continents are denied the sacraments, especially the Eucharist, for lack of priests. In Latin America, urban parishes often number 50,000 Catholics and countryside chapels are visited by a priest only two or three times a year. In the United States and Europe the number of priest-less parishes is rapidly increasing.

Today an urgent need is for concerned Catholics to demand of their bishops, including the Bishop of Rome, their right to "the word of God and the sacraments." Vatican II stated in its *Decree on the Ministry and Life of Priests* that "No Christian community can be built up unless it has its basis and center in the celebration of the most Holy Eucharist" (*Decree on the Life and Ministry of Priests,* 6). That the church must provide the Eucharist for its members may mean a married priesthood in the not too distant future. (See Chapter 15, section 1)

Since the council, Catholic lay men and women seek a larger role in the church and ask for a voice in the decisions that affect them. Yet, there is a not so subtle movement to tone down this new vision of church as the people of God lest the status of the clergy suffer. It is significant that the Extraordinary Synod of Bishops in 1985 failed even to mention the people of God in its final report. This distancing from the ecclesiology (theology of church) as people of God is a characteristic of "the **restoration**"[12] mentality prevalent today.

Significant Vatican II Renewal Achievements

- Emphasizing church as *mystery* captures St. Paul's contagious enthusiasm for Christ and his indefatigable zeal for evangelization, enriches Catholics' mature spirituality, shifts people's preoccupation with the sinfulness of the church to its attractive profound real nature and existence.
- Church as *sacrament* of the risen Christ challenges Catholics, members and leaders, to mirror Christ and his compassionate love in words and action and to accomplish his work today.
- Church as *body of Christ* including all Christians challenges Catholics to achieve Christ's prayer for unity of the separated Christian churches and to overcome divisive polarization within the Catholic Church.
- Church as *people of God* restores Catholic women and men to their role and ministry in the church, safeguards their rights, and lessens exaggerated clericalism,
- Recovering and emphasizing the *communion* theology of the church has far-reaching consequences for her renewal.

- A *pilgrim* church, in need of healing and help on its journey to the Lord, is a more humble church in constant need of renewal and reform.
- *Pilgrim people* form a church immersed in history. A truly renewed church is challenged to divest itself of accumulated 'baggage' of no longer tenable practices, laws, and theological formulations.[13]

Christ's Church is Unique

Of all the great cultures and religions in the history of the world, the Christian church makes the incredible claim that its founder is both God and man, the historical Jesus of Nazareth. It believes that Jesus' death by crucifixion brought salvation to the human family and makes the extraordinary claim that Jesus was raised to life by the power of God and lives today present to his millions of followers. Christians believe that the risen Christ and the Spirit Jesus sent to his disciples after his resurrection are present, guiding and helping them in manifold ways. In answering the deepest yearnings of the human heart for meaning and transcendence, the Christian church offers humankind hope in this world and the next.

We can describe this church as a human-divine reality made up of women and men, saints and sinners in which God is present and active. As such it has inspired millions of people through almost 2000 years to have *faith* in a transcendent God whom no one has seen, to believe in the extraordinary event of the **Incarnation** that God entered history by taking on human flesh in the God-man Jesus of Nazareth; to cling to the Christian virtue of *hope* that after this earthly pilgrimage their high vocation and destiny is an eternity of happiness and peace with God and their loved ones; and to *love* God and each other according to the example of Jesus. In so doing, this church has produced countless saints and **martyrs** who have lived lives of extraordinary heroic goodness and suffered torture and death as witnesses to Jesus Christ.

The Christian church is also unique in its size, made up of 2.25 billion people, embracing the Catholic, Orthodox churches, the Anglican communion, and the many varied Protestant churches and evangelical groups sharing the common bond of baptism.[14] Moreover, it is the largest among the many religious of the world.[15] In addition the Christian church is unique in its ability to survive in the face of overwhelming odds. It weathered the fierce Roman persecutions when Emperors like Nero and Diocletian tortured and killed thousands of Christians. It survived two cataclysmic ruptures in its own body: in the 11th century splitting into the western Roman Catholic and eastern **Orthodox**; churches and in the 16th century **Reformation** in Europe fracturing into the existing Catholic Church and multiple Protestant communities.[16] In the **Age of Enlightenment** in 18th century Europe it survived the frontal attack on the possibility of faith and belief in God. In our own times both the eastern Orthodox and western Catholic and Protestant churches survived devastating persecution under communist regimes in Russia and Eastern Europe and under Nazi "cleansing" in western Europe. Christians believe the church continues to exist because its founder the risen Christ promised it would survive through the centuries.

A prominent characteristic of the church is its extraordinary vitality worldwide today. It is growing by leaps and bounds in Africa and some parts of Asia. In mainland China with its 1.33 billion people (mid-2008) there is a relatively small but fervent group of Protestant and Catholic Christians, the possible harbinger of a future great harvest.[17] Yet a painful reality is the Christian Church's present division into many separate churches.[18] It is a sinful church in constant need of renewal and reform.

The Catholic Church

Within the church of Christ, the Catholic Church occupies a unique place. With the Orthodox she is an apostolic church reaching back to the 12 Apostles chosen by Jesus; as such she preserves the structure of bishops, reality of the Eucharist and the sacramental system, and the totality of God's revelation in Jesus Christ. In possessing the bishop of Rome as its foundation rock of unity, the Catholic Church makes the unique claim to be the fullest expression of the church Jesus established. Thanks to the modern ecumenical movement and a new positive approach to the Catholic Church, many Anglicans and a number of Protestants sense that in a future-united church which Christ prayed for, even the pope should in some way be present!

Significant current events in the Catholic Church are worth mentioning. The once slumbering church in South America has been awakened by liberation theology with its tens of thousands of base Christian communities whose members fervently live the gospel message of love and liberation and who have died by the thousands as martyrs for justice and charity. Throughout the world, the Catholic Church is in the forefront of the fight for freedoms, human rights, and the God-given dignity of the human person. In Latin America and the United States, the Catholic Church faces the enormous challenge of the Pentecostal and evangelical churches who preach the "born again" religious experience. For them, one is not a true Christian, a previous baptism and present belief notwithstanding, until one has had the Spirit-given conversion experience and makes an adult total commitment to Jesus Christ and thus is "saved." The Pentecostal churches are strongly missionary, offering their members personal love of Jesus their savior, familiarity with the Bible, powerful preaching, experience of community and a disciplined life. The Catholic Church has much to learn from them.

Though the nearly 2000-year history of the Catholic Church is beyond the scope of these pages, knowledge of its remarkable history is indispensable to understand today's church and her Vatican II renewal. Several readable recent church histories are mentioned at the end of this chapter, which both younger and older Catholics as well as our sister and brother Christians will find informative, stimulating and non-triumphal!

For Discussion

1. Does knowing and appreciating the church as mystery and as people of God change your opinion of the Catholic Church?
2. Do you think the Catholic Church fosters community? What more can be done?
3. How have you experienced the risen Christ present in the church?
4. What should/can Catholic lay women and men do to help renew the church? to reach out to youth and to others who feel marginalized by the church?

Further Reading

Bokenkotter, Thomas. *A Concise History of the Catholic Church,* Revised and Expanded Edition. Garden City, NY: Doubleday, 2005. The best comprehensive history available of the Catholic Church's tumultuous history. Interesting reading, very informative and including Vatican II.

Clark, Matthew H. *Forward in Hope: Saying AMEN to Lay Ecclesial Ministry.* Notre Dame, IN: Ave Maria Press, 2009. In a time when the numbers of priests are declining rapidly, Bishop Clark sees the lay ministry as critical to maintaining a vibrant faith community. He examines with optimism the ways the laity can transform the daily functioning of local parishes and the opportunities for increased lay input in the workings of the Church.

Dulles, Avery. *Models of the Church.* New York: Doubleday, 2000. In this updated version of his classic best-selling book, Fr. Dulles (later Cardinal) writes of the mystery of the church in terms of 'models' which illuminate aspects of how the Church functions in the world and in the lives of the faithful today: the Church as an earthly institution, a mystical communion and fellowship, a sacrament, the herald of Christ's message to the world, and as servant to all.

Rausch, Thomas P. *Towards a Truly Catholic Church: An Ecclesiology of the Third Millennium.* Collegeville, MN: Liturgical Press, 2005. Beginning with an analysis of Vatican II documents *Lumen Gentium* and *Gaudium et Spes*, Rausch provides an illuminating story in ecclesiological structures of the church as 'people of God,' 'body of Christ,' 'temple of the spirit,' and 'communion.' He stresses that the mystery of Christ is revealed in the community of the faithful and sees ecumenism as critical for the communion and unity of the people of God.

Footnotes

1 The original draft of the *Constitution on the Church* , *LG*, made the hierarchical church of pope and bishops its first chapter. After spirited debate, the final document became Chapter 1, church as Mystery; Chapter 2, as People of God,; Chapter 3, as Hierarchy to emphasize that the hierarchy is within the church, not above it.

2 The bishops emphasized that the reality of the church as sacrament is essential to the church's very "own nature and universal mission." LG 1. The church is meant to be both an example to the world and the means of bringing the human family to God and to live in unity.

3 The world is charged with the grandeur of God. It will flame out, like shining from shook foil; It gathers to a greatness, like the ooze of oil Crushed ... nature is never spent; There lives the dearest freshness deep down things. And though the last lights off the black West went Oh, morning, at the brown brink eastward, springs - Because the Holy Ghost over the bent World broods with warm breast and with ah! bright wings." Norman Mackenzie, ed., *The Poetical Works of Gerard Manley Hopkins* (New York: Oxford University Press, 1990), 131.

4 A valid baptism uses water and the Trinitarian form "in the name of the Father, and of the Son, and of the Holy Spirit.'

5 See LG, Chapter 1, number 7 for a beautiful development of Paul's writing on the Body of Christ.

6   The council spoke of the four presences of Christ in the Mass:: in the Scriptures proclaimed, in the Christian community present, in the priest acting in the person of Christ, and in the consecrated bread and wine.

7   The institutional model prevailed in the church for over four centuries since the Council of Trent 1545 – 1563. Because the Protestant Reformers attacked the authority of bishops and pope, the Counter Reformation Catholic Church emphasized the hierarchical, institutional nature of the church and its authority.

8   Andrew Greeley, *A New Agenda* (Garden City, N.Y.: Doubleday, 1973), 49.

9   Vatican II devoted a separate document, *Decree on the Apostolate of the Laity*. It described the laity's twofold apostolate as participation in the internal life of the church and in the renewal of the temporal order.

10 Michal Lawler, *A Theology of Ministry* (Kansas City: Sheed and Ward, 1990), 79.

11 As priest they offer themselves and their ministry to God; as prophet they witness Jesus' values by their lives; as king they work to establish God's kingdom of justice, love and peace.

12 Restoration, a term first used by Cardinal Ratzinger, refers to the effort to return to or restore some pre-Vatican II practices, to re-interpret Vatican II, and to put obstacles in the way of its program of renewal.

13 Examples are terms like curia, pontiff, province from the Roman Empire; Greek philosophical categories to express the nature of Christ; cultural approach to sex, status of women, etc.

14 The Christian Church is entered through baptism, therefore made up of all baptized believing Christian people. Consequently, it is a broader reality than any one existing church, Catholic or Orthodox or Anglican or Protestant. The second Vatican Council recognized the baptisms in these other churches as valid; thus Catholics began to call Christians sisters and brothers, rather than the demeaning "heretics and schismatics" as in their non-ecumenical past.

15 Christians, 2,280,616,000; Muslim 1,553,188,700; Hindus 942,871,000; Buddhists 462,625,000; Chinese Universalists (Folk Religionists) 454,404,500; Tribal Religionists 269,723,000; New Religionists 63,684,100; Sikhs 23,758,300; Jews 14,824,000; others, Shamanists, Confucians, Bahais, Jains, Shintoists 41,224,000. (Encyclopedia Britannica, Book of the Year, mid-2010, 302.)

16 Prior to the Reformation the still united western Catholic Church managed to survive its major leadership crisis of the 70-year-long Western Schism when three men claimed to be pope to the confusion of the Christian world. It also survived periods of especially corrupt leadership in the 10th and 12th centuries and in the 15th and 16th when popes and bishops were unworthy men.

17 There are roughly 14 million Catholics in China divided between the "underground church" and the Catholic Patriotic Association church (though the numbers are probably much larger) and more than 40 million Protestants thanks to the phenomenal growth of Pentecostal conversions.

18 Roman Catholics 1,150,661,000; Protestants 419,795,000; Orthodox 270,227,000; Anglicans 86,051,000; others, small house churches and mega churches, various sects 320,668,000. (Encyclopedia Britannica, Book of the Year, mid-2010).

Chapter 4:
Momentous Change: Liturgy / Sacraments

The liturgy is … an exercise of the priestly office of Jesus Christ. (SC 7) … the summit toward which the activity of the Church is directed; the fount from which all her power flows. (SC 10)

...every liturgical celebration, because it is an action of Christ the Priest and of his body which is the Church, is a sacred action surpassing all others. (SC 7)

In passing *The Constitution on the Sacred Liturgy, SC,* by an overwhelming vote of 2169 for, 46 against,[1] the bishops at Vatican II "set in motion a programmatic reshaping of virtually every aspect of Roman Catholic liturgy unlike anything that had ever happened before."[2]

Why such a momentous change? Because liturgy, the way Catholics worship, the way they relate to God and to each other, the way God's salvation comes to them, is at the very center of Catholic lives. Vatican liturgist Piero Marini insists that "Celebrating the liturgy is itself the primordial source of renewal in the church … the future of liturgy is the future of the church."[3] In the light of the crises in the church today, it is important to see how this major change came about, how the council bishops were able to so completely reform such a vitally important part of the Catholic Church's life, and to understand the "reform of the reform" that is dominant today.

Prior to the First World War, a vibrant liturgical renewal began in the Benedictine monasteries throughout Europe. Dom Lambert Beauduin, a Belgium monk of the abbey of Mt. Cesar, promoted the recovery of an ancient understanding of the liturgy as the priestly offering and work of Christ and of his Mystical Body on earth and of the full participation of the people as flowing from the nature of the liturgy and of the church.[4] At monastic abbeys like Solesmes in France and Maria Lach in Germany, Benedictine monks experienced the dignity and beauty of the church's liturgy in their community worship. Liturgical scholars began study of worship in the early church, publishing in liturgical journals read by many.

Before the council, pastoral bishops began to ask for changes in the liturgy to restore the community-oriented liturgy of the early church and the peoples' involvement in worship. This was a dramatic change from the unchanging Mass of the Council of Trent over 400 years ago that emphasized Latin, the priest as celebrant, correct external rubrics, and a passive laity as "mute spectators."[5] The text on the liturgy presented to the bishops at the first session of the council in 1962 reflected this monastic liturgical renewal. It elicited a spirited debate that lasted three weeks with 328 speeches called interventions by the bishops plus 297 written submissions.[6]

The hot button issues for the minority conservative bishops were the use of Latin and whether bishops' conferences have authority over the church's worship. The intervention of Maximos IV of the Melkite Catholic Patriarchate won high praise from the council bishops.

> The almost absolute value assigned to Latin in the … Latin church strikes us from the Eastern church as strange. Christ after all spoke the language of his contemporaries. … All languages are liturgical. … The Latin language is dead. But the church is living, and its language, the vehicle of the grace of the Holy Spirit, must also be living because it is intended for us human beings not for angels.[7]

The Constitution on the Sacred Liturgy, SC, (Sacrum Concilium)[8]

The **paschal mystery** of Christ's saving death and resurrection continues in the church through the sacred liturgy of the Eucharist, the great thanksgiving prayer of the church and the memorial of Jesus' paschal mystery, and in the sacraments. The liturgy is the action of Christ himself and of the baptized people of God. It is meant to transform Christians precisely because in liturgical worship baptized Christians meet and experience the person of Jesus Christ. "... every liturgical celebration is an action of Christ the Priest and of his body the church."(7)

To appreciate the momentous reform program of the Vatican II bishops, I quote the straight-forward, often eloquent words of the Constitution. These passages are taken from the Introduction and first Chapter, "The Nature of the Sacred Liturgy and its Importance in the Life of the Church," (Numbers 1-46 and Chapter Three, "The Other Sacraments." (59-82).

- *Sacred Nature of the Liturgy:* "Every liturgical celebration because it is an action of Christ the priest and of his body which is the church is a pre-eminently sacred action." (7)
- *The Most Important Renewal Principle.* "It is very much the wish of the church that all the faithful should be led to take that full, conscious, and active part in liturgical celebrations which is demanded by the very nature of the liturgy, and to which the Christian people ... have a right ... by reason of their baptism." (14) "In the restoration and promotion of the sacred liturgy the full and active participation by all the people is the aim to be considered above all else.' (7)
- *Purpose of the Reform.* "To import ever-increasing vigor to the Christian lives of the faithful; to adapt to the needs of our age; to encourage the union of all who believe in Christ." (1)

- *Importance of the Reform.* It is where "the work of our redemption takes place." Through liturgy Catholics "express in their lives ... the mystery of Christ and the real nature of the true church. ... The liturgy builds up those in the church ... to the fullness of Christ." (2)
- *Four-fold Presence of Christ.* "He is present in the Sacrifice of the Mass in the presence of his minister [the priest], in the Eucharistic species [bread and wine], ... in Scripture read in the church ... when the church prays and sings." (7)
- *Unique Place in the Church.* "The liturgy is the *summit* toward which the activity of the church is directed; it is also the *source* from which all its power flows.' (10)
- *Reform of Liturgical Texts and Rites.* The texts should "express clearly what they signify [so that] the Christian people understand them easily and take part in them." (1) The rites...should be short, clear and free from useless repetition .... within the peoples' comprehension." (37)
- *Scripture Renewal:.* "Sacred Scripture is of the greatest importance in the celebration of the liturgy" (24). "The treasures of the Bible are to be opened up more lavishly." (51) "The homily is strongly recommended ... [as] part of the liturgy itself ... and must not be omitted." (52)
- *Liturgy is Public.* "Liturgical services are not private functions but are celebrations of the entire church." (26)
- *Cultural Variety.* "The church does not wish to impose a rigid uniformity." (SC 37) ...provision shall be made for adaptations to different groups, regions, and peoples especially in mission countries." (38) "...elements from the traditions and cultures of individual peoples might be admitted into divine worship." (40)
- *The Vernacular.* "A wider use may be made of it ... to be decided by local bishops." (36).

- *Holy Spirit in Liturgy.* "Enthusiasm for the promotion and restoration of the sacred liturgy is a sign … of the movement of the Holy Spirit." (43)
- *Peoples' Responsibility.* "… that the liturgy produce its full effects, it is necessary that the faithful come to it with proper dispositions…" (11)

Sacraments are Liturgical Actions.

'The purpose of sacraments is to sanctify people, to build up the body of Christ, to worship God. … They presuppose faith. … nourish, strengthen, express it … confer grace. … It is of greatest importance the faithful easily understand the symbolism of the sacraments.' (59)

Sacraments are privileged encounters with Christ where Catholics meet and experience Jesus and his saving power in each sacrament. When Catholics approach sacraments with faith and desire, sacraments are transformative. In explaining Christ's action in each sacrament, theologians describe sacraments as *symbolic* rituals, actions using words and primordial elements like water in baptism, oil in confirmation, ordination and anointing of the sick, bread and wine in the Eucharist, which make present the spiritual effects of each sacrament.[9] In this way the visible ritual action points to and makes real Christ's invisible action.[10]

All religions use symbolic rituals as doorways to the spiritual world to express their relationship to the divine. For example, Native Americans practice the sun-dance, the sweat lodge, and the vision quest. Religious Jews and Christians bless food before eating. Muslims turn to Mecca and prostrate themselves to pray. Catholic parents trace the sign of the cross on their children's foreheads before they go to sleep. Young people sit in the lotus position, hands outstretched, in meditation. To be human is to use rituals.

How Catholics Experience Their Sacraments

- *As Celebrations.* Celebration lifts our spirits, revives and restores us, bonds us with others; so effective liturgical sacramental celebration revives our faith, restores our hope, inspires us to love God and the community about us, giving a foretaste of heaven. Baptism, first communion, confirmation and marriage are joyful family celebrations. Eucharist and ordination are festive celebrations of the entire Christian community. Reconciliation and anointing the sick are consoling celebrations of God's loving care and solicitude.
- *As Heightened Experiences of Daily Life.* Our experiences of forgiving another person or of being forgiven is intensified when we experience Jesus' forgiveness in the sacrament of reconciliation. Our experience of friendship and love in family meals or with special friends is heightened in the sacrament of the eucharistic meal.
- *As Bonds* uniting Catholics in a world of disbelief and hopelessness, of greed and hate but still suffused with the compassion and love of Jesus Christ.
- *As Encounters with Christ.*[11] When the church baptizes or confirms or forgives sins, it is the risen Christ who baptizes, confirms and forgives. Sacraments draw their spiritual power from Jesus' paschal mystery of his suffering, death and resurrection for the salvation of all people.
- *As Christ's Actions and Ours.* We join the risen Christ in his offering to the Father of his saving suffering and death.
- *As Transformative.* The purpose of sacraments is to transform us into Christ, to effect change in our attitudes and values and

our way of living. To achieve this conversion, we must come with faith and the sincere desire to receive the graces Christ offers and be willing to change. Otherwise, sacraments are magic and superstition.

Catholics value and love their sacraments. The Catholic Church is a sacramental church.

Evaluation of the Renewal of the Liturgy since the Council

The liturgical renewal has been hugely successful. The majority of Catholics appreciate the Mass in English with the priest directly addressing them, value the emphasis on Scripture, participate more fully, and experience being part of the worshipping Christian community. Many receive communion under both species of bread *and* of wine. "The council's desire for full, active and conscious participation has been realized in much of the church throughout the English-speaking world ... especially evident in the growth of lay ecclesial ministry and liturgical leadership ... [and] in recovering the intrinsic relationship between liturgy and life – worship that flows into social outreach to the poor and disenfranchised."[12] However, liturgical scholars call attention to a loss of the transcendent and look to recovering a sense of mystery and silence in post-Vatican II liturgy.

The renewed rituals of baptism, marriage and anointing of the sick have taken on new meaning as family and parish spiritual experiences. The emphasis on reconciliation with those around us as well as with God, the healing compassion of Christ, the less legalistic approach toward confessing sins, and the opportunity for face to face confession have enriched the newly-named sacrament of Reconciliation, though Catholics' use of this sacrament has drastically declined.

One of the most successful renewal practices of Vatican II has been the restoration of the ancient catechumenate for adults, called Rite of Christian Initiation for Adults (RCIA). (64) By the third century persons were prepared for baptism by a lengthy period of two or three years of instruction in the Christian faith culminating in the period that later became Lent and climaxed in the night before Easter by the initiation sacraments of baptism, confirmation and the Eucharist. (See chapter 5). Gradually this practice fell into disuse throughout the church. Today the earlier practice in modified form in the RCIA is generally a year-long program in each parish made up of *catechumens* preparing for first baptism or of already baptized *candidates* seeking full communion with the Catholic Church celebrated at the Easter Vigil Mass.

In recent years, however, a "reform of the reform" by which the original liturgical renewal/reform of Vatican II has been replaced by a series of Vatican documents and actions that constitute this new liturgical reform movement. Two results have been the Vatican's encouragement of the Tridentine Mass in Latin with the priest-celebrant facing away from the people and the new translation of the Roman Missal introduced in the United States in Advent 2011. This reform of the reform is seen as turning away from the "full, conscious, active participation of the people of God" and the council's emphasis on the worshipping community.

For English-speaking Catholics, the Roman Curia's Congregation for Divine Worship and the Sacraments (CDW) rejected 16-years work by liturgical scholars of ICEL (International Commission for English in the Liturgy) commissioned by eleven English-speaking national bishops' conferences to translate into English Pope Paul VI's Roman Missal. Liturgical scholar Keith Pecklers in "The Process of Liturgical Translation" chronicles the long non-collegial process by which the original membership of ICEL was replaced by CDW, ICEL statutes changed, the bishops' conferences over-ruled and Vox Clara

(Clear Voice) created to oversee a totally new translation by a different ICEL membership.[13]

For those committed to the renewal of Vatican II, CDW's unilateral action represented a serious twofold repudiation of the Vatican Council: the authority of national bishops' conferences over the liturgy and the practice of collegiality, a major theme of Vatican II.

March 16, 2001, CDW formally rejected ICEL's 1988 English Sacramentary translation with the publication of *Liturgicam Authenticam (Authentic Liturgy),* the fifth instruction on translating liturgical texts called "The Right Implementation of the Constitution on the Sacred Liturgy of the Second Vatican Council." It established a new set of principles of translation, *formal equivalency* (literal) to replace ICEL's *dynamic equivalency,* the effort to convey the overall sense and meaning of the Latin text in each language. Pecklers noted that *Authentic Liturgy* was addressed primarily to ICEL and the English-speaking world ... especially regarding the issue of inclusive language."[14]

CDW's expressed purpose of formal equivalency is better to bring out the "sacred mysteries of salvation" and achieve a unity of wording in the many language translations. An unhappy result has been literal, almost word-for-word translation from the Latin. Strong negative reaction to the new English translation of the Mass soon followed. In the United States, an article by Seattle pastor Fr. Michael Ryan, "What If We Said, Wait?" elicited 22,000 lengthy, thoughtful objections to the new Mass translation from deeply-concerned liturgical experts, priests and sisters, lay lectors and Eucharistic ministers, and parish staff from eleven English-speaking countries.[15] Bishop Donald Trautman, chair of the U.S. Bishops Liturgy Commission, spoke and wrote in favor of the ICEL translation, pointing out the inadequacy for English-speaking people of the literal translations from the Latin. "If the Roman Missal does not speak to our culture, the church in the United States will suffer."[16]

The new translation is now a reality. Bishops' conferences and diocesan offices of worship and the Catholic people are encouraged to use it, in liturgist Pecklers' words, as "a *kairos* moment – a fresh opportunity for the church to be renewed in its worship of the triune God." He states "the church is offering us an important invitation ... to evaluate our liturgical practice and to reflect on how we can better improve our worship so that it more profoundly exhibits the ecclesiological, liturgical, and theological vision of the Second Vatican Council."[17]

Of Special Interest: The Church's Liturgical Year

By living the church's liturgical year, Catholics recall and experience the life of Jesus and the great variety of canonized Saints. Sundays throughout the year celebrate major events in Christ's life and weekday Masses follow readings from both the Hebrew and Christian Scriptures or commemorate Saints' lives. To enrich the liturgy with the Scriptures, three Bible passages were chosen, one each from the Hebrew Scriptures, from the letters of Paul or of other writers, and from one of the four Gospels. Readings from the Synoptic Gospels are arranged in a three-year cycle: A from Matthew, B from Mark, and C from Luke. John's Gospel occurs throughout the liturgical year.

The liturgical year begins in late November or early December with the four Sundays of Advent whose three readings prepare us for the coming of Jesus our Savior. Christmas Day celebrates his humble birth with succeeding Sundays dedicated to his hidden life at Nazareth. On the six Sundays of **Lent**, the church stresses penance for sin and baptism in memory of the catechumens' final preparation for baptism. Lent prepares Christians for "the great week," the holiest of the liturgical year. Thursday of **Holy Week**, a single Eucharist celebrates the Lord's Supper, Jesus' gift of his body and blood and his washing the disciples' feet; on Good Friday Christians enter into the sufferings of Jesus leading to his cruel crucifixion that saved humanity from sin. The Saturday evening Easter vigil and Masses on Easter Sunday, the greatest feast of the liturgical year, celebrate the resurrection of Christ the Lord, his victory over death and the guarantee of our own future resurrection. Forty days follow to commemorate the period of Jesus' visible risen life on earth, climaxed by the two great feasts of Ascension Thursday celebrating Jesus' glorification in heaven and nine days later of Pentecost Sunday to commemorate Jesus' sending his Holy Spirit on the Apostles and the beginning of the church. The "Ordinary" Sundays until Advent recall the public life of Jesus, his teaching, miracles and healings.

The popular liturgical cycle called the *Proper of the Saints* occurs on week days throughout the year. This calendar of canonized saints covers almost 2000 years and includes both men and women, young and old, martyrs and "confessors," founders and members of religious orders, and persons from every continent and most countries of the world. Individual countries and each religious order and congregation celebrate their own saints on special days. For example, Mexico and the United States celebrate with festive Masses and mariachi bands the feast of Our Lady of Guadalupe on December 12 when in 1531 a brown-skinned Mary appeared to the peasant Indian Juan Diego outside of Mexico City.

For Discussion

1. Why did Vatican II need to recover an older practice of liturgy and sacraments? Give examples.

2. How do rituals mediate or accomplish spiritual realities? What are the most important differences between the Catholic sacraments and non-Christian rituals?

3. Do you think Mass said in local, colloquial language is preferable to Mass said in Latin? Why? If you were traveling to a country whose language you do not speak, does your opinion change?

4. Do you really believe that you can meet God, "encounter" Christ in the sacraments? Why? What are the most important gifts sacraments give you.

Further Reading

Osborne, Kenan B. *Sacramental Theology, A General Introduction.* New York: Paulist Press, 1988. Osborne offers a readable as well as detailed study of the history and development of the Catholic sacraments from the early times of the church through the reasons for their renewal at Vatican II. Central to his study is an understanding that 'the church itself is a basic sacrament,' and the necessity of the sacraments for the faith life and spirituality of the faithful. He also offers ecumenical approaches to understanding the centrality of the Catholic sacraments.

Ferrone, Rita. *Liturgy: Sacrosanctum Concilium.* Mahwah, NJ: Paulist Press, 2007. This book focuses on the Vatican II document "The Constitution on the Sacred Liturgy," examining and explaining how exactly the liturgical changes reformed and revitalized the way parishioners' participate in the Mass. She points to the importance and the future of liturgical renewal for "the times in which we live." A great introduction for Catholics born after Vatican II.

Mitchell, Nathan D. *Meeting Mystery: Liturgy, Worship, Sacraments.* Maryknoll, NY: Orbis, 2006. This is a vibrant discussion of the meaning of the liturgy and sacraments, written in the context of a post-modern multicultural and globalized world. For Mitchell, the liturgy is about the connections between God and us, as well as between ourselves and one another through both space and time.

Noll, Ray R. *Sacraments, A New Understanding for a New Generation.* Mystic, CN: Twenty-Third Publications, 1999. For a new generation of believers wondering about the meaning and practical value of the sacraments, this book offers clear and concrete explanations and answers in a readable and student-friendly book. He explores the sign, meaning, and experience of each of the seven sacraments in the church and in the lives of the faithful.

Pecklers, Keith F. *Worship, A Primer in Christian Ritual,* 2003, and *The Genius of the Roman Rite, On the Reception of the New Missal,* 2009. Collegeville, MN: Liturgical Press. These very readable and informative books by a modern liturgical expert are essential reading to understand both the importance and the way ritual works in the Mass and sacraments and the history, personalities and issues behind the new translation of the Roman Missal.

Footnotes

1   The vote "represented a great breakthrough despite last-minute attempts in certain circles of the Roman Curia to sideline the process in favor of a rubrical, centralized, and rigidly immutable Roman liturgy celebrated in Latin." Keith F. Pecklers, *The Genius of the Roman Rite, On the Reception and Implementation of the New Missal.* Collegeville, MN: Liturgical Press, 2009), 26.

2   John W. O'Malley, S.J. *What Happened at Vatican II* (Cambridge, MA; Harvard University Press, 2008), 139.

3   Pecklers, *op.cit.,* 115.

4   Richard R. Gaillardetz and Catherine E. Clifford, *Keys to the Council, Unlocking the Teaching of Vatican II,* Collegeville, MN: The liturgical Press), 2012. 23-34. Beauduin was critical of the state of the liturgy of his time: laity passive at Mass, the liturgy considered the prerogative of the clergy, and adoration of the Blessed Sacrament as the highest form of worship!

5   The Council of Trent Mass was in Latin unintelligible to most and silently spoken by a priest "up there" with his back to the people and separated from them by the communion rail, emphasizing the strict distinction between priest and people who were thus passive spectators often filling their time praying the rosary or reading prayer books.

6   See O'Malley, *op.cit.,* 129-141 for his interesting, revealing account.

7   *Ibid,* 136.

8   Austin Flannery, Gen. Ed. *The Basic 16 Documents, Vatican Council II* (Northport, N.Y.: Costello Publishing Co., 1996) 117-161.

9   Theologians explained that each sacrament causes its distinctive spiritual effect precisely *by signifying* that spiritual reality. For example. Baptism by total immersion of a person in water *signifies* his/her death to all sin; the baptized person coming out of the water signifies his/her new life like Christ emerging from the tomb with his new risen life. Ultimately, of course, it is the power of the risen Christ and the Holy Spirit that achieves the spiritual reality. Vatican II

insisted that the renewal of sacraments as symbolic rituals demands they "express more clearly the holy realities they signify"(SC 21) so that "the faithful easily understand the symbolism of sacraments. (SC 59)

10 The eminent systematic theologian Karl Rahner insists that it is precisely in and through the real symbol that Christ's action in sacraments become present. See his article 'Theology of Symbol' in *Theological Investigations 1V.* See also Louis-Marie Chauvet's *Symbol and Sacrament: A Re-Interpretation of Christian Existence,* the classic on the subject of symbol..

11 Belgium Dominican Eduard Schillebeeckx proposed this new theological insight in his 1960 book *Christ, the Encounter with God.*

12 Pecklers, *op.cit.,*40-41.

13 *Ibid.* 61.

14 Pecklers, *op. cit.,* See also Robert Mickens informative three-article series in *The Tablet* that chronicles in detail this long story: "Unlocking the Door of the Vernacular," June 18, 2011, 11-12; "How Rome Moved the Goal Posts," June 25, 2011, 8-9; " A War of Words," July 2, 2011, 8-9.

15 Michael G. Ryan, "What if We Said, Wait?" *America,* December 14, 2009, 17. The countries represented are Australia, Canada, England and Wales, India, Ireland, New Zealand, the Philippines, Scotland, South Africa and the United States.

16 See *National Catholic Reporter,* November 13, 2009, pp 1 and 14, for his October 22 address at the Catholic University of America, Washington, DC. See also his "How Accessible are the New Mass Translations," *America,* May 21, 2007.

17 Pecklers, *op.cit.,* 91.

Chapter 5:
New Life, Forgiveness, Friendship

S acraments are the lifeblood of the Catholic Church, the consolation and joy of Catholics, their source of strength and hope in the struggles of daily life. Three special sacraments bring *life* in abundance, offer healing *forgiveness* and seal the *friendship* of intimate love. By its renewal of the sacraments of baptism, reconciliation and marriage, Vatican II greatly enriched the spiritual lives of Catholics.

Baptism - New Life

It is the year 150, Smyrna, Asia Minor, the night before Easter Sunday. In flickering candle-light, 33 catechumens, men and women and their sponsors, are gathered around a sunken pool of water. It was an experience they would never forget. That Holy Saturday night they fasted and prayed, turned to the darkened west to renounce Satan and to the east where the sun rises to commit themselves to Christ, the light of the world. Then, as dawn approached, the catechumens (candidates for baptism) were stripped of their clothes, entered the sunken baptismal font, and were immersed three times; after each immersion they professed faith in the Trinity, first in the Father, then the Son, then the Holy Spirit. Coming up out of the water, their five senses were anointed with the oil of chrism and the Holy Spirit was asked to give them his power. The newly baptized in Christ then put on a white garment and took a lighted candle. Thus attired, they left the baptistery and entered the church where the assembled Christian community welcomed them warmly with the kiss of peace. As the dawn broke, the joyful Easter eucharistic celebration began and the new Christians received the body and blood of Christ for the first time.

In scenes like this throughout the Mediterranean world, catechumens were initiated into the Christian community to begin their journey as followers of Jesus Christ. It was a life-transforming event, the climax of three long years of preparation in which they learned the central Christian beliefs and how to pray. During it, they made the momentous decision to give their lives to Christ, to renounce a former sinful life, and to risk dying for the crime of being a Christian.

It should be noted that in Rome 150 A.D. baptism was more likely done in a household church in a pool of general use probably in the courtyard. After the baptism, the new Christians would enter a large interior room and celebrate the Eucharist, probably the agape socioreligious meal.

Let us try to appreciate the powerful sacrament that is baptism and the extraordinary experience it was for those early Christians. Christ became the inspiration and model of their lives as they took the noble name of Christian. Baptism was their *christening*: their sharing Christ's own divine life and a mystical real sharing in the paschal mystery of his death and resurrection.[1] By their immersion in the baptismal pool, all their past sins, no matter how great or ugly, were totally taken away as the new life of Christ flooded their being. This new life is a second birth making them a new creation. (2 Cor. 5:17) Armed with the Holy Spirit's gifts of faith, hope and love they begin their Christian journey as disciples of Jesus to the glory of heaven and receive their mission to spread the good news of Christ and build his kingdom of justice and love.

Through baptism people join the Christian church as on that first Pentecost in Jerusalem when 3000 persons were baptized. Baptism unites all Christians – Catholics, Orthodox, Anglicans, and Protestants

– and is the basis of the ecumenical movement.[2] Christians recognize this bond when they pray in the Creed: "We believe in one baptism, in the communion of the saints, in the resurrection of the body, and life everlasting." For Paul Lakeland "Vatican II rediscovered the sacrament of baptism for the institutional church. ... [It] changed everything for ordinary Catholics by making clear ... that we all are equal in baptism, that baptism is our entry into mission, that we truly 'own' our church."[3] Baptism is *the* great sacrament of the church, too often under-appreciated by those baptized as infants.

Origin of Baptism

Following Jewish proselyte baptism and John the Baptist's baptism for repentance of sin, the church used water as the means of obtaining these extraordinary benefits of baptism. Water is a powerful cosmic symbol, both life-giving and life-destroying, apt for Christ giving new life to the baptized and destroying all their sins.

The early church developed its theology of baptism from the New Testament gospels and the writings of St. Paul. The three synoptic gospels – Matthew, Mark, Luke -   describe Jesus' baptism by John in the Jordan River: coming out of the water, Jesus receives the Holy Spirit, hears a voice assuring him he is pleasing to God, and then is driven by the Spirit into the desert where through severe temptations he discovers and embraces his life vocation (Mt 3:13-17; Mark 1:9-12; Luke 3:21-2) Two effects of baptism are described in the *Acts of the Apostles* when on Pentecost Sunday Peter answers the crowd's question "What are we to do?" "Repent and be baptized every one of you and be baptized in the name of Jesus Christ so that your sins may be forgiven; and you will receive the gift of the Spirit." (Acts 2:38)

In letters to his Christian communities in Asia Minor, St. Paul developed his theology of baptism through images familiar to his hearers.

Cleansing from Sin: "you have been washed, consecrated, justified in the name of the Lord Jesus Christ and in the Spirit of our God.' (1Cor 6:11)

A New Creature and a Birth: "For anyone who is in Christ is a new creation." (2 Cor. 5:17)

Clothes Metaphor and Bond of Unity: "All you who have been baptized into Christ have clothed yourselves with him. There does not exist among you Jew or Greek, slave or free, male or female. All are one in Christ." (Galatians 3:27-8)

Member of Christ's Body: "For in the one Spirit we were all baptized into one body."

All Are Equal: "In one Spirit we were all baptized, Jews as well as Greeks, slaves as well as citizens, and one spirit was given us all to drink." (1 Cor. 12:13)

Death and Life in Christ: "Are you not aware that we who were baptized into Christ Jesus were baptized into his death? Through baptism into his death we were buried with him, so that just as Christ was raised from the dead by the glory of the Father, we too might live a new life. If we have been united with him through likeness to his death, so shall we be through a like resurrection." (Romans 6:3-5)

Renewal of Baptism

In renewing the ritual of baptism, Vatican II called for revision of the rites both for adult baptism (*SC* 66) and infant baptism (*SC* 67) to emphasize the distinctive nature of each, particularly the responsibility of parents and godparents in infant baptism. The actual revision was left for later commissions which produced the *Rite of Baptism for Children* in 1964 and the new *Rite of Christian Initiation for Adults* (RCIA) in 1972.[4]

The essence of the sacrament of baptism is the water ritual and the words "(Name), I baptize you in the name of the Father and of the Son and of the Holy Spirit." The complete baptismal ceremony is a memorable multiple ritual including reading from Scripture, blessing of the baptismal water by recalling the times God used water in the history of Israel, a solemn renunciation of sin and profession of faith, and three impressive symbolic actions.

- *anointing* with healing oil." We anoint you with the oil of salvation in the name of Christ our Savior. May he strengthen you with his power... "
- holding a *lighted candle* symbolizing Christ the light of the world. "You have been enlightened by Christ. Walk always as a child of the light and keep the flame of faith alive in your heart."
- clothing with *white garment* to signify the baptized's purity of soul and new life in Christ. "(Name)... you have become a new creation and have clothed yourself in Christ. Take this white garment and bring it unstained to the judgment seat of our Lord Jesus Christ so that you may have everlasting life."

In the case of infant baptism, a beautiful prayer of blessing for both mother and father concludes the baptismal ritual.

The renewed ritual of baptism is a deeply meaningful family event. Grandparents, uncles and aunts and family friends come from afar to participate in this great sacrament. Vatican II's revised ritual is often a moving spiritual experience, especially for the parents. The reception afterwards is a family celebration of joy and gratitude flowing from their Christian faith in this religious event that has drawn them together.

The Rite of Christian Initiation for Adults (RCIA)

In renewing the ancient **catechumenate** as described in chapter 4, **RCIA** has become one of the most successful renewal practices to come from Vatican II. Its success comes from the dynamics of creating a prayerful sharing Christian community. Each catechumen and his/her sponsor share their spiritual journey, discuss openly and with trust the questions they have about Catholic beliefs and practices, pray together, and form friendships. While learning Catholic teachings and practices, they experience the bond of a Christian community. The Easter Vigil on Holy Saturday night is the highlight when the catechumens officially join the Catholic Church by receiving the three sacraments of baptism, confirmation and Eucharist. It is a joyous occasion in the presence of the parish community and relatives and friends.

Issues Related to Baptism

Recovery of Immersion. For the first thousand years of the Catholic Church, immersion was the ordinary way of baptizing, dramatically expressing death to sin and the new life of Christ. The later practice of pouring water on one's forehead symbolizing cleansing or washing does not adequately express Paul's powerful symbol of dying and rising with Christ. Baptism thus brings about a mystical, ontological union between the baptized and Jesus' very death and resurrection. For St. Paul, baptism marks the end of the power of sin and of the devil over the baptized and brings about the new creation in the life of Christ. Vatican II encouraged full immersion for infants and adults alike. A large baptismal pool is an increasingly common sight at the entrance of Catholic churches.

Original Sin. The teaching of the Catholic Church is that baptism remits all sin including Original Sin. Since all are born with Original Sin, what happens to infants who die without baptism? Theologians posited a place or state called Limbo since Hell would be unjust punishment. However, the existence of Limbo is questioned by theologians including then Pope Benedict XVI. Since 1950, theologians have reconsidered the meaning of Original Sin, emphasizing God's salvific will, that God wants all to be saved whom God created out of love. Accordinly, it is pastorally prudent to emphasize the many rich benefits of the sacrament of baptism rather than the removal of Original Sin.

Necessity of Baptism for Salvation. The Catholic Church teaches that baptism is necessary for salvation. At the same time, God wants all to be saved, God's grace is available to all people, and the working of that grace is unknown to us. Sacramental theologian Kenan Osborne observes that "the main issue is not with [the necessity of] baptism but with Jesus [as Savior of all by his death and resurrection] ... This is the dominant and controlling idea behind the statement that baptism is necessary for salvation."[5]

Infant Baptism. New Testament baptism is adult baptism and involves personal faith. St. Paul's references to the effects of baptism refer to the baptism of adults. It is not known when the church started baptizing infants. By the year 200, probably earlier, the church began to baptize infants. When asked why, St. Augustine proposed washing away Original Sin. As a result, Catholics came to view the main effect of baptism as 'getting rid' of Original Sin, thus obscuring the many wonderful graces given at baptism. Because of the theological ambiguity of an infant receiving a sacrament that involves adult faith commitment, Vatican II emphasized that the rite of adult baptism is normative as best expressing the full meaning of the sacrament of baptism.

In practicing infant baptism, the church stresses that infant baptism brings the infant into the Christian community so that the child's life of faith can be nourished in the formative years, that faith is indeed present in the vicarious faith expressed by parents and spouses in the ritual and that St. Paul baptized whole households presumably including children.

Reconciliation-Forgiveness[6]

"Though your sins be as scarlet, they will become white as snow." (Isaiah 1:18)
… his father caught sight of him and was deeply moved. He ran out to meet him, threw his arms around his neck, and kissed him. … Let us eat and celebrate because this son of mine was dead and has come back to life. He was lost and is found. Then the celebration began. (Luke 15:20-24)
"Forgiving is not forgetting … it's a second chance for a new beginning."

Bishop Desmond Tutu

A teen-age son, bored with life at home, talked his old father into giving him his rich inheritance. He went off to the city, spent his money on wine, women and song. After a while, he wound up friendless, hungry, and lonely. He remembered his old father and how good life was there. "Coming to his senses at last, he said … "I will return to my father and say to him, Father I have sinned against God and you; I no longer deserve to be your son."

The Dutch master-painter Rembrandt captured this moving scene of the prodigal son kneeling shoeless and in tattered clothes, his head buried in his father's embrace, and the old man, head bent lovingly toward his son, hands spread tenderly on his son's shoulders in a gesture of love and total acceptance.

Jesus told this beautiful parable of repentance and forgiveness to show the kind of God his Jewish listeners and we have today: totally forgiving, full of tender love for weak people who sin, celebrating when we return to our loving God.

This intensely human scene powerfully illustrates what the church's sacrament of Reconciliation can be: a sinner's reconciliation with those offended; an experience of God's forgiveness and healing love; a joyful celebration. The prodigal son felt a strong need to return to his father and to hear his words of forgiveness and receive his reassuring embrace. We too need the reassurance and "proof" of God's forgiveness when we candidly relate our sins to Christ's minister, the priest, and hear the words of absolution: "...through the ministry of the Church, may God give you pardon and peace; and I absolve you from your sins, in the name of the Father, and of the Son, and of the Holy Spirit." The church's sacrament of Reconciliation recalls and repeats again that first Easter evening after his resurrection when Jesus appeared to his disciples and said:

"Peace be with you. As the Father has sent me, so I send you." Then he breathed on them and said: "Receive the Holy Spirit. If you forgive men's sins, they are forgiven them; if you hold them bound, they are bound." (John 20: 22-23)

Our culture has a great need to recover a sense of sin. Sin is real in our lives. It alienates us from God, from others, and even from our better selves. We feel the need to shed guilt, to be forgiven and to be reconciled. In receiving the sacrament, we experience, often with strong emotion, the personal healing of Jesus as he forgives us with unconditional love, floods our soul with joy and with the feeling of being clean and ready to start afresh.

As we consider this important sacrament, we look first at the church's past and present understanding of mortal sin and the role of conscience; then, how Vatican II renewed this sacrament; finally the surprising development of this ritual of forgiveness through the centuries.

Sin: Old and New Understanding

In the early church, only three sins were considered mortal (from Latin *mors*, death): murder, adultery, apostasy or repudiating the church. But from the Middle Ages on, lists of sins as mortal or venial began to be drawn up to help priests in the confessional judge the gravity of sins. The result was a legalist mentality[7] and an emphasis on individual actions. A definition of sin as a free, deliberate action, word, thought or desire that violated God's commandments developed.

Before, during and after Vatican II, influenced by Scripture, by insights from psychology and anthropology and by the council's emphasis on the primacy of conscience, moral theologians developed a new understanding of sin as *relationship* rather than as individual acts. Sin came to be seen as breaking one's love-friendship relation to God and to God's people, ultimately a failure to love.

The past over-emphasis on mortal sin and individual acts often caused Catholics to see mortal sin where it did not exist. Yet common sense indicated that religious persons did not lightly break their relationship with God over and over again, thus to be constantly in danger of Hell. In this context, moral theologians developed the fundamental option theory.

*The **Fundamental Option** Theory.* In the light of evidence from psychology, of a more complete understanding of human motivation and of decisions coming from one's deeper core consciousness, of the Hebrew Scriptures' idea of sin as rupture of the Jews' covenant relationship with their God, moral theologians proposed the fundamental option or choice to explain mortal sin. A fundamental option is the most basic choice a person can make: a decision to *totally* reject God, however understood, from one's life by choosing self first in all areas of life; or conversely, to put God and others before self. It is "fundamental" because the decision comes from the inner core of one's consciousness and affects the most basic values and actions of one's life.

To make such a decision against God and others would qualify as a mortal or death-dealing state of sin for it completely destroys one's love-relationship with God. Viewed in this way mortal sin is of rare occurrence among those whose life direction is for God and others. Actions, however, are important in this approach. A series of grossly selfish actions can lead over a period of time to that definitive act that finally ruptures one's love relationship with God.

Three points regarding the fundamental option are to be stressed. First, it is a theory, not a doctrine to be accepted as official Catholic teaching. Second, there are actions that may not constitute a fundamental option but which are grave, serious sins traditionally called mortal. Because of this ambiguity, this theory has critics today. Third, the fundamental option is not limited to sin. To choose habitually to live Jesus' gospel of love toward God and fellow humans is to make a *positive* fundamental option. This is a gradual process, involving a life-long effort of conversion. Such personal conversion is a major goal of the new rites of reconciliation.

Forming Conscience. **Conscience** is not an inner feeling but the practical moral *judgment* about the rightness or wrongness of a choice that confronts a person: whether to do this or avoid that here and now. Even though one's judgment may be wrong because of lack of information or differences of honest opinion or the complexity of the issues, a person must follow his or her sincere conscience since conscience is the final norm of conduct and the basis of God's judgment of human actions. In *Gaudium et Spes* Vatican II has the following beautiful description of conscience:

> Deep within his conscience man [sic] discovers a law which he has not laid on himself, but which he must obey. Its voice, ever calling him to love and to do what is good and to avoid what is evil, tells him inwardly at the right moment: do this, shun that. For man has in his heart a law inscribed by God. His dignity lies in observing this law, and by it he will be judged. His conscience is man's most secret core and his sanctuary. There he is alone with God, whose voice echoes in his depths. (GS 16)

The council's metaphor for conscience is *sanctuary*, that sacred place where a person meets God and the safe place where no outside authority may intrude. The council's major contribution is its insistence on the *primacy of conscience*, "on this single moral imperative ... always follow your formed and informed conscience."[8]

Obviously, forming one's conscience correctly and sincerely is necessary and of great importance for proper moral choices. For Christians, this involves many factors: knowing the values that Jesus preached and lived in the four Gospels, learning the church's teaching on specific points, weighing evidence from the social sciences and increasingly today from medicine and psychology, asking advice from those in a position to know, personal prayer, and listening to the Holy Spirit. After the publication in 1968 of the papal encyclical *Of Human Life* condemning contraception on the basis of argumentation from the natural law, many married Catholics followed a process of conscience-formation similar to the above to make a practical judgment on how to respond to the encyclical. Many priests in the sacrament of confession respected their sincere conscience judgment even when it went against the papal teaching.

Social Sin. The pre-Vatican II emphasis on sin as individual acts tended to ignore the reality of social sin, those unjust structures of society that are destructive and inflict evil. Vatican II's *Pastoral Constitution on the Church in the Modern World* cautioned against a "merely individualistic morality" (GS 30) and spoke of social justice in terms of the structures of society. Examples of social sin are racism, sexism, militarism, environmental pollution and so forth. Deliberately participating in social sin is material for the sacrament of reconciliation. "One of the most important insights [from Vatican II] is that no sin is ever private and individual but always has a social effect ... and can infect our communities, our cultures, and especially our economic structures and institutions." [9]

Vatican II Renewal of the Sacrament of Reconciliation

The council bishops asked for a revision of the "rite and formulas" of the sacraments better to express their "nature and effect." (SC 72). For the sacrament of reconciliation the result was three new rituals or ways for Catholics "to go to confession. "

The *first rite* involved individual confession and absolution as in the past, but greatly improved the ritual to allow face-to-face dialogue between the penitent and the priest. The impersonal dark confessional "box" gave way to a "reconciliation room" with chairs and an inviting atmosphere. The priest welcomes the penitent. A different manner of confessing sins is encouraged. Rather than going through a 'laundry list' of sins and imperfections, the penitent mentions only those sins or failures that are most significant and harmful to oneself and to one's relationship with God and others. The priest, avoiding a legalistic or moralizing manner, may offer encouraging advice. He then gives a "penance" to be performed later, like choosing a prayer or

Bible reading or doing a good work tailored to the person's individual needs. After the penitent expresses sorrow for sin and a determination to do better, the priest absolves his/her sins by pronouncing these words:

> God, the Father of mercies, through the death and resurrection of his Son, has reconciled the world to himself and sent the Holy Spirit among us for the forgiveness of sins; through the ministry of the church, may God give you pardon and peace, and I absolve you from your sins, in the name of the Father and of the Son, and of the Holy Spirit.

A brief prayer of thanks concludes the ritual.

The *second rite* involves a group reconciliation service consisting of hymns, Scripture readings, prayers, and an uplifting talk to dispose the group to experience sorrow for sin and trust in God's loving mercy and to help the penitents examine their conscience. Individual confession of sins and absolution by the priest follow.

The *third ritual* features a communal reconciliation service as in the second rite but permits private confession to God rather than to a priest followed by *general* absolution to all present. This third rite is restricted to situations where the number of people is too large for individual confession with the stipulation that if mortal sin is involved the individual confess at an available later time.

In offering these three rites, the council bishops had two goals in addition to forgiveness of sin: that the penitent experience Jesus' healing forgiveness and be motivated to begin the serious work of conversion.

Conversion from sin and deeply imbedded attitudes and habits is a long process and does not come easily. It involves strengthening one in the fundamental option for God and for others and in the lifelong struggle to overcome selfishness and to act out of love. The goal is more than avoiding certain sinful acts, though this is important; rather the new rites seek to deepen one's relationship with God, to choose afresh God over self, to let love guide one's dealings with others. In the work of conversion, the guidance and encouragement of a skilled spiritual adviser is important.

So that sacramental confession and absolution may be a joyful personal religious experience of Jesus' forgiveness and healing and bring peace of mind and soul to the penitent, it is important that the priest-confessor no longer act primarily as judge, as in the older practice, but as a healer, a reconciler, a source of encouragement and hope. As in the parable of the Prodigal Son, this means conveying the old father's loving forgiveness and acceptance of his prodigal son.

The Vatican II renewal emphasized the dimension of *reconciliation* to stress the fact that this sacrament reconciles us not only with God but also with the community of the church. Reconciliation thus stresses the social dimension of sin through the harm it does to the Christian community. The early Christians were acutely aware that sinful members who gave bad example weakened the community and made evangelization of non-Christians more difficult. Public sinners were excommunicated, that is, expelled from the community.

Remarkable Historical Development of This Sacramental Rite

More than the other six sacraments, this ritual of penance or "confession" has undergone dramatic changes since the time of Jesus and the Apostles. This informative historical overview is an example of how church discipline and practice developed over the centuries and therefore points to the possibility of further change in this sacramental ritual in the future.

The Example of Jesus. Forgiving sin and reconciling sinners to his Father was central to the ministry of Jesus. Jesus preached forgiveness, "not 7 times but 70 times 7." He forgave Peter who denied him three times and even those who crucified him. Before the 4th century, baptism was the primary way sin was forgiven. Gradually early church leaders, following the example of Jesus and relying on his promise "I assure you ... whatever you declare loosed on earth shall be loosed in heaven" (Mt. 18:18), began to deal with sins of its members.

The 4th to 6th centuries was the period of rigorous penances. Sinners confessed serious sins to the bishop, generally public sins like murder, adultery or apostasy from the faith. The bishop enjoined lengthy penances that could last for years, involving fasting, wearing coarse penitential garments, abstaining from sexual relations, and not receiving communion. This forgiveness generally happened once only! Subsequent sinners were left to the mercy of God. Three things stand out in this practice: how seriously the early church took the reality of sin; its realization that sin severely damaged the Christian community; and its conviction that one of its most important ministries from Christ was to forgive sin and help the sinner in the process of conversion.

After the sixth century, a new form of private confession was developed in the monasteries of Ireland where monks confessed privately to their abbot. These Celtic missionary monks fanned out over Europe by the hundreds, evangelizing and baptizing the hordes of barbarians that over-ran Europe, teaching their form of private confession to a priest with absolution from sin first and a penance performed afterward. This practice proved immensely popular due to its privacy, availability, its leniency, its healing and consolation. At first the Church tried to outlaw it but gradually the Irish practice prevailed. By the year 1000 public penance had completely disappeared.

The Council of Trent (1545-1564) formulated the official teaching on the sacrament which remained unchanged until the Second Vatican Council.

What can be said about the remarkable historical development of this sacrament? Can it provide insight into our present situation? Even though the church offers three new rites for the sacrament, Catholic people on the whole are not attracted to the sacrament. It may be that the church has not yet discovered the best way to satisfy the religious needs and cultural realities of today's Catholics. It may be that Catholics need large doses of instruction and motivation to rediscover the reality of sin in their lives and the positive benefits of this sacrament. It may also be that priests need to make confession a more joyful, personal religious experience of God's forgiveness and healing love like the old father's loving forgiveness of his prodigal son.

Many pastorally-concerned priests want the church to permit and encourage the use of the third rite of general absolution without conditions attached. The changes begun by Vatican II can help point the way. The church has changed the ritual dramatically over the centuries to meet the spiritual and psychological needs of her members; she can do so again.

A startling development in the post-Vatican II church was that the great majority of Catholics simply stopped using the sacrament. Why? The reasons are not clear. Theologian Monica Hellwig thought Catholics did not find that the sacrament met their spiritual needs. Some think the exaggerated emphasis on sexual sins gave neurotic guilt feelings making confession onerous. Others feel the impersonality of reciting lists of sins and often non-sins to an invisible priest in a dark confessional contributed to the decline.

The new emphasis on sin as relational may have caused Catholics to conclude they were not committing mortal sins. Or Vatican II's emphasis on personal conscience resulted in more mature conscience-formation among Catholics. Perhaps Catholics just got tired of confession after being forced to go regularly as children by well-meaning parents and teachers in Catholic schools?

However, there is something positive in this development. For many years prior to Vatican II, monthly, even weekly confession was the norm. What may have motivated this practice is what church historian Jay Dolan termed a 'culture of sin' in the Catholic Church. In contrast, the present rejection of frequent confession may indicate a healthy spiritual maturity on the part of Catholics. Yet, those Catholics who come regularly or when they experience the need for forgiveness and healing and encouragement continue to highly value this sacrament of reconciliation.

Marriage, Sacrament of Intimate Friendship

"At the beginning of creation God made them male and female. ... and the two shall become one....Therefore let no man separate what God has joined." (Mark 10: 6-12)

"A man will leave father and mother and be joined to his wife and two shall become one flesh. This is a great mystery ... Christ and the church." Ephesians 5:31-2

The Catholic Church's teaching on the sacredness of a sacramental marriage in Christ is a huge value for people in today's cheapening of love, high divorce rate and failure to honor permanent commitment. In this joyful sacrament, Jesus joins a man and a woman in the sacred bond of a permanent, faithful covenant of love-friendship that recalls and mirrors the total, self-giving, never-ending faithful love Jesus has for his church, the People of God, proved by his suffering and death on a cross. The married couple are challenged and strengthened by grace from their sacrament to love each other with the quality of Jesus' love. An awesome sacrament.

In *The Pastoral Constitution on the Church in the Modern World,* the bishops at Vatican II spoke in eloquent terms of the beauty and sacredness of marriage and married love. Their vision of marriage renewal came only after a long and heated debate at the council between those bishops who fought for a traditional legalistic understanding of marriage while Northern Europe bishops championed a personalist approach. We consider the council's rich teaching of a Christian sacramental marriage which the bishops described as an "intimate partnership of life and love." (GS 48).

The Second Vatican Council's Renewal of Marriage

The bishops significantly modified and enriched Catholic teaching on sacramental marriage in two ways. Prior to Vatican II Christian marriage was considered a legal *contract* between husband and wife. Since the language of contract was impersonal, highly juridic, limited to rights and duties, and lacking in spirituality and relationship, the bishops envisioned marriage as a *covenant* of love and friendship. A covenant is a friendship love agreement between persons. In the history of salvation God made solemn covenants with the Jewish people which bound God to love and protect his chosen people and they to love, worship and obey God alone. Jesus made a new covenant with his Christian people in giving himself on the cross out of his total unselfish love for them.

To look on marriage as friendship love-covenant changes everything. Marriage becomes a deeply spiritual commitment of love in which the spouses agree to love each other without limits and to be faithful to each other as God to the Jewish people and Jesus to all for whom he died.

Secondly, Catholic teaching before Vatican II held that children or procreation was the primary purpose of marriage with the mutual love of husband and wife a secondary purpose. This hierarchy of purposes caused many practical difficulties. Having as many children as possible came to be the Catholic ideal in marriage with the mutual sexual love of the spouses relegated to a secondary and therefore inferior position in the marriage, a stance opposed to the experience, convictions, and often capabilities of Catholic couples. Vatican II modified this position by stating that both mutual sexual love and procreation are equally *primary* purposes of Christian marriage.

> ...children are the supreme gift of marriage and greatly contribute to the good of the parents themselves. ... But marriage is not merely for the procreation of children; its nature as an indissoluble covenant between two people and the good of the children demand that the mutual love of the partners be properly shown, that it grow and mature. (*Gaudium et Spes* 50)

The bishops at Vatican II described covenantal Christian sacramental marriage in eloquent and profound terms that reveal why the Catholic Church defends so tenaciously sacramental marriage between a man and a woman.

Holiness of Marriage and Family (GS 48). "The intimate partnership of life and love ... established by the Creator." "God himself is the author of marriage." "The intimate union of marriage as a mutual giving of two persons..." "... the partners mutually surrender themselves to each other..." "Christ our Lord has abundantly blessed this love" "Authentic married love is caught up into divine love..." "Spouses therefore are fortified and ... consecrated for the duties and dignity of their state by a special sacrament."

Married Love. (GS 49) "The Lord, wishing to bestow special gifts of grace and divine love on married love...leads the spouses to a free and mutual self-giving, experienced in tenderness and action and permeating their entire lives..." In a paragraph beginning "Married love is uniquely expressed and perfected by the exercise of the acts proper to marriage," the council praised the spouses' sexual union as "noble and honorable," as "fostering the self-giving it signifies" and as "enriching the spouses in joy and gratitude." The council stressed the "equal personal dignity" of "man and wife in mutual and unreserved affection." The bishops encouraged the spouses to "pray for a love that is firm, generous and ready for sacrifices."

In its renewal of Christian sacramental marriage, the council has thus set a high ideal for married spouses in what it terms "their lofty calling." (GS 47)

Another aspect of the richness of Christian sacramental marriage is its intimate relationship to Jesus Christ and to the church as described to us by St. Paul.

Christian Sacramental Marriage is "Marriage in Christ." St. Paul referred to Christian marriage as a mystery. "Husbands love your wives even as Christ loved the church and handed himself over for her. ...This is a great mystery but I speak in reference to Christ and the church" (Ephesians 5:25- 32). The mystery Paul refers to is twofold: the total, unselfish, permanent, faithful love of Jesus for his Christian people sealed by his sufferings and death on the cross; the love Christian spouses have for each other that should mirror and imitate the quality of Christ's total unselfish love. Paul sets a lofty example and model for spouses in their sacramental marriage.

For married couples today, the risen Christ in his covenantal love for his body the church not only gives the example of faithful love but helps the spouses love unselfishly, to be faithful "till death do us part," to care lovingly for their children, to make their marriage a success.. "He abides with them in order that by their mutual self-giving the spouses will love each other with enduring fidelity as he loved the church and delivered himself for it." (GS 48)

The Church's Pastoral Care for
Sacramental Marriages

Since a Christian sacramental marriage is a marriage in Christ, a lofty vocation, a great mystery according to St. Paul, and an "indissoluble covenant" (GS 50), the Catholic Church takes sacramental marriage very seriously in her effort to follow Jesus' ideal of a permanent faithful union, in her theology of marriage as a sacrament, and in her discipline concerning marriage. The following are a few of the ways the church seeks to help the spouses as they strive to live their covenantal relationship.

Preparation for Successful Sacramental Marriage. Commitment to the covenantal relationship of a Christian sacramental marriage calls for couples who are emotionally, mentally, and spiritually mature. For this reason, and to ensure as far as possible permanent, happy, and fulfilling marriages, dioceses in the United States provide marriage preparation programs. The couple are asked to see their parish priest six months before the wedding; in this initial interview the pastor verifies their freedom to marry, their understanding of the commitment they are about to make and their psychological maturity. The couple then set the date for their wedding and reserve the church. They sign up for a marriage instruction program usually consisting of three or four meetings with other engaged couples led by an experienced married couple, a priest who presents the church's teaching on marriage, and an expert on finances and legal questions. Engaged couples generally find these sessions most helpful.

The couples are also encouraged to make a weekend engaged couples retreat to deepen their relationship with each other and the risen Christ, to develop the habit of prayer, and to put their coming marriage in the hands of the Lord. They find it very important and helpful to identify clearly the *expectations* they have of themselves, of their partners and of their marriage. Since expectations are crucial to harmonious living together, couples find very helpful for a successful and happy marriage a "marriage expectations" test taken separately and then discussed together.

After the Wedding – A Touch of Realism. The wedding ceremony, important and beautiful as it is, is only the beginning of the marriage. The full Christian sacramental marriage is the couple's daily living their covenental love with each other; or as one couple put it, "It's in the day-to-day loving that our marriage comes alive." Couples have the assurance that the risen Lord is with them on their life journey, sanctifying their sexual love, sustaining them in the ordinary give and take of family life, and empowering them to be examples of love to each other, to their children, and to all their friends. To help spouses grow in love and trust and communication, the Catholic Church has developed the highly successful Marriage Encounter, a weekend program facilitated by experienced married couples and a priest in which the spouses learn to shed their defenses and talk to each other on a deep level of trust. For marriages in serious trouble, a program called *Retrouvaille* or rediscovery has been successful in saving spouses' marriages.[10]

Special Marriage Situations

*Marriage **Annulment.*** It's often objected that annulments are the Catholic divorce. However, granting annulments is the church's attempt to care pastorally for Catholics whose first marriages have failed and at the same time to preserve the integrity of a sacramental marriage.

In granting an annulment, the church states, after lengthy investigation by a diocesan marriage tribunal, the first "marriage" was not in fact a valid or real sacramental marriage because one or several of its canonical requirements for validity were not present. Before the Vatican Council conditions for an annulment were very strict resulting in few annulments. However, the council's teaching on marriage as covenant and partnership of love enabled the church's canon lawyers to recognize that psychological or religious immaturity could make it impossible for one or both partners to make the commitment needed for a lifelong partnership of love that constitutes a covenant marriage in Christ. Clearly in modern society, many people find it very difficult to make a personal commitment; they may lack psychological maturity. If such immaturity can be shown to exist *before* the marriage, strong grounds exist for granting an annulment. However today, some tribunal officials and canon lawyers in the United States are questioning whether the cumbersome and painful, often demeaning process of annulments, is the best way for the church to deal with the dilemma of divorce and remarriage.

Inter-Christian and Inter-Faith Marriages. Thanks to Vatican II the Catholic Church has made such marriages easier and a source of joy, peace and God's blessings. Thus a minister of another Christian church can witness the marriage of a Catholic with another Christian in the church of that pastor. The same holds for marriage of a Catholic and a Jew or member of another non-Christian faith or a person with no religion.

Another benefit of the Second Vatican Council is that, out of respect for the conscience and religious convictions of the non-Catholic partner, he or she no longer must promise in writing to have the children baptized and reared as Catholics. The Catholic partner likewise need not promise in writing to convert the other partner; it is sufficient that he or she is willing to make such an effort provided that it not endanger or put undue pressure on the harmony and success of their marriage. The reasons behind these major changes from pre-Vatican II practice are the Catholic Church's new ecumenical respect for other Christian churches and her conviction concerning religious liberty and the primacy of conscience championed by Vatican II.

The Catholic Church recognizes these marriages as valid; the only condition is that the local bishop dispense the Catholic party from the church law regarding such marriages, a dispensation always given.

An "Ecumenical Marriage." Such inter-Christian and interfaith marriages pose a problem for those partners who take their own religion seriously: in which church or religion will the children be baptized and brought up? will they go to a Catholic school? will they worship in a Catholic or Protestant church, a synagogue or mosque? In such ecumenical marriages, serious couples are attempting practical actions that respect both churches or religions: rather than splitting the family, they attend each other's worship on alternate weeks. They believe that God blesses their decision. In the case of inter-Christian marriages, the couples' experience of lived ecumenism at the grassroots family level may in God's providence help the separated churches in their pilgrimage to full unity.[11]

Same-Sex "Marriages." In the struggle of gay men and gay women for the federal government and states to recognize their unions as marriage, the United States bishops and other Christian groups vigorously oppose their efforts in order to protect the integrity of Catholic sacramental marriage, for the church is convinced it must respect the sacredness of a sacramental marriage between a man and a woman. The church, however, respects the civil rights of gay men and women to enter a civil union.

For Discussion

1. What does your baptism mean to you now? How can you make it an important part of your Christian life?
2. What do you think the Catholic Church should do to attract people including youth to use the sacrament of Reconciliation?

3. Is the Catholic Church's prohibition of remarriage after divorce too strict? Why or why not?

4. Do you think the Catholic Church's stance on gay marriage is realistic in to-day's world" How can Catholics begin to reconcile church teachings on homo-sexuality with those members of the church who do not identify themselves as hetero-sexual?

Further Reading

Bosio, John. *Loving Together: The Catholic Blueprint for a Loving Marriage.* New London, CT: Twenty-Third Publications, 2008. Bosio explains how the love of Christ is key to the loving relationship in marriage. He uses real-life sto-ries to illustrate the struggles and triumphs couples have had in overcoming selfishness to find true Christian love in their marriages.

Catoir, John T. *Where Do You Stand with the Church? The Dilemma of Divorced Catholics.* New York: Alba House, 1996. He provides straightforward answers to questions many divorced Catholics have, such as why the church requires annulments, whether divorced Catholics can still receive the sacraments, the annulment process and its practice in the church today. He also sympathetically discusses the struggle of Catholics with broken marriages to maintain their ties to the church.

Johnston, Catherine, Daniel Kendall, Rebecca Nappi. *101 Questions and Answers on Catholic Married Life.* New York: Paulist Press, 2006. This book answers questions on Catholic married life, discussing the church's stand on difficult issues such as homo-sexuality and divorce. A good introduction to the post-Vatican II church's teaching on marriage.

Muldoon, Tim. *Longing to Love, A Memoir of Desire, Relationships, and Spiritual Transformation.* Chicago: Loyola Press, 2010). A beautiful story of a young couple falling in love and staying in love through difficulties and tragedy.

Mick, Lawrence E. *Living Baptism Daily.* Collegeville, MN: Liturgical Press, 2004. This is a book worth reading! It is written for RCIA and baptismal teams and parish staff to enrich their ministry. The author has a knack for simple, straight-forward presentation of the practical spirituality of baptism that reflects solid scholarship and considerable pastoral experience."

Nouwen, Henri. *The Return of the Prodigal Son; A Story of Homecoming.* New York; Doubleday, 1992. Moving account of his personal conversion by sitting in front of Rembrandt's painting of the Prodigal Son, his insights and healing. Fresh look at our heavenly Father's unconditional love and forgiveness of his children.

Walsh, Christopher J. *The Untapped Power of the Sacrament of Penance: A Priest's View.* Cincinnati, OH: Servant Publications, 2005. Lively and practical discussion on recent decline in use of the sacrament, need to renew it for today's young adults, the question and misconceptions Catholics and converts have, the gifts of the sacrament, and the need for priests to make confession a healing experience.

Footnotes

1 "By baptism men are implanted in the paschal mystery of Christ. They die with him, are buried with him, and rise with him, and rise with him." (SC 6)

2 See Joseph F. Eagan, S.J. *Baptism and Communion Among the Churches* (Rome: Gregorian University Press, 1974).

3 Paul Lakeland. *Catholicism at the Crossroads. How the Laity Can Save the Church.* New York: Continuum, 2007. 5.

4 The Council stressed that adult baptism, rather than infant baptism, is the norm since baptism of adults was the practice in the early church involving their faith response.

5 For the question *how* the vast number of people are saved who have not heard of Jesus or had the Gospel preached to them, theologians developed the *votum Christi*, desire for baptism; accordingly, a sincere following of one's conscience suffices for the desire of baptism and thus for their salvation. In Vatican II's *Constitution on the Church*, the bishops discussed the salvation of Catholics, Orthodox, Protestants, Jews, non-Christian believers and atheists. Theological developments, begun with Vatican II, open the way to ecumenism and greater dialogue between all faith traditions.

6 The pre-Vatican II name for this sacrament was penance. Reconciliation recovers the social reality of sin as hurting the Christian community. The early church was acutely aware that sinful members' bad example weakened the community's ability to evangelize non-Christians.

7   To steal up to a given amount was a venial sin, over that mortal. To miss a portion of the Mass was venial, beyond that mortal. Anything involving sex for the unmarried was mortally sinful. The result too often was guilt-ridden Catholics.

8   James T. Bretzke. *A Morally Complex World, Engaging Contemporary Moral Theology* (Collegeville, MN: Liturgical Press, 2004), 109.

9   Bretzke, *op. cit.,* 201.

10   The program consists of a weekend at a retreat center or hotel followed by six sessions every other week over a 90-day period. It is led by three couples themselves recovering from a troubled relationship and by a priest. The key to its success, like Alcoholics Anonymous, is "listening to self-disclosure stories, recognizing the need for honesty with oneself, making a personal inventory, putting one's trust in God, acknowledging that personal selfishness is a root cause of one's problems, taking spiritual steps, granting forgiveness, aiming to change oneself rather than one's spouse, ridding oneself of resentment and finally, as a last step in recovery, participating in a ministry of helping others." Ed Gleason, "Recovery for Troubled Marriages," *America* (October 10, 1992) : 253.

11   See George Kilcourse. *Double Belonging, Interchurch Families and Christian Unity.* New York/Mahwah, NJ: Paulist Press, 1992).

Chapter 6:
Jesus' Greatest Gift

At the Last Supper ... our Savior instituted the eucharistic sacrifice of his body and blood ... to perpetuate the sacrifice of the cross throughout the ages ... and to entrust to ... the church a memorial of his death and resurrection: a sacrament of love, a sign of unity, a bond of charity, a paschal banquet in which Christ is received ... and a pledge of future glory is given to us.
Constitution on the Sacred Liturgy (SC 47)

As often as they eat the Supper of the Lord they proclaim the death of the Lord until he comes. (SC 6)

These two passages express why and how the Eucharist (Mass) is Jesus' greatest gift to his people: the first highlights the Eucharist as the memorial of Jesus' saving death and resurrection given at his Last Super; the second emphasizes Vatican II's teaching of the fourfold real presence of the risen Christ in every Mass – in the priest-celebrant, in the three Scripture readings, in the sacramental signs of bread and wine, and in the gathered worshipping community.

This is why the Eucharistic celebration is the very heart of the Catholic Church and the life-giving source of Catholics' spiritual lives. This is why millions and millions of Christians in every corner of the world for almost 2000 years have celebrated Eucharist with devotion and often great personal sacrifice - a phenomenon unparalleled in the history of religion - because on the eve of his suffering and death, Jesus asked his followers "Do this in memory of me."

Gerald O'Collins describes the Eucharist in these graphic words: "The Mass is charged with the powerful presence of the crucified and risen Christ."[1] For Jeremy Driscoll what happens at the Eucharist is "a huge event ... God acting to save us ... concentrating the entirety of his saving love for the world into this ritual action and words of the eucharistic liturgy."[2] In addressing a vast crowd of young people at the 2005 World Youth Rally in Cologne, Germany, Pope Benedict XIV made this dramatic statement: [Consecrating the Eucharist] "is like inducing nuclear fusion in the very heart of being, the victory of love over hatred, of love over death."

In each Eucharist the risen Christ, made present by the Holy Spirit in the prayer before the words of consecration, offers his death on the cross to the Father for the salvation of all people. Each Eucharist, done in memory of Jesus' paschal mystery, is a divine reality, a mystery, believable only by God's gift of faith received at baptism and nourished by parents, family and the church. The 2005 Synod of Bishops called the Eucharist "a mystery to be believed, to be celebrated and to be lived."[3]

Eucharistic Ecclesiology of Vatican II

The Second Vatican Council recovered an earlier understanding of the profound link between the church as the body of Christ and the Eucharist. Christ's church is understood as coming into being each time the people of God, the body of Christ, gather to hear the Word of God, to offer Jesus' paschal mystery, to share the Lord's Supper. In celebrating Eucharist the body of Christ the church celebrates their communion with God and with each together. The central meaning of the Eucharist is love, God's love poured out through Christ's paschal mystery to his body the church. The Eucharist is accordingly the church's great prayer of thanksgiving.

Vatican II Reform of the Liturgy

To bring the full riches of the Eucharist to the Catholic faithful, the Second Vatican Council dramatically changed and renewed the Catholic Mass, unchanged since the Council of Trent over 400 years ago.[4] Carrying out the will of the council, Pope Paul VI in 1969 decreed the new Roman Missal be used throughout the universal church as "the sole legitimate form of the Eucharist."

Before the council, the term Eucharist had referred almost exclusively to the sacrament of the real presence of Christ in the consecrated bread and wine. Since the council, the Eucharist has come to mean the entire Mass composed of two principal parts, Liturgy of the Word (three Scripture readings, homily, Creed, prayer of the faithful) and Liturgy of the Eucharist (presentation of gifts of bread and wine, preface prayer, eucharistic prayer of thanks, the Lord's prayer, greeting of peace, communion meal.) Brief introductory rites precede the Liturgy of the Word and a very brief concluding rite follows the Liturgy of the Eucharist. Throughout this book, Eucharist refers to the entire Mass.

The following statements from Vatican II's *Constitution on the Sacred Liturgy, SC,* describe the major changes the bishops mandated for Catholics' worship at the Eucharist.[5] They constitute a significant break from the past.

- "Christian believers are not to be present as strangers or *silent spectators* … They are to take part in the sacred action, *actively, fully aware*, and devoutly. Offering the immaculate victim, not only through the hands of the priest but also *together with him*, they should … offer themselves." (SC 48). (italics added) Conscious, active participation became the basic criterion for renewal.
- "The rite of the Mass is to be revised … duplications omitted … parts lost in history to be restored." Part of the revision was the

deletion of multiple rituals like signs of the cross, bows, genuflections, precise location of hands, etc.

- "The treasures of the Bible are to be opened up more lavishly..." (51) The Liturgy of the Word became an essential of the Eucharist; previously offertory, consecration and communion were considered essential parts; missing one meant non-attendance at Mass!

- "The homily is strongly recommended since it forms part of the liturgy itself." (52) Reflection on the Scriptures rather than "sermons" of the priest's choice became the norm.

- "The prayer of the faithful is to be restored after the gospel and homily..." (53) This emphasized both the participation of the people of God and their prayer of petition.

- "... communion under both kinds (bread and wine) may be granted ... to the laity ..." (55) At his Last Supper Jesus passed the cup to his disciples; drinking from the cup expresses the full meaning of the Eucharist as meal.

- "Concelebration ... manifesting the unity of the priesthood ..." was restored. (57) Priests celebrating the Eucharist together rather than alone is an ancient practice.

- "When churches are built, let great care be taken ... for the active participation of the faithful." (124) The goal is "noble beauty rather than sumptuous display."

- "Religious singing by the faithful is to be skillfully encouraged." (118) Singing is prayer and joyful praise and worship of God.

- "The two parts ... the liturgy of the Word and the Eucharistic liturgy ... form one single act of worship." (56) The importance of attending/participating in the *entire* Eucharist!

These two principles, "Liturgical services are not private functions but are celebrations of the Church" (SC 26) and "the full and active participation by all the people is the aim to be considered above all else," (SC 14) are the basis for the council's renewal of the Eucharist. The following changes express and put these principles into practice: the community prays the *Confiteor, Glory be to God, and Creed* aloud, and answers other prayers in dialogue with the priest; a third Scripture reading was added followed by a homily on the Scripture readings; the communion rail separating the altar from the community was removed and the altar turned so that the priest faces the community closer to and leading the people; the people following Jesus' commands "Take and eat," receive the host in their hands instead of receiving only on the tongue and "Take and drink," receive the precious blood from a chalice or glass; the baptized people of God act as eucharistic ministers and exercise the ministry of lectors.

A new terminology reflecting an older theological understanding of the Eucharist arose: table replaced altar to describe the Eucharist as the Lord's meal to offset past *exclusive* emphasis on sacrifice; the priest is referred to as "presider" to express his relationship to and with the community in the entire Eucharist and to avoid past identification of the priest as the sole offerer of the sacrifice and the Mass as "his Mass"; the tabernacle became the place of reservation recalling the early church practice of reserving consecrated bread to be brought to the sick; the sanctuary is no longer the private reserve of the clergy, a practice that served to emphasize clergy-lay separation and clergy superiority in the Body of Christ.

We turn to aspects of the Eucharist to appreciate better the multiple riches of the council's renewed Eucharist. These reflections illustrate the Eucharist as center of Catholics' spiritual lives.

Reflections on the Riches of the Renewed Eucharist

Eucharist is where we meet Jesus Christ, our personal Friend. The Second Vatican Council taught that the risen Christ is really present in four ways in each Eucharistic celebration: in the Christian community gathered for worship; in the Word of God, the three Scripture readings; in the consecrated bread and wine through the power of the Holy Spirit and the words of the priest; and in the person of the priest who acts "in the person of Christ" as he prays the Eucharistic prayer and repeats Jesus' words over the bread and wine. In doing this the priest represents the Christian community before God.

The Real Presence of Christ

[Christ] is present in the sacrifice of the Mass . . . 'the same one now offering, through the ministry of priests, who formerly offered himself on the cross,' [and] especially under the Eucharistic species. ... He is present in his word since it is he himself who speaks when the holy Scriptures are read in the church. He is present finally when the church prays and sings, for he promised: 'Whenever two or three are gathered together for my sake, there I am in the midst of them (Mt 18-20). *Constitution on the Sacred Liturgy (SC 7)*

In the Sacramental Signs of Bread and Wine at Each Mass. Some Catholics and many other Christians think the bread and wine merely remind us of Jesus at the Last Supper. From the earliest days of the church, however, Catholic faith has consistently held that the *risen* Christ, by the power of the Holy Spirit, is really sacramentally present under the signs of bread and wine. Explaining *how* this can be is a separate question, one which has occupied theologians for centuries. It is beyond the scope of this chapter.

A strong evidence for the real presence of Christ in the consecrated bread is the famous chapter 6 of St. John's Gospel where he describes the dramatic scene in which half of those who had followed Jesus as his disciples ceased to "walk with him." When Jesus told them "My flesh is real food and my blood real drink," they left him, an indication they understood that Jesus meant his real self.[6]

This passage was fulfilled at the Last Supper[7] when Jesus took bread and wine and solemnly stated "This *is* my body" and "This *is* my blood." These are statements of identity. Because Catholics have so believed through the centuries, they have been strengthened by receiving Jesus' body and blood on their journey through life to eternity. In times of suffering and sickness, death of loved ones, and personal tragedies, Catholics experience the powerful help of Jesus' body and blood in Holy Communion. Holy Communion is our privileged time to be alone with Jesus our personal friend, to speak intimately with him, to thank him, to ask for his healing for ourselves and for our loved ones. In these ways Eucharist deepens our personal friendship with Jesus and relationship with God..

It is important to realize that Christ is not only present in each Eucharist but supremely active. As the risen Christ, he offers again and again his suffering and death and his glorious resurrection in Palestine long ago, as an infinite sacrifice for the salvation of every person God created. Thus another name for the Eucharist is the Holy Sacrifice of the Mass. The privileged role of each baptized Christian is to offer Christ's perfect offering to his Father. It is the greatest action Christians are privileged to share with Christ.

Eucharist is the best way we fulfill our fourfold responsibility to our great and awesome God: To *worship* God, that is, to acknowledge, praise and adore the God of majesty and immensity; to express our *sorrow* for our many sins and our selfishness and to receive our compassionate God's forgiveness; humbly and confidently to *ask* for the help we need each day in our pilgrim journey; above all, to *thank* our Creator God for the gift of his Son Jesus who suffered, died and rose to be our salvation, for his gift of life and for all the blessings we receive each day. The Greek word *eucharistia* means thanksgiving; Catholics are "Eucharistic people."

Individual parts of each Eucharist are especially helpful to express this four-fold relationship. During the penitential rite and the threefold "Lord Have Mercy" as Mass begins, we express *sorrow* for our sins and thanks for God's forgiveness. In "Glory to God in the highest," we *praise* and *worship* God with enthusiasm and joy. After the consecration we proclaim with *gratitude* "Christ has died, Christ is risen, Christ will come again." In Jesus' own prayer, the *Our Father*, we pray for our daily needs.

Eucharist is where we experience community and where Christian community comes alive. Catholics who worship together Sunday after Sunday form a genuine community whose members care for each other, love each other and welcome all people. Being part of a welcoming, caring community frees us from the isolation of modern life, supports us in times of hardship and grief over loss of loved ones, and strengthens our faith, inspires our hope, and leads us to love.

During the eucharistic prayer the presider prays "May all of us who share in the body and blood of Christ be brought together in unity by the Holy Spirit." Eucharist is a prayer for the unity of the Christian community. Dorothy Day once said: "At the Eucharist rich and poor kneel side by side, all equal." Christians of all social and economic and racial backgrounds become one in Christ and with each other when they come to the table of the Lord. The popular spiritual writer Ronald Rolheiser calls attention to the family aspect of the Eucharist "…where we come together to be with each other, to share ordinary life, to celebrate special events with each other, to console and cry with each other when life is full of heartaches."

Eucharist is the community's friendship meal. The 12 Apostles and other disciples remembered the intimate friendship meals they had with Jesus on the hillsides of Palestine and by the lake of Galilee after his resurrection. They remembered at their last supper with Jesus how he had said "I have greatly desired to eat this Passover with you before I suffer." (Luke 22:15) The early Christians referred to the intimate gatherings each Sunday in their house churches as **agape** or love meals. The Eucharist is thus pre-eminently the sacrament of Christian love – love of God, love of the risen Christ, and love of each other. Kenan Osborne quotes the striking statement of Jerome Murphy-O'Connor "There can be no Eucharist in a community whose members do not love one another."[8]

In renewing the eucharistic liturgy, Vatican II restored the church's earlier emphasis on community worship. Prior to the council, the priest was the center of attention. Separated from the people of God by an altar railing and with his back to the people, the priest "read" the Mass in Latin while the people were passive spectators, often saying their own devotional prayers or the rosary. The message conveyed was that the Mass belongs to the priest, not the community. For the pre-Vatican II ecclesiology emphasized the hierarchy, represented by the priest, to be church rather than the people of God. However, Vatican II insisted that the Eucharist is the action of both people and priest. Eucharist is meant to be community, not exclusively private or me-and-God prayer.

In such a renewed Mass, community starts at the church door when greeters exercise their important ministry by welcoming each person. As the priest processes up the aisle, the introductory song establishes the experience of community. In the sung *Glory be to God*, with one voice the community praises God. After the homily the community expresses aloud its shared faith in the Creed and in the intercessory prayers petitions God for the needs of the present and wider Christian community. Praying aloud together the Lord's prayer while standing is for many an experience of being a Christian community. To prepare to receive Jesus' body and blood, the community members offer each other *shalom*, Jesus' own peace. For those who participate with understanding and faith, the entire Eucharist is a profound experience of Christian community.

Eucharist is where Sunday after Sunday Catholics' spiritual lives are nourished by the living Word of God in three Scripture readings. The first reading is from the Old Testament in which Christ is prophesied as the coming Messiah; the second is from the letters of St. Paul where Paul presents the risen Christ as the great example for Christians in his far-flung churches; and the third, the gospels of Matthew, Mark, Luke and John in which Christ is the dominant figure.

In stressing the Word of God in Scripture, Vatican II effectively restored the Bible to its rightful place in the church and in Catholic spirituality and emphasized that the Eucharist essentially consists of both the Liturgy of the Word and the Liturgy of the Eucharist, "so closely connected that they form one single act of worship." (SC 56) To come late for the Scripture readings is to have missed a major portion of the Mass!

Catholics participate fully in Eucharist by paying close attention to the Scripture readings as a valuable opportunity to deepen their knowledge of Christ and their commitment to him. Through the Word of God we come to admire and love the person of Jesus, we make his struggles our own, and we grow in Christian faith, hope, and love.

Eucharist is meant to transform us, to change us more and more into what through our baptism we already are, the Body of Christ, to become more loving and caring persons and to follow Christ in establishing God's reign of justice, love and peace in our daily lives and in our world.

Transformation involves personal conversion. Eucharist is a powerful help and motivation for this difficult work. As grain is transformed into bread and grapes into joy-giving wine, and bread and wine are transformed by the Holy Spirit into the body and blood of Christ, so Sunday after Sunday we are gradually transformed by the Word of God and the body and blood of Christ into his faithful friends and disciples. For Christ is the powerful spiritual food and drink given to strengthen us in our difficulties, to give us patience and peace in our sufferings, and to help us become joyful, happy, peaceful people.

Eucharist is for celebration, for prayer, for justice, for mission. The Second Vatican Council meant Eucharist to be Catholics' joyful *celebration* of God's unconditional love for each of us, of Jesus' saving death and resurrection, of forgiveness of all our sins and of our confident hope of eternal life.

Each Eucharist is meant to be an experience of *communal prayer*. As a community, we pray each time we join community-singing, profess the Creed and say Our Lord's own prayer the Our Father; we pray when at the priest's invitation "Let us pray" he recites the opening prayer, the offertory and post-communion prayers in our stead; and we pray when with the priest we pray silently the longer Eucharistic prayer and respond in song the great AMEN, our agreement to the entire eucharistic prayer.

The Eucharist calls us to the works of *justice* in our daily living. As we gather around the Eucharistic table and afterwards outside the church, we disregard the distinction between rich and poor, noble and peasant, aristocrat and servant, straight and gay, and all ethnicities and nations.

At the Last Supper Jesus washed the feet of his disciples to give them the dramatic lesson that Eucharist is meant to result in service to others, especially to the poor and those suffering. Thus, at the end of the Eucharist, the priest sends the community on *mission* when he announces "GO" "to announce the Gospel" or "to glorify the Lord by your life": GO into the world, into your next week to live your faith, to bring Christ's good news of God's unconditional love for all people, to aid the poor, to work for justice and peace. We accept this mission when we say "thanks be to God" and mean it! The final song celebrates our community Eucharist together and sends us out joyfully to live our Christian mission.

Parish: Celebrating Eucharist Today

Each week in countless parishes across the country people gather to give thanks, celebrate Eucharist, share faith, support one another, learn Gospel values and gain strength to be servants in their everyday lives. ... Children learn their faith. ... young adults become active members in those parishes that invite their involvement and pay attention to their unique needs and hopes ... active Catholics find a home in parishes that proclaim 'all are welcome,' ... 'come, be at home.' Divorced and separated, gay and lesbian, elderly and homebound, the disaffected, the poor and the lonely – are having their needs cared for.[9]

This describes the many vibrant, successful Catholic parishes throughout America led by creative pastors and their staffs.[10] Yet this, unfortunately, is not typical of many parishes.

Many Catholic parishes are caught in a church system that is not working. Priests are being spread too thin and are becoming exhausted and frustrated. Pastoral staffs ... are growing impatient with a church structure that asks for their allegiance and obedience, while at the same time, not providing them with a chance to participate in its decision-making. ... Many who attend Mass leave church uninspired and undernourished ... as they drift away from the church, they take their children with them.[11]

As a result, Mass attendance by Catholics in the United States and elsewhere has been dropping dramatically. Many have stopped attending out of anger at the sexual abuse scandal and disillusionment with the bishops' leadership. (See chapter 15, section 2) Statistics reveal that large numbers of Catholics join evangelical groups they perceive as better meeting their spiritual needs. A renewed parish liturgy that creates a caring Christian community celebrating joyful, prayerful liturgies centered on Jesus Christ is the first step to retain Catholics and attract those who have left. The following are proven ways to make parish eucharistic celebrations vibrant, engaging and welcoming.

- First and foremost, each parish makes the Sunday Eucharist its highest priority, investing the necessary funds and personnel. The goal is nothing short of celebrations of the highest quality for parishioners according to Vatican II's renewal of the Eucharist. Much depends on the celebrant and the quality of the music.
- Successful parishes provide quality homilies that meet the spiritual needs and concerns and challenge the intellectual level of today's parishioners. Carefully prepared succinct homilies, no more than 8-10 minutes, which explain but not merely repeat the Scripture with practical application to daily living. A substantial, joyful, challenging message of one or at most two major points is the ideal homily. Successful homilists start their preparation early in the week, with input from the liturgical committee. Some parishes create opportunities for occasional homilies by both lay men and women so that their talents and experience of Catholic living enrich the faith life of the parish community.
- A significant help is for the priest-celebrant and the parish liturgy committee to meet early in the week to plan the different Sunday Masses, choose songs able to be sung and familiar to all, and reflect together on the readings to help the homilist.
- Where possible, individual Masses are planned on special occasions for young adult married couples with children, for often overlooked singles, and for couples celebrating anniversaries.
- To attract young people and provide for their unique spiritual needs and interests, parishes provide a teen Mass at least once a

month that is planned by the young people along with the priest-celebrant often followed by a fun social leading to service projects and/or social action. In youth-sensitive parishes, such Eucharists and social gatherings are the heart of successful youth programs after Confirmation that are led by a youth leadership group which acts as a counter to negative peer pressure often present.

- Carefully-trained lectors who *proclaim* and *interpret* the Sunday Scripture readings make the Word of God come alive for their hearers. Studies indicate Catholics expect expert lectors and an effective sound system!

- The priest-celebrants as skillful presiders lead the community in prayerful, joyful worship and create a sense of community, thus providing the encouragement and inspiration the community needs for their daily struggles. They avoid folksiness and improvisation that detract from the nobility of the liturgy and call undue attention to the priest. Celebrants who rush through the Mass with seeming little devotion or passion disappoint and turn away parishioners.

- Since God's people deserve and have the right to receive both the consecrated bread and wine in order to experience the full meaning of the eucharistic meal and to honor Jesus' command "Take and eat, Take and drink," pastoral parishes provide the cup at each Mass and encourage the people of God to appreciate and use this gift of Jesus.

- Successful parishes employ the ministry of greeters at the beginning of the Eucharist to create a welcoming community and to set the tone for the celebration. The greeters individually greet as many people as possible, ideally calling them by name. Greeters are carefully chosen; not everyone is an effective greeter. Ushers do not double as greeters.

- A reasonable flexibility combined with creativity by the presiding priest and the parish liturgy group to adapt local culture and a style of worship meaningful to parishioners characterizes parishes with successful liturgies.

A valuable and much-needed parish project today might be an out-reach program by both teen-agers and older Catholics to those teen-agers and adults who no longer attend Mass. Discussions with them might include the following: encouraging them to give serious thought to why they stopped attending and to what they are missing; inviting them to attend the Eucharist with a renewed faith in Christ's presence and action in the Mass, with the desire to grow in their relationship with God and Jesus Christ, with the realization of their need for God and their responsibility to worship and thank God. Such personal discussions might lead these persons to discover again or for the first time the great gift of the Eucharist and the experience of worshipping with the Christian community.

Liturgist Keith Pecklers raises serious questions concerning the Eucharist today. In discussing communion services led by members of the laity instead of a Mass, he asks "how high a priority does the church give to the Eucharist? ... If the Roman Catholic Church wishes to seriously reaffirm the centrality of the Eucharist as the very heart and lifeblood of its existence, then it will need to face some serious choices. The most immediate and obvious is the ordination of married men." Failure to act "will result in a future church that is no longer Eucharistic."[12] See Chapter 15, section one.

Eucharist and Cultural Adaptation. The Second Vatican Council endorsed, though cautiously, the principle of adapting the liturgy to various cultures. The council stated that "the Church has no wish to impose a rigid uniformity" because "she respects and fosters the spiritual ... gifts of the various races and peoples ..." (SC 37). Thus "... the revision ... should allow for legitimate variations and adaptations to different groups, regions, and peoples, especially in mission lands" (SC 38). This obviously is a dramatic change from the 450-year practice of one unchanging form of worship throughout the Catholic world.

As a result various cultures have introduced into eucharistic worship practices and symbols important in their culture. Some examples. African bishops encourage native music, clapping of hands, and joyful dance. At a recent Mass in Lusaka, Zambia, attended by an overflowing crowd in the cathedral and concelebrated by a large number of bishops, a special group danced as part of the entrance procession, again during the *Gloria* and while bringing the offertory gifts of bread and wine to the priest. To express their joyous gratitude at the end of Mass, members of the congregation began to dance during the thanksgiving period after Holy Communion. Drums have also been introduced as well as brilliant African designs for the priests' vestments and church furnishings. In India, native customs, symbols and rituals have become a part of the Mass: priest and worshipers sit on the floor in the lotus position, Indian music and songs are used, the priest makes solemn offerings of flowers, incense, fire and water.

Brief History of Eucharistic Celebrations.

The way Catholics have celebrated Eucharist has changed dramatically through almost 2000 years. This fact gives the lie to the criticism that Vatican II changed "the way the mass always was." We look at the remarkable development of the Eucharist from its earliest days.

Graphic images leap to our minds as we visualize the amazing variety of settings for eucharistic celebrations in response to Jesus' command, "Do this in memory of me": a group of Christians in a Roman home of a well-to-do Christian spontaneously praying the eucharistic prayer, recalling stories about Jesus, listening to a letter from St. Paul, repeating Jesus' words at the Last Supper, and then together joyously eating the consecrated bread and drinking from the cup, confident that the risen Jesus was once again in their midst.

More formal Eucharists, now with set prayers and readings before large crowds in spacious Roman basilicas given to the newly freed Christian Church by the Emperor Constantine; pageantry-filled Masses in Latin in the soaring stone cathedrals of Europe in the late Middle Ages; nocturnal Masses said secretly in the manor houses of persecuted Catholics in Elizabethan England by "Mass priests" who hid by day in their "priest holes" behind wood paneling; Masses said by brave Irish priests in the Irish countryside on "Mass stones" during the persecutions; Masses hurriedly said with a few scraps of bread and drops of wine in Nazi prison camps of World War II; chaplains' Masses in trenches or on jeep hoods or on beachheads for troops about to "move up."

Popes John Paul II and Benedict XVI celebrating Eucharists on colorful raised platforms before hundreds of thousands of Catholics on pastoral visits to all five continents; the solemn papal Christmas Mass televised to the world in majestic St. Peter's church and poor missionary Masses in straw roofed, dirt floor chapels in Africa or the mountains of Latin America; the hundreds of thousands of Masses celebrated every Sunday in parish churches throughout the world.

Deeply moving personalized Eucharists during youth retreats or marriage encounters or cursillo weekends; resurrection hope-filled funeral Masses and joyous Eucharists of Christian marriage; incense-filled Divine Liturgies in Orthodox Churches presided over by bearded, richly robed priests amid incense, chanting and lengthy prayers; the Lord's Supper celebrated in Protestant churches with ever increasing frequency

Each of these Masses testify to the enduring reality that the Eucharist is the heart of the Catholic Church and Jesus' greatest gift to his Christian followers.

For Discussion

1. In what concrete ways can parish communities make Sunday Eucharist a *celebration* in which everyone is an active and vital participant?

2. How would you overcome boredom at Sunday Eucharists when the same ritual is performed Sunday after Sunday? What attitude or convictions or values might you bring to the Eucharistic celebration? What might you *do* when present?

3. Do you think the bread and wine truly become the risen Christ or are mere symbols? How would you show they are more than mere symbols?

4. Do you think that incorporating unique and various cultural and ethnic traditions at Mass serve to unite or divide the Christian community at large? Why?

Further Reading

Bernier, Paul. *Living the Eucharist: Celebrating Its Rhythms in Our Lives.* Mystic, CN: Twenty-Third publications, 2005. Fr. Bernier examines how the Eucharist is intimately connected to the way we live out our lives in the everyday world and calls on us to examine the rituals that surround this sacrament.. The celebration of the Eucharist is meant to draw us into an intimate sharing of the life of Christ.

Driscoll, OSB, Jeremy. *What Happens at Mass.* Chicago, IL: Training Publications, Archdiocese of Chicago, 2005. This readable, straight-forward and informative guide to the Mass is ideal for personal spiritual reading and use by parish study groups, college Newman clubs and adult education courses. It draws one to a deeper understanding of this Mystery of Faith.

Hellwig, Monica. *The Eucharist and the Hunger of the World.* New York: Paulist Press, 1976. The communal sharing of food is a central action of the Eucharist and reveals the interdependence of the entire human family. Hunger for justice, peace, the very real physical starving of millions of poor, and spiritual hunger are all interlinked and a part of this communal meal.

Irvin, Kevin W. *Models of the Eucharist.* Mahwah, NJ: Paulist Press, 2005. Using a post-Vatican II perspective, Msgr. Irwin provides ten models with which to understand the Eucharistic Celebration and its centrality in Catholic life: Church as Eucharist, Cosmic Mass, Effective Word of God, Memorial of the Paschal Mystery, Covenant Renewal, Lord's Supper, Food for the Journey, Sacramental Sacrifice, Work of the Holy Spirit.

Sweetser, Thomas P., *Keeping the Covenant, A Call to Pastoral Partnership.* New York: Crossroad Publishing Co, 2007 is a complete course and description of how to become a vibrant and alive parish in the 21ˢᵗ Century. It begins with moving leaders and people into mission, continues with collaborative structures that link all aspects of the parish together, provides practical means for effective planning and deals with concrete issues such as decision-making, fruitful meetings, life-giving transitions and multicultural challenges. It points the way to a parish becoming a covenant, making a pledge to be faithful to God and to one another in service.

Footnotes

1   Gerald O'Collins, S.J. *Living Vatican II: the 21st Council for the 21st Century* (New York: Paulist Press, 2006. 70.

2   Jeremy Driscoll, OSB, *What Happens at Mass.* (Chicago, IL: Liturgy Training Publications, 2005), v.

3   "The Sacrament of Love." *Synod of Bishops on the Eucharist,* 2005.

4   The pre-Vatican II Mass was unchanging, rubrical, clergy-oriented and unintelligible. See Joseph F. Eagan, S.J., *Restoration and Renewal, the Church in the Third Millennium,* (Kansas City, KC: Sheed and Ward, 2005), 32.

5   SC, Chapter 2, "The Sacred Mystery of the Eucharist," Numbers 47-58.

6   "I myself am the living bread come down from heaven ... The bread I will give is my flesh for the life of the world. At this the Jews quarreled among themselves saying, 'how can he give us his flesh to eat?' Thereupon Jesus said to them ... my flesh is real food and my blood real drink. Whoever feeds on my flesh and drinks my blood remains in me and I in him." (John 6:51-56)

7   "On the night when he was betrayed, he took bread and gave you thanks and praise. He broke the bread, gave it to his disciples and said: Take this, all of you, and eat it: this is my body which will be given up for you. When supper was ended, he took the cup. Again he gave you thanks and praise, gave the cup to

his disciples, and said: Take this, all of you, and drink from it: this is the cup of my blood, the blood of the new and everlasting covenant. It will be shed for you and for all so that sins may be forgiven. Do this in memory of me." (Words of consecration during Mass)

8   Kenan Osborne, *Community, Eucharist, and Spirituality* (Liguori, MO: Liguori, 2007), 1. His basic theme is that "the formation of a vibrant community is the foundation and pre-condition for both the actual eucharistic celebration and a meaningful eucharistic spirituality.'

9   This is a slightly edited version in the Introduction to *The Call to Pastoral Partnership* by Fr. Thomas Sweetser, founder of the successful Evaluation Project that has helped 225 parishes across the United States.

10 Paul Wilkes, *Excellent Catholic Parishes, The Guide to the Best Places and Practices.* (Mahwah, NJ: Paulist Press, 2001).

11 Sweetser, *op.cit., xiv.*

12 Keith F. Pecklers, *Worship, a Primer in Christian Ritual.* (Collegeville, MN: Liturgical Press, 2003), 202-03.

Chapter 7:
Church Leadership

Almost daily bishops and the pope are in the world press. The highly publicized revelations of the failure of bishops in the United States, Canada, Ireland,[1] Germany, Austria and Belgium to defend children from priest abusers has brought Catholic bishops as well as the pope to the center of attention throughout the Western world. Frustrated and angry Catholics ask "How could this happen? Is something seriously wrong in the church? In its leadership?" Many Catholics have lost confidence in their bishops and in the leadership of both bishops and the pope. Bishop Kevin Dowling of South Africa acknowledged their concerns and feelings that "church leadership, instead of giving an impression of its power, privilege and prestige, should rather be experienced as a humble, searching ministry together with its people."[2] The Cardinals who elected Francis I pope agreed before they entered the conclave that church governance was their major concern.

Catholics' questioning and anger are understandable. Some are even beginning to ask such basic questions as Why bishops? Are they needed[3] What is their role in the church? Their authority? On what is it based? Why a pope with so much authority and power? What about his infallibility?

In the context of this crisis, it is important that Catholics understand the role and authority of bishops and of the pope, appreciate Vatican II's fresh teaching on both, and maintain respectful balance. This chapter reviews the historical basis for bishops and the pope, explains Vatican II's teaching on their leadership role in the church, and reflects on the great good the Holy Father and the American bishops do today for Catholics and in the world. The question of much-needed reform of the Roman Curia and the office of pope is discussed in chapter 15 under urgent challenges.

Bishops, Successors of the Apostles[4]

Jesus Christ, the eternal pastor, established the holy church by sending the apostles. ... He willed that their successors, namely the bishops, should be the shepherds in his church until the end of the world. (LG 18)

In the person of bishops ... the Lord Jesus Christ ... is present in the midst of the faithful. (LG 21)

Basis of the Office of Bishops

Jesus personally chose 12 men called Apostles, trained them, gave them the mission to establish his kingdom first in Israel and later throughout the world: "Make disciples of all nations ... baptize them ... teach them ..." (Mt 28:19-20) After Jesus' promised Spirit descended on the Apostles in Jerusalem Pentecost Sunday, Peter and the other Apostles began preaching the good news about Jesus and his salvation to the Jews and later Paul to the Gentile non-Jews. After the death of the original Apostles and of Paul, only gradually did the office of bishop develop in the church.

The word bishop from the Greek *episcopos* means overseer. His role is to care for the faith life of the community of Christian believers and maintain their unity. We know little about those who began to exercise this care or oversight in the early period after the Apostles passed from the scene. Only by the year 115 at Antioch in Syria was the threefold ministry of bishop, priest and deacon in place. By the year 175 the structure of a single bishop recognized as the successor of the Apostles and assisted by presbyters (priests) and deacons had spread throughout the early church.

After the church gained freedom under Constantine, bishops became increasingly powerful figures. They preserved the church from doctrinal error, were the principal celebrants of the Eucharist, maintained communion with other bishops, and ruled their local churches with full authority. Bishops' influence grew through the centuries. Side by side in the great squares of European and South American cities were the seat of civil government and the bishop's palace and his cathedral where his chair (*cathedra*, symbol of his spiritual power) had a special place similar to a king's throne. Bishops thus came to be called "princes" of the church. In the Middle Ages bishops were men of wealth and power, often as civil rulers filling the vacuum of civil leadership owing to the barbarian invasions. This obviously led to many abuses and ultimately to the Protestant Reformation.

Fortunately throughout church history many bishops were men of great learning and saintliness as well as strong leaders: St. Augustine, bishop of Hippo, North Africa, and St. Ambrose, bishop of Milan, Italy, to mention only a few. Bishops have been heroic apostles in spreading the gospel of Christ and powerful defenders of the church against kings, oppressive governments and dictators out to destroy the church. Scores of bishops and most of the popes during the first three centuries died heroic deaths as martyrs under the Roman Emperors' fierce persecution of Christians.

Today we think of great-souled bishops who have staunchly stood up against communist oppression to defend their Christian flock: Archbishop Wyzinski of Poland, Cardinal Archbishop Mindszenty of Hungary; Bishop Walsh, martyred Maryknoll bishop in China; Archbishop Dominic Tang of Canton, China, imprisoned for 22 years by Mao's communists; and most recently Archbishop Oscar Romero of El Salvador who was murdered for defending the human rights of his impoverished *campesino* flock.

Vatican II Teaching on Bishops

The council's teaching on the role and authority of bishops has far-reaching consequences for the health of today's Catholic Church. *Bishops are successors of the 12 Apostles chosen by Jesus.* This succession is the basis of bishops' authority and importance in the church. Yet nowhere in the Christian scriptures are found the literal words "successors of the Apostles." Nor do historical records exist from the first century of Apostles actually appointing successors.[5] The council relies on the following theological reasoning: In solemn words Jesus gave the apostles the "great mission": "Full authority has been given to me both in heaven and on earth; go, therefore, and make disciples of all nations. Baptize ... [and] teach them ... And know that I am with you always until the end of the world." (Mt. 28:18-20) This mission is to last until the end of the world. The Apostles will die. Thus the council states "For this reason the Apostles took care to appoint successors..." (LG 20)

Apostolic succession means that the mission given by Christ to the Apostles continues in the church in the person of bishops. In treating this succession, *Lumen Gentium* is careful to avoid the impossibility of showing that today's bishops can trace their ordination back to a specific Apostle or that there exists an unbroken line of bishops back to the Apostles. The earliest that some ancient dioceses can trace their succession of bishops is the 3rd or even 2nd century, since historical records are lacking for the 1st century. Accordingly, the council refers simply to "the office of those ... appointed to the episcopate in a sequence running back to the beginning of the church." (LG 20) This sequence or succession is of vital importance because it guarantees that the teaching of the Apostles received from Christ, the apostolic tradition, is passed to the present without error.

To stress the importance of this succession, Vatican II made an official *dogmatic* teaching: "This sacred Synod teaches that *by divine institution* bishops have succeeded to the place of the apostles as shepherds of the church and that he who hears them hears Christ and he who rejects them rejects Christ and him who sent Christ." (LG 20, emphasis added) Divine institution means that God, not humans, has set up the office of bishops in the church. Bishops are thus *essential* to the church established by Christ. This solemn teaching also has important ecumenical implications to be treated in chapter 11.

Ministry and Authority of Bishops

The Second Vatican Council described the threefold ministry of bishops as "teachers of doctrine, priests for sacred worship, and ministers of government." (LG 20) Bishops receive this threefold office of teaching, sanctifying and governing from the Holy Spirit by episcopal ordination through a ritual of three bishops in the apostolic succession placing their hands on the head of the person being ordained. Their authority "which they exercise personally in the name of Christ is *proper* (that is, to the bishop alone), *ordinary*[6] by virtue of his office from ordination, and *immediate*" (from Christ and his Spirit, not from the pope). (LG 27) Thus bishops may not interfere in the affairs of another diocese nor are they "to be regarded as vicars of the Roman Pontiff, for they exercise a power they possess in their own right." (LG 27) Their authority has practical significance for the renewal of the church today.

Teaching Authority. "Bishops, as successors of the Apostles, receive from the Lord ... the mission of teaching ...(and) preaching the Gospel … (LG 24). "They are authentic teachers … endowed with the authority of Christ." (LG 25). When teaching "in communion with the Roman Pontiff … in matters of faith and morals, the bishops speak in the name of Christ and the faithful are to accept their teaching and adhere to it with religious assent of soul" (LG 25). The term for this authoritative church teaching is *magisterium,* or teaching office. The church understands the bishop as the official teacher in matters of faith and morality in his own diocese.

Catholics sometimes ask the exact nature of bishops' teaching authority. The council gives a carefully stated answer. "Although individual bishops do not enjoy the prerogative of infallibility, they can nevertheless proclaim Christ's doctrine infallibly," that is, without error when they teach as a "college" in union with the pope (LG 25). "The infallibility promised to the church resides also in the body of bishops when that body exercises supreme teaching authority."

Sanctifying Authority. Bishops "promote and protect the entire liturgical life of the church." (Christus Dominus, CD 15) Bishops provide for the spiritual care of the faithful, ensure they receive sacraments, oversee their proper conferral, and lead worship in the cathedral.

Governing Authority. This is a ministry of church discipline, of overseeing the church's resources and personnel, especially priests and parishes, to be exercised with "love and solicitude." (CD 16)

Episcopal Collegiality

Commentators on *Lumen Gentium* state that Vatican II's most important achievement was to recover within the Catholic Church the doctrine of episcopal collegiality, an example of development of doctrine. Its basis is a theology of **communion**, that the universal Catholic Church is conceived as a communion of local churches (dioceses) led by bishops as successors of the Apostles.

Individual bishops are the visible source and foundation of unity in their own particular churches … in and from these that the one and unique Catholic Church exists. For that reason each bishop represents his own church, whereas all together represent the whole church in a bond of peace, love and unity. (LG 23)

Episcopal collegiality means that the pope and bishops together form a "college" or group and thus together share leadership over the entire church.

The Roman Pontiff, as the successor of Peter, is the perpetual and visible source and foundation of the unity of the bishops and of the multitude of the faithful. The individual bishop is the visible principle and foundation of unity in his particular church. … In and from such individual churches there comes into being the one Catholic church. (LG 23)

After extensive and heated debate at the council, in three critical votes the bishops approved these pivotal teachings on bishops: Whether every bishop who is in communion with all the bishops and the pope belongs to the body or college of bishops: yes, 2,049; no 104. Whether the college of bishops succeeds the college of the apostles and, together with the pope, has full and supreme power over the whole church: yes, 1,808; no 336. Whether the college of bishops, in union with the pope, has this power by divine right: yes, 1,707; no, 408. The sizeable "no" votes show the complexity of the issues and the opposition of traditional bishops fearful of lessening papal authority.

Episcopal collegiality establishes the principle of collegiality based on the council's solemn teaching that "bishops, successors of the Apostles, together with Peter's successor, the Vicar of Christ and visible head of the whole church, govern the worldwide church. (LG 18) Today, 1.3 billion Catholics throughout the world through their bishops being in communion with the bishop of Rome are united in an immense Catholic family.

The reality of collegiality and of being in communion with the pope has practical importance in China today. In 2010 the Catholic Patriotic Association controlled by the Chinese government forced the ordination of three Chinese Catholic bishops without the prior approval of Pope Benedict XIV. Though valid, these ordinations were illicit; consequently the newly ordained bishops are not within the universal communion of the Catholic Church because not in communion with the bishop of Rome, the center of the church's communion.

Being in communion with the pope was also crucial in mainland China when Mao and the communists came to power. Chinese bishops and priests were given a stark choice: renounce their unity with and loyalty to the pope or go to prison. Many Chinese bishops, priests and lay Catholics chose to remain in communion with the pope and thus went to prison suffering untold hardships for over twenty years. One such was Bishop Dominic Tang.

I was privileged to meet with Bishop Tang of Canton, (now Quanzou) China, in 1980. He had just been released from prison after 22 years, seven of which were in solitary confinement in an effort to "break" him. He was presently confined to the parish house next to the large grey stone gothic-style cathedral which ironically was "his" cathedral prior to his imprisonment. When we had a moment of relative privacy from the communist officials, he whispered to me: "Tell the Jesuits in Hong Kong that I am still loyal to the Holy Father." He had gone to prison and suffered much through those long years to remain "in communion with" the pope. His slim book, *His Inscrutable Ways*, which reports on his first years as bishop of Canton and the difficult prison years including solitary confinement, is an eloquent witness to his love of God and the great value he put on being "in communion" with the bishop of Rome.

Summary of Vatican II's Teaching on Bishops

- Bishops are an *essential* part of the church of Christ. Neither the Catholic Church nor the Orthodox churches nor the Anglican Communion would ever lose the order of bishops.
- The Catholic Church is thus **hierarchical** or priestly in nature, governed by leaders ordained in the sacrament of holy orders. According to the church's canon law, only the ordained can exercise authority. The Catholic Church is not a democracy, though it can and should use democratic procedures and welcome capable lay Catholic women and men into collaborative ministry for the well-being of the church.
- Bishops enter the apostolic succession through a valid sacramental ordination. This reality has important implications for the Catholic Church's search for unity with other Christian churches, whose ordinations she considers seriously lacking.
- Bishops are supreme in their own churches or dioceses, receiving authority directly from Christ. Only for grave reasons and rarely does the pope act in the affairs of local churches or remove a bishop from his diocese.
- The council immensely upgraded the role and authority of bishops within the Catholic Church through the *principle of collegiality* by which bishops form a team with their brother bishops and the pope. "The episcopal college together with its head the pope is the subject of supreme and full power over the universal church." (LG 22)
- Vatican II affirmed the authority of an ecumenical council. "The supreme authority with which this college is empowered over the whole church is exercised in a solemn way through an ecumenical council."(LG 22) The teaching and renewal program of Vatican Council II is thus authoritative for all Catholics today. This casts in a different light the current restoration movement,

its "reform of the reform" of the liturgy and of Vatican II, and its interpretation of the council as primarily a continuation of the past.

Contemporary Issues concerning Bishops

Choosing Bishops.[7] Considerable dissatisfaction exists today on how bishops are chosen. Priests and people and sometimes the local bishop have little or no input in the bishop they receive, often with tragic consequences as in Holland and Austria. In Ireland "mediocre bishops" were blamed for the widespread sexual abuse of minors.

National Conferences of Bishops.[7] Vatican Council II mandated the formation of conferences of bishops in each country "to foster the church's mission" and "to provide bishops opportunity to exercise in a joint manner their pastoral office." The United States Conference of Catholic Bishops (USCCB), meeting three days twice a year in Washington, D.C., has produced impressive documents, especially *The Challenge of Peace* in 1983 and *Economic Justice for All* in 1986 and letters on a number of issues[8] to guide priests and laity. However, the authority of these conferences has been downgraded, severely limiting their ability to lead and to address urgent local issues. One example: Vatican II gave bishops and national bishops' conferences explicit authority over the liturgy, yet the Congregation for Divine Worship over-ruled ICEL, commissioned by English-speaking bishops' conferences to translate the Mass and sacramentary, and created its own body, *Vox Clara.* (See Chapter 4, Evaluation.)

Apostolic Succession. This is a difficult and emotionally-charged issue in the Catholic Church's relationship with Anglican and Protestant churches. Pope Leo XIII officially stated that Anglican orders are "absolutely null and void" because their bishops are not part of the apostolic succession.[9] Protestant ministers are likewise judged to be outside the apostolic succession of the validly ordained. The Catholic Church recognizes only bishops of Orthodox churches and the Swedish Lutheran church as being in the apostolic succession of bishops.

The famous World Council of Churches' 1982 Faith and Order document *Baptism, Eucharist, Ministry* invited those churches that do not have bishops to recover the historic episcopacy as a major step toward the reunion of the Christian churches. Chapter 11 discusses BEM's promising ecumenical proposal: if apostolic succession is understood *primarily* as passing on *the apostolic tradition*, then churches in the Anglican Communion and Protestant churches that possess the Christian faith expressed in the apostolic tradition might be affirmed part of the apostolic succession.

Awesome Responsibility of Bishops

"For you I am a bishop; with you I am a Christian. ... The day I became a bishop, a burden was laid on my shoulders ... The honors I receive are for me an ever present cause of uneasiness ... being set above you fills me with alarm; being with you gives me comfort."

St. Augustine

As leader of his local church and overseer of its priests and people, the bishop is responsible for the quality of Christian life throughout the diocese. As official teacher, he is responsible for proclaiming the Gospel of Christ to his people and for safeguarding their Catholic faith from error. He is likewise responsible for the proper celebration of the Eucharist and all the sacraments within the diocese. (LG 26) He shares responsibility for the universal church with the bishop of Rome. As "father" of his priests, he has a special care for their well-being spiritually, physically and psychologically. In addition to all this, he bears ultimate responsibility for the financial health of the diocese and its many parishes and multiple apostolic organizations and ventures. It is an awesome responsibility and immense burden for one limited person to carry.

It is thus clear that bishops have an extremely important, indispensable role in the church. The council uses a striking metaphor from St. Ignatius, the second century martyr, to express how Christians should relate to their bishops. "The faithful must 'cling to their bishop' as the church does to Christ and Jesus Christ to the Father, that all may harmonize in unity." (LG 27)

Bishops worldwide serve their people, often heroically under many difficulties, with great energy and dedication as effective pastoral men. In eras of intense political pressure and persecution, they have fought courageously and unselfishly for the church and those under their care. They are men of prayer, deeply spiritual, devoted to Jesus Christ and to the Church the Body of Christ. Such men reveal that bishops can and do honor the church and their vocation, though they rarely grace the pages of the media.

Archbishop Oscar Arnulfo Romero of El Salvador was such a bishop. A conservative, traditional churchman, Bishop Romero became archbishop of San Salvador during a turbulent period of death squads and massive injustice and oppression of the poor. After the murder of his friend Jesuit Rutilio Grande, champion for the rights of his 30,000 parishioners, Romero realized the reality in El Salvador and became a strong voice for the poor.[10] He traveled all over the archdiocese, listening to his priests and the poor, ministering and encouraging them. Under his leadership the church became fully collegial.

Each Sunday at the 8:00 AM cathedral mass, in a homily heard on transistor radios throughout Central America, he denounced the oppression of the poor and read the names of peasants and priests murdered the past week by the military and the death squads. He was criticized by his fellow bishops, the wealthy, and the Vatican for being "political" and even Marxist. He wrote "the church would betray its love for God and its fidelity to the Gospel if it stopped being a defender of the rights of the poor."

The last year of his life Archbishop Romero received constant death threats. Two weeks before his death he stated: "As a shepherd I am obliged to give my life ... for all Salvadorans ... I offer my blood to God for the resurrection of El Salvador and for my people's liberation. A bishop will die but God's church which is the people will never perish." (See chapter 10, liberation theology)

March 24, 1980, while saying mass in a chapel attached to a hospital, he was assassinated by a single bullet from a gunman hired by the government. "The voice of those who have no voice" became a martyr of justice for his people. The people of El Salvador and beyond call him Saint Romero and pray to him for his intercession with God in their daily lives. In dirt-floor hovels of the poor throughout El Salvador are crude altars with a picture of "our bishop," a true shepherd who gave his life for his flock.

Peter in the Church

"You are Peter, the rock on which I will build my Church." (Matthew 16:16)

"The Roman Pontiff, as the Successor of Peter, is the perpetual and visible source and foundation of unity both of bishops and of the whole company of the faithful."

Lumen Gentium, 23

Perhaps no other spiritual leader and world figure has attracted so much coverage in the media or caused such strong emotions both positive and negative as the Catholic pope. In addition, the historical development of the papacy or office of the pope within the Catholic Church is complex and much debated.

The papacy is the oldest living institution in the Western world. Of all the Christian churches, only the Roman Catholic Church has the papacy. Thousands attend the pope's weekly audiences and rush to take photos or grasp his hand as he walks up the center aisle. Hundreds of thousands attend his Masses on his worldwide pastoral journeys. Pope John Paul II became a kind of media star and was seen by perhaps more people than any other human. Diplomats and heads of state visit the pope as head of Vatican City, as world leader, and spokesman for moral values.

Yet serious questions surround the pope. Is the papacy a human invention since early historical evidence is lacking for the popes *as successors of Peter?* During later periods individual popes were seriously unworthy of their high office. The Protestant Reformation was precipitated by the misuse of authority by the Renaissance popes. In the modern effort to unite the separated Christian churches, the papacy is considered the greatest obstacle, as Pope Paul VI once stated. Moreover, can a mere man be infallible? Can a 2000-year institution like the papacy respond to the increasing calls for change?

So today major questions persist. Is the papacy essential to the Catholic Church? Did Jesus establish the office of pope or is it a historical development? Must a future united Christian Church include the pope? What is the best way for the pope's authority to be exercised today? Does the papacy need reform?

Why a Pope? The Rock and Keys Metaphor

Whenever St. Peter is pictured in mosaics high on the walls of the great European churches, he always holds a set of large keys in his hands. These are his identification. In St. Peter's in Rome, high above the floor in four-foot golden letters in Latin and Greek running the length and breadth of the giant basilica are Jesus' words to Peter, beginning with: "Blessed are you Simon...." These words are taken from the famous passage in which Jesus gives Peter a new responsibility and special role among the Christian people.[11]

> Simon Peter spoke up: "You are the Messiah, the Son of the Living God." Jesus agreed and said to him: "Blessed are you Simon, son of Jonah. Flesh and blood has not revealed this to you but my Father in Heaven. And I tell you, you are Peter and on this rock I will build my church, and the powers of death shall not prevail against it. I will give you the keys of the kingdom of heaven, and whatever you bind on earth shall be bound in heaven and whatever you loose on earth will be loosed in heaven." (Mt. 16:16-19)

The context of this pivotal event is important. Jesus had just asked his disciples who people thought he was. All were silent. Only Peter, thanks to a personal divine revelation, identified him as the Messiah, the longed-for Jewish anointed savior. In reply, Jesus changes Simon's name to Peter, the Greek name for rock *(petra)*. In Semitic custom to change a person's name is to give him a new vocation or mission; thus God changed Abram's name to Abraham, signifying he was to become the father of the Jewish people (Genesis, 17:5). Peter is to be the rock foundation on which Jesus is to "build my church," a foundation so strong as to endure against powers out to destroy it.

The second part of Peter's vocation or responsibility is to exercise spiritual authority in the church, symbolized by keys that open and close buildings, an authority supported by God ("bound ... loosed in heaven").[12]

From this famous text, Catholics and a growing number of Protestant scholars and ecumenists conclude that Peter has a unique, special role in the church conferred by Jesus. Peter is mentioned 114 times in the Gospels, far more than any other Apostle. He is presented as the spokesman of the other apostles; his name always appears first in a list of the Apostles' names; he is present at special incidents in Christ's life. In the first half of the *Acts of the Apostles*, Peter dominates the pages: he gives the first Christian "sermon" to the Jews, he works the first recorded miracle of the Apostles, he visits many of the newly-founded churches, and he presides over the first Council of Jerusalem. Raymond Brown, the eminent American Catholic biblical scholar, refers to "a trajectory of images of Peter" in the New Testament, that is, Peter grows in importance from Gospel to Gospel indicating that the early Christian communities realized more fully as the years passed the special role Jesus had given Peter.[13]

Two Scripture passages indicate that Peter's role as rock and keeper of the keys is to continue in the church. In Matthew 16:16-18, Jesus promises that the powers of death will not destroy his church beyond Peter's lifetime. In Matthew 20: 18-20 Jesus sent his Apostles including Peter to preach the Good News until the end of time. Accordingly, successors to Peter are needed that the mission continue.

But who are these successors? We have seen that bishops forming the episcopal college are the successors of the Apostles. Can we also conclude that the popes are the successors of Peter? The question is complex. Historically, documentary proof is lacking that a *single* monarchical bishop existed in Rome during the first century and beyond. Scholars today accept that a group of presbyters or priests led the church in Rome before and after Peter's martyrdom in Rome. What happened is a gradual *development* over several centuries of a single bishop of Rome exercising Peter's role in the church.[14]

The Bishop of Rome as Successor of Peter

While the Roman Church did not exercise an exclusive authority over other churches in the early centuries, from the very beginning, the church at Rome was recognized as having a special place among the other Christian churches because it was the church of Peter and Paul who lived and were martyred in Rome and because it held the treasured tombs of the two Apostles. From the letters of Clement of Rome (ca. 95 AD) and Ignatius of Antioch, modern-day Turkey, (ca. 110) and later Irenaeus (180) and Tertullian (213), we learn that on controversial questions other churches looked to Rome as having faithfully preserved the faith of the Apostles. Around 375 the bishops of Rome first began *formally* to claim succession from Peter. The high point of this development was Pope Leo I (d. 461) who developed a theology of the bishop of Rome as successor to Peter and of the Roman church's prerogative (primacy?) over the churches of the West. At the Ecumenical Council of Chalcedon, 461, which officially stated the church's understanding of the nature of Christ, the council fathers declared "Peter has spoken through Leo."

From this gradual development, we are able to conclude that the bishops of Rome are in fact the successors of Peter: Peter was martyred in Rome in the year 64 or 67 making it an Apostolic Church respected by all other churches; these churches came to recognize the special nature and authority of the Roman Church and its bishops; no other bishop claimed to be Peter's successor or acted as foundation of the unity of the churches with spiritual authority. Catholics believe that this gradual development took place under the inspiration of the Holy Spirit promised by Christ to his church.

Office of Peter in Vatican I and Vatican II

Because the pope's ***primacy*** or firstness of authority within the Catholic Church is essential to the Church and because this claim to primacy is misunderstood by Catholics and a source of contention with the Orthodox, Anglicans and Protestants and a serious obstacle to unity with them, we treat Vatican I and its official teaching on the pope's primacy and his infallibility.

We first treat *Vatican Council I (1869-70)* and its dogmatic *Constitution on the Church of Christ, Pastor Aeternus, Eternal Pastor,* which stated the council's official teaching on the pope's primacy. "We teach and declare that according to the testimony of the Gospel the primacy of jurisdiction over the whole church of God was immediately and directly promised to and conferred upon the blessed Peter by Christ the Lord." Jurisdiction refers to making laws binding on all; immediate means an authority not depending on anyone else. *Pastor Aeternus* continues by describing the pope's infallible teaching office.

We teach and define that it is a divinely revealed dogma: that the Roman Pontiff, when he speaks *ex cathedra,* that is, when, acting in the office of shepherd and teacher of all Christians, he *defines,* by virtue of his supreme apostolic authority, doctrine concerning *faith or morals* to be held by the universal church, *possesses* through the *divine assistance promised to him in the person of St. Peter,* the infallibility with which the divine Redeemer *willed his church to be endowed* in defining doctrine concerning faith or morals: and that such definitions of the Roman Pontiff are therefore *irreformable* because of their nature, but *not because of the agreement of the church* (emphases added).

Several important aspects of this highly technical official teaching need to be emphasized. Vatican I does not state "the pope is infallible" but that he is "empowered" with the infallibility Christ gave his church, that is, the pope exercises a power belonging not to himself but to the church. The pope can exercise this infallibility only when he speaks in his role as pastor and teacher of the universal church. He can speak only on matters of faith, on God's revelation through Jesus, and of morality; these "definitions" cannot be changed (irreformable) in later years.

It is obvious that its use is limited. In addition to this definition at Vatican I, papal infallibility has been used only twice – the Immaculate Conception of Mary in 1854 and the Assumption of Mary into heaven in 1950. If the principle of collegiality is fully observed, the likelihood of future papal infallible statements is diminished. Pope John XXIII is supposed to have joked "I won't make any infallible statements, therefore I'm not infallible!"

This doctrine of papal infallibility has caused much debate within the church and outside. One fourth of the bishops at Vatican I "had misgivings" about it, considering it was unnecessary, an obstacle to union with other Christians, and needed further explanation. Several doubted its truth. The opposition of Protestants and the Orthodox is twofold: the doctrine appears to be of human origin to give the pope more power and prestige and is open to abuse. For Catholics, the doctrine caused the phenomenon of "creeping infallibilism" in which average Catholics mistakenly took all official papal statements and documents as infallible, a misunderstanding operative today causing division within the church. Theologians have questioned why the church needed this new dogma after 1800 years' existence without it. Church historians also pointed out that the dogma was historically conditioned, that is, a strong movement in the church called **ultramontanism** urged the definition in order to strengthen the diminished authority of the papacy at that time and that Pope Pius IX exerted pressure to have it defined.

The Second Vatican Council (1962-65)

Though *Lumen Gentium* fully accepted Vatican I's teaching on the papacy, the Second Vatican Council put that teaching in an entirely new light.[15] The council used the language of Scripture to define the role of the pope, in contrast to Vatican I's juridical language of primacy and jurisdiction: "The Lord made Peter alone the rock-foundation and the holder of the keys of the church (Mt 16:18-19) and instituted him shepherd of his whole flock (John 21:15);" (LG 22) "...the office which the Lord confided to Peter alone as first of the Apostles, destined to be transmitted to his successors, is a permanent one ..." (LG 20); "The Roman Pontiff, as the successor of Peter, is the perpetual and visible source and foundation of unity both of bishops and of the whole company of the faithful." (LG 23)

As we have seen, Vatican II stressed collegiality, that bishops form the episcopal college with the bishop of Rome and thus have full and supreme authority in governing the universal church with him. From their episcopal ordination and not from the pope, bishops have full authority over their own local church (diocese). The council thus restored the older ecclesiology of *communion* whereby bishops are responsible both for the unity of their own local churches and create the communion of all the churches by being in communion with the Bishop of Rome.

Vatican II clarified the teaching of Vatican I on infallibility by stating that the college of bishops could teach infallibly in communion with the pope, that infallibility is strictly limited to divine revelation, and that no new revelation is possible. The charism of infallibility given to the bishop of Rome is *immunity from error* regarding divine revelation and to those truths that are necessary to preserve and explain divine revelation, termed the "secondary objects of revelation." [16]

One might say that the council bishops created a limited checks and balances in the government of the church, a practice that has somewhat fallen into disuse since the council.

How the Pope Exercises the Petrine Office in the Worldwide Church

Most simply put, the role of the pope is *to be Peter* in the Church today. His most appropriate title is therefore successor of Peter; other titles like Roman Pontiff, Vicar of Christ, Patriarch of the West, Holy Father, and "His Holiness" accrued to him later. The title bishop of Rome is appropriate because he is in fact the diocesan bishop of the city of Rome.[17]

- *To be the Center and Guarantee of Unity.* Thus 1.3 billion Catholics worldwide are united by their individual bishops being in communion with the pope. Accordingly, the bishop of Rome must in some way be the unifying force in a future united church. In the Lutheran-Catholic dialogue in the United States, the Lutheran participants of ELCA (Evangelical Lutheran Church of America) asked their churches to acknowledge "the possibility and desirability of the papal ministry, renewed under the Gospel and committed to Christian freedom, in a larger communion" of the Roman Catholic and Lutheran churches.[18]
- *To be the universal teacher and protector of the Christian Tradition* from Christ through the Apostles. The pope and all the bishops have "the duty to promote and to safeguard the unity of faith" (LG 23) for they are "authentic teachers ... endowed with the authority of Christ." (LG 25) Thus bishops in union with the pope form the *magisterium* or teaching office in the church. The Christian Tradition includes the truths of faith (doctrine), worship (sacraments), and morality (right and wrong actions), popularly termed creed, cult, and code. St. Paul and the Catholic Church throughout its 2000-year history have put high priority on unity and purity of doctrine.

- *To be the final decision-maker, but collegially.* This means consulting the bishops of the world before making a serious teaching. Pope Pius XII did this in proclaiming the Assumption of Mary a dogma to be believed by Catholics.[19]
- *To have "full and supreme authority"* in governing the universal church but together with the worldwide bishops who form the episcopal college. This establishes the principle of collegiality, considered the most important accomplishment of the Second Vatican Council.

Governing the Worldwide Catholic Church

In his government of the universal Church, the Bishop of Rome is aided by a large, uniquely dedicated supporting staff. *The Roman Curia* is the vast bureaucracy composed of nine congregations, each headed by a Cardinal[20] and many pontifical councils.[21] *Cardinals* personally appointed by the pope and bearers of the coveted 'red hat' are his special advisers whose role since 1159 AD is to elect the pope. *Nuncios* are trained diplomats who represent the pope to a state or civil government. *Apostolic Delegates* are personal representatives of the pope to the bishops of each country; by presenting candidates to be chosen bishops by the pope, they have great influence.

The pope lives and works in Vatican City, the smallest state in the world occupying 108.7 acres. As an official state recognized by the nations of the world, it has political relations with most countries, exchanges ambassadors (nuncios), and enters into ***concordats*** to protect the rights of the church.

The pope thus has a dual role: his spiritual leadership as successor of Peter and bishop of Rome and his political role as head of Vatican state. His extraordinary world influence as spiritual leader of 1.3 billion Catholics and as a world spokesman for religious and moral values make him a doubly valuable person for heads of state who come in large numbers to speak with him.

Current Issues Involving the Papacy

Some bishops, many priests and women religious, theologians and church historians, and educated lay Catholics are increasingly concerned with the failure of collegial relationships throughout the church. They cite the over-centralization of authority in Rome; the Vatican's failure to discuss critical issues like clerical celibacy, married priests, women's role in the church, the growing shortage of priests and loss of the Eucharist; the movement to restrict and re-interpret the renewal of the Second Vatican Council and to restore some pre-Vatican II practices. They believe that many of the problems in the church today stem from the failures of collegiality and governance. For further issues, see Chapter 15, "Urgent Issues," especially section 9, Reform of the Papacy.

Catholics' Devotion to the Pope

Though aware of issues involving the papacy and at times critical of its exercise, Catholics nonetheless have great esteem and devotion for the person of the pope. They see Peter in the pope as foundation of Catholics' unity worldwide; they are convinced the papacy is essential to the Church established by Jesus himself; they take seriously one of the pope's titles, Vicar of Christ,[22] as visibly representing Christ, and they accept the pope as their Holy Father in the faith, responsible for safeguarding the unity of their faith and for proclaiming it ceaselessly to them.

John Allen, Rome correspondent for the *National Catholic Reporter,* recounts a chance meeting late one night in St. Peter's large empty square when he came on Cardinal Schonborn of Vienna who was standing alone looking up at the lighted window of Pope John Paul II's apartment. Allen asked why he was there. The Cardinal replied. "Because Peter is here. He was crucified alongside this obelisk when it was in Nero's circus just over there. Peter is also up there in the papal apartment watching over the Church, just as he has been for two thousand years. It's an awesome sensation ... a tradition back to Christ himself and to the head of the Apostles."[23]

A Matter of Balance

There is a danger that criticism of bishops in the United States and of popes John Paul II and Benedict XVI obscures their real accomplishments and the quality of their leadership for the church today. One can acknowledge their intellectual brilliance, obvious spirituality, encyclicals affirming social justice, their apostolic journeys and strong messages to world leaders and overall leadership of 1.3 billion Catholics. One can point to Benedict XVI's well-received statements to world leaders, his two encyclicals on love and hope, his courageous social teaching and care for the environment, his prolific writing and personal spirituality.

Similarly the American bishops deserve appreciation and gratitude for their strong social justice leadership, and their commitment to the poor, to religious liberty, to human dignity and the sacredness of human life, the family and marriage. The United States Bishops' Conference provide Catholics' articulate leadership through statements on a wide range of issues and needs. The American bishops carry on under overwhelming pressures of shortage of priests, parish realignment, constant financial problems, and the burden they carry of the sexual abuse tragedy.

For Discussion

1. Why are bishops so important in the church?
2. How would you evaluate today's bishops?
3. Why is Vatican II's insistence on the principle of collegiality in governing the worldwide Catholic Church so important and necessary in the church today?
4. Explain to a non-Catholic friend why the pope is essential to the church.
5. Can you accept papal infallibility now that you understand its stringent conditions?

Further Reading

Pottmeyer, Hermann. *Towards a Papacy in Communion: Perspectives from Vatican Councils I and II.* New York: Crossroad Publishing Co., 1998. This book explains the teachings of Vatican I and II regarding the papacy, dispelling some common misconceptions, emphasizing that the institution of the papacy is called to reform by Vatican II, and stressing the theology of communion as a way beyond a centralist understanding of papacy and an opening for dialogue on papal primacy.

Quinn, John. *The Reform of the Papacy: The Costly Call to Christian Unity.* New York: Crossroad Publishing Co., 1990. The former archbishop of San Francisco, Quinn boldly explores how reform of the papacy and the Roman Curia is needed to answer Christ's call for the unity of the separated churches. An insightful, important book.

Reese, Thomas J. S.J., *Archbishop: Inside the Power Structure of the American Catholic Church.* San Francisco: Harper and Row, 1989. Reese provides a thorough description of the institution of the archbishop and of the hierarchy at the diocesan level, explaining in detail the power structures, finances, election by the Congregation of Bishops and the pope, as well as education and social services.

Sobrino, Jon. *Archbishop Romero: Memories and Reflections.* Maryknoll, NY: Orbis Books, 1990. A beautiful and inspiring book told with love by Fr. Sobrino who was a close friend of the martyred archbishop; he chronicles Romero's life and courage in the face of injustice and death threats. A wonderful portrait of how Catholic bishops can be a vital spiritual force in the world.

Footnotes

1   A government study of widespread abuse of children in Ireland over many years and of the Irish bishops' consistent concealment and protection of guilty priests in order to protect the church's reputation devastated the Irish people. Pope Benedict XVI publicly admonished them for "grave failures in leadership" which "seriously undermined your credibility and effectiveness." Dublin Archbishop Martin candidly admitted "the church has tragically failed many of its children: through abuse, through not preventing abuse, through covering up abuse."

2   "Catholic Social Teaching Finds Church Leadership Lacking.," *National Catholic Reporter* (July 8, 2010): 1,9-10.

3   A daily communicant parishioner is so upset and angry with the bishops over their failure of oversight that he comes out with expressions like "What good are they? We don't need them. Let's get rid of them," this from an educated and prominent engineer! My rejoinder that there are many fine, outstanding bishops fell on deaf ears. His solution – "stop contributing, turn off the money source."

4   A bishop heads a geographical area called a *diocese;* an archbishop is a bishop of a major city who heads an *archdiocese.* The entire world is divided geographically into dioceses or archdioceses. Some dioceses contain large numbers of Catholics, others relatively few. Some cover vast areas of land or sea. The United States currently has 34 archdioceses and 177 dioceses.

5   For the lack of New Testament evidence regarding Apostles' appointing successors see Raymond Brown, *Priest and Bishop, Biblical Reflections* (Eugene, OR: Wipf and Stock Publishers, 1999), 51-5.

6   The bishop who is called "the Ordinary" has full power of jurisdiction in his diocese to distinguish him from coadjutor or helper bishops who do not.

7   Local diocesan bishops are invited to put names on a list of candidates to be sent to the apostolate delegate. When a vacancy occurs, the delegate is supposed to 'engage in wide-ranging consultations' and to come up with three names, the terna. He sends the names to the Congregation of Bishops in Rome which may or may not consult further and then forwards the names to the pope who makes

the final choice. Interestingly, it was not always done this way. For the first 1000 years or so bishops were either elected directly by the people of a given diocese or nominated by an emperor or king or even feudal lord and then approved by the pope. The 28th canon of Ecumenical Council Lateran II in April, 1139, states that bishops shall be elected by cathedral chapters. Even as late as 1829 the pope appointed bishops in only 24 dioceses outside the papal states

8   *To Teach as Jesus Did*, 1972; *The Many Faces of Aids*, 1987; *Biblical Fundamentalism*, 1987; *Brothers and Sisters to Us, Racism in Our Day, 1979; Women in the Church and Society*, 1994; *Ministry with Young Adults* 1996; *Lay Ecclesial Ministry*, 1999; *Adult Faith Formation*, 1999; *To Hunger and Thirst for Justice*, 1999; *Welcoming the Stranger Among Us*, 2000; A *Call to Solidarity with Africa*, 2001; *Charter for the Protection of Children and Young People*, 2002; *Marriage and Same Sex Union* 2003; *Comprehensive Immigration Reform* 2006; *Ministry to Homosexual Persons*, 2006; *Forming Consciences for Faithful Citizenship* 2007; *Catholic Health Care Services*, 2008, and many statements on countries (Iraq, Kenya, Sudan, middle East, African Refugees, East Timor) and annual Labor Day Statements.

9   The commission called by Leo XIII to decide the question of Anglican orders voted 5-4 for their invalidity. Cardinal Mary del Val cast the deciding vote under pressure from Cardinal Vaughn of England who argued that a verdict of validity would undermine the Catholic Church and its new freedom to function in England.

10   Romero once said "When the Church hears the cry of the oppressed, it cannot but denounce the social structures that give rise to and perpetuate the misery from which the cry arises … . We must not seek the child Jesus in the pretty figures of our Christmas cribs. We must seek him among the undernourished children who have gone to bed at night with nothing to eat, among the poor newsboys who will sleep covered with newspapers in doorways." Joe Jenkins, *Christianity* (Oxford: Heineman Educational, 1995), 68.

11   Scripture scholars agree that this passage, if not Jesus' actual words, are either a memory in the tradition or Mathew's insertion as part of the growing awareness in the New Testament period of Peter's role as rock of unity. In referring to this New Testament evidence, Raymond Brown observes that "Christians

are divided most along denominational lines, on whether the development of the papacy should be considered as God's plan for the church; but given the New Testament evidence pertinent to the growth of the image of Peter, it is not easy for those who reject the papacy to portray the concept of a succession to Peter as contradictory to the NT. Raymond Brown, *An Introduction to the New Testament,*(New York: Paulist Press, 1975). 225.

12 "There are debates about what is meant by this binding/loosing. Is it the power to forgive/not forgive sins (as in John 20:29) or to teach what must be observed...?" Brown, *op.cit.,*189.

13 *Ibid.* 67-77.

14 See the classic study of the German scholar Klaus Schatz, *Papal Primacy from Its Origins to the Present,* Part I, The Development of the Primacy in the First Five Centuries," Collegeville, MN: The Liturgical Press, 1996, 1-40. "It is clear that Roman primacy was not a given from the outset; it underwent a long process of development whose initial phases extended well into the fifth century." *Ibid.,* 36.

15 See Schatz, *Ibid* 169-70, Part IV, section IV. "After 1870: Is There a Future? " 1. Between Vatican I and Vatican II. 2. The New Accents of Vatican II and Lack of Integration (of authority: the college of bishops with the pope and the pope alone.).

16 For a scholarly exposition of truths not formally revealed but necessariy connected with revealed truths and the development since the council "with regard to the infallibility of the magisterium when it speaks *definitively* about these truths (the secondary objects of infallibility) "to be held in faith," see Francis A. Sullivan, "Developments in Teaching Authority since Vatican II," *Theological Studies* 73:3 (2012) 579-89.

17 In official documents the term **Apostolic See** means that diocese first occupied by the Apostle Peter and then by his successors; "See" comes from the Latin word *sedes* or chair, the symbol of authority for the one who "sits in the chair of Peter," since a throne is the sign of the king's authority. This idea is expressed artistically in two places in St. Peter's Basilica in Rome: the life-size

black statue of St. Peter actually sitting in a chair with his left shoe worn by the touches and kisses of millions of pilgrims; and the exuberant sunburst monument by Bernini of the chair of Peter behind the main altar.

18 Paul Empie and T. Austin Murphy, editor, *Papal Primacy and the Universal Church,* (Minneapolis, MN: Augsburg Publishing House, 1974), 23, # 32.

19 In 1968 Pope Paul VI seems to have acted without consulting the world's bishops in his encyclical *Humanae Vitae, Of Human Life,* which caused tragic division within the Church.

20 Doctrine of Faith (CDF), Bishops, Divine Worship and Sacraments. Clergy, Evangelization of Peoples, Religious Orders and Secular Institutes, Catholic Education, Oriental Churches, Cause of Saints. (List according to relative importance)

21 The most important are: the Laity, Promoting Christian Unity, Justice and Peace, Dialogue with non-Believers.

22 Theologically no mere human can take Christ's place as the one head of the church. Vicar of Christ became the exclusive title of the pope during the papacy of Innocent III, 1198-1216.

23 John Allen, *The Inside Story of How the Vatican Really Thinks* (New York: Doubleday, 2004),189.

Chapter 8:
Trail Blazers! Men & Women Religious

"Let us do something beautiful for God." Mother Teresa

"Never see a need without doing something about it." St. Mary MacKillop

"For me Christ is everything." Pedro Arrupe, Superior General of Jesuits

This chapter tells the story of amazing women and men, nearly a million worldwide and 75,000 in the United States.[1] They live vowed lives of poverty (possessions in common), chastity (celibacy) and obedience (to a religious superior) in 125 male[2] and 300 women[3] religious congregations worldwide. Their religious communities were in the forefront in embracing *Perfectae Caritatis, (Of Perfect Charity*, PC), the Second Vatican Council's renewal of religious life. With remarkable vision and full trust in the Spirit, they set about the challenging task of "adapting to the changed conditions of our time" and "suppression of obsolete" practices.

As a result, these impressive women and men have become teachers, scholars, psychiatrists, doctors, nurses, play-writers, authors, TV producers, contemplatives, parish pastors, university presidents, teachers and medics in refugee camps, retreat givers, spiritual directors, counselors, agricultural experts, song writers, novelists and poets, hospital chaplains, AIDS counselors, labor union specialists, and so forth. They are indeed trailblazers!

Their accomplishments tend to be mind-boggling: they run networks of elementary and secondary schools, colleges and universities; they write scholarly books and articles of philosophy and theology, the humanities and science; they publish magazines, newspapers, and catechetical materials; are administrators and nurses in hospitals, clinics, leprosaria, and orphanages founded and staffed by their religious communities; they journey to distant lands as missionary priests, sisters, and brothers to proclaim the good news of Christ, to plant the Catholic Church and minister to the physical and spiritual needs of peoples of many cultures; they conduct retreats for thousands of men, women and youth in retreat houses in rustic settings; those specially called by God like **Trappists** for men and **Poor Clares** for women come together in contemplative communities to lead lives of prayer, silence and work offered for the church and the world.

Before considering Vatican II's renewal of these American religious women, we first look at how religious life in the church came about and the kind of life religious live as the source of their amazing activity and the motivation that sustains and inspires them.

Origin of Religious Life and Founders of Religious Communities

Neither Jesus nor the 12 Apostles established religious communities. But already the *Acts of the Apostles* and letters of St. Paul to Timothy showed that religious groups had arisen in the church in response to special needs. Later, God inspired special charismatic individuals like St. Augustine in 5th century northern Africa, St. Benedict in 6th century Italy, both St. Francis in Assisi, Italy, and St. Dominic in France in the 13th century, St. Ignatius Loyola in 16th century Spain,

Mother Teresa in 20th century India, to found religious communities. Such individuals attracted followers who began to live together in voluntary poverty, to practice celibacy, and to minister to people in many ways. At some point a simple rule of life or a more detailed constitution was drawn up and submitted to the pope; with his official approval the group becomes a formal religious order or congregation within the Catholic Church.

Religious Life

Women and men join a religious community in response to a personal call from God. For some the call is the result of a profound religious experience; for most the call comes as a growing attraction and conviction of God's will as the person seeks that will in a process of discernment with the help of an experienced spiritual director. In the past most joined religious communities after high school or college; today most are older and come with a variety of valuable life experiences.

The heart of the religious state in the Catholic Church is personal friendship with Jesus Christ expressed through the three religious vows lived in community. By *poverty* the religious follows the poor Christ in a more simple life without personally owning material things. In sacrificing the great good of marriage and a family, the religious experiences that joyfully living a *celibate* life frees him or her heart whole-heartedly to love God and serve God's people.The vow of *obedience* puts the will of God first in the life of the religious person making possible the extraordinary apostolic flexibility of the apostolic orders and congregations whereby the superior is able to send the religious anywhere in the world to do God's work. One of the glories of religious congregations in the Catholic Church is their extraordinary missionary work and service to the poor and sick.

Religious men and women live in a community sharing all things equally. In this shared life they experience joy and consolation, inspiration and valued friendships and receive support to live their three vows and to serve others generously and with personal satisfaction.

The Second Vatican Council urged each religious order and congregation to recover the *charism* of its founder or foundress - that unique inspiration and call from God to choose specific apostolic works and establish a religious community. For example, St. Francis' charism is his extraordinary simplicity and love of "lady poverty," his love of the crucified Christ and respect for all God's creatures. St. Ignatius' charism is total service of Christ, everything "for the greater glory of God," special loyalty to the church in the person of Christ's vicar the pope, and the *Spiritual Exercises* which give each Jesuit his characteristic Ignatian spirituality. Mother Teresa's charism is sharing Christ's love with the poorest of the poor; Catherine McAuley's is bringing Christ's merciful care to the sick and youth in need of education; Mary MacKillop's is the determination to educate poor children.

Vatican II Renewal of Religious Life

While recognizing the vitality and extraordinary achievements of today's religious communities and of their members, the bishops at Vatican 11 recognized that many practices had become outdated and impeded apostolic effectiveness.

In the *Decree on the Up-to-Date Renewal of the Religious Life, Perfectae Caritatis, Of Perfect Charity, (PC)* the council bishops mandated significant principles for renewal of religious life: return "to the sources of Christian life" and to the "original inspiration of the community and adaptation to the changed conditions of the times" (PC 3). In so doing, Vatican II challenged today's religious to recover and live more fully the vision and charism of the founder or foundress as the best way to renew their community. For effective adaptation to modernity the council urged that "religious be properly instructed ... in the behavior patterns, emotional attitudes, and thought processes of modern society." (PC 18) Their "manner of living, praying and working should be suitably adapted to the physical and psychological conditions of today's religious ... to the needs of the apostolate, the requirements of a given culture ..."

To accomplish these two principles, the council made life in community a priority[4] and realistically directed that "constitutions and rules, custom books and prayer books" be revised and "outmoded rules" be suppressed. (PC 3) These principles stimulated research into the communities' historical roots and documents to recover the original charisms making possible the elimination of "excess baggage" accumulated over the centuries.

The *Decree* "opened up enormous new possibilities" for religious women and men. "For the first time in many centuries the official teaching voice of the church was actually urging religious to turn their faces *toward* the world instead of away from it."[5] Inspired by Vatican II's *Pastoral Constitution on the Church in the Modern World,* and its challenge to read the "signs of the times," (GS 4), apostolic religious communities committed wholeheartedly to works for the poor and to social justice.

Thus a "dynamic model" of apostolic religious life replaced the classic model of isolation from the world, the sacredness of the religious habit, and a multiplicity of external rules." One example. A revolutionary change in "the manner of exercising authority and decision-making" occurred in many congregations resulting in a "lively sense of the importance of communal discernment and consequently of the location of authority not only in the superior but also in the community" with "a concomitant relocation of responsibility."[6] The American women religious successfully committed to this method of prayerful discernment in their decision-making.

American Apostolic Women Religious

More than most, American religious women took the Vatican II renewal seriously and incorporated it into their communities.[7] In group meetings congregations rediscovered the vision and energy of their foundress, redefined their mission, changed their religious habits to more secular dress, created Sister Formation programs, sent sisters to earn Masters and Doctoral degrees, and chose new apostolates. In a perceptive article, Sister Joan Chittister, Order of St. Benedict and former prioress of Mount St. Benedict Priory in Pennsylvania, analyzed five facets of religious life that dramatically illustrate women's religious life before and after Vatican II: modes of *spirituality* (from self-repression to self-development); *ministry* (from being the labor force of the church "to being a leaven," a Christian presence, in building a Christian world); *vision of the foundress* (rediscovering the energy lost in the over-instutionalization of congregations); *cultural needs* (addressing the signs of the times: the poor, peace and justice organization, pastoral work); and the *nature and role of women* (re-establish the personal identity of women religious as adults capable of defining and structuring their own lives). This brought about a new understanding and practice of the vow of obedience.[8]

With the support of their religious communities and inspired by Vatican II, individual American religious women courageously embarked on innovative new ministries.

Sisters became hospital and prison chaplains, poverty and immigration lawyers, and medical professionals of all kinds. They assumed ministries in parishes that were increasingly without sufficient clergy. They became tutors of at-risk youth and adults who needed to learn English. They undertook hospice care, plunged into political advocacy and peace work and staffed non-governmental organizations, assumed leadership in the promotion and defense of women; served on boards of non-profits; addressed homelessness in a variety of ways. They became skilled spiritual and retreat directors and founded or staffed spirituality centers. They started alternate schools for the disadvantaged and reached out to AIDS victims, street people, the addicted, the societally or ecclesiastically rejected. They became theologians and artists, scientists and researchers. ... The ministries they undertook began to determine where and how they lived.[9]

Sister Dorothy Stang became a missionary in Brazil where she spent her life fighting for land rights for her impoverished indigenous peoples of the Amazon. Wealthy landowners expropriating the campesinos' land had her murdered. Sr. Helen Prejean is an outspoken anti-death penalty advocate. She authored *Dead Man Walking* and *The Death of Innocents: An Eyewitness Account of Wrongful Executions,* a true-life account of her work with men on death row. She also founded the organization *Survive,* which provides counseling to the families of victims of violence. Sister Jeanine Gramick created a ministry to gays and lesbians whom she asserts are not sick or sinful and deserving of dignity and respect by the Catholic Church. She co-founded New Ways Ministry, a Catholic social justice center for Catholic gays and lesbians. Sisters from different religious communities founded *Network* based in Washington to advocate for just legislation and monitor pending bills by lobbying Congress on behalf of the poor and powerless.

Two Vatican Challenges

Inspired by Vatican II, American religious women in 1968 formed the Leadership Conference of Women Religious (LCWR) whose 1500 members, superiors and counselors of American religious congregations, represent 85% of 57,000 U.S. women religious. In 2001 the Vatican *Congregation for the Doctrine of the Faith* (CDF) expressed concern over some of its policies. In 2008 Cardinal Rode, prefect of the Roman Curia *Congregation for Institutes of Consecrated Life (ICL)* inaugurated an investigation of the American women religious communities that are members of LCWR.[10] He attributed what he considered the sorry state of religious life to "inauthentic renewal based on a profoundly misguided interpretation of Vatican II" and decried "the pseudo-aggiornamento that followed Vatican II."[11] The religious women were totally surprised and profoundly disturbed, particularly in the light of having carried out so thoroughly and successfully the renewal mandated by Vatican II. Some wondered why they were singled out rather than males involved in the priest abuse tragedy.[12] The Cardinal's judgment on Vatican II renewal mirrors the polarization within the American church between the forces of renewal and restoration.

To their credit, the American sisters cooperated with the Vatican investigation, using it as an opportunity to deepen their appreciation and commitment to their charism. With Cardinal Rode's retirement, his successor, Archbishop Joao Braz de Aviz of Brazil, promised to "rebuild a relationship of trust." "We have begun to listen again," he said.

In a scholarly response to the Vatican investigation of women religious life, in 2010 Sr. Sandra Schneiders, a member of Servants of the Immaculate Heart of Mary and professor of New Testament Studies and Christian Spirituality at the Jesuit School of Theology in Berkeley California, wrote a scholarly 39-page, five-part essay on the history of religious life as a prophetic form of religious life.[13] She sees the ICL investigation as part of "the struggle between religious and the hierarchy" as being "at its core a struggle over the nature of religious life itself which is necessarily determined by how one understands the church in its relation to the world." After carefully examining the history of religious life, she describes the emergence of a new form of "non-monastic ministerial religious life" of women religious. For her, "the very heart of ministerial religious life is its participation in the prophetic mission of Jesus," since "Jesus came to pour out his life for the salvation of humanity, [and] to inaugurate the reign of God on earth."

She understands that Vatican II's renewal of religious life "was intended specifically to foster greater engagement of women religious in the modern world ... to put their enormous gifts as educated modern women in the active and public service of the reign of God." Her statement, "we read *Perfectae Caritatis* through the lenses of *Gaudium et Spes* and *Lumen Gentium,*" aptly expresses the inspiration for "a new form of non-monastic prophetic ministry."[14] Accordingly, "Prophetic ministry is integral to our identity and vocation ... and not by delegation of the hierarchy."

Looking to the future, six hundred Sisters representing LCWR's women religious congregations met August, 2011 for a different kind of annual meeting: a period of contemplative prayer to "open us to a deeper place within ourselves" so "we can create with God the future God intends" for our ministry, in the words of St. Joseph Sr. Carol Zinn. Most Precious Blood Sr. Mary Whited said "It is now time to stop and evaluate all the transformation that has happened since Vatican II and to determine what the Spirit is calling for now."[15]

The second Vatican challenge occurred April 18, 2012 with CDF's "Doctrinal Assessment of the Leadership Conference of Women Religious"[16] announcing that three American bishops led by Seattle Archbishop J. Peter Sartain would review LCWR's programs, affiliations with organizations like the nuns' social justice lobby Network, and would revise LCWR's statutes. CDF's concern was the content of addresses at LCWR's annual assemblies, its policies of "corporate dissent, its alleged "radical feminism, and its failure to promote church teaching on abortion, women's ordination, homosexuality and same-sex marriage, as championed by the American bishops.

At their annual meeting August 7-10, 2012 in St. Louis, 900 LCWR sisters met to formulate their response to CDF. After extensive discussion and days of prayer, they concluded that "the assessment had not been truthful to their experience" and voted unanimously for continuing dialogue to explain their Vatican II vision of women's prophetic ministerial form of religious life, "an authentic expression of this life that must not be compromised." They look for "open and honest dialogue ... that may lead not only to increasing understanding between the church leadership and women religious but also to creating more possibilities for the laity and particularly for women, to have a voice in the church."[17]

In her closing optimistic address, Sr. Pat Farrell, OSF, past LCWR president, said "these religious women see themselves not as being in opposition to the hierarchy but rather as a timely, needed pastoral vision and life and a feminine voice in the church." She pointed out that the Sisters' "solidarity with the poor," and their "ministry at the margins" and "participative and collaborative leadership models" they developed for religious life at the encouragement of Vatican II is "the gift we now bring to the church, a "new vision and new hope."[18] She affirmed that "we look forward to a future full of hope" and believe "we are being readied for a fresh in-breaking of the reign of God."[19]

Much appears to be at stake for the American church in this disagreement between the American sisters and the Vatican's CDF. Some see it as an authority question; others as competing visions between that of the renewal of the Second Vatican Council and of the magisterium's interpretation of the council. A hopeful sign is the respectful yet firm response of LCWR's leadership and their committing to dialogue and CDF's exercise of collegiality in assigning American bishops to mediate a pastoral solution that respects the convictions and values of each.

Is it possible that LCWR's unprecedented challenge and firm response to the Vatican CDF and the sisters' defense of a new prophetic form of women's religious life is a unique opportunity for the church to embrace as gift for church renewal?

An American Success Story[20]

This chapter would not be complete without a well-deserved tribute to American religious women. Their fascinating story may be of particular interest for those who have not experienced grade or high school education from the sisters or been privileged to know individual sisters. The "good sisters" are the unsung heroes of the Catholic Church in the United States. They originally sailed from Europe in groups of three and four during the 18th and 19th centuries with battered suitcases and hearts full of generosity and love to a strange and difficult land. They settled in major cities or the adjoining countryside and without money or buildings began opening schools and orphanages and hospitals. The first intrepid group were the Ursulines (founded by St. Angela Merici in 1535 in Italy) who settled in New Orleans in 1727 and soon became an integral part of the life and history of this booming Mississippi river city. They cared for Civil War soldiers and prayed for the outnumbered troops of Gen. Stonewall Jackson, prompting him later to enter the convent walls to pay a thank-you visit to the nuns.

From such humble beginning in the United States, these courageous dedicated women attracted scores of young American girls and women to join their communities. Soon the little wooden convents grew into large 4-5 story, multi-winged motherhouses and one-room schools and clinics developed into large schools and hospitals. As the numbers of nuns increased, the motherhouses sent bands of two or three sisters into the frontier of ever-expanding America to found new convents and schools and hospitals and orphanages. By the early 1900's virtually every major U.S. city had large convents full of sisters who staffed girls' high schools and women's colleges and hospitals: between 1896 and 1955 they had founded more than 100 colleges for women and had built most of the Catholic hospitals. This remarkable growth of institutions serving the expanding Catholic immigrant population is one of the most remarkable success stories in the history of the Catholic Church.

The school system itself was an extraordinary achievement. Older Catholics today remember with a mixture of awe and affection their days in parochial schools under the stern discipline of the nuns. Poor immigrant Catholics were able to attend these schools because tuition was low thanks to the poverty of the nuns whose salary was hardly enough to live on. Scores of Catholic men and women owe their knowledge and practice of the Catholic faith and their strong loyalty to the Church to their parochial school training.

The nuns were a visible, respected part of American life. Each congregation was identified by fascinating different habits and wimples, the latter revealing only pinched faces; these wimples were marvelous creations of black or white headdress and white starched front covering neck and part of the chest! Wherever nuns went, they received much respect from both Catholics and Protestants who recognized their selfless dedication. Older Catholics view with nostalgia the absence of the sisters' immediate public identity and visible witness to their consecrated lives now that the habits and wimples have been replaced with secular dress or knee-length skirts and a simple head dress often resembling nurses' caps. They tend to yearn for the "old days" and feel twinges of sadness when large convent buildings are sold and girls' schools closed for lack of sisters. For "their" nuns were the glory of the Catholic Church in the United States since they, more than any other group, were responsible for the education of millions of immigrant Catholics and the enormously successful Catholic parochial school system and the care of millions in a nation-wide network of hospitals.

The modern sister is an impressive person -- highly educated, often possessing a doctorate, deeply apostolic, attuned to the modern world, committed to justice and human rights especially for the poor and oppressed, profoundly spiritual withal. The modern sister is likely to be a skilled university professor or hospital administrator, medical doctor in missionary lands, member of "network sisters" lobbying in Washington for human rights and just laws, a social worker in the poorest areas of American cities or in the *favelas* of Latin America, and pastor of a parish.

The legacy of women religious in America is graphically captured in *Women & Spirit: Catholic Sisters in America,* the touring exhibit sponsored by LCWR. It premiered in Cincinnati in 2009 and has been seen by thousands in the Smithsonian Institute and Ellis Island Immigration Museum in New York, in Dallas, Cleveland, Dubuque (Iowa), Los Angeles, South Bend (Ind) and finished in Sacramento in 2012. It tells the story of the Sisters' leadership in education, health care and social services and features hand-written letters from President Thomas Jefferson reassuring the nuns of Catholics' practice of religion in the newly purchased Louisiana Purchase territory and from President Stonewall Jackson thanking the Sisters for nursing wounded soldiers in the Civil War. The exhibit shows how Catholic sisters helped shape the early history of America.

Cokie Roberts, news analyst and author, spoke this tribute to American religious women. "From the time the Ursulines arrived in New Orleans in 1727 up to today, women religious have made an incalculable contribution to this nation. Running schools, hospitals and orphanages from America's earliest days, these women helped to foster a culture of social service that has permeated our society. Over the centuries these courageous women overcame many obstacles – both physical and cultural – to bring their civilizing influence to every corner of our country. Understanding and celebrating the history of women religious is essential to understanding and celebrating the history of America."

Two Founders, Three Foundresses

The many larger-than life canonized Saints and martyrs, their amazing adventures and labors in far-away missionary lands, their contributions to education and social justice, to health care and dedication to the poor, make the history of these religious women and men fascinating and informative. We consider the two largest religious orders of men and three congregations of women.

St. Francis of Assisi (1181-1226) and the Franciscans (1210 . . .)

Francis was born the son of a wealthy merchant of Assisi in Tuscany. As a young man he led a worldly life. But a year as prisoner of war in Perugia and moved by the wretched lives of beggars and lepers in Assisi, he began a new life. He became a hermit and devoted himself to the care of lepers and to rebuilding churches in and around Assisi. On Feb. 24, 1209, while hearing a reading from the 10th chapter of Matthew, he felt a call to live in total poverty and to preach Christ. Disciples soon joined him. On a trip to Rome with his 11 followers, he received the pope's approval for a new religious group. It grew steadily. Young men were attracted to Francis' infectious enthusiasm, his gaity and love, his life of total poverty, his burning love of Jesus, and his simple but powerful preaching.

As the number of friars increased, Francis sent them out in pairs beyond the Alps and across the sea. It became necessary to establish some form of organization and in 1217 provinces were set up. In

1223 the pope approved the final version of Francis' rule for his new religious order. The friars were to preach the gospel, obey it literally in a life of total poverty, care for the sick and suffering, give up everything for Christ, accept no money and beg for their needs.

Francis wore out his body by penance and fasting. His sympathy and love extended to all people including Muslims to whom he preached and actually visited in Africa on a peace mission. Everything reminded him of God. When sick and nearly blind toward the end of his life, he composed a song of praise and thanks to God, the *Canticle of Brother Sun.* His special devotion to the humanity of Jesus led to his giving the Christian world the Christmas crib.

His last years were filled with mystical experiences. Two years before he died Oct. 3, 1226, he received the stigmata, the marks of Jesus' wounds on his hands and feet and side. Only two years later, in 1228, his old friend and "Cardinal Protector" of the order, Pope Gregory IX, solemnly canonized him. He lies buried in the crypt of the magnificent church begun that year. Heroic life-size frescos depicting scenes from his life by the Florentine painter Giotto grace the upper church of the Basilica of St.Francis.in Assisi. Francis is probably the best known and most loved of all Catholic Saints. Today, 15,130 Franciscans Friars Minor live his example and the rule of poverty and service to the poor.

St. Ignatius Loyola (1492-1556) and the Society of Jesus (Jesuits, 1540-1773 and 1814-)

Ignatius of Loyola, a Basque nobleman and courtier, was wounded at Pamplona fighting the French. In 1521, while recovering at his family castle, he experienced a religious conversion. Deciding on a new life, he spent a year as a hermit in a cave in Manresa, Spain, where he received a series of mystical experiences which he recorded in a notebook. They became the basis for his *Spiritual Exercises,* a classic of Catholic spirituality.

Realizing he needed an education to preach Christ, he joined a class of children to learn Latin and attended universities in Spain and Paris. At the University of Paris he gathered six disciples. These "friends in the Lord," banded together to follow Christ. Ignatius drew up a plan of life which Pope Paul III approved in 1540 and was later elected the first general superior of the "Company of Jesus," the name he insisted on despite much opposition. During his 16 years as general, Ignatius founded 33 colleges and seminaries while the new society grew rapidly to about 1000 members, often as a result of young men making his *Spiritual Exercises*. He sent his close friend and early companion, Francis Xavier to India. Xavier baptized tens of thousands in southern India and Indonesia and founded a flourishing Jesuit mission in Japan. After 11 laborious years traveling tirelessly, he died in 1552 on a lonely island attempting to enter China. He is known as the greatest apostle since St. Paul.

Education and missionary work became the major Jesuit apostolate. By early 17th century 15,000 Jesuits were conducting more than 500 colleges and seminaries for the nobility and middle class of Catholic Europe. Jesuit missionaries travelled to the Philippines, Morocco, Ethiopia, the Congo in Africa, Brazil and Paraguay, Japan and China where Mateo Ricci used his scientific knowledge and mastery of Chinese language and culture in the imperial court. Well-known missionaries are Saints Isaac Jogues and John de Brebeuf to the Iroquois in upper New York state, the explorer Marquette in the Upper Mid-West and Eusebio Kino who founded missions in upper Mexico and present-day Arizona.

The Jesuits' vast educational and missionary effort came to a tragic end when Pope Clement XIV suppressed the Jesuit order in 1773, pressured by the leaders of the Enlightenment and the monarchs of Portugal, Spain, France and Naples. Thirty years later

Pope Pius VII restored the Jesuits in 1814. The order grew steadily to 15,000 members despite being banned by anti-clerical governments in Latin America and by Chancellor Otto von Bismarck in Germany. In 1964 Jesuits numbered 36,000 laboring in more than 100 countries worldwide. Inspired by their charismatic Fr. General, the Basque Pedro Arrupe, two general congregations committed Jesuits to work for justice and the poor, resulting in the murder of 45 Jesuits. In the United States Jesuits conduct 27 universities,[21] 42 high schools, and Nativity schools grades 6-8 and Cristo Rey high schools for Hispanic and Black students as part of their commitment to the poor.

A number of 20th century Jesuits have made major contributions to Catholic theological renewal, particularly Pierre Teilhard de Chardin of France, Bernard Lonergan of Canada, and Karl Rahner of Germany. Several Jesuits, notably Daniel Berrigan and John Dear of the United States, lead social-protest and antiwar movements.

Catherine McAuley of Ireland (1778-1841)

This indomitable woman founded the Sisters of Mercy in 1931 dedicated to the education and care of poor homeless women and children. Her parents both died when Catherine was quite young; she was taken in by a Quaker couple until adulthood. Catherine's holiness inspired them to convert to Catholicism. Using the rich inheritance they left her, she followed a call from Christ to found a school for the poor and for homeless women and children of Dublin. She attracted many young women who joined her to work for the poor. Her Sisters were dubbed 'Walking Sisters' for seeking the homeless in streets and alleyways. Though she lived her entire life in Ireland, the religious congregation she founded spread worldwide. She wrote poetry, letters and a constitution for her sisters. Her dedication to education especially for the poor continues to inspire women who serve in Mercy schools, colleges and hospitals worldwide. She found "peace in the Cross, joy in suffering, prayer in action and action in prayer." She was canonized a Saint in 2010.

St. Teresa of Calcutta (1910-1997)

Although Albanian by birth, Mother Teresa entered the Sisters of Loreto in Ireland in 1928, and was sent to be a missionary in Calcutta in 1929. In 1946, on a train to Darjeeling, India, she experienced a special call from God to work for the "poorest of the poor." Her transparent love of God and her heroic love for the sick and dying outcasts of Calcutta attracted first a handful and then gradually hundreds of young women to join her in her work for the poor in the new congregation she founded in 1950. Her sisters wear the familiar habit of a white sari with a blue border, the garb of the poor. In 1963, she also founded the Missionaries of Charity for Brothers, and in 1984 the Missionaries of Charity Fathers; later she established Lay Missionaries of Charity for lay Catholics dedicated to service of the poor. She also established Co-Workers of Mother Teresa and the Sick and Suffering Co-Workers, both open to people of different faiths in service of the poor. These groups became established internationally as word of Teresa's good works spread. She was awarded the Nobel Peace Prize in 1979 for her utterly selfless work with the poor and the inspiration she gave to those of all faiths and cultures. Her prayer was "Make us worthy, Lord, to serve those people throughout the world who live and die in poverty and hunger. Give them through our hands, this day, their daily bread by our understanding love, peace and joy." After her death in 1997 her writings revealed her constant inner suffering of the absence of God. She was canonized a Saint in 2007.

St. Mary McKillop (1842-1909).

Called the "ideal saint for our time, robust, pioneering, courageous," at age 24 she founded the Sisters of St. Joseph dedicated
to live in poverty and teach poor children. She established schools,
convents and orphanages for the poor all over South Australia and
havens for unmarried mothers and ex-prostitutes. Because she insisted
that her religious congregation be self-governing, a local bishop
excommunicated her for "insubordination." Her schools were closed,
her sisters disbanded. She submitted humbly trusting in God. She
went to Rome, submitted the rule she had written for her sisters to the
pope and won from the Vatican approval of the principle of self-government. During her lifetime, Mary established 160 Josephite houses
and 117 schools for 12,000 students. When she died her congregation
numbered 1000 sisters. Pope Benedict XVI canonized her a Saint Oct.
17, 2010. Imitation of Christ through acceptance of suffering and her
love and service of the poor marked her saintliness.

For Discussion
1. What do you think are the reasons why fewer young men and women are joining religious communities today?
2. In your opinion what needs to be done so that the religious life would once
   again become an attractive, challenging, fulfilling vocation?
3. Find out about the exciting missionary adventures and accomplishments of
   Francis Xavier in India and Japan or Mateo Ricci to the Chinese Emperor in
   Beijing or the heroic life and martyr deaths of Edmund Campion in England or
   Isaac Jogues in New York state or Miguel Pro in Mexico.

Further Reading

Chittister, Joan. *A Fire in These Ashes: A Spirituality of Contemporary Religious Life*. Franklin, WI: Sheed and Ward, 1995. Sister Chittister asks the following probing questions in this book: "What, if anything, constitutes the spirituality of contemporary religious life? What is the work of religious life now? What are the virtues demanded of religious now that take character and test commitment, that make the world closer to the reign of God and bring a person closer to the Truth of life?"

Failka, John J. *Sisters: Catholic Nuns and the Making of America*. New York: St. Martins' Press, 2003. Wall Street journalist John Failka takes a fascinating look at the history of Catholic sisters in the United States. From caring for orphans and prostitutes during the gold rush, building hospitals and schools for the destitute, and being at the forefront of the civil rights movement, Failka provides a stunning portrait of the best the religious life has to offer.

Sammon, Sean D. *Religious Life in America: A New Day Dawning*. Alba House, 2002. Sammon calls on the Catholic religious communities to heed the signs of the times, and offers practical suggestions for renewal of vocations and the religious life. The author sees a real spiritual hunger in today's youth, one which the religious life is capable of fulfilling. Insightful questions for discussion and action close the end of each chapter.

Schaltz, Larry. *Brothers: An Inside Look*. Winona, MN: St. Mary's Press, 2002. Brother Larry offers a short (65 page) meditation on how he discerned his vocation to become a religious brother, his journey into the religious life, the challenges and rewards of his vocation and how he lives out his call in community with his fellow brothers while remaining very much involved and grounded in today's challenging secular world. An excellent and readable first-person overview of religious life.

Schneiders, Sandra M. *Prophets in Their Own Country: Women Religious Bearing Witness to the Gospel in a Troubled Church*. Maryknoll, NY: Orbis Press, 2011. She draws on her biblical scholarship to study the life of Jesus as a prophet and examines the distinctive characteristic of women religious life today. In reviewing the Vatican's 2009 investigation of women's religious congregations, she answers two questions: why is the Vatican investigating the sisters and why do the sisters object so strongly.

Footnotes

1 Religious sisters, 746,814 worldwide, 55,944 in the United States; Religious men 189,841 worldwide, 17,213 in the United States. *The CatholicAlmanac* as of Jan. 1, 2010.

2 The 15 largest religious orders of men in 2009: Jesuits 18,711; Salesians 16,215; Franciscan Friars Minor 15,130; Franciscans (Capuchins) 11,092; Benedictines 7,558; Society of the Divine Word, 6138; Dominicans 6,002; Redemptorists 5, 552; Brothers of the Christian Schools 5,226; Societies of Mary Immaculate (Oblates) 4,467; Franciscan (Conventuals) 4513; Marist Brothers 4,057; Discalced Carmelites 4004; Vincentians 3442; Claretians 3050. *The Catholic Almanac,* 2010.

3 Ten largest families of religious women. Carmelites 18,207; Charity Sisters 11,297; Salesians 14,420; Franciscan Sisters 14,025; Mercy Sisters 10,654; Claretians 9483; Missionaries of Charity (Mother Teresa) 5973; Dominican Sisters 5,656; School Sisters of Notre Dame 5973; Adoration of the Blessed Sacrament Sisters, 4654.

4 Class distinctions were to be abolished and religious were encouraged "to carry each other's burdens" to be "a true family gathered together in the Lord's name since "from it results great apostolic influence." (PC 15)

5 Timothy O'Connell, ed. ,*Vatican II and Its Documents, An American Reappraisal* (Wilmington, DE: Michael Glazier, 1986), 82-83.

6 *Ibid.,* 89.

7 Comments of two young women religious: "My religious community is steeped in Vatican II, is committed to the well being of women and promotion of all gifts of women. I was drawn to our international richness and diversity. Members of my community are visionaries and committed to justice, prayer and spirituality." ... "The congregation is forward thinking, not tied to old ideas of what religious life is about. They are interested in serving God's people and enjoying the life we are given. The sisters are committed to a solid prayer life, to preserving Mother Earth, to help women achieve their full potential, and to spread the Good News to all. And the sisters are committed to good, wholesome fun!" in

"Recent Vocations to the Religious Life: A Report for the National Religious Vocation Conference," Mary E. Bendyna and Mary L. Gautier, August, 2009.

8   Joan Chittister, "Rome and American Religious Life. *America.* (Jan. 4-11, 2010): 12.

9   Sr. Sandra M. Schneiders. "The Past and Future of Ministerial Religious Life," *National Catholic Reporter* (Oct. 2, 2009): 3a.

10   Its task was "to look into the quality of life of women religious in the United States who are members of apostolic religious institutes" which include 50,000 women religious.

1   Francene Cardman. "Vatican II Revisited," *America* (Jan 4-11, 2010): 12. "Cardinal Rode believes, in his own words, that the Council precipitated the first 'worldwide crisis in the history of the church and that women religious, in his view, are primary promoters of that crisis in the United States." See Sandra Schneiders, page 1 in article referred to in footnote 13.

12   Sister X. "Cross Examination, Why is Rome Investigating U.S. Nuns? *Commonweal* (October 9, 2009): 7-12.

13   Published in *National Catholic Reporter*, http:// ncronline.org/print.

14   See Sandra Schneiders, IHM, *Prophets in Their Own Country: Women Religious Bearing Witness to the Gospel in a Troubled Church* (Maryknoll, NY: Orbis, 2011). Listed in Further Reading.

15   Monica Clark. "Women Religious Meet to Examine Spirit's Call. *National Catholic Reporter,* (August 5, 2011): 1,6.

16   Congregation for the Doctrine of the Faith, "Doctrinal Assessment of the Leadership Conference of Religious Women," *Origins* (April 26, 2012): 751-56.

17   Sr. Pat Farrell, OSF, "Navigating the Shifts," Presidential Address, to LCWR Assembly, Aug. 10, 2012, and Thomas Fox, "LCWR's response offers a new

vision for being church," Aug. 11, 2012, http: ncronline.org/users/Thomas-c-fox, "LCWR response offers new vision for being church."

18 Sr. Pat recognized the "inherent existential tension between the complementary roles of hierarchy and religious" and opted for "an environment of open dialogue for building up of the whole church." She called attention to "the paradigm shift of our day," as heralding "a hopeful future for our church and our world.

19 "What the sisters envisage – and what the Vatican is clearly complaining about – is a new church where leadership and ministry are cooperative endeavors." *The Tablet,* 18 August 2012, 12.

20 Ursulines came to America in 1727; Carmelites to Maryland in 1740; Visitation Sisters, Washington, DC, 1799; Sisters of Charity, Philadelphia, 1809; Sisters of Loreto, Kentucky 1812; Religious of Sacred Heart, St. Louis 1813; Third Order St. Dominic, Springfield, KY 1822; Sisters of St. Joseph, St. Louis 1836; Sisters of Providence, Indiana 1840; Sisters of Mercy, Pittsburgh 1843; Third Order St. Francis, Milwaukee 1849; sisters of St. Benedict, St. Mary, PA 1852; Presentation Nuns, San Francisco 1854; Little sisters of the Poor, Brooklyn 1868; The Poor Clares, Cleveland 1875.

21 Prominent universities are Georgetown, Boston College, Fordham (New York), Marquette (Milwaukee), St. Louis, Loyola of Chicago, and in California, Santa Clara, Loyola-Marymount, University of San Francisco.

Chapter 9:

Why Church? The Great Mission

"Go therefore and make disciples of all nations." (Mt. 28:18)

"The Lord founded his Church as the sacrament of salvation." (*Ad Gentes* 5)

These statements by Jesus and the Second Vatican Council capture the "great mission," a seeming mission impossible given the Catholic Church and each Christian today.

It is the year 35 A.D. Jesus of Nazareth has surprised all by rising from the dead after a cruel crucifixion and appearing often to his close followers. As he was about to leave this world, he made them a startling promise. "You will receive power when the Holy Spirit comes down on you: then you are to be my witnesses in Jerusalem, throughout Judea and Samaria and to the ends of the earth." (Acts 1:8) Climaxing his powerful preaching and dramatic healings, he asked his eleven Apostles to meet him at a mountain in Galilee. There Jesus gave these former fishermen their mission.

Full authority has been given to me both in heaven and on earth; go, therefore, and make disciples of all nations. Baptize them in the name of the Father, and of the Son, and of the Holy Spirit. Teach them to carry out everything I have commanded you. And know that I am with you always until the end of the world. (Mt 28:18-20)

The mission Jesus gave his Apostles and through them the Catholic Church and all Christians is to evangelize the entire world, to bring the good news of God's great love and plan of salvation in and through Jesus Christ and his church to every person everywhere.

The powerful preaching of the church's two greatest evangelizers, Peter to Jews and Paul to Gentiles, brought thousands to accept Christ and "the way" of this early band of Christians, as it was called. That first Pentecost Sunday Peter boldly addressed "devout Jews of every nation."

> Men of Israel, listen to me. Jesus the Nazarean was a man whom God sent to you with miracles, wonders and signs as his credentials. These God worked through him in your midst, as you well know. He was delivered up by the set purpose and plan of God: you even made use of pagans to crucify and kill him. God freed him from death's bitter pangs, however, and raised him up again, for it was impossible that death should keep its hold on him. ... Let the whole house of Israel know beyond any doubt that God has made both Lord and Messiah this Jesus whom you crucified."[1] Acts 2:22-24, 36

St. Paul indefatigably preached Christ throughout Greece and Asia Minor, establishing Christian communities in major cities. Chapters 13-28 of Acts of the Apostles contain example after example of Paul's effective evangelization as do his many eloquent letters to his churches in Thessalonica, Ephesus, Colossus, Corinth, Philippi, Galatia and to Christians in Rome. One example.

> Men of Athens. ... As I walked around looking at your shrines, I even discovered an altar inscribed 'to a God Unknown.' What you are worshipping in ignorance, I intend to make known to you. For the God who made the world and all that is in it, the Lord of heaven and earth, does not dwell in sanctuaries made by human hands. ... it is he who gives to all life and breath and everything

else ... he is not far from any one of us. 'In him we live and move and have our being' as some of your own poets have put it ... we ought not to think of divinity as something like a statue of gold or silver or stone ... he is going to judge the world with justice through a man he has appointed whom he has endorsed by raising him from the dead. Acts 17:22-31.

In its long history the Catholic Church has been eminently successful in carrying out Jesus' awesome mission to evangelize all nations. The Mediterranean world soon became Christian through the evangelizing efforts of lay apostles and priests alike announcing the good news.

In succeeding centuries to the present, zealous missionaries travelled to far lands to bring Christ to millions, often with great hardship and at the cost of their lives. The brothers Cyril and Methodius evangelized the Slavic people 1000 years ago. St. Francis Xavier, the Jesuit apostle of the Indies, is said to have baptized over one half million people, founding churches throughout Asia and Japan. The North American martyrs, heroic French Jesuits, brought Christ to the Iroquois, Mohawk and Huron indigenous peoples of New York State and Canada, finally to suffer extremely cruel martyrdoms. Franciscan friars evangelized the Indians of South and Central America. Jesuit priests Pere Marquette brought Christianity to Indian tribes of the Upper West, Pierre de Smedt to native Americans of the Far West and Eusebio Kino to the Indians of Sonora Mexico and southern Arizona, each of whom are honored with their statues in the Capitol rotunda in Washington representing Wisconsin, Missouri and Arizona. The new American missionary society of Maryknoll priests and sisters brought Christ to China and now labor heroically in Latin America and Africa after their expulsion from China. Maryknoll associates, lay men and women and married couples, give two or more years to live and work as foreign missionaries. Thousands of priests and sisters lived under great hardships and dangers to proclaim Christ in Africa, Alaska in the dogsled days, and in the South Pacific Islands.

Evangelization has taken on a new importance in the Catholic Church today. Vatican II insisted that evangelization is the "fundamental task" of the church, the vocation of each Catholic by his/her baptism. (Ad Gentes 35) Benedict XVI, following Pope John Paul II, has committed Catholics to the 'New Evangelization,' nothing less than the transformation of today's society. Today, the success of Pentecostals and evangelicals in Latin America and throughout the world challenges the church.

Evangelization

Evangelium is the Latin word for good news; the English equivalent is gospel. The four Gospels by Matthew, Mark, Luke and John are accounts of the good news about Jesus Christ. Jesus came to announce this astounding good news of God's great love for the human family. Evangelization is the church proclaiming the good news about God's love and God's plan of salvation in the person of Jesus Christ. In its strict meaning, evangelization is aimed at non-Christians; accordingly the church does not evangelize fellow Christians, the Orthodox, Anglicans, Lutherans and so forth.

The Second Vatican Council enriched the church by emphasizing three aspects of evangelization: the missionary task of preaching the good news of Jesus Christ and planting the church where it has not existed before; the practice of inculturation so that the church is "rooted in the social life of the people [and] conformed to its culture;" and the calling by their baptism and the gifts of the Holy Spirit to evangelize as missionaries.

Pope Paul V1

Inspired by the Second Vatican Council, Pope Paul VI on the 10th anniversary of the council gave Catholics an in-depth prophetic understanding of evangelization called *Evangelii Nuntiandi, EN, Announcing the Good News.*[2] His letter has special relevance for the New Evanglization. Paul described evangelization as "the grace and vocation of the Church, her deepest identity. She exists to evangelize." (EN14) The following are major emphases of Paul's important document.

- *The Content of Evangelization* "The clear proclamation that in Jesus Christ ... salvation is offered to all as a gift of God's grace and mercy." (27)
- *"The profound link between the Church and evangelization."* (5) Evangelization necessarily leads to entrance into a Christian community, the church, "the channel of God's grace" which "perpetuates Christ's sacrifice of the Mass." (14)
- *Transformation.* Evangelization is nothing less than a profound transformation resulting in a 'new humanity' through the power of the Gospel. This involves "a *metanoia* or conversion, a radical change of mind and heart," (10) "new persons living according to the Gospel." (18)
- *Evangelization is Disruptive.*[3] Paul VI prophetically recognized that "the split between the Gospel and culture and between Gospel love of neighbor and respect for God and his kingdom and today's culture of consumerism and greed, practical disdain for the dignity of each person and the sacredness of human life, is the drama of our time." (20)
- *Human Development.* Paul VI broadened the scope of evangelization to include "the millions of human beings condemned to remain on the margin of life: famine, chronic disease, illiteracy, poverty, injustices in international relations and commercial

exchanges, situations of economic and cultural neo-colonialism sometimes as cruel as the old political colonialism" (30).

- *Magnitude of Evangelization.* The pope extended evangelization to include the billions "who have never heard the Good News of Jesus Christ," "the immense sections of mankind who practice non-Christian religions" and "the drama of atheistic humanism." (52, 53, 55) In calling attention to "the very large number of baptized people who for the most part have not formally renounced their baptism but who are entirely indifferent to it," (56) The pope anticipated the 'new evangelization' of John Paul II and Benedict XVI.

The Second Vatican Council taught that "the Catholic Church has one sole purpose, that the **kingdom of God** may come and the salvation of the human race be accomplished." (GS 45)

Evangelization and the Kingdom of God

In the Lord's prayer, Jesus taught his disciples to pray "Our Father . . . thy kingdom come ... on earth as it is in heaven." During his life in Palestine, Jesus tirelessly preached and worked to establish God's kingdom. His first recorded words in Mark's Gospel as he began his public ministry were: "This is the time of fulfillment. The kingdom of God is at hand." (Mark 1:15) In the synagogue at Nazareth, he read the passage from Isaiah to illustrate what God's kingdom involves.

"The spirit of the Lord is upon me; therefore he has anointed me. He has sent me to bring glad tidings to the poor, to proclaim liberty to captives, recovery of sight to the blind and release to prisoners, to announce a year of favor from the Lord." (Luke 4:18-19)

Jesus graphically spelled out what he meant by God's reign in his famous eight beatitudes, identifying himself with the hungry, the naked, the sick, strangers, those in prison. (Mt. 5:3-12) In Mathew's Last Judgment Jesus made eternal life depend on helping these very persons (MT 25:31-46)

During his public ministry, Jesus told parable after parable to illustrate the priceless value of God's kingdom. When asked the two greatest commandments of the Jewish law, he answered "... you shall love the Lord your God with all your heart, with all your soul, with all your mind, and with all your strength. This is the second, "You shall love your neighbor as yourself" (Mark 12:30-31). For Jesus, the reign of God exists wherever and whenever people know, love and worship God and love others by treating them justly and living at peace with all. Jesus thus insisted that the kingdom of God is "within you" when people practice such love.

Evangelization and Salvation

The opening words of *Ad Gentes* announce that God sends the church to be the "universal sacrament of salvation," a new name Vatican II gave the church. *Sacrament* refers both to how the church mirrors Cod's unconditional love and will to save all people and that the church actually accomplishes salvation through its many rich spiritual resources. *Salvation* is eternal life with God in heaven and on earth salvation is the life God wills for each person, a life befitting human dignity lived in justice and peace. That the church is the *universal* sacrament of salvation means that the church is present in all countries and cultures and reaches out to all as Jesus did, to sinners, the poor, to those who suffer and exist on the margins of society, to gays and lesbians, and even to her critics.

Evangelization and Inculturation

In its *Decree on the Church's Missionary Activity, Ad Gentes, AG, To the Nations,* the Second Vatican Council spoke of "the work of implanting the church" in the culture of the people she evangelizes. (AG 10) In bringing the Gospel to foreign cultures, missionaries are to respect their culture, their customs, family traditions, religious practices and myths. The result of effective evangelization is an inculturated local church that expresses the Gospel and the Catholic life according to its own style of worship, its own symbols and art, its own theological understanding, and led by its own native priests and bishops. Thus is born a "new creation."[4]

A dramatic example of successful inculturation was the work of the Italian Jesuit Matteo Ricci in the seventeenth century in China. He mastered the Chinese language and became a noted Confucian scholar. As a result of his brilliant mathematic and technical skills, the Emperor invited him into his court and gave him permission to preach Christianity. In the church's tragic dispute over Chinese rites, he judged that the Chinese practice of home shrines and burning incense before the ashes of ancestors did not constitute divine worship of their ancestors. Rome's judgment against these rites led to the persecution of Christians and the end of the promising Catholic missionary effort.

Today, inculturation means that all good elements of that culture are preserved and find a place in the church, thus enriching it. The happy results of such inculturation are many. The Catholic Church will not be perceived and experienced as a foreign import, as in China and Japan and much of Asia today; in times of persecution, such a church may be expelled or simply wither and die. Second, Christianity will more easily be understood and more fruitfully and joyously lived in an inculturated local church which meets the religious needs of its people and attracts "converts." The older evangelizing church and the newer local church are both changed and enriched. Thus the Catholic Church becomes in fact a global church, multi-cultural and truly catholic.

I experienced two inculturated Masses. In Ghana, West Africa, in an open-air church packed with men and women, young and old, I marveled at the joyful celebration: exuberant singing, the whole congregation clapping to rhythmic drumbeats, young girls gracefully dancing as they brought the gifts of bread and wine to the altar, the colorful priests' vestments of African designs. In Madurai, India, I participated in a joyous, deeply religious Mass replete with Hindu elements: rose petals, water and incense, both priests and people seated on the floor in the lotus position.

The New Evangelization[5]

Benedict XVI made the new evangelization his major goal as pope. He described its purpose as combating the "cultural and moral climate of secularization and agnosticism" [in Europe and beyond] and "to re-evangelize formerly Catholic lands with the joyous discovery of the faith." He told members of the Roman Curial Congregation of the Faith "we are facing a profound crisis of faith, a loss of the religious sense which constitutes the greatest challenge to the church today."[6] Accordingly, Benedict characterized evangelization as "reproposing the Gospel to those who are convinced they already know the faith which holds no interest to them. It is the courage to invite our contemporaries to hear the message of Christ as if for the first time!"[7] He emphasized that it is a summons to an authentic and renewed conversion to Jesus Christ and an opportunity to "rediscover the journey of faith" and to experience the joy of personal friendship with Jesus and the treasure of faith in the Catholic Church.

For the new evangelization and the year of faith to achieve their promising goals, several considerations appear important: the bishops enlist the laity as equal partners and effective evangelization requires humility and removal of obstacles to receiving the church's message.[8] At the Synod, Archbishop Bernard Langley of England said the first step has to be "an act of profound listening" and Filipino Archbishop Villegas warned that "evangelization has been hurt by the arrogance of its messengers." Reception is facilitated when the church is perceived to be a welcoming community that manifests sensitivity to the feelings, convictions and common sense judgments of Catholics and of those who have left the church. It might be asked, does the church come across as humble, welcoming, inclusive? Can effective evangelization of the West occur as long as women and others are perceived as excluded?

Evangelization Today – an Evaluation

Is the Catholic Church today a *credible sacrament of salvation* to its own members, to other Christians, and to the world at large? Though the Second Vatican Council encouraged a church of diversity and inclusiveness, there remain many Catholics, especially women, the divorced and remarried, gays and lesbians, who feel alienated from the institutional church. The perceived rigidity of the church, its centralization of power and its continued reluctance to change are obstacles to evangelization and have resulted in frustrated Catholics leaving the church and discouraged non-Catholics from entering it. There exists the thinking that a smaller, more faithful and orthodox church is to be desired, a mentality in apparent opposition to a church that calls itself Catholic, a "big tent church" open and welcoming to all. Many would frame the question this way: does the Catholic Church as the sacrament of salvation mirror the humble, loving Christ who came to serve and not to dominate, who welcomed the sinner and who washed the feet of his disciples at the Last Supper?

In terms of inculturation, do the local churches of Africa and Asia enjoy the freedom to experiment, to make their own pastoral decisions, create their own liturgical worship and theology and discipline?

What is the recent record of *inculturation* in the United States? The literal translation from Latin of the Roman Missal into words and expressions foreign to contemporary English usage and to the way Catholics are accustomed to pray and worship has caused much concern among English speaking liturgists, priests, lay ministers and ordinary Catholics. Bishop Donald Trautman, former chairman of the American Bishops' Committee on Liturgy, stated: "If the Roman missal does not speak to our culture, the church in the United States will suffer."[9]

Is it possible that the church has become so absorbed with its internal affairs that its energy spent on areas like sexual ethics, same sex marriage, abortion as a single issue, important and urgent as these are, leaves little energy for its primary mission of evangelization, a mission explicitly given by Jesus as his last act on earth? A major challenge in America and Europe today is the large number of Catholics who have been baptized and confirmed but never been evangelized.

Has the Catholic Church *lost its missionary zeal?* Have Catholics failed in their baptismal vocation to evangelize? On the surface it appears they have since Catholics as a whole do not match the evangelizing zeal of both clergy and laity of evangelical and Pentecostal groups, of Mormons, Seven-Day Adventists and Jehovah Witnesses, of the Assembly of God and Church of Christ who go in great numbers to evangelize Latin America, Africa and more recently Russia and Eastern Europe. Avery Dulles comments that American Catholics are "wary of evangelization for a variety of reasons." "They distrust the biblicism, the individualism, the emotionalism, and the aggressive proselytism of certain Protestant evangelistic preachers;" since faith is a free, personal private response to God they are reluctant to appear to pressure anyone; too often Catholics have believed "simply on the authority of the Church" rather than experiencing the Gospel as an "extraordinary piece of good news" to be shared with others; "too many Catholics seem never to have encountered Christ" in a personal, familiar way.[10]

How today can the church inspire Catholic young people with the same missionary spirit of evangelical and Pentecostal youth? How create the missionary attraction and excitement of traveling to a foreign country to tell people about Christ? Or how enlist for missionary vocations the idealism and generosity of Peace Corps, America Corps and Jesuit Volunteer members and similar groups?

Yet, there are encouraging signs. Both young and old consciously evangelize by the witness of their daily lives and in creative and hidden ways. A growing number of lay Catholics, married couples and young people, volunteer for ministry in the United States, in Latin America, and elsewhere. Priests and sisters continue to labor heroically in missionary countries, often giving their lives as martyrs of charity. Countries with many vocations like India, Korea, Nigeria and the Philippines send priests and sisters as missionaries. In America college students have formed groups that evangelize others through discussion groups, retreats and social activities.

A Contemporary Question

Should the church evangelize religious Jews, Hindus, Buddhists, Muslims and Native Americans? Clearly the church must proclaim the good news about God's plan in Jesus Christ to all peoples of the world. It "is duty-bound to proclaim that Jesus Christ … is the way, the truth and the life and the one Savior of all." The church does not force conversion on anyone and respects the culture and religion of all peoples. In Asia where Catholics are a small minority among other religions and cultures, evangelization consists in witnessing the love of God by serving the needs of all, "a powerful and effective form evangelization." (EN 21). Thus is the seed of faith planted with God giving the increase. Shortly after Vatican II, the bishops of Asia created the *Federation of Asian Bishops' Conferences (FABC) and* committed themselves to the triple dialogue with culture, with religions and with the poor as their way of evangelizing as a tiny minority among a sea of non-Christian religions.

For Discussion

1. If the Christian Church is God's plan for the human family, in what sense is the Catholic Church *necessary* for their salvation?
2. As sacrament of salvation, what does the Catholic Church need to do today to reach out to Catholics who feel alienated or marginalized by the church?
3. To what extent *can* the American Catholic Church inculturate American customs and values? What elements *should* it inculturate to be more authentically American yet Catholic?
4. How can you live the church's call to evangelize today?

Further Reading

Bevens, Stephen B. and Jeffry Gros. *Evangelization and Religious Freedom: Ad Gentes, Dignitatis Humanae.* Mahwah, NJ: Paulist Press, 2008. The authors examine these two ground-breaking Vatican II documents, explaining in detail their radically new understanding of evangelization and inculturation. They also focus on the reception and implementation of these documents forty years after Vatican II.

DiSiano, Frank. *The Evangelizing Catholic: A Practical Handbook for Reaching Out.* Mahwah, NJ: Paulist Press, 1999. Fr. DeSiano outlines concrete and workable actions faithful Catholics and Catholic parishes can take that more effectively reach out to alienated Catholics. He concentrates on personal as well as parish evangelization, stressing 'peer relationship' and that both parish practices and individual parish members need to show enthusiasm of faith and dedication to live that faith in community.

Hillman, Eugene. *Toward an African Christianity, Inculturation Applied.* Mahwah, NJ: Paulist Press, 1993. Fr. Hillman uses his experience with the African Masai peoples, describing how their deep religiosity, belief in the spirit world, unique culture, arts, music and enthusiasm are critical to retain and maintain in order to achieve an authentic evangelization. He also addresses the Church's past errors in evangelization, including the colonialization and domination and forced conversion of other nations.

United States Conference of Catholic Bishops. *Catholic Evangelization in an Ecumenical Society.* Washington, DC: USCCB Publishing, 2004. Ecumenism is a part of Catholic identity. This book examines Jewish-Christian relations, ecumenical issues and interreligious dialogue.

Footnotes

1   Other examples of Peter's powerful evangelizing preaching: Acts 3:11-26; 4:8-12; 10:34-43.

2   *Announcing the Good News* is the result of the 1974 Synod of Bishops meeting on the topic of evangelization.

3   "Through this witness Christians stir up irresistible questions in the hearts of those who see how they live: Why do they live this way? What or who inspires them? Why are they in our midst? Such a witness is a silent proclamation of the good news [and] an initial act of evangelization." EN 10.

4   Term of Fr. Pedro Arrupe, former charismatic superior general of the Society of Jesus who championed inculturation for Jesuit missionaries. "...the incarnation of Christian life and of the Christian message in a particular cultural context, in such a way that this experience ... becomes a principle that animates, directs and unifies the culture, transforming it and remaking it so as to bring about a 'new creation.'" Quoted in T. Howard Sanks, *Salt, Leaven and Light. The Community Called Church* (New York: Crossroad, 1992), 194.

5   The 2012 Synod of Bishops emphasized that the goal of the new evangelization is to call every Catholic to a personal renewal of faith and to share that faith with others. "New Evangelization begins with ourselves as practicing

Catholics, inviting us to deepen our relationship with Jesus Christ. It extends to those who have left the church, whom we miss, inviting them to come back home. It reaches out to those who have not met the Lord inviting them to encounter Jesus Christ. This synod touches everyone, calls all to awaken the faith, to discover what the church teaches and to inspire others to know Jesus Christ. ... Works of charity and justice are at the heart of the new evangelization." The bishops spoke of "relighting the church's missionary fires" through "injecting a new missionary spirit in the parishes." "Accent on the New," *America* (Nov. 5, 2012): 8.

6   Retired bishop Francis Quinn considers that the "overarching crisis of faith in today's church ... is not faith in God, not faith in Jesus Christ, but faith in the institutional church." Francis A. Quinn, *America* (Apr. 7, 2003): 14.

7   Congregation for the Doctrine of the Faith, "Pastoral Recommendations for the Year of Faith," *Origins* (January 19, 2012): 513-19. "The Year of Faith will be a propitious occasion to make Vatican Council II and the Catechism of the Catholic Church more widely and deeply known."

8   Obstacles often alleged to reception are the church's image of rigidity and resistance to change, refusal of discussion and dialogue on issues of concern to the people of God, language that implies criticism or rejection of groups of people, pre-judgment and lack of sensitivity to their needs and conscience decisions.

9   Donald W. Trautman, "How Accessible Are the New Mass Translations?" *America*, (May 21, 2007): 11.

10   Avery Dulles, "John Paul II and the New Evangelization," *America*, 166 (Feb. 1, 1992): 71.

Chapter 10:
Spirituality and Spiritualities

Lord, send out your Spirit and renew the face of the earth.
Psalm 104

We are not human beings having a spiritual experience. We are spiritual beings having a human experience.

Teilhard de Chardin

The spiritual life does not remove us from the world but leads us deeper into it.

Henri Nouwen

A phenomenon of our age is intense interest in **spirituality**, despite or perhaps in opposition to pervading secularism and aggressive atheism. People yearn for meaning and religious experience in their fast-paced, increasingly individualistic isolated lives. Enter bookstores and the spiritual section is replete with books on meditation, Eastern prayer, mystics, Christian spirituality, angels, Saints and New Age Spirituality. Scores of people today are discovering in their search for a meaningful spirituality the rich Catholic spiritual tradition. Christian spirituality is founded on the belief in a personal God of unconditional love and expressed in commitment to Jesus Christ and the conviction of the presence and activity of his Spirit in one's life. Christian spirituality influences Christians to a way of life that endeavors to love and respect others and the world created and loved by God. For spirituality provides a reference for how a person looks at life in terms of values and attitudes toward ultimate reality however understood.

Rich Vatican II Spirituality

Vatican II greatly enriched the spiritual lives of Catholics by recovering aspects of Christian life de-emphasized through the centuries. We describe nine such "spiritualities" influenced by the Second Vatican Council.

Spirit Spirituality. In a sense the council rediscovered the Holy Spirit, the third Person in the Trinity of Persons comprising God, by emphasizing throughout its documents the inspiration of the Spirit in all aspects of the church's life: in each of the sacraments, in the lives of individual Christians and in the church's recognition of the Spirit's presence and activity in other Christian churches, world religions and cultures, and the world. The Spirit Jesus gave at Pentecost lives in the church today and in the lives of Christians inspiring them with the gift of faith, the power to hope and the ability to love. Thanks to the council, Catholics have become accustomed to pray regularly to the Spirit for enlightenment and help in finding God's will and making difficult decisions.

A dramatic presence of the Holy Spirit in the post-Vatican II church is the sudden rise of the **Catholic Charismatic Renewal**.[1] It began in 1967 during a weekend retreat at Duquesne University, Pittsburgh, when a group of students and professors experienced the gifts of the Holy Spirit. The renewal spread to Notre Dame University and the University of Michigan and then rapidly throughout the Catholic world. Bishops and priests were at first skeptical. Official church approval came in 1975 when 10,000 Catholic charismatics were received by Pope Paul VI in Rome who said "The Church needs her perennial Pentecost. She needs fire in the heart, words on the lips, prophecy in the glance."

The soul of the charismatic renewal is baptism in the Spirit which "is meant to be a life-changing experience of God's presence." This is not the sacrament of baptism which occurs only once; rather it is a stirring up, "a release of the graces already received in baptism and confirmation." Patti Gallagher Mansfield, one of the original group at Duquesne, lists the effects of baptism in the Spirit: "a deepening awareness of the presence and love of God and the Lordship of Jesus Christ; a growth of intimacy with God in prayer; a hunger for God's word and the sacraments; a love for the church; a new power and desire to witness; a growth... in peace, love, joy; a call to purification and holiness; a desire for Christian unity; a call to serve the needs of others."[2] Other effects of baptism in the Spirit are **glossalalia** (speaking in tongues or words/languages generally not understood by the speaker or other charismatics); mental healings of fear, guilt, anger, hurtful memories and sometimes physical healings; prophecy, not of the future but conveying God's messages. However, these are secondary to the extraordinary on-going experience of God's presence and love and the enormous inspiration of the Spirit to live a profound Christian life.

Christ-centered Spirituality. Thanks to the council, the person of Jesus Christ has regained his central place in the spiritual lives of Catholics. Prior to Vatican II the exuberance of devotion to the Saints at times overshadowed the centrality of Jesus Christ in Catholic life. For example, the indigenous peoples of South and Central America tended to see Jesus as a far-away figure, whereas the Saints and Mary are viewed as members of the family, humans they can go to for help in sickness, with an unfaithful spouse, during a poor harvest and in times of famine and floods. Often superstition intermingled in this **popular religiosity.** In the *Constitution on the Sacred Liturgy,* the council stressed Christ's work as Savior and Redeemer in the paschal mystery of his suffering, death and resurrection and spoke eloquently of Christ's presence and activity in the church, especially in the Eucharist.

Liturgical Spirituality Centered in the Eucharist. Vatican II restored the church's public worship to its pre-eminent place in the spirituality of Catholics. In the past, novenas and holy hours, adoration and benediction of the Blessed Sacrament had often assumed more importance than the Mass itself. Today Catholics celebrate significant events like weddings, funerals, anniversaries, and birthdays with a Mass. The high point of the world travels of Popes John Paul I and Benedict XVI and now Francis is always a public Eucharist attended by large crowds. In Third World countries the poor often walk days to attend such celebrations. The Eucharist has become the core of Catholic life and the most important spiritual action of Catholics, thanks to the Second Vatican Council.

Biblical Spirituality. St. Jerome, the 4th Century Scripture scholar, said "ignorance of the Bible is ignorance of Christ." The *Dogmatic Constitution on Divine Revelation* devoted its sixth chapter to "Sacred Scripture in the Life of the Church" and urged that "access to sacred scripture should be widely available to the Christian faithful." (DV 22) In the reform of the liturgy, the council affirmed that since "sacred scripture is of the greatest importance in the celebration of the liturgy" … "it is essential to promote … lively appreciation of sacred scripture." (SC 24). Accordingly, after the council a third reading from Scripture was added and the Liturgy of the Word and the Liturgy of the Eucharist became the two principal parts of the Mass, with the traditional sermon being replaced by a homily to explain the Scripture readings and apply them to the daily lives of the congregation. In responding enthusiastically to this "rediscovery" of Scripture, Catholics formed parish bible groups, and joined Protestants in studying and praying the bible. The Word of God in the Scriptures has become a valued part of Catholic spirituality.

This World Spirituality. The Pastoral Constitution on the Church in the Modern World was a "game changer" for Catholics by inspiring them to create God's kingdom on this earth and to find God and imitate Christ in their day-to-day lives. Catholics' spirituality thus moved from an individualistic, me-and-God emphasis to a this-world spirituality in which concern for social issues of war and peace, hunger and homelessness, justice, human rights and human dignity became a vital part of one's relationship to God and Jesus Christ. Before Vatican II "the world" was too often considered evil and to be avoided. But a "signs of the times" theology that recognized God as present and active in the world and saw Christians' vocation as carrying out God's plan for the human family inspired Catholics to view the world in a new light. As a result, Catholics are in the forefront of social justice issues, world peace, political life, ecological and environmental concerns and care for the poor and disadvantaged. Frs. Dan Berrigan and John Dear demonstrating against the militarization of American life and for world peace, Katy Kelly risking her life for the victims of war in Iraq and Afghanistan, Cesar Chavez' tireless struggles for just wages and safe, decent working conditions for migrant Hispanic workers are just a few of the many Catholics inspired by Vatican II to work for justice, human dignity and rights, and a better world.

Ecumenical Spirituality. The *Decree on Ecumenism* created an about-face in the lives of Catholics who came to know and appreciate their fellow Christians in other churches, to pray and collaborate with them and to work for the restoration of unity among the still divided churches. Thus was born a distinctive ecumenical spirituality.

Commitment to Christian unity has expanded Catholics' understanding of the one Church of Christ and of Christ's prayer for unity resulting in a new way of relating to Christ and to other Christians. Ecumenical spirituality sees Christian disunity as a scandal that cannot be allowed to continue and takes very seriously Christ's Last Supper prayer for unity as a personal challenge to work perseveringly despite setbacks for Christian unity. With this new appreciation for other Christian churches and their members, Catholics refer to Protestants and Orthodox as brothers and sisters in Christ, cooperate with them in social action and works of charity, and come together in ecumenical prayer services. The partners in Catholic-Protestant marriages often attend each others' worship and raise their children to respect both churches. Catholic priests and Protestant ministers and pastors witness inter-church weddings.

Creation Spirituality. An important development since Vatican II is the growing awareness of the imminent serious threat to the planet and the urgent need for action. From this has risen among Catholics a spirituality that values the rich bounty and goodness of God's creation and recognizes Christians' moral responsibility to preserve and safeguard creation. Popes John Paul II, Benedict XVI and Francis have spoken and written forcefully for the environment as have the American bishops. A missionary to the Lakota people in South Dakota, drawing on Native Americans' pervasive religious relationship to nature, describes their spirituality of creation:

> Everything that exists is good. Because it is good, it is beautiful with its own unique kind of beauty. Because it is good and beautiful it is lovable. Because it is all of this, it is sacred: reflecting the presence of God within it and around it. ...In creation spirituality the earth itself is sacred. ... Humans have a sacred obligation to natural creation, to be its caretakers, not its plunderers. To treat

anything in creation merely as an object to do with as we wish is a sacrilege. ... all creation is saturated with the presence of the cosmic Christ who continues to work with us and with all creation.[3]

Marital Spirituality. The Second Vatican council spoke eloquently about the covenant love of husband and wife. The council stressed that the spouses' mutual sexual love, their pledge of life-long love and fidelity, their daily self-sacrificing love for each other and their children constitutes their high spirituality and the way they experience God and achieve holiness. Married couples realize that they, not the clergy, are ministers of the sacrament of marriage, thus conferring God's grace on each other; in so doing, the risen Christ bonds their love and promises his on-going grace and blessings. Vatican II devoted an entire chapter to "The Dignity of Marriage and the Family" in *Gaudium et Spes.* Especially noteworthy are the beautiful numbers 48 on "the Holiness of Marriage" and 49 on "Married Love."

Lay Spirituality. For the first time, Vatican II emphasized the unique spirituality of Catholic lay women and men. Based on their baptism in Christ and sharing his priesthood, they are called to a high degree of holiness in their daily lives of family, work, civic and social involvement and through collaborating with the clergy in the pastoral and spiritual life of the parish. The council bishops devoted chapter 4 of *The Constitution on the Church* to "The Laity" and one of the 16 council documents to the *Apostolate of the Laity.*

In devoting an entire chapter in *The Constitution on the Church* to "The Call of the Whole Church to Holiness," the Second Vatican Council made a remarkable statement that is both an enormous vote of confidence in and challenge to each and every Catholic: "... all Christians in any state or walk of life are called to the fullness of Christian life and the perfection of love ..." (LG 40) *By* their baptism into the body of Christ and gifted with the power of the risen Christ and his Spirit, all Christians are capable of a high degree of spirituality: married couples, house-wives, single persons, businessmen and women, politicians, professional athletes, bartenders, construction workers, pop-stars, gays and lesbians, students and teen-agers! Prior to Vatican II, the average Catholic tended to think holiness was for clergy and religious and Saints but "not for me."

The large number of lay women and men whose lives of great love of God and of their neighbor testify to Vatican II's call to holiness and to be a leaven for the transformation of the world: Dorothy Day, the founder of the **Catholic Worker** and of hospitality houses for the poor; Franz Jaggerstatter, the Austrian farmer who defied the Nazis and was martyred as a result; Cesar Chavez who dedicated his life to the plight of the poor and exploited Mexican-American farm-workers; deeply spiritual Dag Hammarskjold, the Swedish former Secretary-General of the United Nations; Jacques Maritain, the influential 20th century Catholic philosopher and his wife Raissa; all married couples whose love and lives of self-sacrificing love witness to a high degree of spirituality. We include also all those women and men, young and old, who accept physical and mental suffering with real faith; recovering alcoholics and their humility and total trust in God; many young people in their struggle with peer pressure and the allure of drugs, sex, and money.

The Holy Spirit and Four Church Spiritualities

At his Last Supper on earth, Jesus promised to send his Spirit to his followers. "I will send him to you ... he will guide you to all truth ..." (John 16:7) "The Paraclete, the Holy Spirit ... will instruct you and remind you of all I told you." (John 14:26) After his resurrection

Jesus repeated his promise: "… within a few days you will be baptized with the Holy Spirit." (Acts 1:5) Jesus' promise became reality that Pentecost.

> When the time for Pentecost was fulfilled, they [the disciples] were all in one place together. And suddenly there came from the sky a noise like a strong driving wind, and it filled the entire house in which they were. Then there appeared to them tongues as of fire, which parted and came to rest on each one of them. And they were filled with the Holy Spirit and began to speak in different tongues, as the Spirit enabled them to proclaim. (Acts 2:1-4)

Fifty years ago this same Spirit inspired Pope John XXIII to call the Second Vatican Council. He placed the work of the council under the guidance of the Holy Spirit: "Renew your wonders in our time, as though a new Pentecost and grant that the holy church … may increase the reign of the Divine Savior, the reign of truth and justice, the reign of love and peace."[4] During the four years of the council, the assembled bishops continually experienced the guidance of the Holy Spirit, confident that their program for the renewal of the Catholic Church was the work of the Spirit. Today the council is the Spirit's enduring gift to the Catholic Church.

Jesus' Spirit is present and alive in the one Church of Christ, inspiring a rich variety of spiritualities. The different Christian churches are living manifestations of the Spirit's action in their members and leaders. We consider the rich spirituality characteristic of four religious families.

Catholic Spirituality is aptly described as being sacramental, eucharisitc, hierarchical, Marian and Saint-oriented. Through experiencing the seven sacraments, Catholics are characterized by what is called the Catholic imagination, the habit of encountering the invisible God in the world about them and within their own experience. The Eucharist is the heart of Catholic spirituality, the ritual by which Catholics worship and praise God and most intimately experience the saving action of the risen Christ. Hierarchical means Catholic spirituality is priestly, depending on priests and bishops to bring them sacraments, and preserve their faith and unity in the Catholic tradition. Catholics' special devotion to Mary, the mother of Jesus, and to myriads of Saints is well-known.

Within the Catholic Church, a variety of religious orders, each with distinctive spirituality, greatly enrich Catholics' spiritual lives. *Franciscan* spirituality is characterized by devotion to the humble self-emptying Christ, to "lady poverty" and to the poor in imitation of its saintly founder St. Francis of Assisi. It is a contemplative and mission-oriented spirituality that emphasizes an apostolic way of life through preaching supported by community life of prayer and liturgy and commitment to intellectual excellence and social justice. *Benedictine* spirituality based on St. Benedict's monastic rule of the 4th century has been followed even to modern times in a variety of communities. *Domincan* spirituality emphasizes preaching and intellectual excellence supported by community contemplative living marked by prayer, poverty and study of the Word of God. *Jesuit* spirituality has profoundly influenced the church and millions of Catholics for 450 years and continues to do so today. It deserves explanation.

Jesuit Spirituality is based on the Spiritual Exercises of its founder, St. Ignatius Loyola (1492-1556) and comprises the following elements: deep personal love of Jesus Christ expressed in the order's title, the Society of Jesus; service in collaboration with God expressed by *men for others*; spiritual discernment in choosing the best way to serve God and others in world-wide apostolates; more generous and magnanimous service of God and the human family expressed in the Ignatian *magis*, more; *friends in the Lord* or fraternal companionship as necessary support for an apostolic way of life; *finding God in all things*, the integration of prayer and service and of contemplation and action which enables the entire Society and each Jesuit to seek God in every work and event; commitment to work for justice throughout the world, especially for the poor, expressed in *the faith that does justice.* Fr. Pedro Arrupe, the saintly and much loved Superior General of the Society from 1965 – 1981, warned that the price of working for justice would be costly. Since 1965, 51 Jesuits have been murdered worldwide, including the six Jesuit priests of the University of Central America (UCA) in 1989 because of their voice for justice for the poor of El Salvador.

Thanks to the council's *Decree on Ecumenism,* Catholics have a new appreciation for the rich spiritual traditions of Christian families other than Catholic. In considering the following three, we omit many of merit, like Quakers' prayer of silence before God and total commitment to peace and Pentecostals' experience of the gifts of the Holy Spirit expressed in baptism in the Spirit, speaking in tongues, healing and joyful spontaneous prayer and worship of God.

Orthodox Spirituality is a rich mix of the sublime and the down-to-earth. **Orthodox** Christians have great devotion to the Holy Trinity based on their doctrine of the divine indwelling through baptism; to the Holy Spirit who dwells in each baptized person; to Jesus the eternal Word as redeemer and creator who is pictured in majesty from the apse of Byzantine cathedrals as the bearded Christ holding the book of the Gospels, his right hand raised in blessing; to the Gospel whose book always lies open on the altar for veneration as an icon of the living Word in the midst of the people; to Mary as *Theotokos,* the Mother of God, and to the Divine Liturgy whose public worship has been the main strength and unifying force of Orthodox Christians through centuries of persecution.

Orthodoxy expresses its sublime spirituality in a profusion of colorful, down-to-earth ways. The Divine Liturgy, often two hours or more, is celebrated with much chanting and singing, lengthy prayers, clouds of incense by bearded priests in colorful rich vestments reaching to the ankles. Orthodox Christians kiss the many two dimensional painted **icons** or images of Christ, of Mary and of the saints, venerating them as windows or ways into the eternal and as divine images of heaven on earth. Venerating icons, many of which are art treasures, is the most visible characteristic of Orthodox spirituality. Vividly aware of the communion of saints, Orthodox Christians honor their saints and martyrs and speak of departed Christians not as dead but "sleeping." All these elements of Orthodox Christian piety are means toward the ultimate end of divinization through the "divine indwelling" and of salvation.

The tragic schism between Eastern and Western Christianity finalized in 1054 deprived Roman Catholicism of this rich Orthodox spirituality. In referring to the hoped-for reunion of Orthodoxy and Roman Catholicism, Pope John Paul II prayed for the day when the Christian Church can "breathe once again with both lungs!" See chapter 11, the section "The Challenge Ahead."

Anglican Spirituality is characterized by solemn, joyous liturgical worship and stately hymns and is nourished by a rich tradition of devotional books and theological and historical scholarship. The inspirational King James translation of the Bible, the much loved *Book of Common Prayer,* the Eucharistic liturgy called the Holy Communion or Holy Eucharist (and by some the Mass), the Sunday services of Morning and Evening Prayer (Evensong), all have formed the spiritual lives of generations of Anglicans.

Anglican spirituality has been influenced by major historical movements within the Church of England: by stern Puritanism with its insistence on morality and the individual's responsibility before God;

by Methodist spirituality inspired by John and Charles Wesley who introduced a "methodical" approach to God characterized by frequent private family and public prayer and meditation on the Bible, celebrating the Lord's Supper "at every opportunity," joyous hymn singing and meditating on hymns sung and sermons heard, care of prisoners and the poor; and by the 19th century Catholic Oxford Movement led by the brilliant preacher and writer John Henry Newman, later Cardinal and recently now named Blessed by Benedict XVI, and by other scholars who also turned to the **Fathers of the Church** to study the formative years of the church and to reinforce this early Catholic heritage within the church of England.

Anglican spirituality reflects a Catholic appeal to tradition along with the Protestant spirit of independence, freedom of the individual, reliance on the Bible, and conciliar decision-making rather than hierarchical authority.

Lutheran Spirituality has been formed and is still influenced by the intense spiritual struggles and prodigious scriptural and theological contributions of Martin Luther and his experience of the grace of God. Lutheran spirituality stresses the sinfulness of the human condition and the all-enduring mercy of God through Jesus Christ whose suffering and death saved weak, helpless sinners justified or made pleasing to God, not through their own merits, but in the merciful love of God manifested in Jesus. Christ is the great mediator before God; no others are needed. All Christians share in the priesthood of Christ through their baptism. Lutheran spirituality is centered on word and sacrament: the Bible that contains Christ the living Word of God and the two sacraments of baptism and the Lord's Supper. Luther developed a spirituality of the freedom and responsibility of the Christian and of the triumph of the cross in Christian life. Lutheran spirituality is characterized by total devotion to the triune God and to the gospel that declares the pattern of Christian life in the world.

Distinctive Catholic Spiritualities

Catholic Feminist Spirituality. The convergence of two events gave rise to Catholic Feminist Spirituality: women's demands for a life and identity of their own as a result of Betty Friedan's book *The Feminine Mystique* in 1963 and the Second Vatican Council empowering women in its insistence that they, the people of God, are the church and that their baptism is the source of their rights and ministry in the church.

Feminism holds that women and men are dehumanized by patriarchal structures that subordinate women and that women should have equal economic, political and social opportunity and be accorded the same dignity and rights as men. Catholic feminists point out that both Scripture and theology are historically conditioned, rising out of a male-dominated culture that served to oppress and dehumanize women. An impressive group of women scholar theologians like Anne Carr, Diana L. Hayes, Elizabeth Schussler Fiorenza, Elizabeth Johnson, Rosemary Radforth Reuther, Sandra Schneiders and many others write from the perspective of women's experience. They are concerned with unmasking **patriarchy** in society and in the church by which males have all the power and decision-making and control women's lives. They ask that women's gifts be recognized and used in the church. Catholic women are convinced, despite struggle and controversy, that Catholic feminism is inspired by the Holy Spirit and has great potential to enrich the church. Catholic feminism and the spirituality that nourishes it is a serious, legitimate reality in today's church. Chapter 13 treats Catholic feminist liberation theology and chapter 15 further describes the Catholic feminist movement and the question of women's ordination to the deaconate.

Life Spirituality. In response to the 1973 Supreme Court decision affirming a woman's right to abortion, a vigorous pro-life movement for the sacredness of unborn life championed by Catholic men and women, priests and bishops, has risen. Influenced by Chicago's Cardinal Joseph Bernardin's "consistent ethic of life," his "seamless garment" of life from conception to natural death, by Catholic social teaching emphasizing human dignity, and by revulsion at the callous disregard for human life in wars, genocide, capital punishment, terrorism, and aborted human life, an impressive spirituality of life has developed among American Catholics.

Black Catholic Spirituality. African American Catholic Spirituality is an emerging voice in the Catholic Church in the decades following the Civil Rights movement. African Americans see in the Scriptures their own struggle and persecution which they have expressed so movingly in the Negro spirituals. According to the Benedictine monk Cyprian Davis, black spirituality has four unifying characteristics: contemplative, holistic, joyful, and communitarian.[5] Dominican M. Shawn Copeland explains each.

It is contemplative because the African American apprehension of religion mystically surrenders to the dark numinous power of God to hallow a home in the heart and soul, to infuse the whole person with awe of God's transcendent presence and with ecstatic joy at the intimacy of God's immanence. It is holistic because the African American personality is di-unital, and retains the capacity to manage ambiguity. This personality is gifted with a fundamental regard for person, for the human over products or things. Black spirituality is joyful resting in the power of God to protect, to defend, and to save; and this joy animates works of love and compassion, of reconciliation and peace. Black spirituality is communal and expresses itself in social concern and social justice: and this communitarian dimension opens Black Christians to all, excludes none."[6]

Other theologians in this field include Toinette Eugene, Peter Sarpong (Archbishop of Accra, Ghana), Sheila Briggs, Diana L. Hayes, and Sr. Jamie Phelps, OP.

Latino/Latina Catholic Spirituality. The Latino/a voice in the Catholic Church has been long overlooked in spite of the vast numbers of Spanish-speaking Catholics in the Americas. Latino spirituality is centered around four main themes: "La Familia, Mestizaje, Popular Religiosity, and Festive Hope.[7]

The family is a central organizing principle in the spiritual lives of Latino/a Catholics. *Mestizaje*, or 'mixing,' refers to the racial mixture of Spanish and the variety of native cultures of the Americas and the marginalization that this mixing produces when the *mestizo* interacts with the dominant culture. As a result, Latina/o spirituality emphasizes the needs of the poor and marginalized. *Popular religious devotions*, as to the Virgin of Guadalupe, form a major part of Latino/a spiritual practice. *Festive Hope* is the manifestation of a spirituality that reaffirms itself and strengthens the bonds of family and community with religious festivals celebrated such as Saints' days, Holy Days, baptisms and marriages There are many voices of Catholic Latino/a spirituality, such as Fr. Virgilio Elizondo, Miguel Diaz, Ada Maria Isasi-Diaz, Arturo J. Banuelas, Fernando F. Segovia, Michelle A. Gonzalez, Maria Pilar Aquino and Fr. Allan Deck.

Inter-religious Spirituality. Vatican II's *Declaration on the Relation of the Church to Non-Christian Religions (Nostra Aetate)* for the first time officially acknowledged the presence and activity of the Holy Spirit in Judaism, Islam, Hinduism and Buddhism: "The Catholic Church rejects nothing of what is true and holy in these religions." (NA 2) The declaration honors the heritage and spiritual ties that bind Christians to Jews who "remain very dear to God for the sake of the patriarchs" and that God's plan of salvation began with the patriarchs, Moses and the prophets." (NA 4) "The church has high regard for Muslims [who] worship God who is one, living and subsistent, merciful and almighty, the creator of heaven and earth who has also spoken to humanity." (NA 3) "In Hinduism people explore the divine mystery and express it in the limitless riches of myths … and seek release from the trials of the present life by ascetical practices, profound meditation and recourse to God in confidence and love." (NA 2) Buddhism … proposes a way of life by which people can … attain a state of perfect liberation and reach supreme illumination … with divine help." (NA 2)

The Holy Spirit is also present and active in the large number and variety of native religions and cultures. God's "providence, evident goodness, and saving designs extend to all humankind." (NA 1) "Throughout history to the present day is found among different peoples a certain awareness of a hidden power … even a recognition of a supreme being or still more of a Father." (NA 2) Native Americans recognize and worship the Great Spirit like the Lakota Sioux of the Great American Plains who practice the Sweat Lodge, Sun Dance and Vision Quest.

These many manifestations of the presence and power of the Holy Spirit witness to Jesus' lavish gift of the Spirit at Pentecost.

Resources of the Catholic Spiritual Tradition

In its long history the Catholic Church has provided a myriad of effective ways to find God, to develop personal relationship with Jesus Christ, and grow in spirituality. To complete this chapter on spirituality, we include a survey of the rich resources found in Catholic spirituality. Paramount is prayer and the different prayer practices the church has developed in its long history.

Prayer and Types of Prayer

Prayer is the oxygen of the spiritual life. As in human friendship and love, there is no personal relationship with God or Jesus Christ without the frequent contact of prayer. Prayer is described as "lifting one's mind and heart to God" or "loving intimate conversation with God" or "intimate sharing between friends." (St. Teresa of Avila) As weak and vulnerable, we need God's constant help; as dependent creatures we owe God worship; as sinners we need to seek forgiveness and to express our sorrow to God; as recipients of God's lavish goodness and many blessings, we need to thank God. The traditional purposes of prayer are petition, adoration, contrition and thanksgiving. (PACT)

Prayer is meant to influence our behavior, to change us. As a result of sincere prayer, we become more compassionate and loving, experience a new freedom, grow in unselfishness, enjoy peace and joy, and come to a deeper awareness of God in our lives. Many of us have been blessed with parents or grandparents, aunts or uncles whose example of prayer still influences us.

Vocal Prayer uses words recited or spoken or sung. We pray privately or with others set prayers like the Lord's Prayer (Our Father), the Hail Mary, the Act of Contrition, Come Holy Spirit, Prayer of St. Francis, the Memorare, and many others. The church provides us with a wealth of such prayers for all occasions. Older Catholics value their personal "Prayer Book."

Mental Prayer involves our mind, will and imagination. In *meditation* we begin by reflecting on truths of faith or on the virtues, on God and the life of Christ, or on our own lives, and then move on to acts of praise and love, sorrow and resolution that engage our will and emotions. The much-practiced *Lectio Divina* or "Godly" Reading is the prayerful reading of a passage from Scripture, a Psalm, or words of Jesus and events from his life. We put ourselves in God's presence, speak to our Lord about the reading, listen to him, and finish by thanking him. We may choose a word or phrase suggested by the reading to be repeated as a mantra during the day.

In the increasingly popular *"centering prayer,"* people focus or center on God present. A person sits relaxed and quiet following three guidelines: be in faith and love to God who dwells in the center of one's being; take up a love word like God, Jesus, Lord, Spirit, love, Friend, etc. and let it be gently present, resting in God in love; whenever one becomes aware of other things, simply gently return to the Lord with the use of the love word. *The Jesus Prayer* or *Prayer of the Heart* from the Christian Eastern monastic tradition consists of repeating phrases like "Lord Jesus, Son of God, have mercy on me a sinner" or "Jesus, have mercy on me" or simply "Jesus" or "Maranatha," "Come, Lord Jesus, Come." Such prayer is easy, able to be made anytime, anywhere, and is very calming.

Contemplative Prayer. In general, **contemplation** is getting in touch with God within us; it is living the present moment in awareness of God always available to us; it discovers the Divine in the ordinariness of everyday lives. The growing interest today in contemplative prayer was evident among university students in the 1960's and '70's who read *Seeds of Contemplation* by the famous Trappist monk Thomas Merton. In his *Spiritual Exercises* St. Ignatius introduced a series of contemplations he called "application of the senses" to Gospel scenes. The retreatant enters a Gospel scene in his/her imagination, slowly and lovingly contemplates the persons, what they are doing, how they are reacting, what they are saying, and then makes a personal application. This loving contemplation is easy and rewarding. *Classical Contemplation* refers to infused passive prayer of mystics as described by St. Teresa of Avila and St. John of the Cross.

In these various forms and methods of prayer, it is important to keep in mind that the greatest prayer of all is the Eucharist when the Christian community assembles to praise and glorify God and to join the risen Christ present in its midst as he offers once again the paschal mystery of his death and resurrection for the salvation of the world.

As aids to advance in prayer and lead a full Christian life, Catholics find periodic retreats, personal spiritual direction, the wealth of spiritual books, the Catholic tradition of sacred art and music, devotion to the Saints, and the multiplicity of devotional practices enormously helpful.

Retreats

Retreats of three, eight or 30 days away from the frenetic pace of modern life in a setting close to nature are a popular form of spiritual rejuvenation and an opportunity for prayer. A well-known and increasingly popular retreat is *The Spiritual Exercises of St. Ignatius,* a series of meditations and contemplations designed to lead the retreatant to an election or choice to follow Jesus Christ. Originally of 30 days duration, it is divided into four periods or "weeks: meditation on the purpose of life and sin and inordinate attachments (way of purification); the public life of Jesus and his passion and death (illuminative way); and Jesus' risen life and heaven (unitive way) climaxed by reviewing God's many gifts in a "Contemplation for Attaining Love." Priests and sisters and increasingly lay Catholics make *The Exercises* in eight days; large numbers of lay men and women make three-day weekend retreats annually in retreat houses in restful non-urban settings.

The *cursillo* is a short course in Christianity of four intense days led predominantly by lay Christians to rediscover Christ. It has been enormously successful in inspiring Catholic men and women and other Christians to live their faith with enthusiasm. *Search* weekends are popular with young Catholics of high school and college age. Through sharing and discussion they experience God and Jesus Christ, and become enthusiastic and motivated to live their Christian lives. In *Marriage Encounter* married couples learn to communicate with each other on a deeper level and to love more intensely

Spiritual Direction. and Spiritual Reading

Spiritual Direction is the time-honored practice in a person's spiritual life in which an experienced priest or sister or trained lay person meets regularly with their directees to guide and encourage them in their spiritual lives. For priests and sisters a spiritual director is considered essential. Today more and more lay people, including young people, are beginning to seek a spiritual director. A popular practice during retreats after Vatican II is the recovery of the directed retreat in which a spiritual director meets with each retreatant to help him/her discover the action of the Holy Spirit during prayer. A "regular confessor" in the Sacrament of Reconciliation may fill the role of spiritual director.

The practice of spiritual reading introduces Catholics into the riches of their spiritual tradition. Daily or regular spiritual reading becomes a powerful inspiration to live a Christian life in today's culture. The wealth of spiritual classics and current spiritual books is seemingly boundless, as a walk through a Catholic or public book store reveals: hundreds of books on Jesus and the Saints, on Christian living, on prayer, mysticism, theology and angels. Popular contemporary spiritual writers are Ronald Rolheiser, James Martin, Joan Chittister, Richard Rohr, Diana Hayes, Kathleen Norris, Sr. Wendy Beckett and the deceased Thomas Merton and Henri Nouwen . Older favorites are St. Augustine's *Confessions,* John Climacus' *Ladder of Divine Ascent,* St. Teresa of Avila's *Interior Castle,* John of the Cross' *Dark Night of the Soul,* Francis de Sales and his *Introduction to the Devout Life,* Brother Lawrence's *Practice of the Presence of God* to name just a few. The spiritual biography "that surpassed all others in popularity" is the "little way of spiritual childhood" by the extraordinary French Carmelite nun, St. Therese of Lisieux (1873-1897), the Little Flower," who died at the early age of 24 after great suffering offered joyously to God for the world and for missionaries in foreign lands.

Sacred Art and Music

Beauty draws us ever closer to God. From the first days of the church, the creation of art and song has been an indispensible part of Christian worship and devotion. In the *Acts of the Apostles,* St. Paul and Silas are described as praying and singing hymns to God while imprisoned (Acts 16:25). Gregorian Chant, classical masterpieces such as Handel's *Messiah,* and popular hymns such as *Amazing Grace* enrich Catholic worship. Paintings and sculptures are immensely important as well. The early Christian catacombs in Rome are covered with paintings and drawings. European churches are dazzling in their use of stained glass, mosaics and frescos.[8] Michelangelo's *Sistine Chapel* frescoes are one of the greatest masterpieces in the history of art. On entering any Catholic church, one views statues and paintings of Christ, Mary and the Saints, the 14 Stations of the Cross and decorative stained glass windows. Priests perform the Mass in embroidered vestments, color-coded for certain days: green for ordinary time, purple for Lent, white for Easter and confessor Saints, red for Pentecost and martyrs, blue for feast days of the Blessed Virgin Mary. Catholic homes often display crucifixes and images of the Sacred Heart, Mary and Saints.

In chapters six and seven of Vatican II's *Constitution on the Sacred Liturgy,* the Catholic Church re-affirmed the rich tradition and vital importance of the arts in its liturgy and devotional practices. Chapter six focuses on sacred music 'of inestimable value' and a 'necessary and integral part' of the liturgy. (SC, VI, 112). Chapter seven treats sacred art, "the noblest activity...oriented to the infinite beauty of God" and of immense value in "turning men's minds devoutly to God." (SC VII, 122)

Vatican II reaffirmed the ancient tradition of veneration of sacred images. Catholics pray in front of statues of the Saints or paintings such as the Virgin of Guadalupe and the Divine Mercy as helps to focus their prayer and contemplation on God. Sacred images ultimately are visual reminders of Christ's incarnation in this world. This fact is especially evident in the Eastern tradition, where the veneration of sacred icons continues to be a vital part of Orthodox prayer and liturgy.

Devotions

Devotion to the Saints[9] almost defines Catholic spirituality. Catholics love their Saints, regularly pray to them, read their lives, place statues of favorite Saints in their homes. Many a garden displays a statue of St. Francis of Assisi. Catholicism is a person-oriented, down to earth religion.

This is especially the case for Mediterranean and Latin American Catholicism. Each city has its saint-protector whose feast day is celebrated often in spectacular fiestas after months of preparation. The fiesta is the major religious event in Latin America and wherever Hispanic culture is found. The early Franciscan missionaries in California gave Saints' name to the string of missions from San Diego (James) to San Francisco (Francis of Assisi): Los Angeles (Our Lady, Queen of the Angels), Santa Monica, Santa Barbara, San Jose, Santa Clara!

Catholic devotion to the Saints is based on belief in *the communion of saints* and in personal resurrection and eternal life after death. Catholics express this belief in the ancient creed: "we believe ... in the communion of saints, resurrection of the body, and life everlasting. Amen." The communion of the saints is the entire body of Christians now on earth (pilgrim church), those in **purgatory** (church suffering) and the saints in heaven (church in glory). Catholics believe that the saints in heaven are vitally interested in their sisters and brothers still on pilgrimage on earth, hear their prayers to them, and intercede with God for them. This vast communion of Christians are united as family in a bond of love.

Who are some of the better known Saints? There are the "*confessor* Saints," those who witness to Christ by their heroic lives: Saint Joseph, Mary's spouse; Augustine, Benedict, Hilda of Whitby, Thomas Aquinas, Bonaventure, Anthony, Francis Xavier, Peter Claver, Peter Canisius, John of the Cross, Francis de Sales, Vincent de Paul, the Cure of Ars, Joan of Arc, Bernard of Clairvaux, Clare and Scholastica, Aloysius, Rose of Lima, and on and on. Then there is the long list of *martyr*-Saints: the Apostles, the virgin Agnes in 3rd century Rome and the teen-ager Maria Goretti in 20th century Italy, the deacon Lawrence, many early popes, Edmund Campion and the 43 English martyrs, Isaac Jogues and the seven North American Jesuit martyrs, the 23 Japanese martyrs, Andrew Kim and hundreds of Korean martyrs, Mulumba and the Ugandan martyrs. The canon or list is in the thousands. This multitude of heroes and heroines of Christ is the glory of Christianity and of the Catholic Church. Their lives make exciting, inspiring reading.

Nowhere is the catholicity of the Church better measured than in its catalogue of the saints. As we browse through the many standard dictionaries of the saints one sees peasants and kings, queens and reformed prostitutes, hermits and people of the world, monks and married folks, men and women who range from the lovable to the fanatic, the learned and the ignorant, the noble and the humble.[10]

In Catholics' devotion to the Saints, the bishops of Vatican II saw the danger of Saints overshadowing the centrality of Jesus Christ in Catholic life. Furthermore, the church's liturgical year seemed to have an overbalance of Saints' feast days. In its liturgical renewal, the church suppressed many feast days of lesser or local Saints to be replaced by ferial or "masses of the day," thus making possible a more continuous reading from day to day of passages from the Hebrew Scriptures, the letters of St. Paul and the four Gospels.

It is well, however, not to lose sight of the millions of saints with a small "s" whose lives of great love, of silent sacrifice, of accepting hardship and suffering with faith, of often literal living the Gospel in imitation of Jesus and serving the poor at home or in distant lands, are powerful examples to those fortunate to know or read about them. Dorothy Day comes immediately to mind. Less known is Canadian Jean Vanier, former Navy officer and university professor, who at 36, seeking to follow Jesus and the Gospel, invited two psychologically disabled men to share a house with him. From this developed the L'Arche communities for severely handicapped persons, now 132 worldwide. "The teaching of Jesus, if it had been followed, would have changed the history of the world – love your enemies," he wrote.

Devotion to Mary

The greatest saint of all is Mary, the virgin mother of Jesus, the God-man. Catholics' love and tender devotion to Mary as "their mother" has been a major characteristic of the Catholic Church since the early centuries climaxing in the "age of Mary" in the Middle Ages. Witness thousands of madonnas by Renaissance painters and Orthodox icons of mother and child; the great European cathedrals bearing Mary's name (Notre Dame of Paris, Our Lady of Chartres, St. Mary Major in Rome); the number of Catholic churches and schools and hospitals called St. Mary's; titles given to Mary (Our Lady, Mother of God, Blessed Mother, Queen of Heaven, the Immaculate Conception, Blessed Virgin); Mary's apparitions at Guadalupe, Lourdes and Fatima; the extraordinary devotion of Mexican Indians to their brown-skinned Virgin of Guadalupe and of the Catalans to their black virgin in Montserrat, Spain; the many feast days of Mary in the church calendar; the countless richly dressed and bejeweled statues of Mary in Latin America and Michelangelo's revered *Pieta* in St. Peter's, Rome; famous Marian pilgrimage shrines all over the world, and much more!

The bishops at Vatican II were aware that such profusion of devotion to the Saints was an obstacle to ecumenical relations with Protestants who objected that it deterred from the central role of Jesus in Christianity. Devotions to Mary in Catholic Europe of the past and also today in the popular religiosity of poorly educated Catholics in Latin America and the Mediterranean world often verged on superstition. So they emphasized Mary's relationship to Christ and her role in God's plan of salvation and in the Church. Accordingly, the bishops rejected the proposed separate document on Mary, instead inserting a chapter on Mary in the *Constitution on the Church* as its beautiful final chapter eight.

The council's teaching on Mary is founded on her "function ... in the plan of salvation." She was chosen by God through the angel Gabriel to be the mother of God (*theotokos* according to the Council of Ephesus, 431 AD), the human mother of Jesus the God-man. This is her pre-eminent title and primary claim to the veneration (not adoration) and devotion of all Christians. Vatican II gave her a new title, "Mother of the Church"; for as Mary brought Christ into the world physically, so the church brings forth Christ through faith, sacraments, grace, and preaching. The council presents Mary as the ideal Christian obedient to God's will. "Be it done to me according to thy word" was her answer to

Gabriel announcing to her that she had been chosen to be the mother of the Messiah. As a true disciple of Jesus, a fellow sufferer in this life, a worthy friend, she is a model for all Christians to imitate.

The council insisted that "there is but one Mediator: ... the man Jesus Christ who gave himself as redemption for all" (1 Tim 2:5-6) and that "Mary's function as Mother of [the Church] in no way obscures or diminishes this unique mediation of Christ." (*LG* 60) Thus Catholics, in recognition of Jesus on the cross saying to the apostle John "This is your mother" (John 19:27), take Mary as their heavenly mother and confidently pray to Mary asking her to intercede with her son for their needs.

Catholics honor Mary in many beautiful prayers and devotions: the *Hail Mary;* the *rosary* consisting of five joyful, five sorrowful, five glorious and five luminous mysteries of the life of Christ and of Mary's part in his life; the *Angelus* traditionally recited three times daily, morning, noon and evening; the *Litany of Mary,* a series of Mary's titles followed by "pray for us"; the *First Saturday* of each month resulting from Mary's appearances at Fatima in 1917. The two-part *Hail Mary* best states the reasons for Catholics' extraordinary devotion to Mary through the centuries: "Hail Mary, full of grace, the Lord is with you; blessed are you among women and blessed is the fruit of your womb, Jesus. Holy Mary, mother of God, pray for us sinners now and at the hour of our death. Amen."

Other Devotions

Over the centuries Catholics have created an almost bewildering variety and richness of both private and public devotions. Many are universal throughout the church; others local to countries and even cities. The following are the most prominent. To *Christ:* the way of the cross (14 stations or stages of Jesus' suffering and death); benediction of the Blessed Sacrament; holy hours before Christ in the consecrated host; prayers to the Sacred Heart of Jesus as symbol of his great love for us and the nine First Fridays of reparation to him; the five wounds of Jesus. To *Mary:* the rosary, litany of the Blessed Virgin, the scapular, special devotions to her under her many titles like Sorrowful Mother, Lady of Perpetual Help, Our Lady of Guadalupe, Our Lady of Fatima, and so forth. To *Saints* (St. Jude, St. Dismas, St. Anthony for lost articles). To the *souls in Purgatory*, loved ones on the way to heaven. Catholics also revere sacred objects such as crucifies, statues, icons, holy cards, and holy water as aids to prayer and devotion.

For most Catholics these many devotions are a significant part of their spirituality. Vatican II did not repudiate these popular devotions; rather it cautioned against the tendency to superstition and magic, emphasizing the central role of Christ and of his saving life, death and resurrection and of the sacraments, especially the Eucharist, in Catholic life

Mysticism and Mystics

There is growing interest, even fascination today, with the phenomenon of Catholic and Eastern mysticism and with men and women mystics. Mysticism is a complex reality that may or may not include ecstasy, visions, altered states. Though mystics exist in various world religions, Christian mysticism involves explicit acknowledgement of God and Jesus. Mystics are persons particularly gifted with God's grace and special call to the mystical state who have intense, direct, transforming experiences of God. They pass through the stages of *purification* from sin and earthly desires, of *illumination* by which the soul understands clearly the mystery of God's love in Jesus, to the stage of intimate *union* with God in love. Mystics surrender themselves completely to God who possesses their soul and transfigures it. Some mystics experience ecstasy during which they are totally absorbed in God, often impervious to the world and physical stimuli, and feel intense joy and love and extraordinary clarity of vision.

The great Spanish mystics, Saints Teresa of Avila (died 1582) and John of the Cross (died 1591), analyzed the mystical experience in their many writings. For example, John spoke of the two stages of the dark night of the soul: the night of the senses and the night of the spirit in which the mystic surrenders to God's purifying action. Well known Catholic mystics are Bridget of Sweden, Catherine of Siena, Julian of Norwich, England (died 1420), the unknown author of *The Cloud of Unknowing*, Bernard of Clairvaux (1153), Francis of Assisi, Ignatius Loyola (died 1556). Mystics are dramatic witnesses to the reality of the spiritual world, to God's powerful love, to the intense joy of paradise and union with God anticipated in this life.

For Discussion

1 In your opinion, have Catholics acquired Vatican II spirituality today? What elements need improvement?

2. Do you think devotion to Mary and the Saints is exaggerated in the Catholic and Orthodox churches? Give reasons for and against.

3. How can art and music play a role in enriching your own spirituality and encounter with God?

4. Describe your own spirituality. What further elements would you like to have in your own spirituality?

Follow-up Suggestions!

1. Attend an Orthodox Divine Liturgy and look at the various sacred icons. How do they enrich the liturgy and your sense of the sacred?

2. Get to know one of the great mystics: St. Teresa of Avila or Thomas Merton, for example.

3. Discover why the rosary is still such a popular prayer after seven centuries.

4. Talk to a Jesuit or religious sister or a lay person who has made the *Spiritual Exercises of St. Ignatius*. Why are these 'exercises' so popular today? Discover their unique spirit and power.

5. Ask a member of the Catholic Charismatic Renewal how this movement has enriched his/her faith experience. Attend a charismatic meeting.
6. Go to the medieval and Renaissance section of your local art museum and check all the paintings and statues of Christ, Mary and angels and saints. What does it all mean?
7. Make the acquaintance of modern 'saints' such as Dorothy Day, Cesar Chavez and Archbishop Romero.

Further Reading

DeMello, Anthony. *Selected Writings with an Introduction by William Dych, S.J.* Maryknoll, NY: Orbis Books, 1999. Tony DeMello was a Jesuit priest-psychologist, retreat giver and spiritual writer from India famous for his stories and parables bringing together the wisdom of East and West to awaken in his listeners awareness of God's presence in their midst. Highly creative and full of irrepressible joy.

Eagan, John, SJ. *A Traveler Toward the Dawn, The Spiritual Journal of John Eagan, S.J.* Chicago: Loyola University Press, 1990. This is an inspiring and deeply spiritual journal by a Jesuit high school teacher who died of cancer after refusing chemo treatment. It appeals to both young and old, lay and religious persons. John tells the story of his rich, interesting life as teacher, counselor and companion of young people and of his experience of God hiking in mountains and in his annual retreats, written with his characteristic humor.

Martin, James, S.J. *My Life with the Saints.* Chicago: Loyola Press, 2007. In this popular and easy-to-read book, Fr. Martin describes with humor and insight how well-known Saints affected his life and spirituality and how people today can live out Thomas Merton's adage, "To be a saint is to be myself." He includes questions and meditations for personal growth and discussion.

Nouwen, Henri, Michael J. Christensen and Rebecca J. Laird. *Spiritual Direction: Wisdom for the Long Walk of Faith.* New York: Harper Collins, 2006. This book is designed for the layperson who desires to deepen his/her spiritual life by learning to open one's heart and to hear God's Spirit through prayer, meditation and community. It is based on a course Fr. Nouwen taught as presented by two of his former students.

Rohlheiser, Ronald. *The Holy Longing: The Search for a Christian Spirituality.* This modern spiritual classic by a priest-psychologist is clear, down-to-earth, practical, utterly honest, full of fresh insights, with excellent examples and stories to illustrate his topics. It challenges readers to adult spirituality in today's world. Spiritual reading at its best.

Footnotes

1   Charismatic refers to the gifts of the Spirit St. Paul mentions in 2 Corinthians, 12:12-4. Renewal indicates that the gifts of the Spirit are given for a profound renewal of the whole Catholic Church , members and leaders alike.

2   Patti Gallagher Mansfield, *As By a New Pentecost: The Beginning of the Catholic Charismatic Renewal* (Steubenville, OH: Franciscan View Press, 1992), 160.

3   Bill Callahan, S.J., "My Experience of Creation Spirituality," *Companion* (Milwaukee: Wisconsin Province of Jesuits, Spring, 1993), 159-61.

4   John XXIII, *Humanae Salutis,* "Convoking the Council," in Walter Abbott, ed., *The Documents of Vatican II* (New York: Guild Press, 1966), 709.

5   Cyprian Davis. "Black Spirituality," *U..S. Catholic Historian ,* 8 (Spirituality, Devotionalism, & Popular Religion, Winter-Spring, 1989): 39-46.

6   Copeland, M. Shawn, OP, "African American Catholics," in *African American Religious Studies: An Interdisciplinary Anthology,* edited by Gayraud S. Wilmore. (Durham, NC: Duke University Press, 1989), 241-2.

7   Alberto A. Garcia. "Christian Spirituality in Light of the U.S. Hispanic Experience," *Word and World* 20, no. 1 (Winter 2000): 52-60.

8   Monreale, Sicily; the Byzantine churches of Ravenna, Italy; La Sainte Chapelle in Paris; the crown of all, Our Lady of Chartre, France.

9   Saints like Francis of Assisi, Ignatius of Loyola, Teresa of Avila, Catherine of Sienna, the Little Flower Theresa of Lisieux, Thomas More patron of lawyers, Maximilian Kolbe, the Franciscan priest who died a martyr of love by volunteering to take the place of a man marked for death by the Nazis in Auschwitz.

The greatest of all the Saints is Mary, the Virgin Mother of Jesus Christ who has inspired Catholics and Orthodox down through the ages as the wealth of paintings and icons testify.

10 Lawrence Cunningham, *The Catholic Faith: An Introduction* (New York/ Mahwah, NJ: Paulist Press, 1987) , 38-39. For informative and inspiring portraits of Saints and saints for each day of the year, see Robert Ellsberg, *All Saints, Daily Reflections on Saints, Prophets and Witnesses for Our Time* (New York, NY:L The Crossroad Publishing Co., 1997)

Chapter 11:
"That All May be One"

"The restoration of unity among all Christians is one of the principal concerns of the Second Vatican Council. Christ the Lord founded one Church. " (*Decree on Ecumenism No. 1*)

"That all may be one, as you Father are in me and I in you; I pray that they may be one in us, that the world may believe that you sent me" (John 17:21)

The amazing story of the effort of the Christian churches to re-establish unity after their 1000-year and 500-year divorce is the interesting subject of this chapter. It is the story of how the separated churches moved from suspicion and hostility to new-found relationships spurred by enthusiastic hopes for future union and then to dashed hope and seeming impasse. It is also the improbable contemporary story of how the Catholic Church, after fifty years remaining aloof, joined the hitherto Protestant ecumenical movement thanks to the Second Vatican Council and immediately assumed leadership by sponsoring the highly successful inter-church theological dialogues. Undreamed of events became common-place: Protestants, Catholics and Orthodox began talking and praying and working together, their theologians achieved breakthrough faith and theological agreements, visible union of the separated churches seemed around the corner.

Why Christian Ecumenism?

The success or failure of Christian ecumenism has enormous consequences today for the world's problems. A united Christianity could be a powerful influence for justice and world peace, for the rights and dignity of women and men, for the eradication of poverty and hunger, disease and premature death.

The inspiration and motivation for the modern ecumenical movement is the prayer Jesus made to his followers on the eve of his death: "That all may be one, as you Father and I are one, that the world may believe." Jesus' concern was the unity of the millions who were to follow him as Christians, a unity essential to their successfully preaching his Gospel. Likewise, St. Paul's over-riding concern was unity among the communities he founded throughout Greece and Asia Minor. This unity was ruptured between Eastern and Western Christianity in 1054[1] and within the western Catholic Church by the Protestant Reformation in the early 16th century and subsequent divisions.[2]

The results of these two tragic events are with us today. The following membership statistics are a dramatic reminder of the magnitude of the ecumenical task ahead.

Christian Churches Worldwide: The Catholic Church, 1,150,661,000; Protestant Churches 419,795,000; Orthodox churches, 270,227,000; Anglican Communion 86,051,000; Marginal Christians 34,643,000. *(Encyclopedia Britannica, Book of the Year,* mid-2010).

United States Christian Churches: The Catholic Church , 70,465,000; Southern Baptist Convention 16,16,088; The United Methodist Church, 7,744,931; The Church of Jesus Christ of Latter-day Saints, 5,974,041; The Church of God in Christ, 5,449,875; National Baptist Convention, U.S.A, Inc. *5,000.000; Evangelical Lutheran Church in America , 4,542,868; National Baptist Convention of America, Inc., *3,500,000; Assemblies of God , 2,914,669; Presbyterian Church (U.S.A.), 2,770,730; African Methodist Episcopal Church, *2,500,000;

National Missionary Baptist Convention of America,*2,500,000; Progressive National Baptist Convention, Inc.,*2,500,000; The Lutheran Church – Missouri Synod (LCMS), 2,312,111; The Episcopal Church, 2,006,343. (The National Council of Churches' 2011 *Yearbook of American & Canadian Churches)* Some entries are 2009. (*estimate)

The modern ecumenical movement to recover unity began in 1910 when Anglican and Protestant church leaders met in Edinburgh, Scotland to explore ways the churches competing for converts in India might unite to more effectively preach the good news of Christ to the masses there.[3] In 1948 the World Council of Churches (WCC) was founded in Amsterdam; today with over 300 Anglican, Protestant and Orthodox church-members, WCC promotes the goal of church union through an impressive number of study and action commissions at the WCC headquarters in Geneva, Switzerland.[4] The Catholic Church joined the ecumenical movement with the publication of Vatican II's *Decree on Ecumenism* November 2, 1964; it is not a member of WCC but has close contacts through a Joint Working Group and Catholic theologians are full-time members of WCC's **Faith & Order Commission.**

Decree on Ecumenism, *Restoration of Unity (UR)*

This Decree effectively committed the Catholic Church to join with Orthodox Churches, the Anglican Communion and Protestant churches in the journey toward the goal of visible unity. Emphasizing that division between the churches "scandalizes the world and damages the sacred cause of preaching the Gospel to every creature," (UR 1) the Decree laid out principles and practice for Catholic ecumenism as the way the Catholic Church would participate in the ecumenical journey. This involved setting guidelines, explaining to skeptical

Catholics the church's about-face in embracing ecumenism, and crafting a new understanding of the church in relation to other Christian churches.

Guidelines for the Catholic Practice of Ecumenism. These challenge the Catholic Church and individual Catholics to change past attitudes and practices. They represent an unprecedented admission by the Catholic Church.

- Reform and renewal of all areas of the church's life. "Christ summons the Church ... to that continual reformation of which she always has need." (UR 7)
- Admit "deficiencies in moral conduct or in Church discipline or even in the way Church teaching has been formulated" (UR 6) and beg "pardon of God and our separated brethren ... for sins against unity." (UR 7)
- "... become familiar with the outlook of our separated brethren ... their respective doctrines ... their history, their spiritual and liturgical life, their religious psychology and cultural background." (UR 9)
- Make "every effort to avoid expressions, judgments and actions that do not represent the condition of our separated brothers with truth and fairness and so make mutual relations with them more difficult." (UR 4)
- Cooperate with separated Christians in social actions "to relieve the afflictions of our times, famine and natural disasters, illiteracy and poverty, lack of housing, the unequal distribution of wealth. Through such cooperation all believers in Christ learn how to esteem each other more and how the road to unity of Christians may be more smooth." (UR 12)
- Personal conversion. "There can be no ecumenism ... without interior conversion." (UR 7) "This change of heart and holiness of life, along with public and private prayer for the unity of

Christians... [is] the soul of the whole ecumenical movement and merits the name of 'spiritual ecumenism.'" (UR 8)

- The one church established by Christ is "primarily a mystery of Christ's presence and activity" (LG, Chapter 1), a reality greater than any existing church including the Catholic Church.

A New Ecclesiology

The Catholic Church formally accepted the proper baptism of other Christian churches which led to recognizing Orthodox, Anglican, and Protestants as part of the body of Christ, members of the one Church of Christ. "All who have been justified by faith in baptism are incorporated into Christ ... [are] Christians ... [and are] sisters and brothers in the Lord." (UR 3)

Accordingly, the Catholic Church recognizes other Christian churches, no longer as mere sociological groupings of Christians, but ecclesial communities bringing the grace of Christ and his salvation to their members. "The Spirit of Christ has not reframed from using them [the separated churches and communities] as means of salvation." (UR 3).

With this new understanding of the Catholic Church in relation to other churches, a new theology of church is born that expresses the Catholic position and plan for achieving union and establishes the basis and goal of theological dialogue with the separated churches and ecclesial communities.

The starting point and basis of the Catholic Church's new ecclesiology or theology of church is the one Church established by Christ. Protestant theology, as a way of explaining its legitimacy after the Reformation, spoke of two churches, the visible divided church and the invisible true spiritual church known to God alone. The council firmly repudiated this two-church theology.

The society equipped with hierarchical structures and the mystical body of Christ, the visible society and the spiritual community, the earthly church and the Church endowed with heavenly riches, are not to be thought of as two realities. On the contrary, they form one complex reality comprising a human and divine element. (LG 8)

The council described this one Church of Christ in its relation to the separated churches in the famous article 8 of the *Constitution on the Church.*

This is the unique Church of Christ which in the Creed we profess to be one, holy, catholic and apostolic which our Savior, after his resurrection, entrusted to Peter's pastoral care... This Church, constituted and organized as a society in the present world, *subsists in* the Catholic Church, which is governed by the successor of Peter and by the bishops in communion with him. Nevertheless, many elements of sanctification and of truth are found outside its visible confines. Since these are gifts belonging to the Church of Christ, they are forces impelling towards catholic unity. (LG 8) (Italics added)

The key phrases are "this Church subsists in" and "elements of sanctification and truth." The council's original first draft read "This unique Church of Christ *is* the Catholic Church," meaning that the one Church of Christ is identical with the Catholic Church. This identification caused spirited debate in the council. Progressive bishops objected that such an un-nuanced identity excluded not only Anglican and Protestant churches but the ancient Orthodox churches from being in some real way part of the one church Jesus established. By substituting "subsists in" for "is", the bishops acknowledged the reality of the Church of Christ existing in the Catholic Church, thus maintained her unique reality, and recognized the ecclesial reality of the other Christian churches (the various national Orthodox churches) and the ecclesial communities (Protestant churches).[5]

To express their ecclesial reality, the council recognized the "elements of sanctification" possessed by the separated churches as "gifts from Christ" that "build up and give life to the church itself ... [and which] exist outside the visible boundaries of the Roman Catholic Church: the written word of God, the life of grace, faith, hope and charity with other gifts of the Holy Spirit." (UR 3) *The Constitution on the Church* added baptism and "other sacraments in their own churches and ecclesial communities, the episcopate, the holy Eucharist, devotion to Mary." (LG 15).

The key point. In denying *exclusive identification* of the Church of Christ with the Catholic Church and her sometimes pre-Vatican II claim to be the *one true church,* this new ecclesiology created the possibility and positive climate for theological dialogue.

For the separated churches to achieve the future united Church of Christ, the council proposed the following model of union.

Fully incorporated into the Church are those who ... accept all the means of salvation given to the Church together with her entire organization, and who -- by the bonds constituted by the profession of faith, the sacraments, ecclesiastical government, and communion -- are joined to the visible structure of the Church and through her with Christ who rules her through the Supreme Pontiff and the bishops. (LG 14)

Accomplishing *full incorporation* and *full communion* is the goal of the theological dialogues.

Theological Dialogues

Immediately after the council finished, the Catholic Church invited other churches to join with her in official theological dialogue.[6]

The Decree on Ecumenism had proposed "dialogue between competent experts from different churches and communities" in which "each explains the teaching of his communion in greater depth and brings out its distinctive features" so that "everyone gains a truer knowledge and more just appreciation of the teachings and religious life of both communions." (UR 4) In this "discussion of theological problems ... each can treat with the other on an equal footing." (UR 9)

These bilateral dialogues between the Catholic Church and other churches represent one of the greatest successes of the council. Their positive goal is to discover both *faith* and *theological* agreement while clarifying disagreements. Theologians research a given topic, write scholarly papers which are distributed to dialogue members in preparation for regular meetings in which the papers are thoroughly analyzed. They explain their church's teaching and theological position and answer probing questions. A report is drawn up and published expressing agreement reached and remaining differences. The participating theologians grew in appreciation of each other's church, discovered shared faith and similar theological understanding and formed enduring friendships.

We treat only the most prominent dialogues.

Roman Catholic-Orthodox Dialogue, 2007

Known as the *Ravenna Report,* the dialogue's ambitious title is *Ecclesiological and Canonical Consequences of the Sacramental Nature of the Church: Ecclesial Communion, Conciliarity and Authority.* It tackled the key issue dividing Orthodox and Catholics: the role and prerogatives of the Bishop of Rome. Both sides agreed that in the first millennium of the undivided church, universal communion of the two churches was maintained among the bishops and among the five major Patriarchs (Alexandria, Antioch,

Constantinople, Jerusalem, and Rome). The Orthodox agreed that Rome, as the church that "presides in love," the phrase of St Ignatius of Antioch (*To the Romans,* Prologue), and its bishop (the pope as Patriarch of the West) occupied the first place *of honor* among the patriarchs. They agreed that the principle of conciliarity (councils or meetings at all levels of the church) as exercised in the early ecumenical councils implies an active role of the Bishop of Rome as first among bishops of the major churches. With the groundwork thus laid for dealing with the key issue of authority still dividing the two churches, they agreed to study in greater depth the role of the Bishop of Rome in the communion of all the churches. However, subsequent reservations voiced by the Orthodox reveal continuing major challenges facing this dialogue.

ARCIC I (Anglican Roman Catholic International Dialogue)

This dialogue began in 1966 when Anglican Archbishop Ramsay and Pope Paul VI stated their intent to "inaugurate … a serious dialogue which…may lead to that unity in truth for which Christ prayed." The commission they created published four remarkable documents: *Eucharistic Doctrine* 1971; *Ministry and Ordination* 1973; *Authority in Church I* 1976 and its 1981 *Final Report.* The member theologians reported "substantial agreement" on the Eucharist, "consensus on essential matters regarding ministry" and agreement on "the need of an universal primacy in a (future) church." The *Final Report*[7] was sent to the various churches within the Anglican Communion and to the Holy See's Congregation for the Doctrine of the Faith,[8] with the recommendation that on the basis of these agreements and convergences the two communions/churches begin serious concrete steps toward union. ARCIC II produced further agreed statements: Salvation and the Church, 1987; Morals, Communion and the Church, 1994; and Church as Communion, 1991.

Lutheran/Roman Catholic Dialogue USA

Begun in 1965 right after Vatican II, this rich dialogue produced eleven   important documents of scholarly quality.[9] In *Differing Attitudes toward Papal Primacy,* Lutheran participants stated that "Lutherans increasingly recognize the need for a ministry serving the unity of the church universal, and challenged their churches "to acknowledge… the desirability of the papal ministry, *renewed under the Gospel and committed to Christian freedom,* in a larger communion which would include the Lutheran churches."[10] (italics added)

Joint Declaration on the Doctrine of Justification

Reformation Sunday, October 31, 1999, in Augsburg, Germany, representatives of the Catholic Church and the Lutheran World Federation (LWF) signed the historic agreement on justification[11] that resolved the central doctrinal issue of the 16th century Protestant Reformation. "Together we confess: By *grace alone*, in *faith* in Christ's saving work and not because of any *merit* on our part, we are accepted by God and receive the Holy Spirit … equipping and calling us to *good works*." JDDJ 15 (Italics added) This agreement is an enormous ecumenical achievement. Twenty-five years of theological dialogues between RCC and Lutheran theologians had resulted in new understanding and re-interpretation of the two churches' 16th century mutual condemnations.

The teaching of the Lutheran churches presented in this declaration does not fall under the condemnations from the Council of Trent. The condemnations in the Lutheran Confessions do not apply to the teaching of the Roman Catholic Church presented in this declaration. (JDDJ 41)

Thanks to persevering theological dialogue, the major issue dividing the Reformation churches and the Catholic Church for 400 years was laid to rest. Two years later the World Methodist Council, after extensive study of JDDJ, signed agreement to the Declaration.

Dialogue among Four Churches[12]

Cardinal Walter Kasper, then head of the Vatican's *Pontifical Council for Promoting Christian Unity (PCPCU),* in 2009 published *Harvesting the Fruits: Basic Aspects of Christian Faith in Ecumenical Dialogue,* an important study of 37 bilateral dialogues spanning 40 years between the RCC and the Anglican Communion, the LWF, the World Methodist Council, and the World Alliance of Reformed Churches.[13]

Harvesting the Fruits discovered "considerable consensus" on baptism and a growing consensus on the Eucharist, affirmed the churches' strong faith in Jesus Christ and the Trinity, the content of the Creed, the relation between Scripture and Tradition and significant agreement on justification. It acknowledged serious differences, "unresolved questions: the nature of the church, authority and who exercises it, the meaning of ordination and who can be ordained, and ethical problems particularly concerning sexuality. A remaining major challenge is *reception*, that the dialogue-churches accept and act on the agreements achieved.

Landmark Ecumenical Events

1982. *Baptism, Eucharist, Ministry (BEM).* The result of thirty years' discussions by theologian members of the WCC's Faith and Order Commission (FOC), including non-WCC-member Roman Catholics, *BEM* is the most important ecumenical document ever published with over a half million copies translated into 31 languages. It represents a ***convergence,*** not yet an agreement, on these three essential fundamentals of the church's faith and structure. FOC sent BEM to WCC member churches requesting their response and urging them to recover the faith and the practice of the undivided church of the first 1000 years concerning infant baptism, reality of Eucharist, the three-fold ministry of bishop-priest- deacon and the "sign of communion with the ancient church through ordination in the historical episcopal succession." One hundred and eighty WCC churches discussed *BEM* for four years; their written reports, over 1000, fill six volumes.[14]

After reviewing the churches' responses, FOC singled out three areas for further study and discussion: the relation between Scripture as norm of faith and Tradition as containing and passing on the apostolic faith to the churches; the reality and understanding of sacraments; and the essential nature of the church.

1995. *Ut Unum Sint (That They Be One), UUS.* In this unprecedented letter, Pope John Paul II invited leaders of all churches to "engage with me in ... dialogue on this subject" [papal primacy] ... "to help me find a way to exercise the office of bishop of Rome in a new way that leads to unity. " Archbishop Quinn considers UUS "a revolution. For the first time it is the pope himself who raises and legitimizes the question of reform and change in the papal office in the church."[15] In emphasizing conversion as the heart of the ecumenical movement, John Paul stressed his own conversion first!

1997 The United Church of Christ, the Presbyterian Church USA, and the Reformed Church of America along with the Lutheran Church merged to form the Evangelical Lutheran Church of America (ELCA).

2005. The WCC World Assembly of member churches meeting at Porto Alegre, Brazil, stated "we confess one, holy, catholic and apostolic church as expressed in the Nicene-Constantinopolitan Creed and affirmed the church is a community of believers created by the Word of God. As follow-up to BEM, FOC published *The Nature and Mission of the Church,* a significant statement on the divisive issue of authority in the church and of the pope.

2007.*Anglicorum Coetibus* (*Anglican Groups*). Benedict XVI offered Anglican laity, priests and bishops the opportunity to join the Catholic Church while retaining their own rich Anglican tradition and practice. In England over 1000 Anglican lay persons, five priests and two bishops were received into the Catholic Church in 2011; in the United States Episcopalian groups have accepted Benedict's offer.

This broad overview of the theological dialogues and the impressive efforts of the churches to respond to Christ's Last Supper prayer and will for unity is a somber reminder of how difficult the journey to actual union is and how tragic the breakup of Christianity in 1054 and the Protestant Reformation have proven to be. The dialogues also reveal the key role of the Catholic Church and of the bishop of Rome, Peter's successor, and pose the question: what is the responsibility today of the Catholic Church in achieving union and doing the serious will of Christ?

The Ecumenical Picture Today

The picture is mixed. At the grassroots, Catholics and other Christians have discovered each other as brothers and sisters in Christ, gained knowledge and appreciation of each other, pray and worship and work together; church leaders have established new bonds of appreciation and friendship; the dialogues have achieved unprecedented faith and even theological agreement. Yet discouragement and frustration exist at the slow progress toward unity and the failure of church leaders to take concrete steps toward actual union. New problems have become obstacles on the path to unity: the re-emergence of denominationalism by churches protecting their institutional concerns and resisting change; divisive moral issues of abortion, homosexuality, same sex marriage, stem-cell research; church dividing questions of women's ordination and recently active gay bishops; major ecclesiological issues of the role of bishops and the pope, apostolic succession, inter-communion, and the essential nature of the church. Thus the ecumenical movement has entered a new phase from the immediate post-Vatican II enthusiasm and hope to the maturity and realism of the dialogues and the presence of the above problems.

The Challenge Ahead

Prospects for Full Communion. The first millennium of Christianity featured the united Church of East and West with their five patriarchs in communion with each other. The second millennium was one of divisions in 1054 and the early 16th century. Will the third millennium feature the restoration of unity envisioned by the Second Vatican Council?

The most promising potential union is between the RCC and the Orthodox who share the same Apostolic faith, the full sacramental system, and bishops in the apostolic succession. However, the Orthodox cannot accept the Bishop of Rome as long as he claims *primacy of jurisdiction* over all churches. Orthodox could accept the pope's exercise of authority as a primacy of *honor* such as existed during the first six ecumenical councils in the early centuries. Pope Paul VI said this arrangement is possible for the Catholic Church. Cardinal Ratzinger spoke of a "new situation" in the exercise of the papacy. Cardinal Edward Cassidy, former head of PCPCU, suggested in a 1993 address to a WCC meeting that it is possible for the pope to retain a juridical primacy over the Catholic Church and a more "symbolic and honorary primacy over other churches."

In UUS John Paul II spoke of a new "way of exercising the papacy … open to a new situation" and recommended the church structure of the first millennium as a way of restoring full communion. However, the Orthodox did not respond to his suggestion because they desire a collegial *synodal* exercise of authority that is their traditional practice. The current centralization of authority in Rome and insistence on the juridical primacy of the bishop of Rome remain major obstacles rendering union between the Orthodox and the RCC unlikely in the near future.

The decision of the Patriarch Bartholomew of Constantinople to attend the inauguration Mass of Francis I, the first such act since the great schism of 1054, is a significant promising step toward unity. The fact that Francis consistently refers to himself as bishop of Rome, and not pope or pontiff, was not lost on the Patriarch. On his part, Francis, the successor of Peter, warmly greeted Patriarch Bartholomew as "My brother Andrew, " referring to him as successor of the Apostle Andrew.[16]

Full communion is the explicit goal of the on-going Anglican-RCC dialogue.[17] Unity seemed promising since the Anglican Communion consists of episcopal sacramental churches. But formidable obstacles have risen. In 2000 Cardinal Ratzinger, as head of the Congregation of the Doctrine of the Faith, stated that the invalidity of Anglican Orders is to be *definitively* held[18] by Catholics, in reference to Pope Leo XIII's judgment in 1896 that "Anglican Orders are absolutely null and void." In addition, the fact that the Church of England and the Protestant Episcopal Church USA ordain women priests and bishops is for the

Catholic Church as well as the Orthodox a serious obstacle to union. Yet, both the pope and the Anglican Archbishop of Canterbury meet annually in genuine fellowship and continue to seek full communion.

Despite the impressive agreements between the Lutheran, Methodist and Reformed churches reported in *Harvesting the Fruits,* full communion with these ecclesial communities seems far off because of major ecclesiological and sacramental differences. Though Catholic dialogues with Baptist and Pentecostal churches have been productive, union with them is virtually impossible for both theological and ecclesiological differences.

Models of Church Union: Ecumenical theologians have proposed various models or ways of imagining future church union. A basic "return to the Catholic Church" model is rejected by all Protestant and most Catholic ecumenists. The "merger" model, suitable for churches with similar traditions as in the newly formed Evangelical Lutheran Church of America (ELCA) in the United States, is too limited and unacceptable to Catholics and Orthodox. The "conciliar model" championed by the WCC envisions diverse churches remaining separate but coming together in councils of churches at local, national, regional and world levels for common worship and decision-making. Though attractive, this model fails to provide for unity of faith, doctrine and sacramental life or episcopal and papal structures.

Virtually all the churches in the dialogues agree that the **communion** model has the most promise for the future union of the one church founded by Jesus as a communion of churches. Communion, **koinonia**[19] a fellowship, a sharing, was the church's form of unity in the first millennium, with bishops and patriarchs in communion with each other through fraternal relationships. In this model proposed by the council, those churches already in *partial* communion with the Catholic Church through baptism, apostolic faith, and elements of the Church of Christ, gradually move to *full* communion. Agreement on the essential structure, ministry and sacramental nature of the church, the goal of the ecumenical movement, is presently lacking and is the major obstacle.

To overcome the current ecumenical impasse, both the Protestant Reformation churches and the Catholic Church will need to make major changes. According to the communion model of moving from partial to full communion, the churches coming from the Reformation will need to recover the essential nature of the one Church of Christ: full Apostolic faith, ministry, and its sacramental reality expressed by the ordination of bishop-successors to the Apostles guaranteeing Eucharist and sacraments. Orthodox churches will need to recognize and accept in some form Peter's successor the bishop of Rome.

For its part, Archbishop Quinn describes the change the Catholic Church will need to make.

> We have to face the fact that in the service of Christian unity, the Catholic Church will have to make significant structural, pastoral and canonical changes. Collegiality, participation of the laity, decentralization and greater openness to diversity are some obvious areas where the Catholic Church will have to make some changes.[20]

Quinn adds that in its relationships to all the separated churches, the Catholic Church must "ask [itself] what things that give offense and create obstacles can be changed or even rejected. ... Given the urgency of Christian unity ... the Catholic Church ... must take the first step."[21] Ecumenist Jared Wicks recognizes that "the special claim that we make, namely of the church of Christ *subsisting* in the Catholic Church, brings a special obligation, an imperative to make what we claim transparently visible to others." He adds "I hope that our Catholic Church will grow and develop in ways to make the discovery and recognition in it of the church of Christ a more natural perception by other Christians." He realistically understands that "movement toward full communion involves the gradual discovery and recognition of the church of Christ present in other communities as they now exist and are developing."[22]

"If Christian unity is to be real in the future, it will come about when changed Protestant churches and a changed Catholic Church find their way together into a unity within the one Church of Christ." These are the prophetic words of Yves Congar, eminent ecclesiologist, theological expert at the Second Vatican Council, and major influence on the *Constitution on the Church* and *The Decree on Ecumenism*.[23]

Ultimately Christian unity is the work of the Holy Spirit. The council insisted that spiritual ecumenism based on prayer and conversion is the soul of the ecumenical movement. (UR 8)

Spiritual ecumenism is the future of the churches' journey to union!

Interfaith Ecumenism: *Nostra Aetate (Our Age)*

Another breakthrough Vatican II document, *Declaration on the Relation of the Church to Non-Christian Religions (NA)*, urged Catholics to "acknowledge, preserve and encourage the spiritual and moral truths found among non-Christians," as well as "their social life and culture" and to enter "into discussion and collaboration with members of other religions." (NA 2) Currently the Catholic Church is engaged in serious theological dialogues with Jewish, Buddhist, Hindu, and Muslim religious leaders and scholars. That members of the great world religions come to respect each other and live in harmony is critical for world peace.

The following worldwide demographics attest to this: Christians, 2,271,727,000; Muslims, 1,449,614,000; Hindus, 913,455,000; Chinese Universalists, 388,609,000; Buddhists, 387,872,000;

Ethno-religionists, 266,281,000; New-Religionists , 106,163,000; Sikhs, 23,988,000; Jews, 15,058,000.
(Encyclopedia Britannica, Book of the Year, mid-2010)

A special value of *Nostra Aetate* is the section on the Jewish religion. The council bishops took several strong positions:

- The Christian claim that Christ as Messiah "fulfills" or completes the Old Testament does not imply the rejection of Judaism by God. "God does not take back the gifts he bestowed or the choice he made," of his special covenant with the Jewish people (NA 4). Today it is ecumenically appropriate to use the terms Hebrew and Christian Scriptures rather than Old and New Testaments, as though the latter supplanted the former.
- Christians may not hold the Jewish people responsible for the death of Christ. Historically the taunt of "Christ-killer" accounted for Christians persecuting Jews through the centuries.
- The council "deplores all hatreds, persecutions, displays of anti-Semitism leveled at any time or from any source against the Jews" (NA 4).

This Declaration is of enormous value today in the light of rising anti-Semitism in the United States and Europe, of anti-Muslim feeling and the rise of Islamic fundamentalism, and of Hindu nationalism and persecution of other religions in India. "The Church reproves ... any discrimination against people or any harassment on the basis of their race, color, condition in life or religion." (NA 5)

Believers' Baptism

Baptist and evangelical "born again" churches practice adult "believers' baptism," that is, only believers who have made a deliberate faith commitment to Jesus Christ are to be baptized. Such churches generally hold that one is not a Christian unless he or she has made such a commitment to Jesus through a conversion experience; thus those baptized as infants are not considered Christians. Union with believer-baptism churches presently appears out of the question.

For Discussion

1. Do you think the future united Church of Christ has any realistic chance of coming about" What steps would Protestant churches need to take? Orthodox churches? the Roman Catholic Church?
2. If the Catholic Church has the principal responsibility for Christian unity, what might the pope do to reunite the Orthodox? Anglicans? Lutherans? Other Protestant churches?
3. Many feel that ecumenism has "hit a wall." Is it possible for church members, and not just church leaders, to re-invigorate ecumenism today? What steps to take?
4. Would intercommunion (Protestants receiving Catholic Eucharists and vice versa) hasten or deter the union of the churches? Why?

Further Reading

Baptism, Eucharist and Ministry. Geneva, Switzerland: WCC, 1982. This first of its kind and very important ecumenical document represents a convergence, not yet an agreement on the three essential fundamentals of the Christian Church's faith and structure.

Kasper, Walter. *Harvesting the Fruits, Basic Aspects of Christian Faith in Ecumenical Dialogue.* New York, NY: Continuum Publishing Group, 2009. Cardinal Kasper discusses the problems of division between four churches in their efforts toward unity in the light of Vatican II's *Decree on Ecumenism.* The questions driving his study are: "Where are we? What has been achieved? What has still to be done? Where can we, and where, should we move ahead?"

Cassidy, Cardinal Edward Idris. *Ecumenism and Ecumenical Dialogue.* Mahwah, NJ: Paulist Press, 2005. This book focuses on Vatican II's *Decree on Ecumenism* and *Declaration on Interreligious Dialogue*, exploring in detail the documents and the events leading up to their composition and the legacy these documents have left in the Church today.

Ratzinger, Joseph. *Church, Ecumenism and Politics.* San Francisco: Ignatius Press, 2008. A significant book on the state of ecumenism today in the Catholic Church from the perspective of Pope Benedict XVI. He focuses on three topics: the contribution and significance of Vatican II's call to unity; the problems and achievements of ecumenical movements in the churches since the council; and an assessment of the Church in society today and its challenges, and of pluralism and freedom.

Footnotes

1   The first major split in the universal church occurred when the Patriarch of the Eastern Byzantine Church broke communion with the bishop of Rome of the West over political more than theological differences; insensitive, arrogant actions by popes and patriarchs and bishops contributed. World Orthodoxy today is divided into separate *national* churches making unity with the Orthodox difficult: 15 independent, self-governing (autocephalous) Orthodox churches in the mid-East, Europe and America; 13 churches with a degree of self-government (autonomous), and 10 more recent "jurisdictions" in communion with world Orthodoxy.

2   This second great split began with Augustinian monk and priest Martin Luther's protest against the preaching of indulgences for money and the excessive worldliness of popes and many bishops. John Calvin in Geneva and John Knox in Scotland became leaders of the Reformed and Presbyterian movements. The Anglican Church in England began with King Henry VIII's differences with the pope over his desired divorce and with payments of taxes to Rome. Around 1650 what became the Methodist church began as a result of the Wesley brothers, both Anglican priests, preaching to inject life and spirituality into the Anglican Church of England. Also around 1650 Baptists appeared in England and Holland in reaction to the state churches there. Pentecostalism, an American phenomenon, rose in Topeka, Kansas, and Azusa, California, when a group of Christians prayed for the gifts of the Spirit and began speaking in tongues.

3   With the end of World War I, these church leaders invited the Catholic Church to join the nascent ecumenical movement. Following the church's "return"

ecclesiology, Pope Benedict XII told them the only way the church could be united was to "become reunited to the visible head of the Church by whom they will be received with open arms!"

4   Commission of Faith and Order for questions of doctrine and church order; World Mission and Evangelism; Church and Society; Dialogue with People of Living Faith; Units for Justice and Service and Education and Renewal. Every seven years WCC sponsors its World Assembly, a colorful two-week meeting of over 1000 delegates representing the worldwide member churches.

5   Both *LG* and *UR* distinguish between *churches* (the Orthodox national churches) and *ecclesial communities* (Protestant "churches") on the basis of Orthodox bishops in the apostolic succession, their sacrament of Holy Orders and the other sacraments. Respecting the council's distinction, in practice throughout these pages I use "churches" to refer to both Orthodox and Protestant. The Anglican Communion is a special consideration.

6   The International Dialogues: Lutheran World Federation, Anglican Communion, World Methodist Council, World Alliance of Reformed Churches, Classical Pentecostals, Coptic Orthodox Church, Disciples of Christ, Orthodox Church, Baptist World Alliance, World Evangelical Fellowship, Mennonite World Conference, Oriental Orthodox Churches, and Informal Conversations with Seventh Day Adventists, and the Salvation Army.

7   *The Final Report, Anglican-Roman Catholic International Commission* (Washington, D.C. U.S. Catholic Conference, 1982) and (Cincinnati: Forward Movement Publications, 1982)

8   CDF's response given after a 10-year delay welcomed the Final Report but noted that "there still remain between Anglicans and Catholics important differences regarding essential matters of Catholic doctrine. Full text in *Origins* 21 (Dec. 19, 1991): 441-47.

9   *Status of the Nicene Creed as Dogma of the Church*, 1965; *One Baptism for the Remission of Sins*, 1966; *The Eucharist*, 1967; *Eucharist and Ministry*, 1970; *Differing Attitudes toward Papal Primacy*, 1973; *Teaching Authority and Infallibility in the Church*, 1978; *Justification by Faith*, 1983; *The One*

Mediator, the Saints, and Mary, 1989; *Scripture and Tradition,* 1995; *The Church as Koinonia of Salvation: Its Structure and Ministries,* 2004; *The Hope of Eternal Life,* 2010.

10   Joseph Burgess and Jeffry Gros, eds. *Building Unity, Ecumenical Documents I* (New York/Mahweh, NJ: Paulist Press, 1989) : 137, No. 32.

11   From Romans 3:20-28, justification refers to what Jesus did for humanity, that is, by his passion, death and resurrection, God judged sinners totally free from sin and pleasing to God. Justification is a pure gift, a grace, in no way dependent on human deeds or merit.

12   John A Rodano "Ecumenical Dialogue in the 21st Century, Some Steps Forward and Some Continuing Concerns." *Ecumenical Trends* (New York: Graymoor Ecumenical & Interreligious Institute, November, 2009: 151-53 and Walter Kasper. op.cit., Conclusions, 196-207.

13   Kasper, *Harvesting the Fruits* (New York, NY: Continuum Publishing Group, 2009).

14   *Baptism, Eucharist and Ministry 1982-1990: Report on the Process and Responses* (Geneva: WCC Publications, 1990). "Never before have so many theological faculties, confessional families, ecumenical groups, local congregations, and discussion groups of lay and ordained persons joined together in studying the same ecumenical document. *Ibid,* 155-56.

15   John R. Quinn, *The Reform of the Papacy, the Costly Call to Christian Unity* (New York: Crossroad Publishing Co., 1999) 14.

16   Fr. Mark Woodruff. "My Brother Andrew." *The Tablet.* March 30, 2013, 8-9.

17   In 1996 ARCIC II published the impressive agreed statement *Church a Communion.*

18   *Definitively* is the language of infallibility. Theologians recognized that this term has introduced a new level of authoritative teaching in the church.

19 Acts 2:42 "They devoted themselves to the Apostles' teaching and the fellow-ship (*koinonia*), to the breaking of bread and the prayers."

20 Quinn, *op.cit.,* 20.

21 *Ibid.,* 22-23.

22 Jared Wicks, S.J. "Lights and Shadows over Catholic Ecumenism." Rome: *Bulletin/Centro Pro Unione.* No. 61, Spring 2002.

23 Quoted in Paul Lakeland. *Church, Engaging Theology, Catholic Perspectives.* 105

Chapter 12:
Best Kept Secret[1]

"Catholic social teaching calls us to recognize that all peoples of the world are our brothers and sisters."

'... three (economic) questions: what does it do *for* people? What does it do *to* people? And how do people *participate* in it" U.S. Bishops, *Economic Justice for All.*

The progressive social teaching of the Catholic Church is one of the greatest contributions the church offers the world and Catholics today. It has much to say to the magnitude of today's societal and economic crises: political gridlock; the increasing gap between the wealthy minority and the vast majority trapped in dehumanizing poverty; over one hundred million refugees worldwide; the suffering and uncertain status of immigrants; the power of supra-national corporations; and government and international organizations. Catholic social thought challenges the power brokers of today's world and calls for a faith response and human compassion to the urgent needs and suffering of each member of the human family created and loved by God.[2]

The church's social teaching has an interesting history stretching over 100 years by forward-thinking popes. As a constantly evolving tradition within the church, it has developed and expanded to meet new problems and crises. The Second Vatican Council, especially in its final document, *The Church in the Modern World, GS,* profoundly influenced the church's involvement in contemporary social questions and individual Catholics' social action.

Catholic Social Teaching: Encyclicals by Six Popes

These letters spanning 120 years contain the rich heritage of Catholic social thought and teaching. They present principles on which a better world order can be built. As such, they are a strong challenge to the dominant culture today and provide a timely critique to the present economic crisis.

As one reads these ten encyclicals, it is helpful to keep in mind the following: each was written in response to the social, economic and political realities of a given period; the teaching has evolved from letter to letter; underlying each letter is the conviction that the Holy Spirit is at work in human history evident by the Council's "signs of the time."[3] Common to each letter are the basic principles of the dignity of the human person and the rights that flow from his/her dignity. Since each letter is long and closely-reasoned, it is helpful to read summaries where possible.[4]

1891. *The Condition of Labor (Rerum Novarum, Of New Things),* Leo XIII. The terrible poverty and exploitation of workers in the Industrial Revolution in Europe prompted Leo XIII to write the church's first social encyclical. He insisted workers have basic human rights to work, to own property, to receive a just wage and to organize into workers' associations.

1931. *The Reconstruction of the Social Order (Quadragesimo Anno, The Fortieth Year* – after Leo's letter), Pius XI. Written in the midst of a severe, world-wide economic depression, the pope addressed the issue of social injustice, condemned the unregulated competition of capitalism and communism's class struggle and "dictatorship of the proletariate," and stressed the social responsibilities of private property and the rights of working people to a job, a just wage, and organizing to claim their rights. He insisted the state has the responsibility to reform the social order and that capital and labor need each other.

1961. *Christianity and Social Progress (Mater et Magistra, Mother and Teacher)*, John XXIII. John issued his first encyclical in response to the severe imbalance between the rich and poor in the world. He treated for the first time the extreme poverty of millions in the non-industrialized nations of Asia, Africa, and Latin America, especially the world's farmers, and the resulting disparity between wealthy and poor nations. He said it was the duty of wealthy nations to help poorer countries. He distanced the Church from right-wing political forces and stressed that the right to own property is subordinate to the principle that the earth's goods are for the use and benefit of all. The effect of John's encyclical was explosive, even by some prominent Catholics: "mater si, magistra no," mother yes, teacher no!

1963. *Peace on Earth (Pacem in Terris)*, John XXIII. With his characteristic world vision and ecumenical spirit, John XXIII for the first time addressed this encyclical to "all people of good will" and not just to Catholics. It followed two Cold War events: the erection of the Berlin Wall in August 1961 and the Cuban missile crisis in October 1962. He insisted that peace must be founded on the social order established by God, an order "founded on truth, built according to justice, vivified and integrated in charity, and put into practice in freedom." He urged that the United Nations be strengthened and insisted that justice, right reason, and human dignity demand that the arms-race cease.

Papal Encyclicals Influenced by the Second Vatican Council

1967 *The Development of Peoples (Populorum Pregressio)*, Paul VI. Responding to the cries of the poor and the hungry and to victims of global and structural injustice, this is the first encyclical devoted to international development. Paul VI proposed a carefully thought-out theology of development for the poor nations of the world. He coined the phrase "development is the new name for peace." The root of world conflicts is poverty, the growing disparity between rich and poor nations that tempts the poor to violence and revolution. Paul stated unambiguously that "the superfluous wealth of rich countries should be placed at the service of poor nations." (49) He condemned the type of capitalism that "considers profit as the key motive for economic progress, competition as the supreme law of economics, and private ownership of the means of production as an absolute right that has no limits and carries no corresponding social obligation." (26) He called for "basic reforms" and the establishment of "an international morality based on justice and equity." (81) He urged Catholics to make a strong commitment to justice and human rights and to participate actively in the struggle for a more humane world.

1971 *A Call to Action (Octogesima Adveniens, The Coming 80th Year,* commemorating Leo XIII's *Rerum Novarum),* Paul VI. In this document Paul VI introduced several important new ideas to Catholic social teaching. Since economic problems call for political solutions, he encouraged individual Christians to become involved in the political struggle for social justice. He acknowledged that the pope and the Vatican do not have all the answers; local churches must have autonomy and freedom to act.

1981. *Of Human Work (Laborem Exercens, Doing Work),* John Paul II. As a worker in a stone quarry in Poland before he became a priest, John Paul II speaks from personal experience. In treating the dignity of work, he was concrete and specific: wages must be enough to support a family; working mothers should be given special care; workers deserve health care, right to leisure, pension, accident insurance, decent working environment; disabled people should be able to work; people have the right to leave their native countries in search of a better livelihood. John Paul strongly supported the right to unionize and while affirming the right to private property, he subordinated it to the right of common use. A detailed spirituality of work closed this remarkable encyclical.

1987. On Social Concerns (Sollicitudo Rei Socialis, Care for the Social Order), John Paul II. Written to commemorate the 20th anniversary of Paul VI's *The Development of Peoples,* John Paul called attention to the failure of development: the widening gap between the northern and southern hemispheres, the global debt that forces nations to export capital, unemployment and underemployment. Underdevelopment abounds because of East-West militarism, imperialism, neo-colonialism, and exaggerated national security concerns. He criticized the West for its growing selfish isolation and the East for ignoring its duty to alleviate human misery. In promoting the arms-race, both East and West contribute to the millions of refugees worldwide and to increased terrorism. He singled out "super-development" in the excessive availability of goods leading to consumerism and waste and called attention to the "structures of sin" and international trade that discriminates against developing countries. He emphasized that the goods of this world are originally meant for all.

1991. The 100th Year (Centesimus Annus), John Paul II. To commemorate the 100th anniversary of the church's first social encyclical, John Paul II reflected on the effect of the Church's social teaching on the events and trends of the past 100 years with emphasis on the collapse of socialism in Eastern Europe in 1987. He stated that the church's social teaching is an essential part of the Christian message. He reaffirmed the state's responsibility to establish a framework in law to conduct its economic affairs, the decisive role of trade unions in labor negotiations, and the church's preferential option for the poor.

2009. *On Human Development in Charity and Truth (Caritas in Veritate, Charity in Truth),* Benedict XVI. *Charity in Truth* is a sophisticated analysis of the global economy and a profound critique of the economic and business practices that led to the 2008 global financial crisis. Against the theory behind secularization in the Western world Benedict insisted on the practice of charity in truth, the truth that love permeates God's creation" and that faith in Jesus Christ is essential for building a successful social and economic order. He emphasized the urgent need of a true world political authority, the reformed and revitalization of the United Nations, solidarity with the world's poor and the moral obligation to help them. The encyclical condemned corruption, exploitation of workers, destruction of the environment, high tariffs by wealthy nations that shut poor countries out of the international market place, and the high cost of medications capable of saving thousands of lives of the poor. Benedict called for a "profoundly new way of doing business," a culture that welcomes and values every human life, and recognizes that "the primary capital to be safeguarded and valued is the human person."

Documents Inspired by the Second Vatican Council

1968. *The Church in the Present Transformation of Latin America in the Light of the Council.* Called by Pope Paul VI to apply the principles of Vatican II to the tragic situation of South America, the Latin American bishops met at Medellin, Colombia, and addressed for the first time a strong message to the peoples of Latin American in 16 areas: Justice, Peace, Family, Education, Youth, Pastoral Care of the Masses, of the Elites, Catechesis, Liturgy, Lay Movements, Priests, Religious, Clergy Formation, Poverty of the Church, Pastoral Planning, Mass Media. They stressed political reform, **conscientization** of all, end to violence and a far-reaching renewal of the Latin American Catholic Church.[5]

1979. *The Puebla Conference Document.* It confirmed Medellin's mandate for the Catholic Church to evangelize the poor, for liberation and the end to unjust structures, for the role of the Base Christian Communities and the vindication of liberation theology, and for the preferential option for the poor and concern for young people.

Inspired by Vatican II's *Church in the Modern World*, the National Conference of Catholic Bishops (NCCB, now U.S Commission of Catholic Bishops, USCCB) has over the years produced many significant documents. Two are particularly outstanding in their content and their method of bishops inviting experts to advise them and critique their various drafts.

1983. *The Challenge of Peace: God's Promise and Our Response."* This controversial document was the result of a long process of consultation with many groups, especially top U.S. administration officials and military and university experts. The bishops took on nuclear war "... a more menacing threat than any the world has known." They ruled out as morally unjustifiable the use of nuclear weapons against population centers, a retaliatory strike, a first nuclear strike.[6] They condemned the arms race as ineffective for peace, as inciting to nuclear use, and as ultimately taking money from programs to help the poor. They stated that the church's traditional just war theory cannot be applied to the massive destructive power of a nuclear war. The bishops developed a theology of peace from the Bible, from systematic and moral theology and ecclesiology, and from the experience and insight of Catholics in the peace movement.

1986. *Economic Justice for All: Catholic Social Teaching and the U.S. Economy.*[7]

This extraordinary document stressed that the basic norm for the health of a nation is how it treats its poor and powerless; that society has a moral obligation to ensure that no one is hungry, homeless, unemployed; that all citizens have responsibility for all members of the human family.

The bishops laid down six moral principles for economic life:

- Every economic decision and institution must be judged on whether it protects or undermines the dignity of the human person.
- Human dignity can be realized and protected only in community.
- All people have a right to participate in the economic life of society.
- All members of society have a special obligation to the poor and vulnerable.
- Human rights are the minimum conditions for life in community.
- Society as a whole, acting through public and private institutions, has the moral responsibility to enhance human dignity and protect human rights.

For these principles to become reality, the bishops called for interior *conversion* which they described as a profound "change of heart" (23), "to think differently and to act differently (25). They asked Catholics "to join with us in service to those in need. Let us reach out personally to the hungry and homeless, to the poor and powerless, and to the troubled and the vulnerable. In serving them, we serve Christ" (26).

The document contained memorable and eloquent passages and phrases: "Every perspective on economic life that is human, moral, and Christian must be shaped by three questions: What does the economy do *for* people? What does it do *to* people? And how do people *participate* in it?" (1) "We are called to shape a constituency of conscience, measuring every policy by how it touches *the least, the last, and the left out* among us." (Introduction 27) "... the justice of a society is tested by the treatment of the poor." (Introduction 16)

2000. *A Renewed Church in Asia: Mission of Love and Service.* Federation of Asian Bishops' Conferences (FABC). They presented a vision for renewal, discussed pastoral concerns, and introduced the "Triple Dialogue" with other faiths, with the poor, and with cultures as the church's way of evangelizing as a tiny minority throughout Asia.

Vatican II and Catholic Social Teaching

The council's new insights and attitude toward the modern world in *GS* brought about a change in the method of the church's social teaching which led to her new commitment.

A New Methodology

- "Viewing the church as the People of God." As constituting the church, all Christians have an active role in translating into action the church's social teaching as their vocation to carry out God's plan for the human family.
- "Reading the signs of the times." The events of the world both reveal God's presence in the world and show God's design for the world
- "Movement away from a narrow adherence to the natural law to greater reliance on Scripture." The Catholic Church's traditional stress on the absolutes of the natural law is replaced with an inductive, historicist approach to human experience, a shift of great significance for Catholic morality. The insights and justice-emphasis of Scripture have become the "new touchstone" of Catholic social teaching.
- "The primacy of love." Reason was the earlier shaper of Catholic social teaching. Now love, the heart of the virtue of justice, is the ultimate motive to act for justice.

- Emphasis on action. The starting point of pastoral and social reflection is people in their struggles, their needs, and their hopes resulting in practical action.

A Four-fold Commitment: to be a prophetic voice for Christian values in the world and an agent for the transformation of society; for the "humanization" of the world the church must work to bring about God's plan for humane living of all members of the human family; for world justice as expressed by the 1971 Synod of Bishops: "action on behalf of justice and transformation of the world (is) … a constitutive dimension of … the Gospel;" and for a preferential option for the poor. By reading the signs of the times that point to the suffering of the marginalized poor of the world, the church has given the highest priority to the plight of the poor.

Basis of Catholic Social Teaching

These seven principles form the foundation for Catholic social thought and teaching[8]

The Dignity of the Human Person. "In the Catholic social vision, the human person is central … The test of every institution or policy is whether it enhances or threatens human life and dignity." "Human dignity … is not dependent on race, creed, color, economic class, political power, social status, culture, personal abilities, gender, sexual orientation or any other dimensions by which people discriminate social groupings. There is a unique and sacred worth present in each person simply because he or she exists."[9] This sacred dignity conferred by God in creation demands full authentic human development that is social, cultural, political and spiritual. Both love of God and of neighbor are essential for full human development. Love of neighbor demands justice and involves respectful dialogue to address differences and conflicts. (*Populorun Progessio*)

The Dignity of Work. Work is the way persons express and develop their dignity. The purpose of work is to enhance the worker's human dignity, support his/her family, and increase the common good of the human community. Labor has priority over capital, people over profits, products, and production systems. Work is part of God's plan for human development and for the reign of God in this world. (*Laborem Exercens*) "In Catholic teaching, the economy exists to serve people, not the other way around."

The Person in Community. The human person is not only sacred but social. The human dignity of each person is best developed and protected in community with others as brothers and sisters, a community of relationships rooted in love and justice. This reality involves each person participating in attaining the common good of all, in liberation from the structures of sin like all-consuming desire for profit and thirst for power that destroy the common good of all. The Church despite its failures is meant to be a visible embodiment of the type of human community God is working in history to bring about - the reign of God. (*Populorum Pregressio*)

Rights and Responsibilities. "Flowing from our God-given dignity, each person has basic   rights... to freedom of conscience and religious liberty, to raise a family, to immigrate, to live free from unfair discrimination, to have a share of earthly goods sufficient for oneself and one's family, to life and to those things that make life truly human: food, clothing, housing, health care, education, security, social services, and employment. Corresponding to these rights are duties and responsibilities - to one another, to our families, to the larger society, and to work for the common good." Catholic social teaching emphasizes each person's right to private property but insists it is not an absolute right while so many persons lack the basics for survival and human development. The principle of subsidiarity must be respected whereby higher levels and governments may not interfere in what individuals and groups can do best by themselves; yet they should intervene when individuals and groups are unable to do so unaided.

Option for those in Poverty. Poor and vulnerable people have a special place in Catholic social teaching. Concern for people in poverty is at the heart of the Judaeo-Christian social vision based on the passionate voice of the prophets for justice and Jesus' vocation to "bring good news to the poor." The Church's "preferential option for the poor" involves a strong judgment against amassing great wealth as a result of an unregulated free market (Pius XI) and "inadmissible super-development resulting in greed and consumerism, the preoccupation with having rather than being."

Solidarity. Solidarity expresses the basis of the church's concern for world peace, global development, environment and international human rights. The core truth of Catholic social teaching is that we are all united as persons created by God. Solidarity means "we all belong to the one human family. As such we have mutual obligations to promote the rights and development of all people across communities, nations and the world ... In particular, rich nations have responsibilities to the poor nations and people with wealth and resources ... to those who lack them."[10] War is the ultimate destruction of human solidarity. Peace, the fruit of justice, exists when human solidarity is respected and lived. Peacemaking is the vocation of Christians.

Care for Creation. Catholic social thought has only recently addressed environmental and ecological concerns. Care for creation means Christians are called to be co-creators with God in the development of planet earth. This involves food production, water essential to human life and dignity, and chemical hazards. War, population growth, industrial pollution, poverty and the mal-distribution of the goods of creation contribute to the destruction of the earth. Rich nations must find ways to simplify their life styles and share with all peoples and future generations.[11]

Catholic Social Teaching Today

Challenges: Catholic social teaching must continue to evolve in order to meet the following pressing new realities of the post-modern world: a wealthy minority and the vast majority living in extreme poverty; governments captive to corporate wealth ignoring the common good; dominance of a single super-power and economic system; rising consciousness of the rights, talents and roles of women; global phenomenon of vocal, articulate social movements; violence of the powerless; transnational corporations beyond the control of national states and the United Nations; exclusive control by market forces over the common good.

The *Best Kept Secret* indicates specific goals Catholic social teaching needs to undertake to meet today's complex challenges.[12]

- The church needs "to develop more fully principles of good governance and subsidiarity" to address corruption and injustices and the new global phenomenon.
- "The Church's teaching in the areas of peacemaking and war needs renewal and reshaping." "The criterion for evaluating

the justification for war and the traditional principles guiding the waging of war need thorough reconsideration (as do) the economic and social costs of war and the arms trade."

- "The Church must respond to the insightful feminist critique that the anthropology upon which its social teaching is built is flawed." A prophetic statement with special significance today.
- "The Church must acknowledge that its social teaching has been dominated by Western European Christian cultural perspectives, values, principles and social constructs." "Cross-cultural and interreligious dialogue must shape future Church teaching on the social order."
- "The Church must develop its social teaching in more open, participatory and accountable   ways. Its methodologies must become more inclusive. ... Teaching intended for the universal Church needs to become more visibly the result of listening to the experience of all the local and regional churches."

An important challenge is for the Catholic Church today to practice in its internal life justice and subsidiarity, essential elements of its social teaching. According to South African Bishop Michael Donahue "applied to the Church, the principle of subsidiarity requires of its leadership to promote and encourage participation, personal responsibility and effective engagement by everyone."[15]

Accomplishments. Thanks to Vatican II's outreach to the world, Catholic social teaching has become a major influence in the life of the Catholic Church in the United States.

- Catholics have become "socially aware," concerned with justice issues at home and globally and sophisticated as to the causes of injustice, for example, the role of wealthy nations of the northern hemisphere through business practices of their transnational corporations. The U.S. Conference of Catholic Bishops' annual statements on important justice issues educate Catholics and press the Congress to support issues of justice.

- Sisters of religious orders and congregations lin increasing numbers have to live and work with the poor in city barrios and in mountain villages of Latin America.
- Individual Catholics, priests and lay people, are becoming social activists, protesting injustices locally and nationally; witnesses like Fr. Dan Berrigan, Dorothy Day and scores of lay activists were frequently jailed for their actions. Catholics of all ages, especially students, demonstrate annually at Ft. Benning, GA, to close the School of the Americas that trained Latin American soldiers who returned to torture and kill their own citizens. College graduates in large numbers volunteer for one or more years' service for the poor and for justice.[14]
- A significant change occurred from the pervading individualist morality and emphasis on sexual sins to a concern for justice, to recognizing injustice as gravely sinful, and to a global vision of human life on the part of the majority of Catholics.
- In Latin America, the Catholic Church shifted from bishops' alliance with the state and the wealthy classes to a voluntary renunciation of special privileges in church-state relationships. In many countries throughout the world the church has become the church of the poor. Pope Francis has emphasized in speeches immediately after his election his concern for the poor and his hope for "a church of the poor." See chapter 18.
- The church's commitment to justice caused tension, misunderstanding, and division within the church and criticism from the rich and powerful and from some conservative Catholic groups.
- In becoming a force for justice throughout the world, the Catholic Church has become a church of martyrs, particularly in Latin America. Priests, nuns, even bishops, and thousands

of Christian men, women, and children have been brutally murdered.

The Church's Commitment to *Social Justice*[15]

Catholic social teaching is ultimately about social justice as expressed in the statement of the 1971 Synod of Bishops. "Action on behalf of justice and participation in the transformation of the world fully appear to us as a constitutive dimension of the preaching of the Gospel, or in other words, of the Church's mission of the redemption of the human race and its liberation from every oppressive situation."

Justice means giving a person what is his or her due, that is, one's basic rights; *social* refers to the relationships between people in society. Social justice deals with the efforts of individuals and groups (governments, nations) to apply human and Gospel values to the structures and institutions of society. Social justice embraces a wide variety of issues in today's world: the contrast between rich and poor; international debt; oppression (colonialism and repressive governments) and struggles for liberation and freedom; violence and non-violence; disarmament; justice for women; racism; human rights (economic, cultural, social, religious); the population explosion; ecology; refugees; unemployment; alternate model of development from the capitalist model; the sex trade in human lives and justice in the church.

The U.S. bishops, in *A Century of Social Teaching,* issued this challenge to American Catholics. "Social justice ... takes flesh in our homes and schools, businesses and unions, offices and factories, colleges and universities, and in community organizations and professional groups. ... We are called to be a leaven, applying Christian values and virtues in every aspect of our lives."

Two Modern-Day Witnesses of Social Justice

Dorothy Day (1897-1980) is one of the most well-known 20th century social activists. She founded the Catholic Worker Movement and the *Catholic Worker,* a newspaper dedicated to teaching Catholic social justice, the plight of the poor and exploited, and the dignity to be afforded all peoples. She described the paper as meant to "comfort the afflicted and afflict the comfortable." She founded a "house of hospitality" to provide food and shelter in the slum neighborhoods of New York City and Catholic Worker communities dedicated to "live a simple lifestyle in community, to serve the poor and resist war and social injustice." A life-long pacifist, she opposed all war and the injustices leading to war. She led an early rebellious, bohemian life, had an abortion and later a child out of wedlock. Originally an agnostic, she experienced a spiritual awakening after the birth of her daughter and converted to Catholicism in 1927. Her former life and her dramatic example of holiness attract many to her life and work and who consider her a saint.

St. Alberto Hurtado, S.J., (1901-1952), devoted his life to the poor and disadvantaged people of Chile, especially the young as director of the Catholic Action youth movement. He opened shelters for poor and hungry children, called the *Hogar de Cristo* (Hearth of Christ), now one of the largest social justice organizations in Chile. He later turned his attention to labor rights and founded the Trade Union Association to educate labor leaders in Christian values. In addition to writing three books on Catholic social justice, he founded the periodical *Mensajero* that called upon the people of Chile to respond to the social problems and injustices of his day. Celebrated a hero in Chile, he was beatified in 1994 and canonized a Saint in 2005. In a letter just days before his early death, Alberto wrote "As I leave to return to God my Father, permit me to confide to you one last desire: that you strive to create a climate of true love and respect for the poor because the poor man is Christ. 'What you do to the least of my brothers, that you do to me.'" (Mt 25:40)

For Discussion

1. Do you think the Catholic Church's emphasis today on social issues is correct and necessary? Or should the church return to a greater emphasis on personal religious life of its members?

2. Is the criticism by John Paul II and Benedict XVI of the abuses of capitalism justified?

3. Do the wealthy nations of the northern hemisphere have a responsibility to the underdeveloped nations of the southern hemisphere? in justice? in Christian love? in solidarity with fellow humans? in practical self-interest?

4. Do you consider the practical suggestions made by the U.S. bishops in *Economic Justice for All* do-able and necessary?

5. What connection do supermarkets bulging with food and department stores with superabundance of clothes have to do with Catholic social teaching and justice?

Further Reading

De Berri, Edward; Hug, James; Henriot, Peter, Schultheis, Michael. *Catholic Social Thought, Our Best Kept Secret,* Fourth Revised and Expanded Edition, Maryknoll. NY: Orbis Books, 2003. The best available overview of the history of the Church's social teaching for students, teachers, lay people and clergy. It is an excellent introduction for anyone interested in learning about the important papal encyclicals and American bishops' contemporary social statements.

Himes, Kenneth R., O.F.M. *Responses to 101 Questions on Catholic Social Teaching.* Mahweh, N.J. Paulist Press, 2001. A readable question-and-answer format; an overview of major Catholic social teaching documents.

Mich, Marvin L. *Catholic Social Teaching and Movements.* Mystic, Conn.: Twenty-Third Publications, 1998. This introduction to Catholic social teaching makes it alive and describes the movements and people who embodied the struggle for social justice.

Neuberger, Anne E. *Introducing Catholic Social Teaching to Children with Stories and Activities.* Mystic, CT: Twenty-Third Publications, 2002. This is actually a great book for everyone! It has lots of stories of people all over he world living Catholicism's dedication to justice and the poor.

Stone, Elaine Murray. *Dorothy Day, Champion of the Poor.* Mahwah, NJ: Paulist Press, 2004. This fascinating new biography tells the story of one of the most significant, interesting, influential persons in the history of American Catholicism. With tact, truth and insight, the author recounts Dorothy's journey from wild and tempestuous youth, to conversion, radical activism and unceasing advocate for the poor and marginalized. A true story that is a delight to read.

Footnotes

1   Edward T. DeBerrie, with James E Hug, Peter Henriot, and Michael Schultheis, *Catholic Social Teaching, Our Best Kept Secret,* Fourth Edition (New York: Maryknoll, Orbis Press, 2003).

2   "Catholic social thought and teaching comprise a rich and textured faith response to the social challenges of contemporary life. It is a living tradition, evolving as people attempt to work out together ways to live their faith in meaningful ways." *Ibid.* 39. "It is a collection of key themes which have evolved in response to the challenges of the day." 14.

3   "The Church seeks but a solitary goal: to carry forward the work of Christ Himself under the lead of the Spirit. ... to carry out such a task, the Church has always had the duty of scrutinizing the signs of the times and of interpreting them in the light of the Gospel." *The Church in the Modern World (GS)*

4   *Catholic Social Teaching, Our Best Kept Secret* is the best available brief treatment of all papal documents from Leo XIII to John Paul II and a selection of the most important statements of national bishops' conferences. Most helpful is the brief outline of each document.

5   "Latin America appears to be living beneath the tragic sign of underdevelopment that not only separates our brothers and sisters from the enjoyment of internal goods, but from their proper human development. In spite of the efforts being made, there is the compounding of hunger and misery, of illness of a massive nature and infant mortality, of illiteracy and marginality, of profound inequality of income, and tensions between the social classes, of outbreaks of violence and rare participation of the people in decisions affecting the common good." *The Church in the Present Transformation of Latin America in the Light of the Council, 25.*

6   The bishops originally condemned the *possession* of nuclear weapons as deterrent against a nuclear strike. Under pressure from the White House and the Vatican which was pressured by German bishops, they modified their position to permit possessing nuclear weapons as deterrent *provided* a sincere effort is made toward full nuclear disarmament.

7   *Economic Justice for All* was a first in that the bishops held listening sessions across the country attended by economists, university professors, business executives and corporation presidents to comment on and criticize its second draft. This process, plus inviting experts to advise them, blunted the often-heard criticism that bishops have no competence to speak on economic issues. The bishops stressed they "speak as moral teachers, not economic technicians."

8   DeBerrie and others, *op.cit.,* "Major Lessons of Catholic Social Teaching," 18-34.

9   *Ibid.,* 20.

10   *Ibid.,* 30.

11   I*bid.,* 33-34.

12   *Ibid., 35-39.*

13   "Social Teaching Finds Church Leadership Lacking," *National Catholic Reporter.* Vol. 46, No. 20, July 23, 2010. Kansas City, MO 64111, 1,9-10.

14 One example, the Jesuit Volunteer Corps (JVC) whose apt motto is "spoiled for life." Young men and women live in communities in simple life style and serve across the United States and in foreign countries.

15 Some Catholics resisted the new emphasis on action for social justice desiring a return to individualistic piety geared toward personal salvation.

Chapter 13:
Liberation Theologies

The spirit of the Lord has appointed me to proclaim good news to the poor. He has sent me to proclaim release to captives and recovery of sight to the blind, to set at liberty those who are oppressed. (Luke 4:18)

"Liberation Theology is first and foremost a profoundly Christian protest against a world in which a pampered minority condemns the majority to a life sentence of misery and helplessness, if not to death. ... The issue is not socialism or capitalism, but rather life or death for millions of human beings."[1]

O ne of the most exciting and significant results of the new spirit engendered by the Second Vatican Council was the rise of liberation theology in Latin America in the early 1970's. It began as a result of the council's call to social action and new awareness of massive poverty and oppression and lack of the most basic human rights resulting in untold suffering and early death for the majority of the people, mainly indigenous groups made up of campesinos working the land or fleeing to the cities seeking work. It represented an extraordinary change in the Catholic Church from its centuries-long alliance with the state and the wealthy elite to a commitment to the poor and oppressed classes. As a result, liberation theologians and progressive church leaders criticized the prevailing economic system in Latin America as unjust and oppressive. Their criticisms also threatened the privileged position of the controlling wealthy classes. Those in power viewed these new Christian views and movements as allied to communist subversion. The military and right-wing death squads responded to this perceived threat by imprisoning and killing thousands of *campesino* leaders (catechists, delegates of the Word, teachers, health care workers, union leaders) and scores of priests and nuns, culminating in the assassination of El Salvador's Catholic Archbishop Oscar Romero on March 24, 1980.

The Second Vatican Council greatly inspired both liberation theologians and the oppressed poor of Latin America. The *Church in the Modern World* spoke of transforming the world and the mission of all Catholics to work for justice and human rights to achieve God's plan for all people, especially the poor. The *Constitution on the Church* gave the church a new name, the 'People of God,' with the result that oppressed *campesinos* realized perhaps for the first time that they too, not exclusively bishops and priests, are in fact the church and so began to act for their rights. According to Argentina liberation theologian Enrique Dussel, Latin America is "perhaps the continent where the council made the most profound and far-reaching impact."[2]

Liberation theology is enormously important. It has inspired a worldwide group of theologians concerned with issues deeply affecting people today. Alfred Hennelly believes they "represent the vanguard, the pioneers ... the cutting edge of a new Christianity for a new millennium." Their 'theologies of liberation' have created a "new consciousness and maturity" in today's Catholics and a new way to be Christian in today's world.[3]

This chapter has special relevance today as a dramatic example of how the Catholic Church and its leaders regain credibility when they put Gospel values first, read the 'signs of the times,' and listen closely to the people of God.

What is Liberation Theology?

Its *Nature*. The Brazilian liberation theologian Leonardo Boff states that the "starting point" of liberation theology is to experience compassion for the "suffering that affects the great majority of the human race." "Liberation theology was born when faith confronted the injustice done to the poor."[4] **Gustavo Gutierrez** defines liberation theology as "a way of speaking about God starting from the situation of the poor in history" and "a Gospel-inspired commitment to liberation of the poor and oppressed."[5]

How does liberation theology differ from traditional theology? Liberation theology starts from the real life situation in Latin America and asks how God and Jesus judge it, whereas traditional theology begins with God's revelation. Liberation theology moves to action to confront massive poverty and injustice and to change the structures of society that cause and perpetuate these evils. Inspired by Christian faith, its motivation is not secular but religious: to build the kingdom of God on this earth and to live God's preferential love for the poor and oppressed.

Its Definition. As *theology,* liberation theology is a reflection on the plight of the poor and oppressed based on God's special love for the poor in the Hebrew Scriptures and Jesus' concern for them in the four Gospels; as *liberation* it is a way to free the poor from their poverty, oppression, injustice, and institutionalized violence.

Its Goal. Liberation theology aims at nothing less than transformation of the present unjust society and the creation of a new society based on justice, human rights, equal opportunity, and participation of all members of society. Its goal is action done primarily by the poor themselves.

Its Three-step Methodology: social analysis to discover the causes of the real-life situation of poverty, oppression and injustice; *prayerful reflection* on the Scriptures and the four Gospels that reveal how God and Christ judge this situation and to learn what a disciple of Jesus should do about it; *Christian action* (*praxis*) to change the unjust situation. This same methodology of "see, judge, and act" is used by both professional liberation theologians in their writings and by uneducated peasants in the base Christian communities but in different ways.[6]

The Heart of Liberation Theology

The Poor. Liberation theology starts with the poor, those specially loved by God and Jesus Christ. The poor teach liberation theologians and pastoral workers what it is to be poor and oppressed, to be loved by God, to have Christian hope in a hopeless situation, to believe whole-heartedly in God's coming kingdom, to be strengthened by the resurrection of Jesus. One learns only by living with the poor. Preferential option for the poor is the foundation of liberation theology. Leonardo Boff explains that this option implies seeing social reality and history from the point of view of the poor; taking up their cause of lack of land, work, education, and protection of the law; committing to their struggles for justice; and recognizing that the poor must be the agents of their own liberation. [7]

Base Christian Communities (CEB's) is where liberation theology is lived and practiced. A CEB is a group of 10-15 poor persons, generally neighbors in a slum favella or barrio, who come together weekly to discuss their experience of poverty and injustice: hunger, expropriation of land by wealthy landowners, lack of running water, open sewage ditches, low pay, lack of jobs, babies dying of dysentery and malnutrition. They discuss a passage from the Bible to find God's judgment of these conditions and to discover hope and inspiration and then decide on a plan of action here and now. Most often their action takes the form of community organizing: developing food co-ops, communal soup kitchens, cooperative farming, recovering expropriated land, getting electricity and sanitation. Each time campesinos have risen up, especially in disputes over land, they have been violently repressed: their leaders pulled from their hovels at night, tortured, and left dead to intimidate the neighborhood; or they have simply "disappeared" never to be seen again. The CEB's are the core of the so-called "Peoples' Church" in Latin America as a result of Vatican II. Latin American bishops at their Puebla, Mexico, meeting highly praised the CEB's and encouraged their formation.

Awareness Raising. Illiterate *campesinos* "become aware" of the causes of their poverty and oppression and realize that God does not want this situation but rather that they act to overcome it. This **"conscientization"** has overcome their centuries-old **fatalism**.

Structural sin. Liberation theology recognizes that sin is not only personal but *social*. When the very institutions of society do violence to the poor (*institutionalized violence*) because they are essentially unjust, they are termed sinful because against God's plan for human persons. One of the major contributions of liberation theology is its emphasis on structural sin and its insistence that liberation and conversion must involve transforming the unjust institutions in a country.

Christian praxis. The major goal of liberation theology is *action* that transforms the unjust structures of society. It is *Christian* action because its motivation is the Christian faith: Jesus' gospel values of justice and love of neighbor, establishing the kingdom of God on earth, and God's preferential love for the poor. In a broader sense Christian praxis involves conversion of the elites and empowering the poor to be agents of their own liberation. Liberation theology stresses that *orthopractice* or correct action is, in the situation of Latin America, of greater urgency than *orthodoxy* or correct doctrinal teaching. For too long in Latin America the church's emphasis had been on doctrinal matters rather than a commitment to acting for justice.

Favored Model of Society. Liberation theology theoreticians criticize both the liberal capitalist system and collectivist socialism. Instead they favor a *participatory* democracy.

We turn to the dramatic events in Latin America in the 1970's and 1980's that gave birth to liberation theology.

Reality in Latin American from which Liberation Theology Rose

From the depths of the countries that make up Latin America a cry is rising to heaven, growing louder and more alarming all the time. It is the cry of the suffering people who demand justice, freedom, and respect for the basic rights of human beings and peoples. ... We brand the situation of inhuman poverty in which millions of Latin Americans live as the most devastating and humiliating kind of scourge. (Latin American Bishops at Puebla, 29)

Robert White, U.S. Ambassador to El Salvador, 1980-1981, described the typical situation throughout Latin America. "The social order ... rested on a tripod of the rich, the military and the church. The rich ran the country. They controlled it through the military and the role of the church was to counsel the poor to accept their lot and to wait for their reward in the next life.[8]

In virtually all Latin American countries we can distinguish five major actors.

The poor and oppressed. These are predominantly **indigenous** peoples: *campesinos* who work tiny plots of land in hostile mountainous areas; transient laborers hired by wealthy landowners to harvest seasonal crops; the urban poor who live in shanty towns without sewage treatment or running water in closely packed flimsy shacks along mud "streets" or clinging to steep hillsides. The poor live on the margins of society. They are the victims of planned illiteracy, lack of health care, little access to the legal system, subsistence wages. Hunger, disease, infant deaths and early death are their lot in life. Especially in Central American countries like Guatemala and El Salvador, to be poor was to be killed -- often whole villages at a time -- by the military or by the infamous "death squads." To be poor, in **Jon Sobrino**'s vivid expression, is to die! This oppression of the poor is no accident; the wealthy classes aided by the military maintained the poor in subjection in order to preserve their privileged life style. Liberation theology sought to change this.

The Oligarchy (literally, rule by a few). In most Latin American countries a small very rich elite controlled a disproportionate amount of land, power and wealth. Behind high walls and electronic gates, these wealthy landowners and industrialists lived in large mansions waited on by their servants; they enjoyed frequent vacations and shopping sprees in the United States and Europe; they sent their children to prestigious universities in "the States." They often controlled the government and were kept in power by the military. This wedding of government, military and oligarchs constitute what liberation theologians call institutionalized violence: the very institutions and structures of society meant to help and protect all citizens were deliberately utilized to exclude the poor and oppressed, thus doing moral and physical violence to them.

The Military. In Latin America the military had become a privileged class, wielding great power and amassing much wealth. Generals of the army became presidents of their countries and ruthless military dictators, like Stroessner in Paraguay, Pinochet in Chile, Somoza in Nicaragua. Alongside the military were paramilitary groups like the National Guard and the Treasury Police. Under the guise of fighting communism, the military and the military dictators conned the United States into providing millions of dollars to support their "dirty little wars" to make their country "safe for democracy." The military was often guilty of gross human rights violations: innocent peasants, campesinos, union leaders, catechists, delegates of the Word, university students, priests and sisters -- anyone guilty of "subversion" in seeking their basic rights, in educating the peasants, in organizing unions -- were tortured and murdered by the thousands. Torture and murder were commonplace in the 1960's and 1970's in Brazil, Argentina, Chile, Uruguay, Bolivia and in the 1970's and 1980's in El Salvador, Guatemala, and Honduras. In countries of Latin America -- a hopeful sign -- military governments have now given way to civilian rule, though the military still commands power to intervene.

The Catholic Church. From the forced colonization of Latin America by the Spaniards and Portuguese in the early 1500's and through most of its history, the Catholic Church has been allied with the state and the wealthy classes of Latin America. In return the Church enjoyed a privileged position in each country, the exclusive right to educate the young and to have priests' salaries paid by the government. Through this alliance the church "legitimized" unjust governments and the military in the eyes of both the rich and the poor. One such example: presidents were formally inaugurated at a grand pontifical Mass celebrated in the cathedral by a cardinal or archbishop who gave his blessing to the new president. Archbishop Romero broke this manipulation of the Church when he refused to inaugurate President Romero -- no relation -- with such a Mass in San Salvador in 1978. Rather than work for the transformation of society itself, the Church had encouraged the peasants to accept their cruel class position in life as God's will with the promise of reward in heaven. This attitude came to be known as **"fatalism"** and became the mindset of the peasants for centuries.

Vatican II and the bishops of Latin America at their meetings at Medellin, Colombia, in 1968 and Puebla, Mexico in 1979 changed this alliance. Both Medellin and Puebla admitted the Church's failures of the past and committed the church to conversion and a *preferential option for the poor.* The Puebla meeting referred to this dramatic change initiated at Medellin in 1968.

We affirm the need for conversion on the part of the whole Church to a preferential option for the poor, an option aimed at integral liberation (No. 1134). Bit by bit the church has been dissociating itself from those who hold economic and political power, freeing itself from various forms of dependence and divesting itself of privileges (No. 623).

In many countries of Latin America the Catholic Church became a force for justice and for the human rights of the masses of the poor; national bishops' conferences produced letters strongly critical of the wealthy elites, the unjust governments, and the military dictatorships. A graphic example of this new prophetic role of the church was in El Salvador where Archbishop Romero became "the voice of those who have no voice," tirelessly worked for human rights and social change, and courageously criticized the government, the military, and the wealthy class, pleading with them to be converted, to respect human rights, to "stop the killing." The result of the church's new role was the killing of "communist" priests and nuns, *campesinos*, various leaders of the poor and finally the murder of Archbishop Romero himself by an assassin's bullet while he was celebrating Mass.

291

Today the Catholic Church following Vatican II is the strongest influence for social justice and human rights in Latin America as its bishops, priests and sisters seek to defend the poor.

Great Powers of the Northern Hemisphere. Transnational corporations and banks, claiming to improve economic growth in Latin America, often had a reverse effect, impeding development for the majority of Latin American peoples and increasing their dependency on foreign investment. These corporations have made enormous profits in Latin America. In decades past, trans-nationals often dominated the local economies: Gulf and Western from sugar in the Dominican Republic, Anaconda and Kennecott Copper in Chile, United Fruit/Brands from bananas in Guatemala, and pharmaceutical companies by dumping drugs banned in the United States in various Latin American countries. As condition for loans, the International Monetary Fund and the World Bank demanded austerity measures that primarily hurt the poor. The already billions of dollars debt of most Latin American countries ate up a high percentage of their annual income to pay the interest, thus inhibiting economic growth and social programs for the poor.[9]

The past recent role of the United States in Latin America is generally not well known. The U.S. government supported with millions of dollars of foreign aid the military dictators of Latin American under the guise of fighting communism. In the School of the Americas in Panama and later and still today at Fort Benning, Georgia, the United States has trained thousands of Latin American soldiers who later became their countries' officers and generals responsible for terrible human rights violations. The painstakingly researched *Cry of the People* by Penny Lernoux gives in great detail this sordid picture country by Latin American country.[10] That this was a deliberate policy on the part of the United Stated is evident from the recommendation of "The Committee of Santa Fe" in its *A New Inter-American Policy for the Eighties* "U.S. policy must begin to counter ... liberation theology as it is utilized in Latin America by the 'liberation theology clergy." "Latin America is vital to the United States; America's global power projection has always rested on a *cooperative* Caribbean and a *supportive* South America ." [11] (emphasis added)

George Kennan, head of the State Department Planning Staff, *Policy Planning Study,* stated on February 23, 1948: "we have about 50% of the world's wealth but only 6.3% of its population. ... Our real task ... is to devise a pattern of relationships which will help us to maintain this position of disparity... We should cease to talk about vague and unreal objectives such as human rights, the raising of living standards, and democratization. The day is not far off when we are going to have to deal in straight power concepts. "[12]

In This Situation, the Catholic Church's Dramatic Change

Medellin, 1968.[13] Pope Paul VI asked all the bishops of Latin America to apply the teaching and spirit of Vatican II to the grave situation in each of their countries. They met in the city of Medellin, Colombia, in the late summer of 1968 and produced a call to action that has profoundly influenced the church and the political events of Latin America to this day. For never before in recent church history had the bishops of an entire continent spoken so forcefully and concretely about poverty, injustice, hunger, suffering, education, the daily needs of their people and committed the church to reform its structures and the "conversion of the clergy." Nor had the causes of such massive poverty and deliberate oppression been so clearly stated. Medellin thus shattered the centuries-old alliance of the church, the rich elites and the military. It committed bishops, priests, all Catholics to nothing less than the transformation of Latin American society. The powerful document produced after weeks of hard analysis of the gigantic problems of Latin American society and of the church itself was aptly titled *The Church in the Present-Day Transformation of Latin America in the Light of the Council.*

"Latin America lives under the tragic sign of underdevelopment ... a compounding of hunger and misery, illness of a massive nature and infant mortality, of illiteracy and marginality, of profound inequality of income ..." [14] (Bishops' opening statement)

The goal of the bishops' reflections was "to search for a new and dynamic presence of the Church" in this transformation (Introd. 8). Its "central theme" was " Latin American man (sic) who is living a decisive moment of his historical process." (Introd. 1) Its context was "The misery that besets large masses of human beings in all of our countries .... [which] expresses itself as injustice that cries to the heavens." (Justice 1)

The bishops were unusually blunt and specific in their analysis of the problems of Latin America and in assessing the blame. "Institutionalized violence" of colonial and present structures "seeking unbounded profits foment an economic dictatorship and the international imperialism of money." Both capitalism and communism "are affronts to the dignity of the human being" and are to be condemned as are "developmentalists" who place "more emphasis on economic progress than on the social well-being of people." The bishops blamed social and economic injustice on those with the "greater share of wealth, culture and power [who] jealously retain their privileges and defend them through violence" thus "provoking explosive revolutions of despair."

As the way out of this situation, the bishops insisted on the absolute need for conversion of heart. "For our authentic liberation, all of us need a profound conversion so that the kingdom of justice, love, and peace might come to us" (Justice 3). Earlier at Bogota, Colombia, Pope Paul VI had challenged the ruling class "What is required of you is generosity. This means the ability to detach yourselves from ... a position of privilege in order to serve those who need your wealth, your culture, your authority. ... Your ears and hearts must be sensitive to the voices crying out for bread, concern, justice, and a more active, participation in the direction of society."[15]

Nor did the bishops spare the church itself from this urgent need for conversion. In Chapter 14, "Poverty of the Church," the bishops stated: "We want our Latin American Church to be free from temporal ties, from intrigues and from a doubtful reputation; to be 'free in spirit as regards the chains of wealth'" (18). "We wish our houses and style of life to be modest, our clothing simple, our works and institutions functional, without show or ostentation" (12). "We the bishops wish to come closer to the poor in sincerity and brotherhood..." (9).

Puebla, 1979.   Eleven years later the Latin American bishops met again as a group in Puebla, Mexico. It appeared that a group of conservative bishops led by Colombian Archbishop Alfonso Trujillo, secretary-general of the Latin American Episcopal Conference, and the Roman Curia's Cardinal Sebastiano Baggio, president of the Pontifical Commission for Latin America, would condemn liberation theology and severely weaken the Medellin document and the church's commitment to justice and the poor.

However, the courageous speeches Pope John Paul II gave during his pastoral visit to Mexico immediately before the Puebla Conference profoundly influenced the bishop-delegates. To 40,000 Indians at Oaxaca the pope told them: "The pope wishes to be the voice of the voiceless. ... You have a right to be respected and not deprived of the little you have, often by methods that amount to plunder. You have a right to throw down the barriers of exploitation."[16] John Paul II boldly challenged Mexico's wealthy landowners:

For your part you have at times left the land fallow, taking bread from so many families who need it. Human conscience, the conscience of the people, the cry of the destitute, and above all, the voice of God and the Church repeat with me: it is not right, it is not human, it is not Christian to maintain such clearly unjust situations.[17]

To the Mexican workers at Jalisco the pope said a Christian "must be a witness and agent of justice" and stated "I want to tell you with all my soul and strength that I am deeply pained by the injustices against workers.[18]

The powerful statements of the pope, the behind-the-scenes papers of liberation theologians, and the strong leadership of Brazilian Cardinal Lorscheider, president of the Latin American Bishops' Conference, of Cardinal Arns, archbishop of San Paulo, Brazil, and of Panama's Archbishop McGrath so influenced the bishops that the final document of Puebla strongly recommitted the church to the poor and to human rights. It made the phrase "preferential option for the poor" a part of liberation theology vocabulary.

The Episcopal Conference of Latin America (CELAM) meetings at Santo Domingo, Dominican Republic in 1992 and at Aparecida, Brazil, in 2007 confirmed Medellin and Puebla and focused on the evangelization of Latin America, Christian culture, promotion of human dignity and development, ways of overcoming extreme poverty, and promotion of a Christian culture.

Opposition to Liberation Theology

When liberation theology broke on the world in the writings of liberation theologians and found expression among the masses in the "peoples' church" and in popular movements for justice, it soon provoked opposition by the dominant classes of Latin America, by economic and governmental interests in the United States, and within the Catholic Church by the Vatican resulting in two letters by Cardinal

Ratzinger of CDF. The following are the major criticisms with response to each.

Liberation theology is *not a true theology.*" Though it does not follow the method of traditional theology, it develops from the Scriptures a theology of God's preferential option for the poor, of Jesus' commitment to establish the reign of God, and of the Holy Spirit's presence in the struggle of the poor for justice and equality. It thus qualifies as a *bona fide* theology.

"It's *Marxist.*" This has been a too facile past complaint and was the concern and criticism of Cardinal Ratzinger in his first "Instruction on Certain Aspects of the Theology of Liberation" in 1984. This document, while legitimately warning of the dangers of Marxism, implied that any use of Marxist analysis is a dangerous embrace of elements of Marxist doctrine (atheism, class hatred, the necessity of violent revolution, one-party control and totalitarian rule). Though early liberation theologians used Marxist analysis to criticize the prevailing economic system and to emphasize the role of the dominant and proletariate classes, they did not espouse the atheistic and materialistic underpinnings of Marxism or its strategies of violence.

"It's *communist and subversive.*" The elitist oligarchies and military of Latin American countries, elements in the United States government and the economic giants with business interests in Latin America branded as communist and subversive liberation theologians and members of base Christian communities and of popular organizations. These could legitimately be termed *subversive* in that they joined in the struggle for a just society and the end to the institutionalized violence of the privileged classes and of the military. But the *communist* label was a momentous rationalization on the part of the elites and the military to justify massive injustices and murders by the "death squads." Certain U.S. government officials and corporation spokesmen used the communist threat to justify frequent military and political intervention in Latin American countries.

"It *incites class struggle, revolution, and violence.*" Though liberation theologians have spoken of the struggle between the dominant and the powerless classes of Latin America, they have rejected violence and revolution both as unchristian and as unworkable in the present situation of Latin America.

"It was *condemned by the Vatican and the Pope.*" John Paul II in his April 9, 1986 letter to the Brazilian bishops, stated "we are convinced, we and you, that the theology of liberation is not only timely but useful and necessary."[19]

"It *sets up a parallel church* hostile to the official hierarchical church." The Vatican and some traditional local bishops in Latin America felt threatened by the popular or "peoples' church" of the base Christian communities and by the scores of diocesan and religious order priests and nuns who worked and lived with the poor. Actually at stake were two different ecclesiologies. Some members of the Roman Curia and some local bishops thought in terms both of rigid authoritarianism, of power and control, and of the old alliance of church and state in which the Catholic Church received special privileges. The newer ecclesiology of the base Christian communities, of priests and sisters, and of Vatican II local bishops, favored Vatican II's "people of God" understanding of church in which all Catholics, including the hierarchy, are equal before God and *are* the church. However, the vast majority of the poor and of the priests and sisters working with them remained loyal and obedient to their local bishop and to the Holy Father in Rome despite disagreements.

Dramatic Examples of "Lived" Liberation Theology

The reaction to liberation theologians on the part of the privileged classes and government officials was tragically evident in the violence they inflicted on those who embodied in their lives the principles and goals of liberation theology

Perhaps the most dramatic example is El Salvador's Archbishop Oscar Romero, assassinated while he was celebrating Mass, March 24, 1980. In his short three years as archbishop, he incarnated to a remarkable degree liberation theology: his preferential option for the poor; his untiring struggle through his Sunday homilies and in all his actions as archbishop for justice, human rights, and the transformation of Salvadoran society; his appeals to the wealthy classes and the military to "stop the oppression" and make a profound personal conversion; his deep faith in the God of liberation as his constant religious motivation. As the death threats against him intensified, he said "If they kill me, I will rise again in the Salvadoran people." Indeed he has. His picture is found in the shacks of the poor everywhere in El Salvador and he lives in their hearts and minds as "Saint" Oscar Romero, "the voice of those who have no voice." "When I feed the hungry, they call me a saint," Archbishop Romero once said; "when I ask why the poor have no bread, they call me a communist."

Another example is the brutal murder by the government of El Salvador of six Jesuit priests, administrators and teachers of the University of Central America (UCA): Ignacio Ellacuria, president; Martin Baro, academic vice-president and social psychologist; Segundo Montes, head of the university's Social Justice Institute; Amando Lopez, Juan Ramon Moreno and Joaquin Lopez y Lopez, and their housekeeper and daughter, Elba and Celena Ramos. On the night of November 16, 1989, a group of uniformed Salvadoran army soldiers armed with M16 assault rifles entered UCA, went to the residence where six Jesuits were sleeping, and shot them at close range. A crudely scribbled sign was left next to their bodies, "See what happens to highbrows who upset people with dangerous ideas."

The Jesuits were killed by graduates of the 'School of the Americas' for "telling the truth, for [their] critical enquiry, investigation and analysis [of unjust social structures and the crimes of the military], for exposing lies, for freeing the truth from its repression in an unjust and oppressive society."[20] The strong words of Ignacio Ellacuria capture the Jesuit martyrs' commitment: "Christians and all those who hate injustice are obligated to fight it with every ounce of their strength. They must work for a new world in which greed and selfishness will finally be overcome."[21]

Other examples among many are those killed for being in solidarity with the "crucified poor." The American nuns Maura Clark, Ita Ford and Dorothy Kazel and lay volunteer Jean Donovan were raped and murdered by Salvadoran soldiers in 1980 for educating and working with refugees from the Civil War. In Brazil in 1988 Chico Mendez was killed for advocating for and organizing rubber-tapper workers. In 1995 Jesuit Engelbert Mveng was murdered while working with liberation theologian Jean-Mark Ela. In 2005 Sister Dorothy Stang was shot because she fought for land and the human rights of the Indians in the Matto-Grosso area of the Amazon. Kenule Beeson Saro-Weiva, Nigerian human-rights advocate, was killed while opposing the exploitation of the native Ogoni people. More than 100 priests and sisters and over 100,000 peasant men, women and children were murdered or disappeared for their fight for justice and basic human rights in Latin America.

Latin America Today

The situation has drastically changed. With the demise of military rule, most countries now experience varied forms of democracy. A new sense of independence from the United States has resulted from the Bolivarian experiments in Venezuela and Bolivia and the new democratic leadership in Uruguay, Chile, Argentina and Brazil. Yet Catholic social teaching has hardly filtered into the minds and attitudes of the wealthy classes who obstinately cling to their privileged positions, thus widening the gap with the poor. The significant number of Opus Dei bishops have tended to oppose liberation theology and the church's commitment to justice and the poor. Throughout Latin America the terrible shortage of priests and the huge presence of the Pentecostal/evangelical movement has provided a major challenge to the Catholic Church.

Yet liberation theology has proved a "well of hope" for the millions of oppressed poor in Latin America. Most Latin American bishops and the institutional church in Rome have officially adopted the "preferential option for the poor"; scores of dedicated religious and laity work with and for the poor resulting in a new appreciation of their popular religiosity. Women theologians have brought a new feminist perspective to liberation theology and more explicit awareness of the special oppression suffered by Latin American women from the *machismo* pervasive in Latin American society and from patriarchal structures.

Liberation theology has transformed the Latin American Church from a too-fatalistic, dormant, often superstitious Catholicism to a vibrant, dynamic, socially-conscious church. Youth especially have been attracted to this church of the Gospel and of action for the poor. Vocations to the priesthood became plentiful. No longer can religion be called the opiate of the poor. Scholar Jeffry Klaiber of Lima Peru indicated that religion has been rediscovered as a vital force in Latin American social and political life and that liberation theology has contributed to the democratization process throughout the continent and also challenged traditional theology.

It [liberation theology] stands as the most dramatic expression of the 'paradigm shift' brought about in post-conciliar theology.

301

It offers a way of doing theology that originates, develops, and culminates in response to the destructive experiences that characterize the lives of the majority of human beings: oppression, injustice, hunger and persecution -- life-threatening factors that are the result of social structures.[22]

The current challenge to liberation theology is how to carry out the option for the poor in the new social and political situations of Latin America and beyond. With the fall of communism, the failure of socialism, and the apparent global triumph of capitalism and a market economy, the "utopian ideal" of a modified socialism is no longer a viable alternative to liberal capitalism. Since the wealthy elites show little sign of conversion and the abuses of liberal capitalism weigh heaviest on the poor masses, the question today is how can liberation theology effect the transformation essential to lifting the poor masses. Violent revolution has been ruled out by all liberation theologians.

Though the work of Latin American liberation theologians of the 70's and 80's was criticized as being narrowly focused on class and economic injustices and neglecting race, ethnicity and gender, yet the methodology of liberation theology and its focus on the preferential option for the poor remains basic and has resulted in a flowering of liberation theologies throughout the world.

Theologies of Liberation Today

Latin American liberation theology has diversified into today's rich variety of *theologies of liberation* led by a group of theologians who "comprise one far-flung brotherhood and sisterhood with an unquenchable thirst after justice for all."[23] Their theologies of liberation deal with issues of economics and the environment, of race, gender and sexual orientation. They represent a wide variety of liberation theologies: Asian, African, Latin American, Hispanic, Black, Feminist and Ecological.

Asian Liberation Theologies.[24] According to Jesuit priest Aloysius Pieris, author of *Asian Theology of Liberation,* the Asian context of liberation theology is Asia's overwhelming poverty, its multi-faceted religiousness, and the reality that after 400 years evangelization Asia is only 3% Christian (including the overwhelmingly Catholic Philippines). Pieris is convinced that Buddhism is the way to understand Asian religiosity and that Asian liberation theology must be a way of living rather than an academic pursuit. Asian Christianity, he believes, must "be humble enough to be baptized in the Jordan of Asian religion and bold enough to be baptized on the cross of Asian poverty; ... the theology of power domination ... must give way to a theology of humility, immersion and participation."[25]

Chung Hyun Kyung focuses her attention on the Korean experience of women. In the Korean idiom, liberation is *Han-pu-ri.* Japanese occupation in World War II resulted in over 100,000 poor women forced into prostitution. Korean neo-colonialism in the 1970's exploited women textile workers. The goal of liberation theology is release from the bondage of Han, defined as the 'collective feeling of oppression and isolation in the face of overwhelming odds and injustice.

African Liberation Theologies. Fr. Benezet Bujo's book *African Theology in the 21st Century,* provides a comprehensive review of liberation theology as it is embodied on the African continent.[26] His basic question is "in which way can Jesus Christ be an African among the Africans according to their own religious experience.[27] The colonization and forced conversion of Africans to Christianity involved a systematic abolishment of traditional African culture and traditions.

Fr. Bujo suggests Jesus as 'Proto-Ancestor' and thus a model of morality for African men and women. The Eucharist as proto-ancestral meal must be the foundation of a church truly African. A true Eucharist vision of ministry leads to the destruction of all clericalism ... and to the abandonment of a pyramidal image of church in which the laity are treated as mere consumers and in which the proto-ancestral life of the Mystical Body cannot circulate.[28]

For the African to escape misery and inequality, silence and oppression, Fr. Jean-Marc Ela contends that African Christianity must incorporate the oral culture, traditions and symbols that form its cultural identity.

Contemporary Latin-American Liberation Theology. [29] The seminal contribution of Gustavo Gutierrez, the 'founder' of liberation theology, was to emphasize that the church's 'preferential option for the poor' embodies the Gospel emphasis on the spiritual and economic welfare of the poor. Thus liberation theology is a "reflection born of the experience of shared efforts to abolish the current unjust situation and to build a different society, freer and more human.[30] Poverty is not a factor of fate or bad fortune but a product of unjust political, economic and social systems.

The author of numerous books written from the situation of poverty and violence in El Salvador, Jesuit Jon Sobrino builds a liberation Christology based on his experience of the oppressed in Latin America as a crucified people who are liberated by the person of the crucified Jesus. In *Jesus the Liberator,* Sobrino stresses that the way God becomes known in this world is for Christians to become involved in the plight of the poor.[31] Liberation theology begins with entering personally into the suffering of millions of humans; its definition is "*love* seeking understanding."

Elsa Tamez, professor of biblical studies, is the best-known woman liberation theologian in Latin America. In her book , *Against*

Machismo, she criticizes sexism by Latin American men and the loss of "incalculable resources" by the marginalization of women.

American Liberation Theology.[32] The founder and leader of this theology is Martin Luther King Jr. thanks to Rosa Parks refusing to give up her seat reserved for whites in a Montgomery, Alabama, bus December 1, 1955. His liberation theology emphasized *praxis:* demonstrations, sit-ins, imprisonments, and many non-violent actions. His theology of liberation is clear in his eloquent speeches, especially his famous *I Have a Dream.* He had a profound influence on the misunderstood Malcom X.

Perhaps the most influential spokesman and champion of the black liberation theology in North America and beyond is James Cone, professor of systematic theology at Union Theological Seminary in New York City. He cites the civil rights movement and its two key leaders, King and Malcom X, as the originators of a "black theology." These two men, according to Cone, revealed that religion and politics could and should mix and that theology, which historically has been a theology of white oppression, needs to be reformed to allow the voice of a unique black reality and experience of God be heard. Cone explores how the experience of people of color in America remained largely ignored and that the first generation of Black liberation theologians have retreated from the 'radical race-critique' that true liberation from oppression demands.[33]

Hennelly considers that Robert McAfee Brown, former Professor Emeritus of Theology and Ethics at the University of California Berkeley, was "the foremost liberation theologian in the United States and perhaps the entire first world." In his usual graphic style, Brown made clear why liberation theology is not a major concern in the United States:

Liberation theology is about "the God of the poor" – and we are not poor. It's about "the view from the poor" – and we're on top. It's about "good news to the poor" – and that's bad news to the rich. It's about the third world – and we live in the first world. It's about social structures as carriers of evil- and those same social structures are very beneficial to us. (Hennelly 245)

With brutal honesty he said that we white males "must accept the truth of the charges that we have been overbearing, destructive, insensitive, sexist, and racist" and that "we must begin to find ways to redress the wrongs we have committed." (249) He listed what third-world Christians are saying to Americans.

They see the hand of our nation at work in such things as the legitimazation of conquest and genocide; the equation of faith with domination and oppression; puppet governments that falsely represent themselves as something other than what they are; forms of transnational capitalism that exploit rather than help the poor. (251)

Hispanic-American Liberation Theology.[34] Once Jesuit Allan Figuero Deck saw the 'preferential option for the poor' in practical, non-theoretical terms, "the poor stopped being more a socioeconomic category for me and became real flesh and blood."[35] For him the key to liberation theology is ceasing to see the minority as 'the other' but as a call to action in Christ's own ministry and crucifixion:

In baptism, the Eucharist and confirmation, we have all been called and chosen to follow that same loving Lord. ... [This] means loving our neighbor, especially the poor and vulnerable. So ... get down and dirty in the work of ... advocacy on behalf of and empowerment of the poor.(Deck 13)

The first wave of liberation theology largely ignored the voice and experience of women. Ada   Maria Asisi-Diaz explains that *Mujerista* theology ... gives a name and identity to Latin-American women and becomes Hispanic women's liberation theology.

> *Mujerista* theology encompasses the way grass-roots Hispanic women understand the divine and grapple with questions of ultimate meaning in their daily lives. ...Because *mujerista* theology is *praxis* (practice), it is the community as a whole which engages in the theological enterprise.[36]

Feminist Liberation Theology.[37]   Elizabeth Schussler Fiorenza is a Scripture scholar whose work is foundational to feminist theology. *In Memory of Her,* she analyzed the oppression of women in the Bible, concluding that the patriarchal biblical tradition needs to be re-figured in order to abolish the overtly patriarchal church hierarchy and society of today. (Hennelly 53-55) Rosemary Radford Reuther, author of *Sexism and God-Talk,* emphasized women's experience since traditional theology is based on male experience. The critical principle of feminist theology is "promotion of the full humanity of women." To dismantle clericalism in the church, she stressed the Gospel teaching of the ministry of service, not power and domination, in order to correct the androcentrism (focus on men) in Christianity and the resulting systemic and systematic oppression and marginalization of women often found in the church.

Professor Elizabeth Johnson analyzed speech about God in her book *She Who Is.* (Hennelly,71-80) She describes the fatal consequences of sexism and the fate of women "badly and sexually exploited, physically abused, raped, battered and murdered." (70) As a Catholic, she is concerned that "women do not participate fully in sacraments, in decision-making, in law and symbol making or in leadership roles ... including governance and liturgy." (74) She pointed out that one of the most powerful forms of patriarchy (father rule) occurs in religion because religion "claims its structure is divinely established and therefore beyond all criticism." (73) For her, liberation from sexism entails both men and women's voices to free the church from social and institutional structures that perpetuate oppression. Clerical domination must be replaced with a feminine-based community and clericalism with women's ministry.

Eco- Theology of Liberation.[38] Many consider the first eco-liberation Catholic to be St. Francis of Assisi. He preached and embodied in his life both the poverty of Jesus along with the unity of all creation, seeing God in every creature, treating the Earth in its entirety as sacramental in nature and viewing Earth as 'brother and sister.'

Modern ecological theologians can be seen as rediscovering Francis' legacy. The body of God is understood as the body of the world and the universe at large. Sallie McFague, professor of theology at Vanderbilt University, author of *Models of God: Theology for an Ecological-Nuclear Age,* proposes the theological model of the Earth as God's body, an understanding that fundamentally alters the way humans interact with the Earth. She stresses that the 'body of God' is not only *in* all His creation but also *is* all his creation. (Hennelly 279-88)

Roman Catholic priest Thomas Berry is considered one of the great pioneers of the ecological movement. His article "The Earth: A New Context for Religious Unity," illustrates the importance he attaches to a profound respect for earth. "…it is clear that the universe as such is the primary religious reality, the primary sacred community, the primary revelation of the divine … the primary referent in any discussion of reality or of value. (271)

In "Economic Systems: Its Effect on the Life Systems of the World," Berry describes what he terms "ecological Armageddon."

The air, the water, the soil are already in a degraded condition. Forests are dying … the seas are endangered. The rain is acid rain.

... an exhausted planet is an exhausted economy. ... Earth is a faithful scribe, a faultless calculator, a superb bookkeeper; we will be held responsible for every bit of our economic folly. ... Only within the ever-renewing processes of the natural world is there any future for the human community. (273-4)

As long as we use "the natural world [as] a resource for human utility, [and] not as a functioning community of mutually supporting life systems within which the human must discover its proper role," we invite disaster, he claims. We must "cherish the reality and nobility of the world *in itself*, not something to be used and exploited." (275-77)

Gay/Lesbian Theology of Liberation.[39] In *Liberation Theology and Sexuality,* Marcella Althaus-Reid explores those at the sexual margins ignored by Latin American liberation theologians of the 1970's and 1980's.[40] On one hand, the colonization and evangelization of the indigenous peoples of the Americas also included indoctrination on sexual mores. Homosexuality was linked with the worst of capitalism and against the giving of oneself in heterosexual family structures. Gay/lesbian liberation offers a crucial voice to this oppressed and marginalized community. Ignoring their voices is a failure to fully comprehend the complexity of standing in true solidarity with the poor and oppressed who experience the tensions of homo-phobia, domestic violence, and intolerance.

For Discussion

1. What is the "option for the poor?" Give examples.
2. Has liberation theology really accomplished that much to change Latin America society? To better the condition of the poor majority?
3. How have liberation theologies embodied the Vatican II imperative to read the signs of the times?

4. Do you think the widening fields of liberation theologies effect change in each of the groups?

Further Reading

Boff, Leonardo and Clodovis. *Introducing Liberation Theology.* Maryknoll, NY: Orbis, 1987. This book by the well-known Brazilian liberation theologians is a clear, readable explanation of questions tackled by liberation theology: oppression, violence, domination and marginalization.

Brown, Robert McAfee. *Liberation Theology: An Introductory Guide.* Louisville, KY: Westminster John Knox Press, 1994. An introduction to liberation theology designed for a reader with no previous experience of it. He weaves together personal stories, in order to illuminate theological and biblical principles behind the liberation theology movement.

Claffey, Patrick and Joe Egan, eds. *Movement of Moment? Assessing Liberation Theology Forty Years after Medellin.* Bern: Peter Lang, 2009. A collection of essays on how liberation theology has impacted the world since the Medellin Conference in 1968. Their focus is the importance of the 'option for the poor' today and current trends in Latin America, Asia, Africa as well as women's equality. Included is a timely chapter on Cardinal Joseph Ratzinger and his view of liberation theology today.

Lernoux, Penny. *Cry of the People.* Garden City, NY: Doubleday & Co., 1980. The sub-title, "United States involvement in the rise of facism, torture and murder and the persecution of the Catholic Church," states the subject of this carefully-researched and documented best one-volume book available on the struggle against the Latin American military dictatorships for human rights for the poor. A must read to understand this period.

Footnotes

1   Kevin O'Higgins. "Liberation Theology and the New World Order," *America* 163 (Nov. 24, 1990): 392.

2   Adrian Hastings, ed., *Modern Catholicism. Vatican II and After* (New York: Oxford University Press, 1991), 319.

3 Alfred E Hennelly, *Liberation Theologies, the Global Pursuit of Justice* (Mystic, CT: Twenty Third Publications, 1995), 336.

4 L. and C. Boff, *Introducing Liberation Theology* (Maryknoll, NY:: Orbis Books, 1987), 2,3.

5 Interview with Gustavo Gutierrez. "I Am a Christian First," *Maryknoll* (November, 1986): 14.

6 Liberation theologians use the social sciences (sociology, economics, political science) in their analysis. Initially they drew on *dependency theory* which viewed Third World underdevelopment as caused by economic policies that favor rich countries in the First World and on *class analysis* (drawing on Marxist analysis) that focused on the domination of poorer classes by elite oligarchies within Latin America. Later analysis broadened and qualified the sometimes over-simplicty of these initial constructs.

7 O'Higgins, *op.cit.*, 393.

8 Robert E. White."Romero Remembered," *Commonweal* (March 26, 2010): 7.

9 See Penny Lernoux, *Cry of the People,* (Garden City, NY: Double Day & Company, Inc., 1980). Chapter 7, "U.S. Capitalism and the Multinationals," *203-80.*

10 *Ibid.* Chapter 6, *"The Doctrine of National Security – the United States Teaches Latin American How," 155-202,* especially 152-66, "Grad School for Juntas" and 181, the "School of the Americas."

11 Lewis Tambs, ed. Committee of Santa Fe, *A New Inter-American Policy for the Eighties* (Washington, DC: Council for Inter-American Security, 1980). External Military Threat, Proposal 3, p. 14.

12 U.S. Department of State, *The State Department Policy Planning Staff Papers 1947-49,* Vol. 2, 1948 (New York: Garland Publishing, 1983).

13 See Lernoux, *Cry of the People,* 38, for an overview of the *Medellin* document.

14 *The Church in the Present Day Transformation of Latin America in the Light of the Council* (Washington, DC: U.S. Catholic Conference, 1973). Its 16 chapters treated in order Peace, Family and Demography, Education, Youth, Pastoral Care of the Masses, Pastoral Concern for the Elites, liturgy, Catechesis, Lay Movements, Priests, Religious, Formation of Clergy, Poverty of the Church, Joint Pastoral Planning, Mass Media. Each was considered from a three-fold perspective: "Pertinent Facts" or "Analysis of the Present Situation"; "Doctrinal Basis or "Reflection from the Bible" or "Church Teaching;" "Pastoral Planning" or " Guidelines" or" Recommendations for Action. "

15 Lernoux, op.cit, 37.

16 Ibid, 429.

17 Ibid.

18 Ibid.

19 "Pope's Letter to Brazil's Bishops," *Origins* 15 (April 9, 1986): 14.

20 Roger Haight, S.J., "The Jesuit Martyrs in El Salvador: Liberation Christology and Spirituality," 36.

21 Teresa Whitfield, *Paying the Price: Ignacio Ellacuria and the Murdered Jesuits in El Salvador (*Philadelphia: Temple University Press, 1995).

22 Jeffry Klaiber, "Prophets and Populists, Liberation Theology, 1968-88," (Lima, Peru: Catholic University Press, 1969)

23 Hennelly, op.cit., 7.

24 Key Theologians: Aloysius Pieris, Raimundo Pannikar, Chung Hyun Kyung, Kosuke Kayama, Choan-Seng Song.

25 Hennelly, *op. cit.,* 205.

26 Benezet Bujo, ed. , *Liberation Theology in the 21st Century (two volumes),* (Nairobi, Kenya: Daughters of St. Paul, 2005).

27 Hennelly, *op. cit.*, 162.

28 *Ibid.*

29 Key Theologians: Gustavo Gutierrez, Juan Luis Segundo, Jon Sobrino, Miguel A. De la Torre, Elsa Tamez.

30 Gustavo Gutierrez, *Theology of Liberation* (Maryknoll, NY: Orbis Books, 1973), Introd.

31 Jon Sobrino, *Jesus the Liberator: A Historical-Theological Reading of Jesus of Nazareth* ((Maryknoll, NY: Orbis, 1993).

32 Key Theologians: James F. Cone, Robert McAfee Brown, Jack Nelson-Pallmeyer.

33 James H. Cone, *Risks of Faith: The Emergence of a Black Theology of Liberation 1968-98* (Boston: Beacon Press, 1999), 133-35.

34 Key Theologians: Allan Figuero Deck, Ada Maria Asisi-Diaz.

35 Allan Figuero Deck. "Faith Doing Justice: Spirituality and Social Action," (USCCB Secretariate of Cultural Diversity in the Church , (February 7, 2010): 7.

36 Ada Maria Asis-Diaz, "*Mujerista:* A Name of Our Own," Christian Century, May 24-31, 1989: 560 ff.

37 Key Theologians: Elizabeth Schussler Fiorenza, Rosemary Radford Reuther, Elizabeth Johnson, Pui-Ian-Kwok, Delores S. Williams, Emile Townes, Jaqueline Grant.

38 Key Theologians: Thomas Berry, Sally McFague, Michael & Kenneth Himes, Chnng Hyun Kyung, Ivone Gebara, Leonardo Boff, Delores Williams

39 Key Theologians: Elizabeth Stuart, Marcella Althaus-Reid, Robert Goss, Ken Stone.

40 Marcella Althaus-Reid, *Liberation Theology and Sexuality* (Burlington, VT: Ashgate, 2006).

Chapter 14:
Living Ethically Today

You must love the Lord your God with all your heart, with all your soul, and with all your mind. This is the greatest and first commandment. The second resembles it: You must love your neighbor as yourself.

Mathew, 22:37-39

The service which moral theologians are called to provide at the present time is of the utmost importance, not only for the Church's life and mission, but also for human society and culture.

John Paul II, *The Splendor of Truth*, no. 111

Ethical existence is the highest manifestation of spirituality.

Albert Schweitzer

Many Catholics today feel the church is out of touch with issues of morality and sexuality. Her teaching is often considered rigid and closed. They wonder and discuss at length how the Catholic Church comes up with its answers to moral questions and whether there is any room for change. An urgent need is for the Catholic Church to develop a teaching on sexuality that is credible to her members today.

Yet, despite criticism, the church's moral tradition is rich. One of the great values the Catholic Church offers its members and the world is the effort of her teaching office to protect moral values important to society and to her members along with the pioneering scholarly research of her often beleagured moral theologians.

As we approach the emotional and divisive topic of Catholic morality, three realities stand out: The complexity of moral questions for which there aren't easy answers: war, economic issues, world trade, environment/ecology, life questions, justice, scientific research, bio-ethics, capital punishment, gay/lesbian relationships, pre-marital sex, in vitro fertilization, sperm and egg donation, stem cell research and surrogate parenting; the gap between official Catholic moral teaching especially in the area of sexuality and the beliefs and needs of Catholics, particularly the young;[1] and the role and scholarly work of professional moral theologians in addressing these issues and the resulting frequent tension with the church's teaching office.

This chapter treats the *nature* of moral theology, its professional practitioners and the church's teaching office that evaluates their work, and shifts in the *development* of moral theology the past fifty years. These provide the context for examining three concrete contemporary popular practices and four major life issues, each much debated with consequences for living ethically.

Morality and Moral Theology, Magisterium and Moral Theologians

Morality deals with what is right or wrong in human actions in the concrete situations of daily life. *Christian* morality discovers what is right or wrong by looking to Jesus Christ and his revolutionary teaching and actions. The good news Jesus brought to our world was *love* – love God and our neighbor as ourselves, our neighbor today being everyone, but especially those in greatest need: the poor, refugees, victims of war and natural disasters, racism and sexism, the sick and aged and those afflicted with AIDS, even our enemies. Ultimately, love is the norm for living ethically.

Moral theology is an academic discipline that seeks a systematic and coherent understanding of one's moral life and actions: a person's motivation, values and virtues, conscience formation, and principles and norms of action for ethical living. Specialized moral theology deals with particular areas such as personal, sexual, medical, bioethic and social ethics.

Since moral living involves a person's relationship to God and eternal salvation, the Catholic Church has both the responsibility and the authority to teach Christian morality. The church's bishops and the pope constitute its *magisterium* or official teaching office.[2] (See chapter 2) In practice, the Vatican Congregation for the Doctrine of the Faith (CDF) in Rome exercises this office through judgments and documents issued to the universal church on both doctrinal and moral questions.

The magisterium is assisted in this responsibility by the indispensable expertise of her *moral theologians*. These professionally-trained persons undergo a long education in basic doctrinal theology and Scripture, plus specialized study of sociology, psychology, cultural anthropology and in some cases economics and medicine, culminating in a doctorate in moral theology or Christian ethics. Drawing on these sources, they propose moral conclusions published as scholarly articles in professional journals or books which in turn are critically analyzed and debated by other moral theologians. The resulting consensus is evaluated by CDF and becomes Catholic teaching in documents issued by the pope or CDF and by individual bishops.

Many mistakingly believe the church's moral teaching is permanent and infallible with no room for change or discussion. However, the church's *ordinary* magisterium, the day-to-day teaching of bishops and the pope, can be incomplete and even erroneous, as church history testifies, and admits responsible disagreement, termed dissent, by moral theologians and by knowledgeable conscientious Catholics. Examples from the past are usury, slavery, religious freedom, and marriage. This kind of responsible questioning is the way change and progress have occurred throughout the church's history. For Catholic ethical living is a journey of faith and grows and develops through the process of mature reflection on life as lived in today's world in the light of Jesus teaching and example.

The importance of moral theologians cannot be exaggerated. They study today's urgent moral questions in depth; they formulate responsible and credible moral judgments, assist church leaders establish moral policy, initiate needed change, and help Catholics make responsible conscience decisions, develop moral character and grow into moral adulthood. That moral theology has undergone development and change as it meets new questions often creates tension with the Church's magisterium.

Before and After Vatican II: Major Shift in Morality

Catholic moral theology is to a great extent based on the **natural law** tradition which recognizes an objective moral order as a human participation in God's eternal law accessible to human understanding by reason. It is considered a universal, objective norm of morality grounded in human nature, reason and God's creation. Before Vatican II, a physicalist interpretation of natural law dominated Catholic moral theology which portrayed human nature and moral action as fundamentally non-changing and static with clearly drawn lines of what constitutes right and wrong in a given situation.[3] Accordingly, by analyzing the physical laws of nature created by God, one is able to deduce what is morally right or wrong. In this approach, to use a contraceptive in sexual intercourse is judged to be morally wrong because it frustrates the God-ordained purpose of the sexual power to procreate life and is therefore intrinsically (of their very nature) evil and does not allow exceptions. Likewise masturbation, homosexual acts, and artificial insemination are judged intrinsically disordered.

In the years before the Second Vatican Council, a group of moral theologians recognized the limitations of this approach and proposed a new methodology called contextual ethics. Redemptorist Bernard Haring in his 1954 three volume *The Law of Christ* based moral theology on Scripture and the primacy of love and shifted the focus from law to the moral agent, the person making moral decisions. Jesuit Joseph Fuchs, professor of moral theology at Rome's Gregorian University, shaped contemporary moral theology by proposing that an action can only be judged moral or immoral by considering its total context: the person's intention in acting and all the circumstances and consequences coming from that action, thus rendering the concept of intrinsic evil problematic.[4]

Evaluation:[5] Contextual ethics provided reasonable common-sense judgments that render Catholic moral teaching more credible to contemporary people. Its critics, however, point out the danger of abuse, rationalization, and relativism and the difficulty of judging which circumstances/consequences are sufficient to justify actions like pre-marital sex, contraception, homosexual actions. Traditional Catholic morality gives clear concise answers presumably available to all. Its disadvantage is its inability to deal adequately with complex moral questions involving both values and disvalues.[6]

The Second Vatican Council encouraged an *historical* and *personalist* approach rather than the classical emphasis on unchangeable eternal truths, thus opening the door to change, especially in regard to natural law ethics. By stressing Scripture and Gospel values, particularly love rather than law as the source and norm for Christian morality, and by following John XXIII's distinction between the substance of faith and various ways it can be presented, the council accepted a pluralism of theologies.

Moral theologians who follow contextual ethics have been called revisionists. We consider how traditionalist and contextual ethicists give different moral judgments to three current hot-button moral issues.

Contraception in Marriage. Pope Paul VI issued his controversial letter *Of Human Life* in 1968. Popularly known as "the birth control encyclical," it is in fact a beautiful tribute to conjugal love and contains much valuable teaching and a sensitive concern for couples. Its controversial teaching is contained in one sentence: "The Church, calling men [sic] back to the observance of the natural law, teaches that each and every marriage act must remain open to the transmission of life." Thus "the direct interruption of the generative process already begun ... (is) to be absolutely excluded as licit means of regulating birth."[7] Contraceptive use in heterosexual sexual intercourse is thus to be considered an intrinsically evil act.[8] This teaching caused personal and social upheaval among Catholics unable to accept its reasoning as contrary to their married experience.

Moral theologians of the revisionist school were unable to agree with the above reasoning. They argued that the *total* married life of the couple should be open to procreation, not *each and every act* of intercourse. Thus a couple's reason or intention for using contraceptives based on all the circumstances of their life determines the morality rather than the individual physical act. Moreover the spouses' consciences must be respected as stated in the majority report of the commission established by John XXIII and Paul VI to study contraceptive use in marriage. [9]

A problem arises with both artificial contraception and *committed* pre-marital intercourse.[10] The church's teaching magisterium states that the use of the sexual faculty is limited only to a heterosexual couple who ensure that the conjugal act remains physically open to the possibility of procreation, the key element. Therefore, anything that physically obstructs this possibility is considered against nature and intrinsically disordered, such as fornication, masturbation, artificial insemination, in-vitro fertilization, and is judged morally illicit.

Pre-Marital Sex. Both traditionalists and revisionist moral theologians condemn casual pre-marital sex as lacking personal commitment and self-giving love, thereby incapable of expressing God's covenant love and Jesus' total self-giving love for his church. Concerning pre-marital intercourse, contemporary sexual ethics distinguishes non-marital (sexual activity outside marriage without intention to marry, termed casual sex or "hooking up") and formal pre-marital sex (sexual activity of the couple who fully intend to marry but are unable to do so for a variety of reasons.)

Because of disagreements over the moral analysis of some uses of artificial contraception and the fact that Catholic couples of child-bearing age practice contraception at the same rate as non-Catholics, as recent polls indicate, some contemporary moral theologians question whether in God's eyes each and every instance of artificial contraception is immoral. Some other theologians, though fewer, would argue that when a couple finds it impossible to marry at this particular time, pre-marital sex of a truly mature, sincere couple genuinely committed to each other and seriously intending to marry, should not be considered constituting moral evil or sin.[11]

Homosexual Activity. On many levels, this is a profound challenge to Catholic moral theology. Though the Catholic Church makes clear that homosexual *orientation* is in no sense sinful and strongly condemns any discrimination against homosexuals, gays and lesbians were incensed when the church termed homosexual orientation "disordered." Other Christian churches fully welcome active homosexuals; the Episcopal Church USA even accepts for ministry *active* gay and lesbian priests and recently two bishops, thus posing an obstacle to future union with the Catholic Church. Same sex marriage is gaining support in the United States and is lawful in some states and in other countries.

Moral theologians recognize that very many gay and lesbian Catholics are sincerely convinced in their own conscience that their love in a stable relationship is ennobling, contributing to their growth as persons, and that consequently their sexual activity is acceptable to God who gave them their sexual orientation. By respecting their good intention and these circumstances, revisionist theologians judge that moral evil or sin should not be imputed to them. However, revisionists do admit the existence of non-moral or pre-moral evil,[12] a disvalue or lack of the good that ought to be present, since homosexual activity cannot achieve the full values of heterosexual relationships in marriage.

Traditional moral theologians argue that such circumstances have no moral bearing since homosexual acts are against God's plan for human sexuality and are intrinsically evil.

A Catholic Theology of Human Sexuality

Polls increasingly indicate that large numbers of Catholics do not accept Catholic teaching on sexuality in the areas of contraceptives, pre-marital sex, and homosexuality. Yet, when expressed in positive terms, the Catholic vision of sexuality is appreciated and valued, especially in today's culture of gratification, easily available sex, promiscuity and infidelity, with all the heartaches and ruined lives that result. In this context, the Catholic theology of human sexuality is a noble ideal and of great value to people today who are yearning for meaning and happiness in their lives.

The Christian theology of sexuality is rooted in the basic Christian doctrines of the Trinity (God is an eternal love relationship of three divine persons), in the Incarnation (God taking flesh in Jesus reveals that our human sexual nature is good), the Resurrection (our bodies have the eternal destiny of risen life), and Original Sin (as weak sinners we need to control our strong sexual desires). Thus the key question in judging the morality of sexual acts is "How I use my God-given gift of sexuality so as to relate most responsibly to God, to myself and to others?" Accordingly, the basic moral criterion for sexual activity is "responsibility in relationships" based on self-giving love.

The Catholic teaching toward sexuality is that genital sexual activity is expressed and protected in the stable, faithful, permanent union of a *sacramental* marriage publicly witnessed between a man and a woman. The Catholic vision of sexuality and of marriage as sacrament is attractive and life-giving: the married couples' mutual sexual activity is sacred mirroring Christ's total sacrificial love for his Christian people and a rich source of God's grace helping them love unselfishly and faithfully on their journey of love.

Discerning Catholics today realize that there is a critical need for a theology of sexuality that is credible for today's educated, responsible, devoted Catholics, one that corresponds to their lived experience and that can gain a hearing from alienated Catholics. A number of recent articles and books attempt to supply this need by exploring sexuality, love and relationships.

Pope John Paul II Responds to Moral Theologians

John Paul II issued *Veritatis Slendor* (*The Splendor of Truth*) in 1993 to affirm the Church's traditional position on morality. Subsequent commentators[13] suggested that the encyclical's underlying purpose was to support and safeguard the encyclical *Of Human Life* and its condemnation of contraceptive use as intrinsically evil. The following are major emphases of *Veritatis Splendor (VS).*

- The goodness or evil of a human act depends "primarily and fundamentally" on its object, on the action chosen, and not on the person's intention or on the circumstances and consequences of the acts.[14]
- Intrinsically evil acts "are such always ... •Intrinsically evil acts "are such always ... on account of their very object and quite apart from the ulterior intentions of the one acting and the circumstances." VS 50
- The encyclical does not reduce the natural law to "bodily physical acts" or "mere biological laws." VS 47
- The subjective conscience may not decide what is good or bad; only an informed conscience can do so. VS 57-61
- *VS* reaffirms the possibility of mortal sin in particular human acts that do not involve one's **fundamental option**.[15] VS 70
- The role of moral theologians is to explain and support the church's magisterium in its moral teaching. VS 110   Public dissent is to be avoided. VS 113

The concern of the encyclical was to reject an alleged relativism and a subjective morality by stressing rather a morality based on the *object* of human acts and to affirm the reality of intrinsically evil acts and the authority of the magisterium to speak on morality.

Reaction to the Encyclical. There was "a hearty welcome by the [Catholic] hierarchy and others who found it a worthy challenge to the pervasive culture of contemporary moral relativism." Revisionist moral theologians, however, felt their positions were not understood or adequately presented and noted that not a single erring theologian was identified. They strongly rejected the charge that they were teaching moral relativism. They rightly saw the encyclical as returning to the traditional classical **manualists'** position of universal, unchanging absolute principles, rather than the Vatican Council's historicist, personalistic approach.

They pointed out that "what distinguished (them) from the magisterium were "philosophical," not theological issues, and that "their disagreements concerned method in general and intrinsic evil in particular."[16]

Though the encyclical was a strong defense of traditional Catholic moral teaching and a rejection of the contextual ethics methodology, the indispensable role of moral theologians to develop a coherent moral theology for the benefit of the Church and for guiding conscience decisions of mature Catholics remains intact. *Veritatis Splendor* deserves respect as an authoritative teaching of the church's magisterium. It is not infallible teaching. Some of its positions depend on human reasoning and may be incomplete, thus open to further development. Its success or failure depends on its *reception*[17] by the entire church including moral theologians, since reception by a significant majority of the church may be indicative of the Holy Spirit speaking through the people of God and an expression of the 'signs of the times.'

The magisterium may need to explain more persuasively why some acts are intrinsically evil and to indicate more clearly those situations where intention, circumstances and consequences do in fact play a part in influencing the morality of human actions. It may need to consult more broadly and in a collegial manner with the bishops of the world and with moral theologians from a wide spectrum in reaching its moral conclusions. It may also need to state its teaching in less certain assertions for the sake of its own credibility.

Revisionist theologians may also need to re-evaluate some of their positions, to present more carefully how their writings are understood, and to bridge the gap between themselves and the magisterium.

Shift to Theological Ethics

After Pope John Paul II's critique of contextual ethics in *VS,* Catholic moral theologians, now termed theological ethicists, sought "to maintain a critical fidelity to church teaching while honoring the experience of the laity"[18] and began to consider a broad array of society's ethical questions. Moral theologizing became global. Theological ethicists from Latin America, Africa, Asia and the United States address such urgent problems in their own countries as oppression and crushing poverty, HIV/AIDS, wars, plight of refugees, social inequality, environment/ecology, racism, economic injustice, bioethics. Liberation and feminine theologies also play a large role in ethical discussions today.[19]

In searching for fresh ways to consider these issues, these ethicists turned to new ways of theologizing: virtue ethics, social ethics, bioethics, marriage ethics, economic ethics, and so forth. In the area of sexuality, for example, Catholic ethicists engage in a wide-ranging discussion that "remains faithful to the Catholic tradition" while at the same time promoting "a robust, publicly responsible and theologically credible sexual ethics." Aware that "the non-reception of church teaching on sexuality damages (its) overall credibility," today's Catholic ethicists are not attempting to articulate an opposite magisterium on sexual ethics but "to explore ethical frameworks that can bring sexuality into a more responsible social context."[20] Their goal is to develop a credible sexual ethics capable of bridging the gap between the magisterium and the majority of Catholics.

In the case of marriage, theologian Lisa Sowle Cahill finds that contemporary ethicists appreciate the "traditional Catholic values of commitment and monogamy, openness to procreation and parental responsibility ... Yet they typically do not focus on debates about specific moral norms for sexual acts, on birth control or on indissolubility ... to formulate a fresh perspective about the theology and ethics of marriage."[21]

In his report "The Open Debate: Moral Theology and the Lives of Gay and Lesbian Persons," theologian James Keenan observes that "moral theologians do not superficially validate personal life styles but rather propose a variety of criteria for assessing the morality of the way ordinary gay and lesbian persons live their lives. The debate [reveals] that the Catholic tradition is rich, human, and capable of being relevant to help gays and lesbian persons find moral ways of living out their lives and the ways they are called to love." Gays and lesbians "help us see that by silencing and marginalizing them, we do harm to them, to ourselves, to the Church and to the Gospel."[22]

Moral theologizing has now become global, part of a "new Catholicity." Six hundred Catholic ethicists and moral theologians, including 200 theologians from the developing world and 89 female theologians representing four continents and 73 countries met in Trent, Italy, July 24-27, 2010 as part of "Catholic Theological Ethics in the World Church. (CTEWC) A subsequent meeting sponsored by CTEWC of Catholic African theologians met 2012 in Nairobi to discuss reconciliation, justice, peace and feminism in the context of Africa.[23]

Four Moral Questions concerning the Sacredness of Human Life

The Catholic Church is today a strong defender of human life in all its manifestations from "womb to tomb." She insists that every human life is sacred because created by a loving God who alone has authority over life and death. It sometimes appears that the church is fighting a losing battle against the assault on human life which has reached epidemic proportions and is often carried out without remorse and guilt or with rationalization and questionable justification. The moral questions concerning human life are complex and becoming increasingly so with each new scientific and medical-biological discovery. Reflection on the goal and purpose of human life and the shifts to contextual ethics and new ways of theologizing cast new light on these four urgent moral issues dealing with human life today.

Abortion. Abortion has become such a highly-charged emotional question that a calm rational treatment is extremely difficult. Without attempting to deal with all the complex issues, we limit ourselves to three points: the contrasting views of pro-choice and pro-life advocates, four clarifying data considered by moral theologians, and a nuanced position of a growing number of Catholic moral theologians.

We distinguish the legal and moral questions. The *legal* question was established in January, 1973, when the United States Supreme Court ruled that an anti-abortion law "that excepts from criminality only a life-saving procedure on behalf of the mother without regard to pregnancy stage and without consideration of the other interests involved" is unconstitutional. A practical effect of this ruling was abortion-on-demand up to the third trimester of pregnancy. The *moral* question for Catholic Christians is what is morally right or wrong according to the church's teaching and principles elaborated by its moral theologians.

In general, pro-choice advocates see abortion as a question of women's rights against a background of social problems.

Anti-abortion laws are thought of as unjustifiable restriction on the personal freedom of pregnant women. Abortion itself is seen as a potential safeguard of the life, health, or convenience of pregnant women, and at the same time as easing social problems resulting from overpopulation and the birth of unwanted and defective offspring. Abortion is often evaluated as a birth control measure and justified on grounds similar to those applied to contraception. Like contraception, abortion is considered a matter to be determined by private moral decision, although it is recognized to have important consequences for society as a whole. Moreover, entrusting abortion to the mother's decision on her doctor's advice is regarded as fair to all religions and ethical differences since no one is obliged to act contrary to his own conscience or creed.

Catholics in the pro-life movement take an entirely different position.

Basic to the Catholic position was the question of the rights, not of the pregnant woman, but of what Catholics generally were careful to call 'the unborn child,' in contrast to their opponents who were equally careful to refer to it as "the fetal tissue." For Catholics the abortion question has always been regarded primarily, and almost exclusively, as a question of the right to life [of the unborn child].[24]

Archbishop John Quinn of San Francisco called attention to the "dehumanizing effect" of abortion in a 1992 homily.

It is a shocking blow to one of the tenderest and deepest and highest of all human instincts, the love of a mother for her child. It shapes, nurtures and expresses the psychology of violence. It is one of the most violent acts imaginable: the destruction of the utterly help-less human child in the sanctuary of the mother's womb.
All science confirms the fact that the life in the womb is human life: genetics, comparative anatomy, biology, physiology. Morality and science converge in the judgment that those who exercise the choice for abortion are in fact exercising the choice to destroy innocent human life.[25]

Olivia Gans, herself a mother, looks at another aspect of abortion in American society today: its "seductive power."

The lure of abortion stems from our society's desire to avoid responsibility, collectively and individually, for our actions and attitudes. Its seductive power is its promise to eliminate a "problem" neatly and simply, as if that problem -- the child -- never existed. ...The greatest feat of abortion on demand has been to make American society content -- if uneasily so -- with accepting death as a way to solve problems. All across the United States there are basically good people who feel that abortion is not good but that nothing else can be done when a mother is poor or a baby is severely handicapped, or the result of rape or incest.[26]

Because the Catholic Church champions human life, it has steadfastly opposed abortion. Yet, complex questions are involved which defy black and white solutions. The church's moral theologians in trying to reach a consensus on such questions consider the following data:

- Catholic scholastic philosophy holds that "a human *person* is constituted by the infusion of a spiritual soul into an appropriate body." It is, however, impossible to determine the exact moment when this occurs.
- From the moment of conception when sperm and egg are united, *human life* begins with all genetic material present. For this reason Vatican II could state that "from the moment of its conception, life must be guarded with the greatest care."[27] However, over 50% of fertilized eggs are not implanted in the womb and come to term. Are these to be considered deaths of human *persons*?[28]
- Catholic moral theology has traditionally rejected *direct* abortion (the deliberately intended destruction of the fetus) while permitting *indirect* abortion (removing a cancerous womb or an ectopic pregnancy to save the mother's life with the non-directly intended result of the death of the child). This is an application of the double effect, that is, the good effect (mother's life) is intended while the bad effect (death of child) is reluctantly permitted.

- The phenomenon of twinning (a fertilized egg divides into two) and combining (two   fertilized eggs become one) that can happen up to 14 or more days after conception. It is difficult philosophically to conceive of one distinct *individual* human *person* dividing into two or of two human *individuals* fusing into one.

Accordingly, the position of some Catholic moral theologians is to permit a *direct* abortion up to two weeks after fertilization for a proportionately serious reason like rape or incest or the mother's life. Reasons such as economic considerations, one's reputation or convenience, the poor timing of a pregnancy, and so forth, are not proportionate reasons for terminating human life. Concerning aborting a deformed fetus or defective child, most moral theologians see no justification for aborting, for example, a fetus with Downs Syndrome.

The complexities of the abortion issue for practicing Catholics made national headlines in 2009 when Sr. Margaret McBride, a Catholic nun working in St. Joseph's hospital in Phoenix, Arizona, was excommunicated by her local bishop for allowing a patient who was gravely ill to have an abortion 11 weeks into her pregnancy. Her prognosis was an almost 100% chance of death if she tried to carry her child to term, resulting in both her and her child dying. The bishop's action led to criticism from both moral theologians and canon lawyers. Ordinary church goers and many in the general public viewed this as grossly punitive. As a result of this case, on December 21, 2010, Phoenix Bishop Thomas Olmsted formally withdrew the 'Catholic' status of St. Joseph's Hospital.

The Terminally Ill. If human life is sacred in its beginning, it is equally so in its final stages. Today as people live longer or are kept alive by artificial means, strong emotional arguments are increasing for *active* **euthanasia** in the case of elderly and senile persons or those in a vegetative state or those who suffer terribly and plead to be released from their misery. The church has always condemned active euthanasia, deliberately causing death by lethal injection or excessive sleeping pills or other means. Moral theologians point to the fact that God alone has dominion over life and death; moreover, they rightly fear the abuses that would likely follow from legalizing active euthanasia, thus giving humans power over life and death. The memory of Nazi extermination camps and scientific experimentation still haunts the human family.

However, in the case of patients in a permanent vegetative state (PVS) kept alive by artificial life support systems, moral theologians have permitted allowing a person a normal death by removing life support systems when there is no hope of recovery. They argue that there is no moral obligation to use *extraordinary* means to prolong life; only ordinary means must be used. However as medical technology has advanced so rapidly, it is increasingly difficult to distinguish between ordinary and extraordinary means since what was once considered extraordinary has become ordinary.

A change occurred when John Paul II in 2004 stated that administering food and water to PVS patients is a natural way [normal means] of conserving life. The Congregation for the Doctrine of the Faith reaffirmed this teaching in 2007: Directive 58 stated there is a moral obligation to administer nutrition and hydration to PVS patients because of their human dignity though the obligation ceases or becomes optional in certain conditions.[29]

Caring for seriously ill elderly loved ones with no chance of recovery is placing increased financial and psychological burdens on families today. It is therefore sometimes tempting to consider active euthanasia. Yet a strong Christian faith in God, in God's mysterious providence in our lives, and in the role of suffering in the lives of those who follow the crucified Christ are powerful helps in such difficult periods of our faith pilgrimage. Despite the heart-rending suffering of persons terminally ill, the taking of one's life or the direct assistance of such suicide is morally wrong.

Capital Punishment. In the past there was general agreement that a murderer forfeited his right to life and that the death penalty was a necessary deterrent. Today there is a movement gathering increasing support to abolish the death penalty.[30] The U.S. Catholic bishops issued a *Statement on Capital Punishment* in 1980 which argued that "neither the legitimate purposes of punishment nor necessity justify the imposition of the death penalty in the conditions of American society." Drawing on their argumentation, the Catholic bishops of California issued the following carefully expressed statement. It illustrates how difficult it is to apply Christian values to complex concrete situations, how the teaching office of bishops provides moral guidelines rather than inflexible commands, and how moral theologians use sociological data as well as religious principles to reach moral conclusions.

...there are serious considerations which should prompt Christians and all Americans to support the abolition of capital punishment. Some of these reasons have to do with problems inherent in the practice of capital punishment, such as the denial of any possibility of reform or of making compensation; the possibility of mistake by the execution of an innocent person; the long and unavoidable delays which diminish the effectiveness of capital punishment as a deterrent and can produce aimlessness, fear and despair; the extreme anguish which an execution brings, not only for the criminal, but for his family and those who perform or witness the execution; the unhealthy publicity and considerable acrimony in public discussion attracted by execution; and, finally, the not-unfounded belief that many convicted criminals are sentenced to death in an unfair and discriminatory manner; e.g., more than fifty percent of those on death row are minorities, virtually all of them are poor. Other reasons proposed by the 1980 *Statement* have to do with important values that would be promoted by the abolition of capital punishment: It would send a message that the cycle of violence can be broken, that we need not take life for life, that we can envisage more humane and more hopeful and effective responses to the growth of violent crime. It would be a manifestation of our belief in the unique worth and dignity of each person from the moment of conception, a creature made in the image and likeness of God. Abolition would give further testimony to our conviction that God is indeed the Lord of life, a belief we share with the Judaic and Islamic traditions. It would be more consonant with the example of Jesus who both taught and practiced the forgiveness of injustice and who came "to give his life as a ransom for many." (Mark 10:45)

Not all Christians may come to this conclusion when they apply general principles and Gospel values to the concrete historical situation. ... We dare to take this position and raise this challenge because of our commitment to a consistent ethic of life by which we wish to give unambiguous witness to the sacredness of every human life from conception through natural death, and to proclaim the good news that no person is beyond the redemptive mercy of God.[31]

A well-known persistent voice against capital punishment is Sr. Helen Prejean. Her book, *Dead Man Walking,* later a movie, documented her work with men on death row. In *The Death of Innocents* she describes her experience watching those wrongfully convicted of crime executed by the state. She heads a national organization to abolish the death penalty and founded *Survive* which offers counseling to the families of the victims of violent crime. She once said, "Is God vengeful? Demanding a death for a death, or is God compassionate, luring souls into a love so great that no can be considered 'enemy?'"

4. *War and Terrorism.* The Catholic Church has developed over the centuries a "just war theory" that reluctantly permitted war if *all* the following conditions were verified:

- The decision for war must be made by a legitimate authority.
- The war can be fought only to defend against unjust aggression.

- War must be waged only as a last resort.
- There must be a reasonable chance of achieving the objective for which the war is waged.
- The good to be achieved by the war must outweigh the evil that will result from it. This is called the principle of proportionality: one cannot "destroy a city to save it."
- The war must be waged according to the principles of natural and international law. For instance, indiscriminate mass destruction of civilian populations is never justified, for whatever reason.

However, the advent of nuclear weapons has changed the picture drastically. In their 1983 pastoral statement, *The Challenge of Peace: God's Promise and Our Response*, the U.S. bishops judged that a "just" nuclear war is a contradiction in terms. Quoting the *Pastoral Constitution on the Church in the Modern World*, "any act of war aimed indiscriminately at the destruction of entire cities or of extensive areas along with their population is a crime against God and human kind [and] merits unequivocal and unhesitating condemnation" (*GS* 80), the bishops condemned the following: the intentional killing of innocent civilians or non-combatants; a "first strike" strategy; the policy of a retaliatory nuclear strike (MAD or mutually assured destruction); a so-called "limited" nuclear war.

As to the arms race, the bishops state that it "is one of the greatest curses on the human race; it is to be condemned as a danger, an act of aggression against the poor, and a folly which does not provide the security it promises."[32] We recall the statement attributed to President Eisenhower at the end of his presidency that "every dollar spent on the arms race is a dollar taken from the poor." The bishops close with these stirring words:

In simple terms, we are saying that good ends (defending one's country, protecting freedom, etc.) cannot justify immoral means (the use of weapons which kill indiscriminately and threaten whole societies) .... Peacemaking is ... a requirement of our faith. We are called to be peacemakers... by our Lord Jesus.[33]

Since the terrorist strikes of 9/11 in New York City and Washington, D.C., the issue of war is even more complex. War is no longer only between nations but between terrorist groups and national governments. Is invading a nation to eliminate terrorist groups or torture to obtain information concerning future attacks moral? The church maintains that because of the dignity of the human person the use of torture is never justified. The United States' bishops have been consistently outspoken against torture, stating that it is "ultimately counterproductive."

Ordinary Catholics Today

How should a sincere Catholic think and act in this period of division and polarization in the Catholic Church today, especially regarding morality and sexuality? What is a Catholic to make of the situation in which the official church teaches one thing about human sexuality and a large number of reputable Catholic moral theologians disagree with some of this this teaching? Is disagreement with the authentic magisterium of the church permissible?[34] What does one make of the fact that over 85% of U.S. Catholics do not agree with papal teaching on contraception in marriage yet consider themselves good Catholics and receive the sacraments regularly without confessing contraceptive use?

There are three possibilities for today's Catholic: follow official Catholic teaching fully even if one has difficulties and misgivings; totally ignore the magisterium's teaching as irrelevant; form one's honest, sincere conscience after prayer and serious consideration of the reasons for both the official church position and that of responsible moral theologians. The first is admirable provided one is knowledgeable, understands the issues, and does not do violence to his or her conscience. *Uncritical, unquestioning* obedience is not the Catholic ideal. The second is immature and reprehensible and does not do justice to the competency of the Church's magisterium. The third seems to be the most reasonable in today's Vatican II Church which encourages Catholics to follow their own informed conscience based on the teaching of the council.

An informed, morally-adult Catholic will understand that the role of professional moral theologians in the Church is to use their training and expertise to deal with complex moral questions, to critique moral positions that are incomplete or no longer applicable, and to propose positions that best take into account comprehensive data from Scripture, church tradition, human experience, and sciences like psychology, biology, sociology, medicine. A Catholic well-versed in the history of the church will realize that the official church has on occasion taken incomplete positions it later repudiated[35] and that it has often been the last to respond to events, theological insights, and major cultural changes. Such a Catholic will not be scandalized or unduly perturbed because he or she is aware that necessary change in the church often came about by responsible disagreement with the ordinary magisterium. Finally, a religiously sensitive Catholic is confident that the Holy Spirit is guiding the church and is able to bring progress and much good out of apparently harmful division and confusion.

For Catholics today, moral theology means little if it cannot meet the challenges and complexities of the 'real world' of contemporary society. Moral decision-making is something all are engaged in when making everyday decisions and when confronted with complex moral problems. Scripture, the tradition of the church, magisterial documents, the 'sense of the faithful,' prayerful discernment, the 'law of love,' and open and transparent dialogue with those whose ideas and persuasions we may not agree with all play vital roles in this process.

Catholic moral theology constantly strives for a more holistic approach to all facets of the human person. It is an embodiment of the love of Christ striving to manifest itself in the world through the hearts, minds and actions of the people of God.

For Discussion

1. One frequently hears that the church's teaching on sexual morality is outdated. In what areas and to what extent can the church change and still be faithful to Christian values and her centuries old tradition and teaching? In what areas can it not change?One frequently hears, especially from young people, that the church's teaching on sexual morality is outdated. In what areas and to what extent *can* the church change and still be faithful to Christian values and her

2. The church's position on gay and lesbian relationships has alienated many Catholics. What can the church do to welcome people of all sexual orientations? The church's position on the morality of gay and lesbian relationships has alienated many practicing Catholics. What can the church do to welcome people of all sexual orientations?.

3. Catholic moral teaching seems to be primarily focused on human sexuality and abortion. Do you think this focus detracts from other important moral issues of our day? How can the Catholic Church take a more holistic approach to morality?

4. Can abortion ever be justified? What are the moral principles involved? What of complex cases such as that addressed by Sister McBride?

5. Where do you stand on capital punishment? What reasons persuade you? Can abortion ever be justified? What are the moral principles involved? What of complex cases such as that addressed by Sister McBride?Where do you stand on capital punishment? What principles/reasons

Further Reading

Bretzke, James. S.J. *A Morally Complex World: Engaging Contemporary Moral Theology.* Collegeville, MN: Liturgical Press, 2004. This readable book in fundamental ethics combines the best in classical and contemporary moral theology. With pastoral sensitivity and many helpful examples, the author explains conscience, natural law and moral norms, how to consider sin and moral failure and to dialogue on differing ethical issues. A valuable introduction to moral theology and theologizing by a skilled teacher.

Curran, Charles E. *Catholic Moral Theology in the United States.* Washington, D.C.: Georgetown University Press, 2007. By one of the premier moral theologians in his usual clear scholarly writing, this book covers the 19th century, the period before Vatican II, developments in moral theology after the council, and chapters on Sexuality and Marriage, Bioethics and Social Ethics.

Gula, Richard. S.S. *Moral Discernment.* New York/Mahweh: Paulist Press, 1997. Gula offers a way for people to find the answer to the question "Is this the right thing to do?" He explains in plain and engaging way the dual role of church teachings and the formation of one's personal conscience in discovering one's own moral responsibilities in today's complex world.

Keenan, James J. S.J. *A History of Catholic Moral Theology in the Twentieth Century: from Confessing Sins to Liberating Consciences.* New York: Continuum, 2010. Keenan traces the major changes in Catholic moral theology from an ahistorical, deductive approach of textbooks to aid priests hearing confessions to revisionist theologians and the influence on moral theology of Paul VI's *Humanae Vitae* and John Paul II's *Veritatis Splendor* to the theological approaches of South American, Asian and African theologians to contemporary virtue ethics. "A remarkable achievement."

Luizzi, Peter J. O.Carm. *With Listening Hearts: Understanding the Voices of Lesbian and Gay Catholics.* New York/Mahwah, NJ: Paulist Press, 2001. Luizzi is the director of Lesbian and Gay ministry for the Archdiocese of Los Angeles. He expresses the Catholic moral teaching that homosexuals are called to celibacy in the Catholic tradition while at the same time offering a realistic pastoral perspective, offering positive, compassionate and loving respect that the church should and must offer gay and lesbian parishioners.

McElroy, Robert W. "War Without End." *America* (Feb. 21, 2011): 11-13. Bishop McElroy points out the moral hazard of American's vast capacity to wage war whose goal is societal transformation and democratization, its inability to bring war to a close, and the moral question of 13 years' major conflict with no clear prospect of success. Applied to Iraq and Afghanistan, he proposes four applications not permitted by Catholic teaching on war and peace.

Footnotes

1   "... the fundamental problem facing the Church is the gulf between the teachings the leadership expresses and the needs and faith of the people of God." James Keenan, ed. *Catholic Ethics in the World Church* (New York: Continuum, 2007), 140-46.

2   *Declaration on Religious Liberty,* Vatican II, No. 14, "It is its [Catholic Church's] duty ... to declare and confirm by her authority the principles of the moral order..."

3   "Physicalism ... states that the person should always follow his nature which will be basically the same for all. Any moral action that would be contrary to the proper end of his abstract human nature ... would be *contra naturam* (against nature) and therefore always immoral, regardless of intention or circumstances. Much of the church's magisterial teaching on sexual ethics, such as Paul VI's encyclical on the Regulation of Births (*Humanae vitae, 1968)* and the Congregation for the Doctrine of the Faith's Instruction on Reproductive Technologies (*Donum vitae, 1987)* utilizes primarily this mode of reasoning and argumentation." James Bretzke, *A Morally Complex World, Engaging Contemporary Moral Theology.* (Collegeville, MN: Liturgical Press), 2004, 36.

4   See Chapter 7, "New Foundations for Moral Reasoning, 1970-89," James Keenan, *A History of Catholic Moral Theology in the Twentieth Century* (New York, NY: Continuum , 2010), 141-172, especially 152-53. Much of the material for this chapter is taken from Keenan's outstanding study.

5   See Joseph F. Eagan, *Restoration and Renewal: The Church in the Third Millennium* (Kansas City: Sheed & Ward, 1995), for "The Great Debate in Catholic Moral Theology Today," 286-90 and 291-94

6   To clarify "disvalues," revisionists make an important distinction between pre-moral and moral evil. Pre-moral evil is a disvalue, an action that lacks goodness that ideally ought to be present. Pre-moral evil becomes real or sinful evil when done from the wrong intention or without a proportionate reason. This distinction is helpful in complex moral questions like removing support systems for terminally ill, artificial insemination, pre-marital sex, homosexual acts in certain circumstances, contraceptive use. Revisionists argue that in an

imperfect world full of ambiguous, conflict situations, some disvalue or pre-moral evil may, indeed must, be permitted to achieve more important values. Examples are telling an untruth for a greater good, or removing an ectopic pregnancy to save the mother's life but reluctantly permitting the pre-moral evil of terminating the child's life – the classic double effect.

7   "That teaching ... is founded upon the inseparable connection, willed by God and unable to be broken by man on his own initiative, between the two meanings of the conjugal act: the unitive meaning and the procreative meaning. ... By safeguarding both ... the conjugal act preserves in its fullness ... true mutual love and its ordination toward man's most high calling to parenthood." *Ibid.*

8   An action "intrinsically evil" is always and everywhere morally wrong regardless of the person's intention or mitigating circumstances. Considered in the abstract, the action is by definition morally wrong; in concrete life situations, different moral judgments are called for.

9   The commission, after months of meetings and hearing the testimony of moral theologians, doctors, scientists, university professors, married couples, bishops and several Cardinals, voted overwhelmingly, 64-4, to petition a change in the church's traditional teaching against contraception. Pope Paul VI accepted the minority report drafted by the four dissenting commission members opposing change in the official teaching based on the specific ordering of each generative act to procreation.

10 I am indebted to moral theologian James T. Bretzke for his insights and presentation.

11 This is essentially the view articulated by Todd Salzman and Michael Lawler in their recent book *The Sexual Person: Toward a Renewed Catholic Anthropology.* Moral Tradition Series. Washington, D.C.: Georgetown University Press, 2008. The book's position has been severely criticized by the United States Conference of Catholic Bishops (USCCB) Committee on Doctrine. "Inadequacies in Theologians' Book [Salzman/Lawler], *The Sexual Person. Origins* 40,21 (28 October, 2010): 328-335.

12 The advantage of this pre-moral, moral evil distinction is that revisionists safeguard the priority and value of heterosexual relationships in marriage while addressing in

a compassionate, understanding way real-life homosexual relationships. Yet because of the complex issues involved and the deep-seated prejudice against gay people, this distinction may not be acceptable to both traditionalist Catholics or gay Catholics.

13 Professors John Finnis and Germain Grisez, writing in *L'Osservatore Romano 8* (February 23, 1994): 6-7, make these statements: "The encyclical identifies its own central theme ... there are intrinsically evil acts prohibited always and without exception." "Certain theories ... notably proportionalism, consequentialism or teleologism, deny that there are any intrinsically evil acts." "John Paul II makes it clear ... that these theories are incompatible with revealed truth." Richard McCormick's lengthy article, "Some Early Reactions to *Veritatis Splendor,*" *Theological Studies* 55, No. 3 (September, 1994): 481-506, reviewed comments in the press and various symposia of scholars and individual studies by moral theologians; he then discussed three critical issues raised by the encyclical: its positive value ("strong indictment of contemporary relativism and individualism"); its central issue, the meaning of "object" (what precisely constitutes the object of moral actions); and ecclesiology, the issue behind other issues ('the Church as a pyramid where truth and authority flow uniquely from the pinnacle ... (or) the concentric model wherein the reflections of all must flow from the periphery to the center if the wisdom resident in the Church is to be reflected persuasively and prophetically to the world.")

14 "The reason why a good intention is not itself sufficient, but a correct choice of actions is also needed, is that the human act depends on the object, whether or not that object is capable of being ordered to God ... ." VS 78.

15 Fundamental option is the most basic moral decision a person can make coming from the inner core of one's consciousness to reject God by putting self before God and others; it would qualify for *mortal* sin meriting eternal punishment.

16 Keenan, *op.cit.*, 128 and 173.

17 See Thomas Rausch, *Authority and Leadership in the Church* (Wilmington, DE: Michael Glazier, 1989), 105-06 for the twofold "classical" concept of *reception* and two instances of non-reception when the church subsequently rejected official teaching: the claim of Pope Boniface VIII in *Unam Sanctam* in 1302 "that it is absolutely necessary for the salvation of all men that they submit to the Roman

Pontiff" and the Council of Constance decree *Haec Sancta* in 1415 on the "supremacy of a general assembly of bishops over a pope." An example of contemporary non-reception of papal and official magisterial teaching is the statement in *Of Human Life* that "Each and every marriage act must remain open to the transmission of life" so that use of a contraceptive is an intrinsically evil act. The majority of married Catholics, moral theologians, priests and many bishops did not and do not accept the teaching. Bishop Christopher Butler of England stated that the widespread non-reception, is "a phenomenon he viewed as 'invalidating' the teaching." See Richard McCormick, '*Humanae Vitae* 25 Years Later," *America 168* (July 17, 1993): 10 and Joseph Komonchak, "*Humanae Vitae* and Its Reception: Ecclesiological Reflections," *Theological Studies* 39 (1078): 221-57

18 See Keenan, *op. cit.*, 158.

19 *Ibid.*, 191-221.

20 See James F. Keenan, "Can We Talk? Theological Ethics and Sexuality," *Theological Studies 68* (2007): 113-131.

21 *Lisa Sowle Cahill*. "Marriage: Developments in Catholic Theology and Ethics, ' *Theological Studies,* 64 (2003), 80.

22 James Keenan, *op. cit., Theological Studies* 68 (2007), 150. Margaret Farley, *Just Love: A Framework for Christian Sexual Ethics* (New York: Continuum, 2006). Her work "represents the best of Catholic theological ethics of the past century." See Keenan, *op. cit.,* 229, footnote 22. Lisa Sowle Cahill, *Sex, Gender, and Christian Ethics (*New York: Cambridge University, 1996).

23 Linda Hogan and James Keenan "Continent in search of the ethical path," *Tablet* (Sept. 15, 2012): 10-11.

24 James Gaffney, *Moral Questions (*York: Paulist Press, 1989)

25 Archbishop John Quinn, homily in St. Mary's Cathedral, San Francisco

26 See *Respect for Life,* 1988 publication of U.S. National Conference of Catholic Bishops.

27 *Gaudium et Spes,* 51

28 According to a Catholic Doctor "a fertilized egg cannot be considered a human person unless it is implanted in the uterus since it cannot continue to exist biologically."

29 Directive 58. "As a general rule, there is an obligation to provide patients with food and water, including medically assisted nutrition and hydration for those who are unable to take food orally. This moral obligation extends to patients in a persistent vegetative state because of their innate human dignity. This moral obligation ceases or becomes "merely optional" when tube feeding becomes excessively burdensome or no longer accomplishes its objective ... ." See Gerald D. Coleman, "What's Extraordinary?" *America* (Aug. 30 – Sept. 6, 2010): 13-16.

30 Use of new technology such as analysis of DNA samples has documented the innocence of many persons convicted and sent to their deaths.

31 "California Bishops on Capital Punishment," *Origins* 15 (Oct. 17, 1985): 301-03.

32 *The Challenge of Peace: God's Promise and Our Response* (Boston: Daughters of St. Paul, 1983), 5 Summary.

33 *Ibid.,* 8 (Summary, II C)

34 See *Why You Can Disagree and Remain a Faithful Catholic,* by Fran Felder and John Heagle.

35 Examples are Pius IX's denying any truth or goodness in non-Christian religions, his condemnation of the separation of church and state and of religious freedom as an objective right and Pius XII's exclusive identification of   the Roman Catholic Church with the Mystical Body of Christ. Vatican II modified or reversed these. See   Rausch, *op. cit.,* 107, footnote 15 above and   J. Robert Dionne, *The Papacy and the Church: A Study of Praxis and Reception in Ecumenical Perspective* (New York: Philosophical Library, 1987). See especially John Noonan . "Development in Moral Doctrine," *Theological Studies* 54 (December, 1993): 662-77 for four examples of changes in the Church's moral teaching: usury, marriage, slavery, religious freedom.

Chapter 15:
Vision of Renewal -Urgent Challenges, Part I

It is the intention of this holy council to improve the standard of daily Christian living among Catholics; to adopt those structures which are subject to change so as better to meet the needs of our time; to encourage whatever can contribute to the union of all who believe in Christ; and to strengthen whatever serves to call all people into the embrace of the church.[1] (SC 1)

T his opening sentence of Vatican II's *Constitution on the Sacred Liturgy* expresses my hope for the Catholic Church in suggesting these 12 challenges. In considering each, I appreciate the complexity of the problems before our church leaders today and their grave responsibility to safeguard the rich Catholic Tradition and preserve the unity of the church. Their love of the church, their pastoral concern, and their abiding trust in the presence and guidance of the Spirit and the risen Christ are reasons for Catholics' optimism and hope in the future.

At the same time, Catholics' love for their church and concern for her future demand we acknowledge the painful problems and very real challenges confronting the church, the people of God. Some were left unanswered by the Second Vatican Council. Others have appeared in the 50 years since the council: serious shortage of priests with the pending loss of Eucharist and sacraments; the failure to carry out the full renewal/reform mandated by the council; the tragedy of large numbers of priest abusers country by country, the suffering of their victims, and Catholics' loss of confidence in their bishops; the unprecedented departure of Catholics; the alienation and loss of Catholic women; the crisis of faith. These seriously harm the church's ability to carry out her mission. Concerned Catholics ask that these challenges be honestly acknowledged no matter how painful and be courageously addressed.

Thomas Rausch speaks for Vatican II Catholics when he asks "will the church begin serious discussion of

> ... the shortage of priests and the right of communities to the Eucharist, a more collegial style of church leadership, allowing the laity some participation in its decision-making processes and the formulation of its teaching, addressing the special concerns of women, minorities, the divorced, and those in mixed marriages, renewing its ethical teaching particularly in the area of sexuality, and allowing for greater adaptation and inculturation at local levels and in different cultures?

He believes "these are challenges as great as any in the church's history, and they arise , not out of a modern secular spirit, but precisely out of those currents of renewal unleashed by the Second Vatican Council."[2]

Part I: Opportunities   1. Eucharist for All Catholics

The Eucharist and the sacraments are at the center of the spiritual lives of Catholics. Catholics often testify that they are able to cope with severe losses, serious illness, and temptations to despair thanks to the consolation and strength they gain from Mass and the sacraments. With the increasing shortage of priests worldwide and parish closings in the United States and Europe, the Eucharist is becoming less and less available to Catholics. The Center for Applied Research on the Apostolate (CARA) gives the following sobering statistics for the United States:[3]

	1975	2005	2009	2012
Total Priests	58,909	42,859	40,606	38,964
Diocesan Priests	36,005	28,702	27,594	26,661
Religious Priests	22,904	14,137	13,072	12,303
Priest Ordinations	771	454	472	480
Parishes	18,515	18,891	17,250	17,944
Without Priests	702	3,251	3,400	3,389

From 1975 to 2012 the Catholic population grew from 48.7 million to 66.3 million with fewer priests to bring them Eucharist. In 2012, for example, there were 459 parishes without a priest which were led by a married deacon or religious brother or sister or a layperson, often a woman.

Two recent examples in mid-West America dramatize the serious crisis of lack of priests for Eucharist and sacraments. A South Dakota bishop was forced to close a thriving rural parish because no priest was available for a large area. Reaction of the faithful was immediate and decisive. They hired a Methodist minister as pastor of their believing community! When two prosperous Catholic parishes in a Wisconsin city were closed for lack of pastors, the parishioners formed one church they called *Christian Community Church* and hired a Protestant minister to pastor their new church community.

The prospect of further loss of the Eucharist may be the most serious problem facing the Catholic Church today and in the future. The church is thus confronted with the question of celibacy and married priests to serve its people who have a right to the Eucharist as baptized members of the body of Christ.

Celibacy and Married Priesthood. The question of celibacy has become a major discussion point in the Catholic Church by priests, a growing number of bishops and Catholics concerned over their loss of the Eucharist. Some have called it the elephant in the drawing room – the issue that everyone realizes is urgent but is not to be effectively discussed or acted upon.

Many bishops asked that celibacy be discussed at Vatican II but Pope Paul VI removed it from the council agenda. The issue could not be avoided. Maximos IV Saigh, Melchite Patriarch of Antioch, wrote to Paul VI: "In case of necessity the priesthood must not be sacrificed to celibacy, but celibacy to the priesthood."[4] At the council a group of African bishops requested Paul VI's permission to ordain their married catechists in order to bring the sacraments to their people. At the Bishops' Synod in 1971 a number of bishops spoke in favor of ordaining married men. Bishops again brought up the question of celibacy at the synod of 2000 despite the prior prohibition it not be discussed. Today, individual bishops are beginning to speak publically for married priests. (See section 8, next chapter.)

There is a problem of major magnitude here. The official church declines to consider a change in what involves church discipline rather than doctrine; yet many Catholics are being denied that right in a church that professes to be a sacramental church and which places the Eucharist at the center of its religious life. In 1988 the United States Bishops approved the *Directory for Sunday Celebrations in the Absence of a Priest (SCAP),* a rite for a lay-led communion service including readings from Scripture, which, however, is not the Eucharist. Some commentators have referred to it as creating the Protestantization of the Catholic Church.

For many centuries celibacy has been an important gift to the Catholic Church. The celibate lives of vowed men and women in religious orders and congregations has given the church scores of canonized Saints, mystics, great apostles and missionaries, martyrs, men and women committed to the poor and marginalized. For these religious, celibate life is an enormous help for intimacy with God and a life of total service. Properly lived, celibacy is a powerful witness to the reign of God.

Those who favor celibacy for the clergy point to theological and practical reasons: the priest acts in the person of Christ who was celibate; celibacy in forsaking marriage and following Christ to serve the people of God symbolizes the "man set apart' for service of God and the church; celibacy enables the priest to serve God with an undivided heart and without the financial realities of supporting a family.

Moreover, to change the almost thousand-year practice of the church carries with it considerable problems: the potential for further division in the church, a two-tier presbyterate; the cost to parishioners to support married priests and their family; the availability of married priests if they are forced to work outside the parish.

Many theologians, lay Catholics, priests and some bishops do not find these arguments, though valid, convincing today. Clearly, there is no essential connection between priesthood and celibacy as the practice of Eastern married rite Catholic priests and Orthodox married priests and of married priests in the church's first millennium testifies. Celibacy is for those called to it and who have *freely chosen* it. The worldwide departure of large numbers of priests from their ministry in order to marry and the reluctance of many young men to become priests because of the celibacy requirements in the western Latin church complicate the question of celibacy. Likewise, that the church lauds celibacy as a "treasure of the church" appears to have lost some of its luster among Catholics by the behavior of abuser priests worldwide.

There are ways to provide for the spiritual needs of Catholics and at the same time preserve celibacy as valuable gift to the church. The most obvious is to permit diocesan priests to marry as was the case in the first millennium of the Catholic Church. Celibacy would still be preserved by religious order priests who intentionally choose vowed celibate life. Another way is to invite married priests who desire to serve the church to return to active ministry as well as those who left the seminary before ordination because of the celibacy commitment: their experience of both priesthood and marriage would enrich the church and its ministry. Finally, the church is able to offer priesthood to the 17,047 married deacons in the United States whose experience and commitment would greatly strengthen the church.[5]

The Catholic Priesthood. A related question since the council is the Catholic priesthood itself. Some authors speak of a crisis[6] in the priesthood owing to significant priest-departures, the lack of vocations to the priesthood, aging over-worked priests, the poor image of priests from the priest-abuse scandal, the alleged preponderance of homosexual priests, the morale of priests who feel the official church is unwilling to address the priest-shortage, and the shift from the *sacral* model (the celibate priest as a sacred person performing sacred mysteries) of priesthood that held sway for centuries up to Vatican II to a *ministerial* priesthood (the priest preaching the Word of God, forming and leading the Christian community, and imitating Christ who came to serve) favored by the council[7] a shift that has caused tension for some priests and for Catholics accustomed to place their priests on a pedestal.

It is important for American Catholics to support their priests today. Many priests in ministry feel abandoned by the hierarchy; because of scandal by their fellow-priests, they feel guilty by association and handicapped in doing effective youth ministry; they were not consulted on the liturgical changes that directly affect them as pastors and celebrants of the Eucharist. They suffer from a rift between older priests disheartened by opposition to Vatican II renewal and younger, assertive priests who call themselves 'John Paul II priests' and who desire a return to the pre-Vatican II cultic way of exercising priesthood. As one older priest said, "We're tired!"

Yet it should be recognized that most priests live their celibacy faithfully and in poll after poll testify to their happiness as priests. A 2009 survey of American priests showed "high levels of satisfaction with their lives and ministry of preaching the Word of God, joy in celebrating sacraments and presiding over the liturgy, and being part of a community of Christians.[8] Today's seminarians and young priests, more conservative than their elder confreres, are effective and joyful persons, deeply committed to the church, to their priesthood and to celibacy.

2. Retaining Catholics[9]

One of every three adult Americans who were raised Catholic have left the church. If these ex-Catholics were to form a single church, they would constitute the second largest church in the nation.

This loss of one-third of those Americans raised Catholic, 22.1 million persons, is alarming. According to the 2008 U.S. Religious Landscape Survey conducted by the Pew Forum on Religion and Public Life, half of those Catholics joined Protestant denominations, the other half remained unaffiliated. Of the former, two-thirds joined evangelical-Pentecostal groups, one-third mainline Protestant churches. Both groups reported their principal reasons for leaving were twofold: "their spiritual needs were not being met" (71%) and "the religious service and style of worship" in their new church. Those who joined mainline Protestant churches were looking for a "less clerically dominated church."

What are the causes of this 'disaster' according to Peter Steinfels?

Liturgical language ... quality of homilies. The shortage of priests. Celibacy. The role of women and their ordination. Transparency and consultation in church governance at every level from the parish to the Vatican. ... Monitoring of Catholic theology. The demand that Catholic citizens and civic leaders be answerable to episcopal judgments.[10]

Cathleen Kaveny, a Catholic, proposes further reasons shared by many Catholics today.

> They have long doubted the wisdom of elements of church teaching on matters of sexual morality (contraception and gay marriage) and of gender roles (all male priesthood). ... These Catholics see no hope of institutional reform. The pope largely views the sexual abuse crisis as a problem of individual sinfulness, not of broader flaws in church teaching and practices. Vatican II is fast becoming a ceiling for reform, not a floor for reform. ... key members of the United States hierarchy are calling for loyal deference to ecclesiastical authority even on matters Vatican II recognized to be within the competence of the laity ... From the perspective of these Catholics, doctrine and practice are not developing but withering.[11]

Many may disagree with her judgments. It should be acknowledged that in some areas the Catholic Church cannot change and still be faithful to Catholic teaching. Yet Steinfels' and Kaveney's words reflect the attitudes and conviction of knowledgeable and devoted Catholics today and have accounted for their disillusionment with the hierarchy's leadership and why they are leaving the church. It is essential that Catholic leadership acknowledge this reality for the future of the church and address those concerns that are legitimate.

There are different views of how to judge this massive exodus from the church. Some judge these former Catholics disloyal in disagreeing with Catholic teaching: their leaving is good riddance; they lack strong faith; a smaller, more spiritual and loyal church will result.

Another more positive view sees their exodus as a wake-up call for the Catholic Church, both members and leaders alike, to address the personal reasons why our brothers and sisters leave us and where we need reform and renewal to be more fully the church of Jesus. Steinfels believes "We have to ask ourselves why so many are leaving. Are they sinners or searchers?"

What does this mean for the future of the Catholic Church? Will this pattern of departure continue as the wave of the future? Will the American church leadership address the concerns of Catholics and their reasons for leaving? Will the large number of Latino immigrants, soon to be the majority of American Catholics, remain or succumb to the outreach, worship and community style of Pentecostals? One thing seems clear: our bishops need to listen to the Catholic people, to their concerns and what they consider important, to their "sense of the faithful" and prayerfully consider what the Holy Spirit may be speaking to the church through these signs of the times.[12]

What might the American bishops do to reverse this decline? Steinfels believes "some kind of acknowledgment from the hierarchy... of the seriousness of the situation ... a sign of determination to address these losses honestly and openly ... to evaluate a wide range of views about causes and remedies."

From his layman's perspective, he suggests what the church needs to do by way of renewal and building the church of the future.

A quantum leap in the quality of Sunday liturgies, including preaching; a massive, all-out mobilization of talent and treasure to catechize the young, bring adolescents into church life and engage young adults in ongoing faith formation; a regular, systematic assessment of all these activities – as well as theologically more complex and controversial matters like expanding the pool of those eligible for ordination and revisiting some aspects of the church's teaching on sexuality.[13]

From the disturbing Pew Research figures, Thomas Reese proposes three lessons. (1) Catholics "are longing for liturgies that touch the heart and emotions. More creativity [in public worship] is needed." (2) "The church needs a massive Bible education program ... If you do not read and pray the Scriptures, you are not an adult Christian." (3) "The Pew data shows that two-thirds of Catholics who become Protestants do so before they reach the age of 24. The church must make a preferential option for teen-agers and young adults or it will continue to bleed." Reese says "the Catholic Church is hemorrhaging members. It needs to acknowledge this and do more to understand why. Any other institution that lost one-third of its members would want to know why."[14]

At present the Catholic Church does not have the benefit of a sociological survey to know accurately the reasons why so many leave the church today. Fr. Byron, past president of the Catholic University of America, suggested the need for "exit interviews" to establish their reasons for leaving as basis for the American bishops to devote their energies primarily to the pastoral needs of American Catholics through creative programs for the young and for parish liturgical celebration. A hopeful sign is Cardinal Timothy Dolan, archbishop of New York and president of the United States Conference of Catholic Bishops, expressing surprise at the magnitude of the problem of departures and promising to address it.

3. Empower the Catholic Laity

Who are the Catholic laity: They are the church, the people of God, today's Catholic men and women who by their baptism are members of the body of Christ the church, sharing in the paschal mystery of Christ, called to personal holiness and given the mission to establish God's kingdom and bring the good news of Christ and the Gospel to their world. The 1987 Bishops' Synod stated that "baptism calls every Christian to participate in the mission of the church," thus enlisting Catholic lay persons co-partners with their bishops and priests in mission to the world and within the church.

The Second Vatican Council spoke eloquently of the apostolic vocation of Catholic lay men and women in its document *Apostolate of the Laity (AA)*. The mission of lay men and women is to this world. They witness Christian values in their married and single lives and strive intentionally to bring about God's kingdom of justice and peace in their public life. Today, this involves political and business life, education and health care, scientific research and activity, the legal profession and the military. American Catholic men and women are already prominent in these fields, often in top leadership positions.

Being the church, the people of God, by their baptism, Catholic lay men and women are called to ministry within the church. Peter Steinfels called attention to "the astounding emergence of a new category of Catholic leadership that has already transformed much of American Catholic life."[15] Today there are over 30,000 paid lay parish ministers working in 60% of the nation's Catholic parishes of whom 80% are women. They staff Catholic schools, run catechetical programs and **RCIA**, prepare people for the sacraments, lead youth groups and outreach to young people, and plan liturgies. Some act as parish administrators in the absence of priests. This represents an extraordinary new reality in American Catholic life.

Yet today the Catholic laity represent under-utilized talent, energy and leadership. Many in the church today speak of empowering the laity as an urgent need for the church's future. American lay men and women are the most highly educated in the history of the church, often products of Catholic education up to and including university and graduate school. They are generous with their time and resources and are devoted to the Church. One pastor observed that they represent the finest asset we have in the American Church today and the source of its strength and vitality.

The following are some ways the church might empower Catholic lay men and women to become in reality the future of the church in what is sometimes described "the age of the laity."

- Seriously listen to their concerns and to the Spirit speaking through their lived experience of married love, family life and decisions of conscience and those many areas within their expertise.
- Collaborate with Catholic women and men in needed outreach programs. (See chapter 18)
- Respect the expertise, prudential judgments, challenges and ambiguities of Catholics in public life and service without exerting pressure, threats of excommunication and withholding Holy Communion.
- Accept without recrimination and discipline Catholics' disagreement from some non-infallible teaching and disciplinary positions, recognizing conscience decisions and the complexity of practical affairs.
- Welcome competent lay Catholics as members of parish councils with genuine consultative voice and of diocesan councils in a decision-sharing basis where they are currently not present.
- By a liturgical rite, designate lay women and men for parish ministry to meet the critical spiritual needs of Catholics today and encourage and positively support them in their ministry and provide sufficient compensation.
- Create occasions for lay preaching to assist overburdened priests and to capitalize on the talents, knowledge and spirituality of Catholic lay men and women.
- Recognize and respect the charisms, religious commitment and dedication to the church by American religious

women (technically laity) and their extraordinary contribution to American Catholicism through their network of schools and hospitals.

For their part, American Catholic laity may still need to overcome habits of automatically deferring to pastors/priests and bishops and begin to speak out forcefully but respectfully when necessary for the good of the church and their fellow Catholics' spiritual needs. This may involve insisting that bishops provide the Eucharist and sacraments to Catholics increasingly lacking them; assuming meaningful roles in parish and diocesan councils, and insisting on their right to make prudential judgments in public life when different from policies of church leadership. For their effective mission to the world, Catholic lay men and women may need to become expert in Catholic social teaching.

4. Catholic Women

The alienation of many contemporary Catholic women from the Catholic Church in the United States and elsewhere is a critical problem. A growing number of Catholic women resent that their gifts are being denied by an all-male hierarchy who make decisions involving them. According to priest-sociologist Andrew Greeley, a million Catholic women left the Catholic Church as a result of this situation. A vital church can no longer survive this situation.

Is it possible that church leaders do not understand or sufficiently recognize the extent of women's alienation? Were they to meet and listen to women as they have to victims of priest-abusers, meaningful steps might be taken to address this alienation.

In this context, it is helpful to put Catholic feminism and the inflammatory question of women's ordination in perspective.

The Catholic Feminist Movement. This movement reflects women's search for equal political, social and economic rights and equal opportunity for women in all aspects of society. Catholic feminists react against **patriarchy**, the institutionalization of male dominance over women. Today's Catholic women are acutely aware of what they consider the long history of patriarchy in the church, of power tied to ordination and of their being excluded solely on the basis of gender. Church leaders seem insensitive to women's experience in liturgy where male language and male presiders emphasize to many women a sense of exclusion, inferiority, and diminished self-worth.[16]

The accomplishments of the Catholic feminist movement in the United States are impressive. It has produced competent, articulate women theologians and Scripture scholars who teach in Catholic and secular universities and colleges and who take their place alongside their male counterparts. They excel in publications of quality and have produced a near deluge of books on feminist themes.[17]

Catholic women consider the ultimate example of patriarchy to be the exclusion of women from the priesthood. Women's ordination[18] has become the focus for a large segment of Catholic women who see it both as a matter of justice and of male domination. Recently some Catholic women, convinced they are called by God to the priesthood and following their conscience while risking excommunication from the church, have taken the initiative to be ordained.[19]

The church's position on women's ordination is stated in two documents: "Declaration on the Admission of Women to the Ministerial Priesthood" was issued by the Congregation for the Doctrine of the Faith in 1977. "The Church in fidelity to the example of the Lord, does not consider herself authorized to admit women to priestly ordination " based on "an unbroken tradition throughout the history of the Church."[20] In 1994 Pope John Paul II issued an apostolic letter to all bishops of the Catholic Church titled "Priestly Ordination Reserved to Men Alone.[21]

Wherefore, in order that all doubt may be removed regarding a matter of great importance, a matter which pertains to the Church's divine constitution itself, in virtue of my ministry of confirming the brethren (cf. LK 22:32) I declare that the Church has no authority whatsoever to confer priestly ordination on women and that this judgment is to be definitively held by all the Church's faithful.[22]

How should conscientious Catholics view this situation of women priests who defy serious official Catholic teaching and the continuing discussion and advocacy of women's ordination by Catholics? Can the Catholic feminist movement and the push for women's ordination be judged, as they contend, a long-range inspiration of the Holy Spirit for the future benefit of the church? Has the official command not even to discuss women's ordination been counter-productive resulting in even stronger anger and action?[23]

Though the ordination of women in opposition to church teaching seriously wounds the unity of the church so valued by Jesus and by St. Paul and guarded throughout the long history of the church, Christian love forbids condemning and pre-judging these women, and counsels respecting their honest conviction of being called by God to priesthood after often long periods of prayer, discernment and spiritual direction.

The church's ban against women's ordination does not extend to women deacons. The ministry of ordained women deacons flourished in the Eastern Church after the latter half of the fourth century, especially their ministry to women and children and their preparation of women catechumens for baptism and accompanying them to the baptismal pool. Canon 15 of the Council of Chalcedon (451) referred to the ordination of women deaconesses.[24] Two bishops at Vatican II suggested that women be included in the restored order of deacon.[25] Much scholarly historical study is being done today on the complex question of women deacons and the possibility and appropriateness of recovering the ministry of women deacons to serve the people of God.[26] Tens of thousands of women already serve the church in diaconal roles; to grant them the sacramental grace of ordination as male ordained deacons have today would greatly enrich the Catholic Church. (See chapter 18)

5. Credible Sexuality

A universally recognized and admired strength of the Catholic Church is its consistent and strong support of moral values under attack in contemporary society. Yet Catholics are increasingly aware of the difference between what the church teaches on sexuality and their lived experience. Both young and old often find that teaching inflexible, authoritarian and unduly negative. Nearly 90% of Catholics disagree on contraception in marriage; increasing numbers question the church's condemnation of sexual expression between *committed* homosexuals and pre-marital sex in a genuinely committed relationship leading to marriage. Most cannot accept that using a contraceptive in marriage is an intrinsically evil act and mortally sinful; they believe that the church's teaching on abortion would be strengthened if contraception were not so vigorously condemned.

Accordingly, an important challenge facing the Catholic Church today is to develop a theology of human sexuality that expresses her members' lived experience, is genuinely helpful in their daily lives, and able to be taken seriously. To accomplish this, the church will be helped by seriously listening to her members, married and single, straight and gay, women and men, and by supporting the church's moral theologians in their difficult task. The pastoral care of her members as well as the credibility of her teaching office is at stake. In this context we consider the church's teaching on contraception and homosexuality. (See chapter 14 for moral principles involved)

Of Human Life and Contraception "

No papal document has ever caused such an earthquake as the encyclical *Humanae Vitae"* wrote Fr. Bernard Haring, Catholicism's foremost moral theologian at the time of the publication *"Of Human Life."*

The "earthquake" is the teaching of Pope Paul VI's 1968 encyclical that each and every act of sexual intercourse in marriage must remain open to the transmission of human life (no. 11) because of the "inseparable connection between the unitive and procreative meaning of sexual intercourse." (no. 12). To frustrate this act by a contraceptive is to act against the natural law ordained by God and thus is termed an intrinsically evil act.[27] (See Chapter 14)

The commission set up by Pope John XXIII to discuss 'the pill' created by the Catholic Dr. John Rock was made up of moral theologians, doctors, scientists, university professors, married couples, bishops and several Cardinals. After lengthy testimony and discussion, the commission voted 64-4 to change the church's opposition to contraception. The bishops and Cardinals present voted 9-3 to draft a report Pope Paul VI.

The commission affirmed that the morality of married couples' sexual activity depended not on each individual act but on the entirety of their married love and their commitment to children. The minority report drafted by the four dissenting commission members opposed change based on the ordering of *each generative act* to procreation. Fearing that a change in the church's traditional teaching would scandalize faithful Catholics and lead them to leave the church, Paul VI followed the minority report. Ironically, his encyclical caused the very results he feared.

That the vast majority of American Catholics disregard the teaching, and a large number of moral theologians and more than a few priests and bishops privately disagree, raises the theological question of "reception": when a large majority fail to accept a teaching, there is reason to question whether it is an authentic teaching guaranteed by the Holy Spirit. Is it possible that the church is here experiencing an example of the 'intuitive sense of the faithful' emphasized in Vatican II?

There also is the philosophical and theological question of the natural law basis of the church's teaching: can the church pronounce definitively on a principle of morality derived from reason rather than Scripture? A 1975 declaration by the Vatican Congregation for the Doctrine of the Faith "Certain Questions concerning Sexual Ethics" reaffirmed the church's teaching.[28]

The teaching on contraception has special relevance today in the use of condoms to slow the spread of AIDS. Moral theologians have invoked the principle of the double effect to permit condom use since the good effect is the avoidance of disease to save lives. Recently Benedict XVI said condom use can be justified in limited circumstances such as a male prostitute to avoid infecting a male client as "first step [toward] ... a first assumption of responsibility.[29] In this situation the condom does not obstruct conception and human life.

We have treated *Of Human Life* and contraception in detail in the hope that it will not be such a stumbling block for younger Catholics who may be unaware of the larger context and positive values of the church's teaching.

Homosexuality

The Catholic Church has been accused of being anti-gay.[30] Its 1996 statement that homosexual orientation, though not sinful, is an "objective disorder,' angered gay men and women who consider it unjust and insensitive to their experience. The perceived condemnation of any sexual act between two members of the same sex as sinful and the inability of the church hierarchy to accept the possibility that homosexuality is not an acquired way of life but a basic inborn characteristic is particularly vexing to the experience of gay people and in the light of recent public awareness of homosexuals in the Catholic priesthood. A tragic problem is the large number of suicides among teen-age Catholics who receive little help in their guilt feelings and the prospect of not being able to live the life the church expects them to.

Homosexuality is a major pastoral and moral dilemma for the Catholic Church. Theologian Thomas Rausch believes "...one of the most difficult questions facing the Christian community today is ... its official inability to recognize faithful and exclusive relations between homosexuals as appropriate expressions of intimacy and love."[31]

The church teaches that sex between members of the same sex, which cannot result in conception and children, violates God's purpose of procreation and thus is a 'disordered' action constituting sin. The moral and pastoral problem occurs when sincere and conscientious gay persons are equally convinced that God has created them in this way, that their love and sexual activity are not displeasing to God, and that God does not intend them to go through life deprived of the intimacy heterosexuals enjoy. An increasing number of Catholic moral theologians do not impute sin to such gay men and women in a stable, exclusive, and faithful love relationship. They ask, should not the moral question rather be determined by the quality of their relationship rather than by individual acts? Other Catholic theologians and many Catholics disagree with this pastoral approach and condemn those who do.

The Catholic Church finds itself in a very difficult position today; it must remain true to its conviction and teaching yet find a way to act in a pastoral, Christ-like way toward gay men and women valued and loved by God. One of the ways this is happening is in parish communities where gays and lesbians are present. A special ministry exists with the blessing of the pastor to reach out to these Catholics to find a community that welcomes them without judgment.

Conclusion. A promising step for the Church to regain its credibility and close the "gap" in its teaching on sexuality is the urgent call by Bishop Klaus Kung of Sankt Polten, Austria, for a church document on human sexuality to be preceded by a commission including married couples to review all problems connected with sexual morality. For the Catholic Church is often at odds with modern psychology and scientific research, a situation that embarrasses Catholics engaged as therapists and psychologists/psychiatrists; it is one of the reasons many are leaving the church.

For this commission to succeed, it should represent a full cross section of the people of God: theologians, married couples, single men and women, gays and lesbians, parish priests. The commission is likely to fall short of achieving credibility and be of help if it is made up exclusively of male celibate church leadership.

6. Healing the Polarized Church

Differences are not intended to separate, to alienate. We are different precisely in order to realize our need of one another. South Africa Anglican Archbishop Desmond Tutu

"Polarization simply means that people no longer dialogue ...It leads to bitterness and much rash judgment ... The whole Catholic tradition of both/and almost always ends up being either/or ... loyalty and disloyalty become the politicized terms ... "[32]

A major crippling tension in the Catholic Church today is over the "correct" interpretation of the Second Vatican Council between those who want the council's renewal to be fully carried out and those who, while not objecting to Vatican II itself, opt for its re-interpretation. The liturgy of the Mass is an example of this polarization. (See chapter 4)

Other areas of tension involve older priests committed to Vatican II and younger conservative restoration priests; pro-life and social justice camps, gender issues, women's ordination, sexual ethics, and the roles of lay Catholics in the church. Today internet blogs are a new source of polarization in mean-spirited comments aimed at fellow Catholics.

A particularly harmful tension within the Catholic Church in America and elsewhere today is between Catholics and church leadership: Catholics upset at bishops for failing the victims of priest abuse, grieving the closure of beloved parishes, and fearful at the looming loss of Eucharist and sacraments; the large number of women alienated by the official church, divorced and remarried Catholics marginalized by exclusion from the Eucharist.

Such tension causes great harm to the Catholic Church. It tends to create two churches destroying the community of love; it gives bad example to younger Catholics; it is an impediment to vocations to the priesthood and religious life; it hurts evangelization and renders the church less attractive to potential converts; above all it obscures Jesus' example of love.

Both Catholic progressives and conservatives love the church deeply but have different theologies of the church and different perceptions of what today is best for the Catholic Church. Both groups are needed: traditionalists to preserve values and practices of the church's heritage; progressives to challenge the church to change to meet contemporary needs. Catholics must overcome as far as possible this polarization for the church to be an attractive, credible sacrament of Christ's love and unity. The need for healing polarization is great.

We reflect here on two further areas that seriously divide the church today: dissent involving church teaching and forms of Catholic fundamentalism.

Dissent from Church Teaching

A serious cause of tension in the church today is conservatives characterizing alleged liberal Catholics disloyal because they disagree or dissent from authentic, non-infallible teaching of the church's magisterium and liberal Catholics failure to appreciate conservative positions and persons. The non-acceptance by Catholics of the encyclical *Of Human Life* brought the issue of dissent to the fore in the United States and beyond.

Permissible or non-permissible dissent involves a host of important questions: the primacy of one's conscience; the vocation and responsibility of theologians and the most appropriate exercise of the church's teaching office. Private dissent as a matter of personal conscience is permissible; the tension today concerns *public* dissent.

The Case against Dissent. The Catholic Church has received from Christ the responsibility to teach her members and aid them in conscience formation. This responsibility is essential to the church's mission and deserves respect and acceptance. Catholic theologians who teach in the name of the church are responsible to follow church teaching. Public disagreement diminishes Catholics' respect and obedience to the magisterium and becomes a source of confusion and scandal to the faithful. These are weighty reasons.[33]

The Case for Permitting Dissent. Church historians, theologians and Catholic laymen and women recognize that some non-infallible official church teaching has in the past been incomplete and even erroneous.[34] The recently beatified John Henry Newman is called the architect of Vatican II because he championed the **development of doctrine** showing how teaching has changed throughout church history.

Dissent for both ordinary Catholics and theologians brings conscience into play. Vatican II stated "in all his activity a man [sic] is bound to follow his conscience," (GS 3), his "most secret core and sanctuary."(GS 16) Catholic theologians whose service to the church is rigorous, scholarly pursuit of truth sometimes recognize incomplete magisterial teaching with which they disagree.

Another aspect of disagreement or dissent is the council's recognition of the sense of the faithful, that supernatural understanding of faith which characterizes the people ... aroused and sustained by the Spirit. (LG 12) Author and psychologist Sidney Callahan, a Catholic, observed that "Catholics who in conscience dissent ... may be responding to what the Holy Spirit intends for the Church." She believes "the Church must work toward respecting loyal dissent."[35]

It is instructive to note that the U.S. bishops in 1969 issued "Norms for Licit Theological Dissent" from the church's magisterium when "the reasons are serious and well-founded, if the manner of dissent does not question or impugn the teaching authority of the Church and is such as not to give scandal." Cardinal Ratzinger of CDF issued a statement condemning *public* dissent.[36]

Catholic Fundamentalism[37]

A more extreme form of polarization that painfully wounds the church and harms Catholic unity is the phenomenon of Catholic fundamentalism. It has been described as a "religious disease that focuses on non-essential matters in Catholic belief" and is often "obsessed with questions of individual salvation and sexual morality while ignoring Catholic Social teaching on issues like poverty, human rights, greed, just war, etc." "Fundamentalists insist on absolute, infallible, inerrant and unambiguous authority ... of official statements of the Roman magisterium ... to be obeyed absolutely." They often write letters to Rome criticizing alleged "disloyal theologians and nuns involved in social justice causes who fail to wear religious garb."

A current example of Catholic fundamentalism in the United States is what has come to be called "Catholic Evangelism." Catholic 'evangelists' stress the distinction between the "culture of life" and the "culture of death." Confident that the American bishops are on their side, they seek excommunication for Catholic politicians they judge do not adhere totally in public life to church teaching. They point to the position of some bishops who imply that Catholics can vote only for the political party that is anti-abortion. This politicization of the church by the action of some bishops has become critically divisive, resulting in more than a few Catholics leaving the church.

Another form of Catholic fundamentalism is integralism, defined in general terms as the belief that religious convictions should dictate political and social action. Archbishop John Quinn described integralism as a "form of petrifying changelessness" that "denies doctrinal development, inculturation and historical consciousness" and holds that "church and doctrine ... must remain unaffected by the present or the future and must admit of no diversity of expression."[38] Citing Archbishop Lefebrve's Society of Pius X, priest-sociologist John Coleman calls integralism, in contrast to the values of conservatism, "incompatible with living tradition." He identifies today's Catholic integralist movements as *Opus Dei, Communion and Liberation* in Italy, and *Tradition, Family and Property* that supported dictatorships in Brazil and Chile, and in the United States *Catholics United for the Faith, True Catholics, The Remnant and The Wanderer Forum*.[39] He warns that "contemporary integralists tend to "turn discipline into dogma," make the church's magisterium the "litmus-test of orthodoxy," and see the post-Vatican II church as a new form of the [nineteenth-century] modernist heresy." He believes "The Catholic tradition of fundamentalism-integralism has come back to haunt us in the post-Vatican II church."[40]

Catholic fundamentalism appears to ignore the deliberate and explicitly positive attitude to the world of the Second Vatican Council in *The Church in the Modern World*.

Healing Polarization

This was the goal of Cardinal Joseph Bernardin's Catholic Common Ground initiative founded along with Msgr. Philip J. Murnion in 1996. They worried that if polarization was not addressed, the church would be "torn by dissension and weakened in its core structures." They took as their founding principle "the call to be one in Christ." That it was rejected is a tragic lost opportunity. There is both a great need and healing opportunity for the United States Catholic Bishops' Conference to plan and commit to a major program for overcoming today's polarization .

Effective ways to heal the corrosive, negative influence of polarization might include a concerted effort in American parishes through frequent homilies that acknowledge the problem and ask for understanding and tolerance based on the example of Christ; a community liturgy of reconciliation; discussion-dialogue groups led by qualified facilitators; and shared social projects that bring polarized Catholics together to aid the poor, the hungry, and the homeless locally. Parishes that adopt a parish in a developing country provide a welcome focus of concern and pride for differing groups. Liturgist Sr. Mary Collins believes "there needs to be a change of heart running through the whole ecclesial body ... to do the work of Jesus for the kingdom of God."

"A healthy Church generates charity. It exhibits tolerance, concern, encouragement. It invites, embraces, forgives. An unhealthy Church generates division. It exhibits righteousness, judgment, arrogance, discouragement. It rejects, excludes, demeans."[41]

7. Restoring the Unity of Christ's One Church

Recovering the lost unity of Christ's one church is an urgent challenge to the Catholic Church. John XXIII made the restoration of unity a major goal in calling the Second Vatican Council. Unity is Jesus' desire and prayer at the Last Supper: "That all my be one as you Father and I are one that the world may believe." (John 12:11) Disunity is destructive of the church's mission. A united Christian Church is a potentially powerfully force for world peace.

Healing that broken unity of Christ's Church is a particularly important challenge to the Catholic Church. Historians recognize that she bears some responsibility for the breakup of the church in the 11th and 16th centuries. The fact that today the Catholic Church claims to be the fullest expression of Christ's church and is the oldest, largest, and most influential, she may have the most responsibility for resolving the current ecumenical impasse and restoring unity.

Chapter 11, That All May be One," in describing "The Ecumenical Picture Today" and "The Challenge Ahead," recognized the many daunting problems facing the churches in their journey to unity: the pope's claim to primacy of jurisdiction for the Orthodox churches; the ordination of women priests and bishops by Anglican and Protestant churches making union with the Catholic Church impossible; and the Catholic Church's model of unity whereby the Anglican and Protestant churches are asked to recover the threefold ministry of priest-deacon-bishop, bishops in the apostolic succession, the sacrament of Holy Orders for the full mystery of the Eucharist, and the other sacraments except baptism.

Accordingly unity between the Catholic Church and the separated churches (Orthodox) and ecclesial communities (Anglican and Protestant churches) appears unlikely. In this situation, the question becomes: what can the Catholic Church, leaders and members alike, do to heal the broken unity of Christ's one church and achieve the restoration of unity, a major goal of the Second Vatican Council?

Jesuit canonist and theologian Ladislas Orsy believes an answer lies in the conversion of the Catholic Church. He proposed two questions; "How can our Church … contribute to the healing of the Church of Christ through a process of institutional conversion? How can it enter into a *kenosis*, an emptying of itself for the sake of others?[42] He identified seven areas of Catholic teaching and practice that pose obstacles to other churches. He believes "ecclesial union is impossible as long as ...

...the church of Christ is conceived as existing *exclusively* in one community or denomination;

...apostolic succession is seen as an "unbroken line of episcopal ordinations from the Apostles to the bishops today" and therefore is accepted as the *only* criterion of valid ordination and of sacraments;

...theological and ecclesial pluralism and the principle of unity in diversity are denied;

...the Roman Curia seeks to exercise total centralized control over the whole church, especially local bishops and their churches.

...the papal office remains un-renewed according to the Gospel of Jesus.

...the Vatican refuses to recognize at least Anglican and Lutheran ordinations and sacraments and to promote Eucharistic sharing;[43]

...**synodical** and conciliar models of church are denied in practice." (affecting the Orthodox)

Union between the Catholic Church and the Orthodox churches holds promise. John Paul II suggested returning to the Church's first millennium when the Eastern and Western churches were in communion through the five major Patriarchs – Alexandria, Antioch, Constantinople, Jerusalem and Rome – living in communion with each other. Were the pope as Bishop of Rome and Patriarch of the West, one of his ancient titles,[44] to offer to forsake in practice his claim of primacy of jurisdiction and to revert to the practice of the first six ecumenical councils, would such an historic overture be what John

Paul II asked the prayers for in his letter *That All Be One*? Despite historical nuances, this might be a viable new way of exercising the papacy for the sake of communion with the Orthodox after 1000 years of estrangement?

In the light of the serious ecclesiological issues involving the Anglican and Protestant churches (treated in chapter 11 and repeated above), what practically can the Catholic Church, leaders and members, do today to work together toward unity?

First, Christians, already profoundly united in the body of Christ because of their baptism, should take every opportunity to celebrate their common life in Christ by mutual prayer and bible study, pulpit exchanges, cooperation in social projects for the hungry and the poor and world peace, and collaboration for Christian values in public life. These areas provide valuable opportunities for Catholic bishops and priests to lead their people in programs of outreach with and to their fellow Christians in the body of Christ.

Second, Vatican II recognized that the enormity of the challenges confronting the separated churches and ecclesial communities could only be overcome through prayer leading to conversion. "This change of heart and holiness [interior conversion, UR 7) along with public and private prayer for the unity of Christians ... [is] the soul of the whole ecumenical movement and merits the name of 'spiritual ecumenism'. " (UR 8)

Ultimately, Christian unity is the work of the Holy Spirit.

A present powerful program of prayer for Christian unity is the annual Week of Prayer for Unity ending January 25, feast of the conversion of St. Paul. Inaugurated by the Episcopalian priest Paul Wattson, founder of the Society of the Atonement to pray and work for the reunion of the Christian churches, this annual week has come to be celebrated by the majority of the Christian churches worldwide.

Not all Catholic parishes in the United States participate in this Week of Christian prayer nor do all pastors and bishops promote it. In the last analysis, only faithful prayer rising to the Holy Spirit from the churches of the world for change of heart and conversion can accomplish the restoration of unity of Christ's one Church. Spiritual ecumenism is the heart of the churches' difficult journey to union in the body of Christ.

Footnotes.

1   Austin Flannery, O.P. Gen. ed. *Basic Sixteen Documents, Vatican Council.* (New York: Northport, 1996.

2   Thomas Rausch, S.J., "Archbishop Quinn's Challenge: A Not Impossible Task." *The Exercise of the Primacy, Continuing the Dialogue.* New York: Crossroad Publishing Co., 1998. 78.

3   *The Cara Report,* Georgetown, MD: Center for Applied Research in the Apostolate. Vol 15, No. 1, Summer 2009, 5.

4   Adrian Hastings, *Modern Catholicism, Vatican II and After* (New York: Oxford University Press, 1991), 221.

5   Since the order of deacon is a unique vocation of service and is not meant to advance to the priesthood, a change of church law would be needed. The urgent need for priests could make this possible.

6   See Thomas Rausch, *Priesthood Today; An Appraisal* (New York/Mahwah, NJ: Paulist Press, 1992) for an informative, balanced treatment of contemporary American priesthood, especially chapter 2, "Priesthood as Ministry."

7   Vatican II in its *Decree on the Ministry and Life of Priests* (#'s 4,6,9) and *Lumen Gentium* 28 rooted the ministry of priests in Jesus' ministry as prophet, priest and king, emphasizing leadership in forming and nurturing the faith community through preaching the Gospel and empowering the laity for their ministry.

8   Mary Gautier, Paul Perl and Stephen Fichter. Chapter 2, "Satisfaction in Priestly Life and Ministry," *Same Call, Different Men. The Evolution of the priesthood since Vatican II (Collegeville, MN: Liturgical Press, 2012).*

9   We treat here the American Catholic Church. The number leaving the church in Europe, particularly Germany and Austria, is very large. See Introduction, FN 3.

10   Peter Steinfels. "Further Adrift, the American Church's Crisis of Attrition." *Commonweal,* (Oct. 22, 2010): Of those unaffiliated, 56 % were unhappy with the church's teaching on abortion and homosexuality; 48 % on contraception; 39 % treatment of women; 33 % on divorce and remarriage.

11   Cathleen Kaveney. "Long Goodbye, Why Some Devout Catholics are Leaving the Church,'" *Commonweal* (Oct. 22, 2005): 8.

12   Michael J Gilligan. "An open Letter to Bishop Robert Finn." *National Catholic Reporter* Vol 45, no. 25 (Oct. 2, 2009): 24.

13   Steinfels, *op.cit.*

14   Thomas J. Reese. "The Hidden Exodus: Catholics Becoming Protestants." Copyright, The *National Catholic Reporter*, (pr. 18, 2011): 4-5.

15   Peter Steinfels, *A People Adrift: The Crises in the Roman Catholic Church in America* (New York; Simon and Schuster, 2005), 330.

16   The Congregation for the Worship and Discipline of the Sacraments in *Liturgicam Authenticam* (2001) rejected inclusive language translations of the Mass and other liturgical texts adopted and promulgated by the world's English-speaking bishops' conferences.

17   Elisabeth Schussler Fiorenza, Rosemary Radforth Reuther, Mary Jo Weaver, Sr. Joan Chittister, Sr. Sandra Schneiders, Ann Carr, Sally Cuneen, Lisa Sowle Cahill, Phyllis Zagano.

18   Concerned with the survival of the Church during the communist control of Czechoslovakia, Bishop Felix Davidek ordained married men and "a small

number" of women including Ludmilla Javorava in order to minister to women in prison and the large number of women religious. For her inspiring story, read Miriam T. Winter, *Out of the Depths,* New York: Crossroad, 2001.

19   The first such ordination occurred on the Danube River, June 2002, when seven women were ordained by a Catholic bishop reputed to be in the apostolic succession, in an effort to ensure a valid but illicit ordination. Later, two of these women were ordained bishops who in turn ordained five women to the deaconate. In 2005 in Canada five more women were ordained to the priesthood and five to the deaconate. As of this writing over 120 women priests and several women bishops minister to small voluntary groups of Catholics in the United States and Europe. The Church's magisterium considers these ordinations not only illicit but invalid because of "lack of matter," that is, maleness being necessary for the sacrament of ordination.

20   'Vatican Declaration; Women in the Ministerial priesthood,' *Origins* 6, no 33 Feb. 3, 1997, 517-24 plus commentary 524-31. The International Biblical Commission mandated by Pope Paul VI to consider this question reported that there is nothing conclusive for or against women's ordination in the Christian Scriptures. Those who favor women's ordination do not see the force of the argument of Jesus' maleness as essential for priesthood. They quote St. Paul's striking statement "In Christ Jesus there is neither Jew nor Gentile, slave or free, male or female..." (Galatians 4:28), stressing that Jesus' common humanity, not his maleness, is the issue. -They argue from experience that women have gifts and charisms to priestly ministry that would greatly enrich the church. Finally, women argue that their baptism into the Body of Christ gives them a right to serve as priests.

21   See *Origins* 24 (June 9,1994): 50-58 for text of John Paul II's "Apostolic Letter on Ordination and Women," an interpretative text by the Vatican and comments by Cardinals Bernardin and Law; Archbishops Buechlein, Keeler, and Weakland; Bishop Hamelin, president of the Canadian Conference of Catholic Bishops, and Matthiesen. Archbishop Weakland's reflections are thought-provoking in their pastoral sensitivity, frankness, and the pastoral and theological questions they raise. He said "As a bishop I will have to ponder what the phrase 'this judgment is to be held definitively' means in terms of its demands on the faithful." In terms of "the pastoral problems I now will face in my archdiocese,"

he asks what effects this declaration will have on four groups: 1. "so many women and men, especially younger women and vowed religious who still see this question as one of justice and equality"; 2. "on theologians who are still concerned about the theological underpinnings of the pope's teachings"; 3. "on those men and women for whom the issue of the way in which the church exercises its authority is already a problem"; 4. "on ecumenical dialogue ... will this declaration mean that full communion is ruled out with all except the Orthodox churches ... [which] may agree with the pope ... but are usually shocked when the pope teaches the bishops and does not speak in union with them."

22 This is a serious exercise of "the ordinary papal magisterium in a definitive way" and thus asks for the binding assent of faith by Catholics. See Francis A Sullivan, S.J. "Developments in Teaching Authority since Vatican II," *Theological Studies* 73 (2012): 581-89.

23 "The truth is that suppression of thought ... has not only driven people away, it has stunted the Church's own development, diminished its credibility." Sr. Joan Chittister. "Silenced or Louder than Ever." *National Catholic Reporter,* Vol 45, No 25 (Oct 2, 2009): 23.

24 "A woman should not receive the laying on of hands as a deaconess under 40 years of age, and then only after searching examinations ... and if after she has hands laid on her and has continued for a time to minister ..." Council of Chalcedon, Canon 15.

25 Bishop Leon Bonaventura de Uriarte Bengoa, OFM of San Ramon, Peru, asked that "deaconesses be instituted"; Bishop Giuseppe Ruotolo of Ugento, Italy, suggested that "the order of deacons be restored and extended to women with the obligation of celibacy." *Acta et documenta Concilio oecumenico Vaticano II apparando; Series prima (antepraeparatoria) (Typis Polyglottis Vaticanis, 1960-61) (ADA), II/II, 121.*

26 Preeminent are the scholarly studies of Phyllis Zagano, a tireless advocate for women deacons in the church. Phyllis Zagano, *Holy Saturday: An Argument for the Restoration of the Female Diaconate in the Catholic Church* (Crossroad, 2000); *Women in Ministry: Emerging Questions about the Diaconate* (Paulist, 2012); "Women and the Church: Unfinished Business of Vatican II," *Horizons*

34/2 (2007), especially pages 213-21; "Whatever Happened to Women Deacons?" *National Catholic Reporter* (Feb 4, 2011): 8A. See also Gary Macy, William T. Ditwig, Phyllis Zagano, *Women Deacons: Past, Present, Future* (Paulist, 2012).

27 In a speech to the 1980 Synod of Bishops, Archbishop John Quinn spoke of "this enormous problem for the Church." He said many persons of good will do not accept 'the intrinsic evil of each and every use of contraception' noting that this understanding is held by 'theologians and pastors whose learning, faith, discretion and dedication to the Church are beyond doubt." Quinn, "New Context for Contraception Teaching," *Origins*, Oct. 9, 1980 263-67.

28 'The precepts of the natural law have absolute and immovable value; (Section IV); "every genital act must be in the framework of marriage" (Section VII); and "every direct act of the moral order of sexuality is objectively serious" (Section X).

29 See Peter Seewald, *Light of the World: the Pope, the Church and the Signs of the Times.*(San Francisco: Ignatius Press, 2010), 118-19.

30 The Catholic Church insists that gays and lesbians be respected and welcomed; Catholic parishes in America celebrate predominantly gay Masses by priests devoted to their spiritual needs.

31 Thomas Rausch, *Catholicism in the Third Millennium.* (Collegeville, MN: 2003 153-4).

32 Rembert Weakland "Introduction " in Pierre Hegy, ed., *The Church in the Nineties, It's Legacy, Its Future* (Collegeville, MN; Liturgical Press, 1993) xxii-xxiii.

33 Joseph Cardinal Ratzinger, "Instruction on the Ecclesial Vocation of the Theologian," (Vatican City: Congregation for the Doctrine of the Church, 1990). Part IV, The Vocation of the Theologian, 6-12 and 27 "... the theologian will refrain from giving untimely public expression to them."

34 Examples are "no salvation outside the church"; justifying executing heretics; modernist Syllabus of Errors condemning democracy, separation of Church and

State; the Galileo case; the practice and teaching on usury and slavery, capital punishment, relation to other Christian churches.

35 Sidney Callahan "Conscience Reconsidered,' *America* Nov. 1, 1986. 251-53. Moral theologian Richard McCormick asked "If the Church is intolerant of dissent, is it not excluding a possible source of correction and improvement as well as error?" McCormick, "The Search for Truth in the Catholic Context" *America* 153 (April 11, 1986) 281.

36 Ratzinger, *op.cit., Part IV, Magisterium and Theology. B. The Problem of Dissent, 32-41, esp. 37-8.*

37 Frank Arnold "The Rise of Catholic Fundamentalism," *America* 156 (April 11, 1987) 297-302

38 John R. Quinn, "Synod '85, Keeping Faith with the Council," *America,* Sept. 21, 1985, 136.

39 John A. Coleman. "Who Are the Catholic 'Fundamentalists'? A Look at Their Past, Their Politics, Their Power." *Commonweal,* Jan. 27, 1989, 44-45.

40 Coleman, *op. cit.,* 42, 44, 46-7.

41 Editorial, *National Catholic Reporter*, March 18, 1988.

42 Ladislas Orsy, 'The Conversion of the Churches; Condition for Unity, A Roman Catholic Perspective," *America* 166 (May 30, 1992); 479-87. This article was inspired by the remarkable work of the Groupe des Dombes, an independent group of Catholics and Protestants in France who issued a challenge to the divided churches "to recognize that their identity is grounded in a continual conversion – without which their unity can never be realized." Groupe des Dombes, *For the Conversion of the Churches* (Geneva: WCC Publications, 1993).

43 A commission created by Pope Leo XIII in 1896 to study the question of Anglican Orders voted 5-4 against their validity. To make such an important judgment depend on a tie-breaking vote made under historical pressure indicates the question deserves to be re-opened, especially in the light of the

Church's commitment to ecumenism made at Vatican II and the theological agreements and convergences achieved through the International Anglican-Roman Catholic theological dialogues. Then CDF head Cardinal Ratzinger stated that the church's condemnation of Anglican Orders is to be definitively held by Catholics. Vatican II considered the ordinations and sacraments of "ecclesial communities" (Protestants as well as Anglicans) to be seriously lacking (*defectus,* UR 22, See Chapter 11)

44 The recent action of Benedict XVI of dropping from the official *Annuario Pontificio* (annual papal yearbook) his title "Patriarch of the West" is interpreted by the Orthodox as the pope no longer considered himself fraternally equal to the other Patriarchs.

Chapter 16:
Urgent Challenges, Part II and III

Part II. Structures **8. Effective Forum for Lay Catholics and Priests**

The recent and past calls for reform of the Catholic Church by concerned lay Catholics, associations of priests, and even by some bishops highlight and affirm the need for some structure in the church whereby its members at all levels can voice their needs and serious concerns with confidence that their voice will be heard and where possible acted upon. They increasingly feel they are up against a church that holds all the power, does not permit disagreement, and refuses discussion of critical issues.

Recent examples of priests and laity and bishops publicly organizing and speaking out for reform point to the need for such a forum in the Catholic Church.

In Austria, June 2011, the Austrian Priests' Initiative, formed in 2006 by the respected Msgr. Helmut Schuller, former president of *Caritas Austria* and former vicar-general of the Vienna archdiocese, took the drastic step of issuing a public "Appeal to Disobedience." The priests pledged to take practical action on a list of reforms: giving Holy Communion to everyone who approaches the altar in good faith including divorced Catholics remarried without an annulment, allowing competent lay Catholics to preach at Mass, and supporting the ordination of married men and women. The original 300 priests quickly grew to 400; their Appeal received support throughout the Catholic world, in particular Brazil, the U.S., Ireland, France, Germany, Italy and Mexico, Msgr. Schuller reported. Its power and appeal, according to *The Tablet* is the "truth" of its reforms and the fact that the priests are "drawing attention to the disconnect between the norms of official church teaching and everyday Catholic life as lived by many of the clergy and laity."[1]

A similar association of 505 priests exists in Ireland which endorsed married clergy, asked for reconsideration of who can be ordained and strongly criticized the new Roman Missal translation. The newly-formed *Association of U.S. Catholic Priests* is dedicated to the "full implementation of the vision and teachings of the Second Vatican Council with special emphasis on the primacy of individual conscience, the status and participation of all the baptized, and the task of establishing a church where all believers will be treated as equals." Their goal is "to support brother priests who find the heavy burdens of priest-scarce ministry over-whelming and to create a collegial voice so priests can speak in a united way."[2]

These associations repeat past calls for church reform. The 1990 *Call for Reform* of the Catholic Church by 4500 Catholic lay men and women including some priests, appealed "to the institutional Church to reform and renew its structures; it was a call to institutional reform that reflects the concerns and desires of many Catholics today. They cited eleven areas of reform: women in ministry and decision-making; priesthood open to women and married men, and return to the ministry of resigned priests; teaching on human sexuality; selection of local bishops; new forms of liturgy, language and leadership; open dialogue, academic freedom, and due process; financial openness; meaningful movement toward reuniting the Christian churches; affirmation of the collegial and collaborative leadership style of the National Conference of Catholic Bishops; a voice for the laity in decisions to close parishes and schools; youth alienated by a church they view as authoritarian and hypocritical. Their contention was that "today's church is crippled by its failure to address fundamental justice issues within its own institutional structures. It thus becomes a stumbling block to its own members and to society."[3]

In 1995, 40 U.S. bishops wrote a 5000-word statement that enumerated serious issues critical for the U.S. Catholic Church that do not get "addressed openly and honestly" and called attention to problems the U.S. Bishops' Conference has in dealing with Rome, particularly "de-emphasizing collegiality, re-interpreting the council (Vatican II), and establishing a vertical ecclesiology" (centralization of church authority in Rome.)[4] Also in 1995, 505,000 Austrian Catholics signed a petition by the group, *We Are Church,* calling for greater democracy and tolerance within the church. Their platform called for a church of co-responsibility of laity and clergy, the people's voice in choosing their bishops, full and equal rights for women, free choice of a celibate or non-celibate way of life for priests, appreciation for the goodness of sexuality, separation of the issues of birth control and abortion. In 2010 during Benedict XVI's visit to Britain, a coalition of groups called Catholic Voices for Reform (CV4R) presented a letter to the pope of their major concerns in the form of six respectful questions.[5]

In addition, individual bishops have spoken out. German bishop Franz-Josef Bode stated that it is crucial to give women more power in the church and to ordain them deacons. Cardinal Cormac Murphy-O'Connor of England said "top-down clericalism is at the heart of the problem" of priest-abuse in the church. Bishop Paul Iby of Eisenstadt, Austria, spoke in favor of making priestly celibacy optional. Bishops Edward Day of Derry, Ireland, called for an end to mandatory priestly celibacy. "I believe there should be place in the modern Catholic Church for a married priesthood and for men who do not wish to commit themselves to celibacy. ... Under the guidance of the Holy Spirit, major decisions must be made." He added "celibacy as an obligation has caused many wonderful potential candidates to turn away from a vocation, and other fine men to resign their priesthood at great loss to the church."[6] Archbishop Robert Zollilsch, president of the German bishops' conference, stated he favors discussing the issue of communion for remarried divorcees. That serious discussion on these issues addressed by bishops at the triennial synods of bishops in Rome do not take place indicates bishops too need an effective forum in the church.

These many calls for church reform on the same issues expressed by the laity, priests and bishops and their pleas for serious discussion and action have largely gone unanswered. Too often the response has been counter-productive calls for obedience and adherence to authority, rather than acknowledgement of serious issues and openness to meaningful discussion. The result is growing frustration by Catholics and their priests, church leaders' loss of credibility, departures from the church, and divisive polarization.

Unlike these many past calls for reform, the significance of the Austrian Priests Initiative is its unprecedented call for disobedience which rose from repeated past frustration and is a last resort for entering into serious discussion with church leaders on issues of grave importance for the church.

The Austrian priests are not challenging the authority of bishops or the Vatican. They respect that the church governance established by Jesus on the Apostles and Peter is hierarchical consisting of bishops, priests and deacons through sacramental ordination and that accordingly the church is not a democracy, though more democratic exercise of authority is a grave need today. Nor are they advocating a form of church government like Protestant congregationalism. Their goal is that the often-expressed concerns and needs of the majority of Catholics and of their priests be addressed in serious discussion with church leaders on issues critical to the present and long range health of the church.

It should be acknowledged that church leaders, aware of the divisive potential of reform movements in the history of the church, of past lay control of parishes in the United States, of the non- congregational nature of the church, and of their serious responsibility to maintain unity in a worldwide church, are understandably cautious and slow to respond. Yet, might the frequency of these calls from such variety of sources within the church be inspired by the Holy Spirit speaking through the people of God, a signs of the times to be taken seriously and acted upon?

9. Church Governance

The scandal of many bishops' failure to deal with priest abusers and protect their victims precipitated unprecedented calls from both bishops and Catholic laity for a serious look at church governance. Bishops spoke of the concentration of all power and decision-making in Rome and prominent Catholic laity called attention to the need for transparency and accountability throughout the church. The issue of church governance became a primary concern during the pre-conclave discussion to elect the new pope.

At the heart of the governance structure of the Catholic Church is the reality of episcopal collegiality, the college or group of bishops worldwide in relation to the pope as bishop of Rome.[7] Many consider the greatest accomplishment of Vatican II is the recovery of the principle of collegiality stated in the council's *Decree on the Pastoral Office of Bishops in the Church,* no 4; "Together with its head ... the Roman Pontiff, the episcopal order is the subject of full, supreme, universal power over the universal church." By extension, the bishops at Vatican II intended that collegial relationships prevail at all levels of the church: bishops and the pope, local bishops with their priests, and pastors of parishes with the people of God.

The reality since the council has been failures of collegiality. Three non-collegial actions negatively affecting millions of Catholics are

Pope Paul VI's encyclical *Of Human Life* condemning contraception in married life; the Vatican Congregation for Institutes of Consecrated Life investigation of religious women in the United States and of their Leadership Conference of Catholic Women; and the Vatican Congregation for Divine Worship over-turning in 1997 ICEL's Mass translation by eleven English-speaking bishops' conferences without consulting the bishops involved. (See chapter 4, Reform of the Reform) Finding a way to make the church's decision-making processes more inclusive and in some way accountable to laity and clergy alike is one of the most crucial issues the church faces, a challenge of immense practical importance for the Catholic Church today[8]

We consider five important practices of governance in the church today.

Relationship between Local Churches and the Vatican

A major contribution of Vatican II was to restore the importance of the local church.[9] Joseph Komonchak described this emphasis as "the reversal of a centuries-long process of institutional and administrative centralization and uniformity in almost all areas of church life." The result since the council has been a remarkable development of vigorous local churches in Latin America, Asia and Africa by bishops of vision and energy in leading their dioceses and in meeting the needs of their people.

However, in the last thirty years the Holy See and the Vatican Congregations have been exerting ever greater control over the local churches and their bishops. Cardinal Kaspar wrote in *America (4-23-01)* that "the right balance between the universal church and the particular churches had been destroyed," a complaint voiced by many bishops worldwide. This centralizing of authority and decision-making in Rome severely limits the ability of local bishops to respond to the pastoral needs of their people and to meet the unique problems of their regions.

The Appointment of Bishops

"Let a bishop not be imposed on the people whom they do not want." (Pope Celestine) "He who has to preside over all must be elected by all ... let a person not be ordained against the wishes of the Christians and whom they have not explicitly asked for." (Pope St. Leo the Great)

The choice of bishops has become a critical issue in the church today.[10] Catholics in the United States and Europe, priests and people alike, are asking for some voice in the bishops they receive. They are unhappy with increasingly conservative bishops who fail to listen to their concerns and who seemingly are unable or unwilling to address their urgent needs, especially the lack of priests to celebrate Eucharist and bishops' failures in transparency and accountability. They are aware that Rome's choice of bishops on the basis of total adherence to Vatican policies[11] has resulted in bishops putting the church's reputation ahead of care for victims of priest-abusers.

It is important for the church to find a way to open the process of selecting bishops to some form of participation by the whole church. Too often in the past "king-maker" archbishops or cardinals unduly influenced the appointment of bishops within a country. Presently Rome's apostolic delegate in a country draws up a list of names sometimes with limited consultation, submits it to the Congregation for Bishops with the pope making the final choice. In the context of Vatican II's emphasis on the importance of the local church and its bishop, on the rights and needs of the laity, and on collegial decision-making, might the pastoral life of the church be greatly strengthened when priests, laity and the local bishop have input on the bishops they receive.

Choice of bishops is for many Vatican-watchers the most important renewal-challenge facing the Catholic Church today since a whole generation of Catholics is affected by the choices made. Margaret Steinfels believes that today "we need bishops who are prepared to listen to people and to consult with them, and not necessarily to agree with them, but to deploy a certain power of persuasion rather than marching orders."

National Bishops' Conferences

Vatican II encouraged the formation of conferences of bishops for each country.

> This sacred synod judges that it would be in the highest degree helpful if in all parts of the world the bishops of each country would meet regularly so that by sharing their wisdom and experience and exchanging their views they may jointly formulate a program for the common good of the Church. (CD 37)

Examples of successful bishops' conferences are the United States Conference of Catholic Bishops (See Chapter 7) and their many effective pastoral letters; Latin America's CELAM which produced the influential Medellin, Puebla and Aparecida documents (See Chapter 13); the Council of European Bishops (CCEE) and the active, creative Federation of Asian Bishops' Conference (FABC).

However, the Vatican has severely limited the authority of these conferences. In 1985 Cardinal Ratzinger of CDF stated that they have do not have teaching authority because they lack "theological justification." In 1998 John Paul II decreed in *The Theological and Juridic Nature of Episcopal Conferences* that a unanimous vote of members is necessary for pronouncements of a teaching nature. The expressed concern was that the relationship between each individual bishop and the pope is to be safeguarded and takes precedence over any 'collegial' action of a bishops' conference! Unfortunate consequences are Catholics ignoring important documents of the bishops they consider unimportant and individual bishops refusing to accept the role of the United States Conference of Bishops in the early emergence of sex abuse cases. In practice, to many Catholics, the issue of national bishops' conferences appeared to be the Roman Curia's fear that strong national conferences threatened its control.

For the collegial functioning of the church and the ability of national churches to meet their special needs and challenges, it is important that national bishops' conferences be strengthened according to the express intention of the council.

Triennial Synod of Bishops[12]

Pope Paul VI instituted the Synod of Bishops to be a manifestation of collegiality and a kind of continuation of Vatican II. The synod is a three-week meeting every three years in Rome of over 200 bishops representing national bishops' conferences worldwide of whom 15% are chosen by the Vatican plus attendance by members of the Roman Curia and non-voting abbots and superiors of religious orders..

The synods have come under criticism from bishops worldwide, some calling them a waste of time: the synods have no decisive vote but only make recommendations to the pope; they do not function in a democratic way but are controlled by the Vatican, especially the Roman Curia; the pope chooses the topic and determines the agenda; each episcopal conference submits material for discussion but may not share its recommendations with other conferences; suggestions and urgent concerns raised by bishops in the discussion groups and sent as recommendations to the pope often do not find their way into the final report written by curial officials and the pope. A joke circulating in Rome described Pope John Paul II absorbed during one of the sessions reading the final report![13] As long as the synods remain strictly consultative and controlled by the Roman Curia, ignore serious concerns of bishops representing many areas of the world, and result in little action requested by the bishops, they fall short of their potential to benefit the church and to function as the bishops at the Second Vatican Council intended.

Authority and Accountability.[14]

Concerned Catholics and bishops in various parts of the world question whether something intrinsic to the Roman Catholic Church, her clerical culture, the manner of governance, the way its leaders exercise authority, or a combination of these, has either caused or abetted the priest abuse tragedy.

Closely related to the ways collegiality needs to be present in the governance of the Catholic Church is the question of exercise of authority by church leaders, an issue that involves accountability and transparency shown by openness and truthfulness. In his "Reflection on Governance and Accountability in the Church," Pittsburgh Archbishop Donald Wuerl defined accountability as transparency in the exercise of authority. In recognizing that "much of the anger of the recent [abuse] scandal is rooted in the secrecy and confidentiality" of bishops, he stated that "openness is at the heart of ecclesial accountability." Responding to Archbishop Wuerl, Peter Steinfels emphasized that "failure of openness is the actual issue in the sexual abuse scandal."

During the 2001 Vatican conference on bishops and church governance, Bishop Nestor Ngoy Katahwa of Congo warned that "as princes of the church" we bishops "maintain sole legislative, executive and judicial powers, ... a temptation for us to act like dictators."

10. Reform of the Papacy and the Roman Curia

Theologians, church historians, educated lay Catholics as well as some bishops, many priests and some religious sisters are giving considerable attention to the office of Peter and its exercise of authority in the Catholic Church today. They are especially concerned with the following critical issues: the increased centralization of authority in Rome and the failure of meaningful collegial relationships between the world's bishops and the pope, a major goal of the bishops at Vatican II; the church's refusal to discuss neuralgic issues like clerical celibacy, married priests, women's expanded role in the church; the serious diminution of respect for papal authority occasioned first by the 1968 publication *Of Human Life* and the alleged late defensive response in removing bishops who failed to care for the victims of massive priest-abuse; the church's pervasive clericalism and the Vatican's perceived culture of secrecy.

The above-mentioned Catholics are further concerned with the following: the official church's slow progress toward the union of the separated Christian churches in response to Christ's prayer "that all may be one" and Vatican II's commitment to Christian ecumenism; the current movement to re-interpret the Second Vatican Council and the Roman Curia's effort to restrict its renewal and restore some pre-Vatican II practices; the alarming lack of priests worldwide to bring Eucharist and sacraments to a growing Catholic population; the failure to hear the voice of the laity who are the church, who are guided by the Holy Spirit, and who have rights guaranteed by their baptism and enunciated by the council; the exodus of younger Catholics from the church in developed countries and their perception of the irrelevance of the church and its leadership. These are serious issues which ultimately are related in various ways to papal exercise of authority and to the Roman Curia.

Such critiques may appear out of place in the light of the past outstanding Popes John XXIII, Paul VI, John Paul II and pope-emeritus Benedict XVI whom almost all respect for his holiness, intellectual brilliance and writing-speaking ability. For some, even to refer to the papacy needing reform is unthinkable and implies criticism for those who hold the office of Peter in the church. However, present calls for renewal-reform concern the *exercise* of the papacy and is not meant to diminish or obscure respect either for the office of Peter or its present or past occupants. (See Chapter 7) An example of respectful discussion of the way the office of Peter operates is *The Reform of the Papacy, The Costly Call to Christian Unity* authored by retired Archbishop John R. Quinn in response to Pope John Paul II's 1990 invitation to help him better exercise his role as pope to achieve unity of the separated Christian churches.

We consider five important areas of reform and renewal.

Reform of the **Roman Curia**. During Vatican II there were repeated calls for the reform of the Roman Curia. In 1994, 40 bishops in the United States signed a public statement criticizing the curia for its policy of obstructing the renewal program of the Second Vatican Council. Cardinal Schonborn of Vienna publicly stated that the curia is "urgently in need of reform." Archbishop Quinn devoted a full chapter, 'Reform of the Roman Curia," in his book referred to above. For him the "overall goal of curial reform is decentralization, subsidiarity and collegiality."

- *Decentralization*. By exercising control over bishops of the world, the curia has dramatically weakened local bishops' governance of their local churches.
- **Subsidiarity**, the principle of Catholic social teaching that what can be done or decided at a lower level of society should not be

taken over by a higher level. Pope Pius XII considered subsidiarity a fundamental norm of justice for both hierarchical church authority and the lay apostolate. Subsidiarity involves local freedom and initiative, since not all decisions need be made at the top. Jesuit sociologist John Coleman observed that "problems are best formulated and solved by those who know and experience them." Applied to the church today, Bishop Dowling stated that "subsidiarty requires leadership actively to promote and encourage participation, personal responsibility and effective engagement by all." He finds that today's "church leadership actually undermines the very notion of subsidiarity."[13]

- *Collegiality.* The centralization of authority and decision-making in Rome has seriously harmed the collegial relationship between the bishops and the bishop of Rome. Dowling stated the problem in these strong words;

> It has become more difficult over the past years ... for the college of Bishops as a whole, or in a particular territory, to exercise their theologically based servant leadership to discern appropriate responses to their particular socio-economic, cultural, liturgical and other pastoral realities and needs; much less to disagree with or seek alternatives to policies and decisions taken in Rome.

What is needed, he says "is a Church where leadership recognizes and empowers decision-making at the appropriate levels in the local church."

Cardinal Franz Konig, the deceased Archbishop of Vienna, wrote in 1995 that "curial authorities working in conjunction with the pope have appropriated the tasks of the episcopal college." Bishops in the 1987 Synod objected that the curia made it difficult for them to address issues of their own churches. A participant of that synod, Oakland Bishop

Cummings said that "subsidiarity and inculturation were a constant theme" of the synod. Quinn summarized the objections bishops from "many countries of the world" have with the curia: "frequent over-ruling of decisions by episcopal conferences; appointment of bishops with little or no participation of the local episcopate and the treatment of theologians."[16] A frequent criticism is that the curia, rather than serving and encouraging the bishops, comes between them and the pope.

Curial reform is an immense undertaking, complex and delicate, accomplished only by a strong determined pope or by an ecumenical council supported by the pope. The most commonly-mentioned suggestions for curial reform are term limits, say of five or seven years once renewable, and at least two years of pastoral work to provide the needed pastoral experience for the isolated and entrenched bureaucracy of curial personnel. In fairness, it should be noted that the curia is not a monolith but made up of many highly competent, hardworking men dedicated to the church and to the pope, men who have given quality years to the service of the church.

Cardinals and *Election of the Pope.* Cardinals are archbishops of major cities throughout the world plus certain curial officials; their role is to elect the pope. In *Reform of the Papacy,* Archbishop Quinn pointed out the danger of a 'rotational papacy' since the pope appoints the majority of cardinals who will elect the next pope. Commentators noted that Benedict XVI's 2010 and 2012 appointments of a majority of European cardinals may ensure a future European pope when by contrast the majority of Catholics are in South America and Africa with problems and needs unique to them. There are serious suggestions today that representatives from national bishops' conferences participate in electing the pope. It is significant that after the Second Vatican Council Pope Paul VI "considered incorporating the elected presidents of the various national councils of bishops into the conclave" that elects a new pope.[17]

Quinn also called attention to the fact that the distinct body of cardinals separate from and above the college of bishops and used by the pope as special advisers diminishes the collegial relationship that bishops should have with the bishop of Rome. He emphasized that "Vatican II had stressed the collegiality of the bishops in governing the church by divine institution [whereas] cardinals are a strictly man-made body which had evolved from the local government of the diocese of Rome."

Papalism is the exaggerated emphasis, almost cult, of the person of the pope at times encouraged by a sense of his impeccability and creeping infallibilism. South African Bishop Dowling refers to "the mystique that has surrounded the pope in the last 30 years, such that any hint of criticism or questioning of his policies or his exercise of authority is equated with disloyalty. ... Because of this mystique, unquestioning obedience by the faithful to the pope is required ... as a sign ... of fidelity of a true Catholic."[18] This mystique may inhibit bishops from pressing the Holy Father for necessary change that affects the people of God.

The Vatican Culture – Romanita. Vatican watchers recognize the reality of the unique culture they term *Romanita* (Romanness) that pervades the thinking and actions of the curia and explains why change of any sort is so difficult. There is an abiding awareness of ancient traditional ways of acting, a fear of hasty decisions, a sense that by waiting problems will be resolved. It is a culture of "family," of rewarding loyal service often independent of competency, of "kicking upstairs" to the Vatican those less than successful in other positions. There is a fierce loyalty to the Holy Father and a determination to preserve the church's reputation, perceived as necessary to achieve her mission. There is a sense of not needing to listen to Catholic laity and local bishops since they lack the world vision and centuries-long experience the Vatican possesses. In many ways Romanness is a rich, venerable, effective culture, but today it is seen by many as inadequate and detrimental to the church.

The Clerical Culture and Clericalism. With the spreading revelation in Europe and beyond of priest abuse and bishops' pattern of failure to protect innocent victims, the abuse crisis is coming to be recognized as a crisis in the clerical/hierarchical culture, a culture that requires maintaining silence. In his 2010 pastoral letter, *Sexual Abuse of the Young in the Catholic Church*, Archbishop Mark Coleridge of Canberra, Australia, called clericalism "a hierarchy of power, not service" and described this special culture as "used to conceal crime and to protect the reputation of the church at all costs."[19]

Clericalism is an excessive emphasis on the role of the clergy in the church's internal life. It implies elitism, the clergy as a special, privileged class superior to and isolated from the laity. It was a factor in the priest abuse scandal on the part of both the priests and many of the bishops. Clericalism was 'dealt a blow' by the teaching of Vatican II on the priesthood of all believers and their common baptism. In the restoration movement since the council, clericalism is making a comeback in an effort to restore priests to an elevated status characteristic of parish life before Vatican II; in some newly-ordained priests making parish decisions independent from the laity; by the Tridentine rite emphasizing the role of the priest over participation of the laity; and marginalizing and excluding women. Bishops have begun to speak out about the dangers of clericalism in the church. Diarmuid Martin, Archbishop of Dublin, stated bluntly "The narrow culture of clericalism must be eliminated."

Part III: 11. Post Modernity Crisis of Faith

We are facing a profound crisis of faith and a loss of the religious sense, which constitutes the greatest challenge for the Church today. Renewal of the faith must therefore be a priority of the efforts of the entire Church today.

Thus spoke Pope Benedict XVI in his report Jan. 22, 2012, to members of the Roman Curia's Congregation of the Doctrine of the Faith. In speeches and in announcing the New Evangelization and the Year of Faith, he identified the current culture of secularism based on relativism of truth and belief as the major threat to Christian faith today. This culture is often referred to as postmodernism, whose major characteristics pose such formidable threat to Christian faith today.

- Postmodernity holds that all truth is relative. The claims of the church as bearer of God's revelation and as authoritative teacher for belief in God and Jesus Christ are rejected. Postmodernity attacks the ability of human reason to arrive at truth.
- A central conviction of postmodernism is ethical pluralism in a morally pluralist society. Morality is what each person makes it to be. No church can speak with certainty about what is right or wrong.
- Absolutes like the existence of universal truth, belief in a transcendental and immanent God, in the uniqueness of Christ, and in essences like the nature of the church and a natural law known to all, are rejected.
- Grand explanations, meta-narratives, like the Judaeo-Christian belief in salvation history and personal salvation through Christ and his church, are suspect. The reality of mystery and religion itself are relegated to the purely natural world of personal, subjective experience.

In today's crisis of faith, the Catholic Church has an abundance of resources to combat today's postmodern culture and to deepen the faith of Catholics.

In public utterances, Benedict XVI made penetrating analyses of today's postmodern, positivistic culture and offered a strong, persuasive defense of reason's ability to attain truth and of the church's authority to speak for the basic truths of the Christian faith. An impressive example was his highly-praised 2012 address to the German Bundestag (Parliament).

Benedict challenged today's culture of positivism that holds what "is not verifiable ... does not belong to the realm of reason ... [so that] ethics and religion must be assigned to the subjective field ... and the classical sources of knowledge for ethics and law are excluded. He defended human nature that "cannot be manipulated at will. Man is not merely self-creating freedom" and "to ignore Christianity's conviction of a creative God as what gave rise to the idea of human rights ... the equality of all people before the law, and the inviolability of human dignity in every person ... would be to dismember our culture."

Protestant theologian Leonard Gilkey listed four reasons why he believes the Catholic Church is "best equipped to come to terms with modernity."

- "Its unique sense of being a people rooted in a tremendous history embracing a great part of the human family and covering a marvelous diversity of cultural epochs and geographical expanses."
- "Its tenacious sense of tradition which anchors it in the past yet allowing it to develop in response to changing times and customs."
- "Its emphatically sacramental approach to the mysteries of life and God."
- "A certain grace and humanity ... particularly catholic ... a pastoral wisdom ... an attitude tolerant toward human frailty without compromising its commitment to the lofty ideals of the Gospel."[20]

To preserve and deepen their faith, Catholics, especially those wavering and considering leaving the church, will find inspiration and help in using the church's time-tested means of sustaining and strengthening the gift of faith: meeting the risen Christ in the eucharistic celebration of his saving paschal mystery; taking advantage of the powerful sacraments, especially reconciliation and marriage, of prayer and spiritual reading, retreats and spiritual direction and becoming familiar with the exciting renewal/reform of the Second Vatican Council. My hope in the preceding chapters and in the following chapter describing core values of the church is to contribute to strengthening and deepening Catholics' personal faith today.

Church leaders play a crucial role in preserving and deepening the faith of Catholics' by not inadvertently placing obstacles in the way for church members to appreciate and value their church and to use the church's rich means of grace.

The Church and Modern Culture

Though the very existence and nature of the church and the faith of Catholics are strongly challenged by this postmodern culture, the Second Vatican Council embraced a positive, confident view toward the world and encouraged the church and individual Catholics to become players in the secular, materialist world of its day.

Vatican II's final document, *The Church in the Modern World, GS,* took a stance of hope toward the world based on Christ and the Holy Spirit "whose grace is actively visible ... not only for Christians but for all people of good will" (GS 22). The bishops humbly recognized how much the Catholic Church "has profited from history and the development of humankind ... [and] from the progress of the sciences and from the riches hidden in various cultures." (GS 44).

The council confidently presented Christ, the Alpha and Omega of history, the key, center and purpose of the whole of human history (GS 10), as the hope and example and the source and the power for the church's involvement in the world. Accordingly, the bishops urged "Christians not to shirk their temporal duties" (GS 43) in building God's kingdom of justice, love and peace in today's world according to God's design for the human family.

Gaudium et Spes (GS) has been criticized in some quarters as overly optimistic toward the world, particularly in the church's present critique of secularism and rampant relativism toward truth. Yet the council's 'reading of the times' in the light of the Gospel provides a realistic faith-filled basis for the church's role in today's society. The first part of the *Church in the Modern World* described "the new age in history," its "present social and cultural transformation, economic disparity, pervasive anxiety and confusion" (GS 4); "the upheaval brought by science and technology" (GS 5); "rapid changes in the social order"(GS 6) and "peoples' attitudes and morals affecting religion" (GS 7). Its long Part II analyzed in detail five urgent problems in today's society: the dignity of marriage and the family, the proper development of culture, economic and social life, the political community, and peace and the world community threatened by war and the arms race. (GS 46-90). This comprehensive analysis is the council's context for the Catholic Church "*in* the modern world."

Benedict XVI stresses that "the renewal of the Church will only come about through openness to conversion and through renewed faith."[21]

12. Conversion

Responding to the previous eleven challenges that are opportunities for transformation involve and demand personal and institutional conversion, perhaps the ultimate challenge facing the Catholic Church today.

Basically, conversion means a radical change in accustomed ways of thinking and acting. For Christians, conversion depends on the Holy Spirit and his grace. The Second Vatican Council's program for radical renewal and reform was essentially a profound call for conversion of both members and leaders alike and in the structures of governance. Such conversion appears to be urgent today, no longer to be put off. Conversion is a *kairos* moment, a period of choice that is an unique opportunity as identified in the introduction of this book.

The call to conversion was at the heart of Jesus' teaching. He challenged his hearers to "love God with all your heart, with all your soul and with all your strength, with all your mind, and your neighbor as yourself (Luke 10:27). Jesus' first recorded words in Mark's Gospel are "the reign of God is at hand. Repent. ..." reform your lives, be converted.

Personal Conversion

For ordinary Catholics, conversion involves answering the Vatican II's call to personal holiness; being nourished regularly by the Word of God and the Eucharist; sanctifying married and family life or single vocation; witnessing and proclaiming the good news of Christ by word and example; consciously living one's baptismal vocation to establish the kingdom of God in the world of business or politics, science or education; enriching the church as active parish members – in a word, seriously embracing the renewal of the Second Vatican Council. In today's polarized church, conversion means progressives and conservatives listening and speaking to each other, putting the best interpretation on each other's words and actions, refusing to condemn or ridicule, and loving each other as fellow disciples of the Lord.

In today's world where greed and selfishness oppress others, conversion is best shown by concern and care and deeds of love for our fellow brothers and sisters in need according to the dramatic judgment scene in the gospel of Matthew 25:31-40. Conversion challenges followers of Christ to take to heart Jesus' parable of the Good Samaritan, who, moved with compassion, cared for the man beaten and robbed by thieves and left to lie on the roadside. Today, conversion means linking Christian faith to justice in the spirit of Vatican II's *Joy and Hope* (GS)[22]

This conversion is already a reality in the lives of countless Catholics today, a result of God's grace and the inspiration of Vatican II's renewal.

Institutional Conversion

Institutional aspects of the church are its visible structures of government (papacy, bishops, curial offices, canon law, biblical commission, and so forth). Institutional conversion in these areas means giving priority to Jesus' Gospel values and the urgent pastoral needs of the faithful over preserving nonessential institutional interests. This involves the willingness to sacrifice or modify those historically-conditioned structures and policies which often rose to meet specific needs or simply reflected secular models and the prevailing culture and are not essential to the church's nature or its mission. When such structures no longer serve the primary mission of the church or fall prey to abuse, the need for institutional conversion becomes apparent.

Institutional conversion may also involve creating new church structures or modifying existing ones. Examples frequently mentioned today are structures of accountability and due process; collegial relationships and democratic procedures at all levels of the church's life; deliberative voice for the triennial synod of bishops and parish councils; married priests and women deacons better to serve the people of God.

Canonist-theologian Ladislaus Orsy observed that the "need for an institutional conversion is there for all to see." He affirmed that "the intense movement of conversion at Vatican II ... slowed down considerably" after the council in accomplishing the needed "transformation of centuries-old structures." He proposed specific areas of institutional conversion:[23]

- Granting the laity "a greater share in the operations of the Church."
- Granting a more effective role to women in the church.
- Give a more effective role to the episcopal college: "a real but unfinished movement of conversion in the Roman Catholic Church."
- The Petrine ministry become a "promoter of diversity": "to promote legitimate differences, to let local churches blossom," "to be restrained in the use of power" ... would be a strong protection against an "excessive centralization that the council certainly wanted to avoid."
- Safeguard the "legitimate autonomy of bishops."

A recent dramatic call for conversion came from Cardinal Carlo Martini, retired Archbishop of Milan from 1979 – 2002, in a remarkably forthright interview he gave as a last testament weeks before his death. Asked what means he would recommend to "combat" the situation in the church today, he said: "The first is conversion: the Church must admit its mistakes and set out on a radical journey of change, starting with the popes and the bishops."[24]

Should the church fail to listen to the voices of its own members, to hear the Spirit speaking through many today, to address injustices within the church, and to end vestiges of triumphalism, clericalism and legalism within the church, she risks losing more members, falling short of her mission, and becoming increasingly irrelevant.

A devoted Catholic layman and student of the contemporary Catholic Church made this prophetic statement, a sober challenge yet message of much hope: "Today the Catholic Church in the United States is either on the verge of decline or thoroughgoing transformation."[25]

For Discussion

1. Discuss the priesthood in the Catholic Church. Consider the values of celibacy. Would permitting priests to marry solve the problem of priest shortage? Do you think women should be ordained in the Catholic Church today? Why? Why not?
2. Should *public* disagreement by Catholic theologians be permitted today? Do their discussions on controversial questions influence the church to change? Can you suggest examples?
3. Is the slow pace of ecumenism today partially owing to the Catholic Church? Why or why not?
4. Do you think the present divisions and tensions are seriously harmful to the Catholic Church today? What do you think *needs* to be done? *can* be done?
5. How can the church re-engage members who have drifted away?

Further Reading

Boyle, Gregory, S.J. *Tattoos on the Heart, the Power of Boundless Compassion.* New York: Free Press, 2010. "An honest, raw and compelling collection from Fr. Greg Boyle's life and work with gang-involved youth. His commitment should teach us all a lesson in compromise, sharing, learning, loving and most important, living life to the fullest." Angelica Huston "An extraordinary reflection of a life totally committed to reshaping and redirecting the lives of countless young gang members." Martin Sheen

Bonavoglia, Angela. *Good Catholic Girls: How Women are Leading the Fight to Change the Church.* San Francisco: HarperCollins, 2006. Written by a journalist and radically progressive in content, this book consists of stories of many faithful Catholic women, both professed religious sisters, women priests, openly homosexual Catholics, and other female laity who have taken bold action to address the church's need for reforms.

Cahill, Lisa Sowle, John Garvey, Thomas Frank Kennedy, SJ. *Sexuality and the U.S. Catholic Church: Crisis and* Renewal. Herder & Herder Book/Crossroad Publishing Co., 2006. These authors present the most recent insights from Catholic theologians and scholars on issues such as celibacy, sex abuse scandal, contraceptives, and homosexuality, opening a dialogue for faithful change within the church.

Kaufman, Philip. *Why You Can Disagree and Remain a Faithful Catholic.* New York: Crossroad, 1995. Kaufman discusses "conscientious dissent" among Catholics, and how a frank and open debate about Catholic institutions and policies concerning homosexuality, birth control, celibacy in the priesthood and the election of bishops can be done while still remaining faithful to the church.

Wuthnow, Robert. *Christianity in the 21ˢᵗ Century: Reflections on the Challenges Ahead.* Oxford: Oxford University Press, 1995 Wuthnow stresses the institutional, ethical, doctrinal, political and cultural challenges facing the church today and in the future that are critical to the church's effective functioning. Sense of community among its members is a crucial response to these issues and makes the church, in the words of Karl Rahner, "the visible sign of salvation that God has established in this seemingly godless world."

Footnotes

1   *The Tablet,* Sept. 23, 2011, 2.

2   Robert McClory. "US priests form new national association." *National Catholic Reporter.* Sept.   2011, 1, 6.

3   "A Call for Reform in the Catholic Church: A Pastoral Letter from 4505 Catholics concerned About Fundamental Renewal in Our Church," Feb. 28, 1990, *New York Times,* Section A, 14-5.

4   Specific issues: priest shortage and morale, women equality in the church, better preaching and liturgy, annulment process, loss of Eucharist, contraception, sexual ethics, public face of the church on abortion.

5   "How can the church draw on the skills and abilities of the laity in moving towards a healthy, accountable and professional church government' How can the

collegiality of the bishops and the importance of the local church be revived? Why is Rome imposing an outmoded liturgy on Britain? How can the church humanize its understanding of God's gift of sexual orientation? How can the experience of the laity and the scholarship of female and male theologians assist the church to understand that the non-ordination of women is purely 'cultural and historical'? *The Tablet,* Sept. 11, 2010, 36.

6   Sarah MacDonald. "Daly calls for end to clerical celibacy." *The Tablet.* Sept. 17, 2011. 36.

7   The Church of the first millennium functioned collegially. The principle of collegiality was passionately opposed by the conservative minority at Vatican II. See John W. O'Malley, *What Happened at Vatican II* (Cambridge, MA; Harvard University oppress, 2008 : 302-05.

8   Thomas A Rausch 'Where Do We Go from Here?" *America*, Oct. 18, 2004. 12-13.

9   "The Church of Christ is truly present in all legitimate congregations of the faithful which, united with their pastors, are themselves called churches in the New Testament." LG 26. "In and from such individual churches comes into being the one and only Catholic Church." LG 23.

10 "Testimony from all over the world points to a widespread dissatisfaction with the present procedure for the appointment of bishops." Quinn, *The Reform of the Papacy.* 133.

11 Under John Paul II, the criterion for choosing bishops was total adherence to the encyclical *Of Human Life* and disapproval of married priests and women's ordination. This criterion guaranteed a less pastoral, more institution-minded world episcopate.

12 The first Synod in 1967 dealt with five separate topics (canon law, 'dangerous modern opinions,' seminaries, mixed marriages, liturgy); the Extraordinary Synod of 1969 on Collegiality; Justice in the World and Priestly Ministry, 1971; Evangelization, 1974; Catechesis 1977; the Christian Family 1980; Reconciliation and Penance, 1983; the Extraordinary Synod of 1985, a Celebration of Vatican

II; Role of Laity in Church and World, 1987; the Formation of Priests, 1990; Consecrated life, 1994; Church in America, 1997; Africa, 2000; Eucharist, 2005; Word of God, 2008; The New Evangelization, 2012.

13   A joke circulating in Rome described Pope John Paul II absorbed during one of the Synod sessions reading the final report!

14   See the informative chapters on governance, accountability and authority by Donald Wuerl, Peter Steinfels, James Heft and Gerard Mannion in *Governance, Accountability and the Future of the Catholic Church* edited by Francis Oakley and Bruce Russett, Continuum Publishers, New York.

15   Bishop Kevin Dowling, "Catholic Social Teaching Finds Church Leadership Lacking," talk given June 1, 2010, Cape Town, South Africa. *National Catholic Reporter,* July 8, 2010.

16   Quinn, *Reform of the Papacy,* 160.

17   "This radical step was, itself a prelude to the idea that the college eventually could be abolished altogether. ... Many council fathers regarded it as a scandal and a theological error that the bishops had so little power in the government of the Church though their order was apostolic in nature while the cardinals wielded tremendous power, privilege, and tenure in their stead." Francis A. Burkle-Young, *Passing the Keys: Modern Cardinals, Conclaves, and the Election of the Next Pope.* Lanham, MD: Madison Books, 1999. 206-07.

18   Dowling, *op. cit.* Papalism began in the Church with Pope Pius IX and the first Vatican Council. The successful World Youth Days, despite the much good they accomplish, are critiqued for excessive emphasis on the pope and not enough on the local church and the collegiality of bishops with the Holy Father. For some this is seen as creating an ecclesiology of papalism for the future.

19   Tom Roberts, *The Emerging Catholic Church: A Community's Search for Itself.* Maryknoll, NY: Orbis Books, 2011. 94-5.

20   *Catholicism Confronts Modernity: a Protestant View, (New York: Seabury Press, 1975).*

21 Talk at Freiburg, Germany, Sept. 24, 2012.

22 Members of the Jesuit order link faith with justice in the phrase that has come to express their contemporary mission "the faith that does justice."

23 Orsy, *op.cit.*, 482.

24 Asked how he sees "the situation in the church," Martini responded prophetically: "The Church is tired in Europe and America because of affluence. Our culture has grown old, our churches are big, our religious houses are empty, the bureaucratic apparatus of the Church multiplies, and our rites and vestments are pompous." *The Tablet*, (August, 2012). In "Prophet for our Times," *the Tablet* editorialized "This saintly man, greatly loved in his own diocese, has spoken truth to power."

25 Steinfels, *op.cit.*, 20. From 1990 -2010 Steinfels wrote the *Beliefs* column for the *New York Times*.

Chapter 17:
The 'Great Soul' of the Catholic Church

Writing in the New York *Times,* Nicholas Kristof had this to say about today's Catholic Church.

"Ordinary lepers, prostitutes, and slum dwellers may never see a cardinal, but they daily encounter a truly noble Catholic Church in the form of priests, nuns and lay workers toiling to make a difference ... overwhelmingly it's at the grassroots that I find the great soul of the Catholic Church. "[1]

What today is the attractive 'great soul' of the Catholic Church Kristof refers to?

After frankly treating the crises and unresolved issues, the problems and challenges facing the church with the potential risk of caricaturing her actual reality, this chapter seeks to balance the picture by calling attention to the extraordinary wealth of gifts and values the Catholic Church offers Catholics, other Christians, and the world; to the great good she does for millions worldwide; to her rich spiritual, intellectual, artistic and literary traditions and teachings; and to her unique ecclesial reality embracing more than a billion sinners and saints united in a world community to whom Jesus Christ, God-in-the-flesh, is present and active.

The following 15 gifts and values express at least in part, I believe, the attractive 'great soul' of the Catholic Church today and give evidence of the Spirit's presence and guidance in the church that is a beacon of hope for her members and the world.

1. *The Unexpected Event of Vatican II*

To appreciate the great value that Vatican II is to Catholics, one has only to consider what it would be like today if Vatican II had not happened: to attend only Latin masses; to live in a triumphalist and clericalist and legalistic church; to be aloof and superior to Protestants and to risk sinning for attending a "false" Protestant service; to look down on Jews and Muslims not to mention Hindus and Buddhists as inferior religiously whose salvation was doubtful; to look to the pope and Roman curia for the answer to every doctrinal, moral and disciplinary question; to be perceived as a church emphasizing law and regulations rather than love and freedom; not to trust one's own conscience in moral questions; the laity defined as the non-ordained and considered second-class citizens in the church, and so forth.

Thanks to the encouragement of Pope John XXIII and inspired by the Holy Spirit, the Second Vatican Council gave Catholics today an extensive program of renewal and reform. Vatican II is proof that the traditionally unchanging Catholic Church could in fact change dramatically. The bishops at the council gave the example that important change, no matter how difficult, is possible today.

2. *The Priceless Gift of Faith*

In an age that scoffs at the idea of belief in God, that is determined to keep prayer and religious objects out of the classroom and Christmas cribs from public view, the Catholic Church confidently defends and teaches the possibility and reality of God and of the gift of Christian faith.

In today's world people seek meaning and answers to life questions: Why am I here? Why so much suffering? What happens after death? People long for meaningful personal relationships, for intimacy, for ways to overcome loneliness. Faith provides answers and the experience of God's consoling presence and of Jesus' loving friendship. Catholics who experience severe losses or serious illness, emotional and physical suffering, often say "without faith I couldn't have survived."

Faith accepts God and his unconditional love made known in Jesus Christ and his teaching. Rather than a set of doctrines, faith is first a personal experience when God becomes real. Such faith is a gift of the Holy Spirit by which persons are able to believe the existence of a loving God they cannot see or grasp, to accept the mystery of God's great love that He sent his Son to take human flesh as Jesus of Nazareth, to believe that Jesus is God incarnate, that he healed people, forgave sins, was crucified, actually rose from the dead, and is present with us as risen Lord.

For many today, such faith is superstition, irrational, impossible. Yet thousands accepted the indefatigable preaching of St. Paul throughout Asia Minor, millions became believers throughout the Mediterranean world, thousands died as martyrs for their Christian faith in the Roman persecutions. Believing Christians today number 2.25 billion, including scientists, writers, philosophers, public figures, artists, athletes and people in every country of the world.

Faith gives strength to cope, hope to persevere. It is indeed a priceless gift given at baptism and nourished throughout one's life in the community that is the Catholic Church.

3. Privileged Access to Jesus

The Catholic Church provides a wealth of ways to experience personal friendship with Jesus Christ: the seven sacraments or encounters with the risen Christ, Catholicism's rich tradition of prayer; a trove of books by Scripture scholars and spiritual writers on the four gospels, the letters of St. Paul; and spirituality; inspiring biographies of Saints as friends whose lives mirror different ways of loving and imitating Jesus; spiritual direction by trusted guides; privileged periods of reflection in different kinds of retreats. (See Chapter 10)

Foremost is the Eucharist, the memorial of Jesus' death and resurrection; his saving sacrificial meal; the pledge and guarantee of our resurrection and of life everlasting; our joyful prayer of thanksgiving and worship of God; the believing Christian community's love celebration; reconciliation with God and with each other; above all, Catholics' privileged access to Jesus Christ, our friend and savior in a most personal way.

Sunday after Sunday Catholics come with faith to meet and experience the risen Christ. In the Liturgy of the Word, we hear his inspiring teaching and experience his healing compassion. In the Liturgy of the Eucharist, we join our offering to Jesus' great self-offering of his saving death and resurrection. Catholics' treasured moment of intimate union and friendship with Jesus Christ is receiving his body and blood in holy communion.

The church's greatest gift to Catholics is the Eucharist. (See chapter 6)

4. *Champion of Planet Earth*

The Catholic Church has become a strong voice for safeguarding the environment as God's creation. Individual Catholic scholars, national bishops' conferences and Popes John Paul II and Benedict XVI have addressed the ecological crisis and humanity's responsibility to protect and sustain our planet before it becomes too late. Pope Francis speaks of "carefully protecting creation."

The Hebrew Scriptures speak of the goodness of God's creation and our responsibility as stewards of God's bountiful world. Catholic creation teaching stresses that nature is sacred as reflecting its creator God. For God created the world out of love and dwells within nature and all living things, keeping them in existence and energizing them in myriad ways. In accepting scientific evidence for evolution, Catholic theology views plant and animal species as sacred and our common ancestry. Humanity's well- being is tied to the health of the cosmos.

Catholic moral teaching recognizes the despoliation of the environment by uncontrolled economic development, the almost total ecological damage from wars, the severe imbalance among rich and poor nations in their use of the world's resources, and from mining and oil extraction and agricultural wastes that pollute rivers, underground water and the land.

To address these ecological crises, Catholic creation teaching stresses the following values: (1) the goods of the earth are given by God to be shared by all; (2) to live in a safe environment is a human right; (3) the diversity of life has inherent value as exhibiting the grandeur and glory of the Creator; (4) aesthetic appreciation of the beauty of the universe is a classic path to knowledge and love of God; (5) any attempt at resolving environmental abuses must not ignore the poor and their right to authentic development; and (6) a new spirit of solidarity among nations is necessary to resolve issues global in scope.[2] The Catholic Church provides many valuable resources on ecology and preserving the environment[3] Over a century ago, Jesuit Gerard Manley Hopkins prophetically captured the sacredness and profusion of nature despoiled by human exploitation.

The world is charged with the grandeur of God.
It will flame out, like shining from shook foil;
It gathers to a greatness, like the ooze of oil
Crushed. Why do men then now not reck his rod?

Generations have trod, have trod, have trod;
And all is seared with trade; bleared, smeared with toil;
And wears man's smudge and shares man's smell: the soil
Is bare now, nor can foot feel, being shod.

And for all this, nature is never spent
. . . Because the Holy Ghost over the bent
World broods, with warm breast and with ah! bright wings.

5. *Powerful Voice for Moral Values*

In today's world of competing values, of greed and its consequences, of moral relativism, of confusion about ultimate values and
the meaning and purpose of life, the Catholic Church stands tall, often
at considerable cost, in proclaiming the dignity of each person and
the sacredness of human life, human rights and justice for the poor,
and safeguarding God's gift of sexuality and the high ideal of chastity for married and single persons. In addition the church emphasizes
the possibility and reality of truth, the legitimate place of religion in
national life, and the pre-eminent role of Jesus Christ and his values
for human living. The church's gift to society is to be an articulate,
prophetic force for important human values.

Today, the Catholic Church is a powerful moral influence in a
myriad of ways. The popes support moral values through encyclical
letters like Benedict XVI's social teaching in *Truth in Charity*, through
annual Christmas Day and Easter messages (*Urbi et Orbi, To the City
and the World)*, and speeches while visiting countries throughout the
world and in meeting with world leaders who come to Rome.

Catholic scholars and theologians articulate Christian morality through their writings in Catholic news magazines like *America,
Commonweal, First Things, National Catholic Reporter, The London*

Tablet, U.S. Catholic and other quality publications. Catholics like Dorothy Day, Fr. Dan Berrigan, Franz Jurgenstratter,[4] Archbishop Romero and Mother Teresa are powerful prophetic voices by their example.

The United States Conference of Catholic Bishops discuss a wide variety of social issues in their letters on the economy, immigration, the environment, poverty, welfare, housing, health care, the death penalty, etc. Annually they produce *Labor Day Statements* and every four years guidelines for presidential elections, like *Forming Conscience for Faithful Citizenship: A Call to Political Responsibility* in 2008. At the beginning of each new Congress, they contact members to promote the bishops' "principles and priorities" as guide for public policy and its moral implications.

As a strong prophetic voice, the Catholic Church is an immense value for Catholics and all people of good will by keeping before the human family high moral social ideals and a clear vision of the meaning and purpose of human life.

6. *Heroic Struggle for Human Rights*

Today the Catholic Church is the acknowledged spokesman and leader in the struggle for human rights based on the God-given dignity of each human person. To guarantee these basic rights, the church in its social teaching (See Chapter 12) champions justice and peace throughout the world.[5] Benedict XVI, like his predecessor John Paul II, and the United States bishops courageously and tirelessly speak out for human dignity and human rights. Pope John XXIII in his encyclical letter *Peace on Earth* enumerated these rights:

Human rights flow from the sacred dignity of each person: to life, food, clothing, shelter, health care, employment with just wage, leisure, freedom of speech, of religion and of association, immigration and participation in society. These rights carry extensive responsibilities for both individuals and governments. (#s 11-27)

His words resonate strongly today in the context of the revolution sweeping the Arab world. Interviews with opposition forces reveal they are fighting for recognition of their personal dignity, for jobs and decent livelihood, for freedom of speech and free association, and for a voice in their society.

The church's struggle for human rights for all people has often been heroic. Archbishop Oscar Romero and scores of priests and lay Catholics in El Salvador courageously fought for poor campesinos' right to land, education, health care, freedom and a decent life. As a result Romero was assassinated March 24, 1980 (See Chapter 7) and scores of priests, campesino leaders and catechists and delegates of the Word were murdered. For their scholarly writings and public statements, six Jesuit priests, administrators and teachers at the University of Central America, were murdered for repeatedly calling for the government to respect the rights of poor and disenfranchised Salvadorans. (See chapter 11)

The Catholic Church's struggle for human rights and the dignity of each person, especially the poor of the world who lack the most basic human rights, is an enormous value the church offers its members and the whole of humanity. It speaks loud and clear that God in his loving plan wills that every human live a decent life befitting his and her God-given dignity and enjoy all the rights coming from that dignity.

7. *Champion of Human Life*

The Catholic Church consistently and courageously fights for the sacredness of human life in all its manifestations. The church founded the first hospitals to care for the sick and dying and established orphanages for the scores of foundlings and orphans in medieval Europe, condemned the crime of infanticide and abortion, and refused to accept soldiers into the catechumenate because their job involved killing. Today, the Catholic Church and evangelical Christians are in the forefront of the battle against abortion-on-demand in the United States. The church's conviction about the sacredness of human life is well-expressed in Cardinal Joseph Bernardin's 'seamless garment' statement, that human life must be protected in all its manifestations from 'womb to tomb.'

Applications of the seamless garment image are pre-and post-natal care for poverty-stricken mothers, effort to end capital punishment and euthanasia, support for peace-making and nuclear disarmament. Allied to these is the church's commitment to help the world's refugees, the tragic victims of regional wars by oppressive governments, and malnourished and dying children.

A characteristic of the modern world is its callousness to human life: the senseless slaughter of millions of innocent people in wars of domination; genocide and ethnic cleansing; the neglect of countless children dying of hunger, malnutrition and lack of basic hygiene and health care; random "thrill killings" by total strangers; rape and death as a weapon of war.

In its tireless efforts to protect human life, the church provides an inestimable value to the conscience of the world by constantly reminding governments and individuals that each human life, no matter how poor or pitiable or handicapped, is sacred because personally created by God and is of incalculable value.

8. Commitment to the Poor

The Second Vatican Council, in its document, GS, *Joy and Hope,* spoke in strong terms about the poor and the "responsibility of those able to help," "… the scandal whereby some nations … enjoy abundances of riches while others lack the necessities of life and suffer from hunger, disease and all kinds of misery;" (88) "… people are bound to come to the aid of the poor and to do so not merely out of their superfluous goods;" (69) "the task of affluent nations is to help developing nations." (69) A special section of *GS* ,"Economic and Social Life … in the Service of Humanity," emphasized "the situation of the underprivileged … [and the] poor … who have to live and work in conditions unworthy of human beings." (63)

The council's concern for the poor became practical reality in Latin America when in 1986 Pope Paul VI called a meeting of the continents' bishops at Medellin, Colombia. The 130 bishops analyzed what they called Latin America's "tragic underdevelopment … of hunger and misery, of illness of a massive nature and infant mortality, of illiteracy and marginalization, of profound inequality of income, tensions between social classes … [and] rare participation of the people in decisions affecting the common good." [6] They worked out a specific program of action to address this need. Eight years later they met again at Puebla, Mexico, and committed the Latin American church to the "preferential option for the poor." Bishops, liberation theologians and thousands of base Christian communities took up the struggle to overcome the continents' massive poverty, oppression and structural injustice affecting the poor. (See chapter 13)

The Catholic Church's preferential option for the poor is a reality throughout the world. Catholic Charities, Catholic Relief Services and Catholic Refugee Service work tirelessly with the poor. In most Catholic parishes in the United States, St. Vincent de Paul members provide nutritious meals, housing and financial assistance to the poor. Religious communities of men and women minister to and live with the very poorest, often in refugee camps under terrible conditions, in the Mid-East, Africa, Asia and Latin America.

The church's care for poor and oppressed women, men and children is an extraordinary value for the human family and a powerful witness to Christ's love for them.

9. *2000-Year Intellectual Tradition*

An influential and appreciated gift and value of the Catholic Church today is her rich intellectual tradition stretching from her creative thinkers and writers of early Christianity to present Catholic philosophers and theologians, scholars, historians and social critics, biographers and novelists. Their prolific writings enrich the intellectual life of Catholics, inspiring and leading some back to the church.

A characteristic strength of this tradition is respect for reason enriched by faith. Pope John Paul II in his encyclical *Faith and Reason* stated that the early great bishop-theologians[7] of both the eastern and western church provided a rational basis for belief in God, that St. Augustine achieved the first synthesis between philosophy and theology, and that St. Thomas, who sought truth wherever found, demonstrated the harmony between faith and reason, praising the link between them since "each without the other is greatly impoverished and enfeebled." Benedict XVI has been an eloquent voice for reason.

The greater-than-life theologians who were the architects of Vatican II,[8] the large number of competent past and present Catholic theologians,[9] famous biblical[10] and moral theologians[11] are part of the same intellectual tradition.

The church's intellectual tradition thrives today in the vast network of Catholic schools in the United States, [12] especially colleges, universities and graduate schools: University of Notre Dame, St. John's University and the 27 Jesuit universities of which the most prestigious are Georgetown, Boston College, Fordham in New York, Marquette in Milwaukee, Santa Clara in California, and those with well-known medical schools, Creighton in Omaha, Loyola of Chicago and St. Louis. In Rome Jesuits operate the 450-year Gregorian University whose graduates number popes, bishops and cardinals, the world famous *Biblicum* that trains Scripture scholars, and the *Russicum* educating Orthodox and Byzantine Catholic scholars.

Two interesting and highly successful American educational innovations are Nativity (grades 6-8) and Cristo Rey (9-12) schools that prepare minority students for college and productive lives otherwise denied them. At present 64 Nativity middle schools and an increasing number of Cristo Rey schools educate Latino, African-American and Asian students from impoverished neighborhoods.

10. *Rich Tradition of Catholic Spirituality*

From its long tradition of spirituality and mysticism, the Catholic Church offers its members, other Christians and today's seekers, an astonishing wealth of ways to seek and find God and meaning in their lives. Chapter 10 describes the treasures of spiritual writings and Saints' lives and the prayer and sacramental resources, retreats and spiritual direction, and the variety of devotions the church provides.

Catholic spirituality is intensely personal. Catholics experience God as LOVE who seeks our love, is concerned for our needs and suffering, a compassionate forgiving God, ever present to us in the grandeur and lavishness of nature and events in our lives. Jesus comes to us as our Eucharistic food and drink, our inspirational teacher and loving healer, above all, our personal friend and savior whose sufferings and death for love of each of us draws us to him in enduring friendship and love.

Unique to Catholic spirituality is trusting, tender devotion to Mary, Madonna, virgin mother of Jesus, a caring mother who answers petitions and comes bearing gifts to her children as Lady of Guadalupe, of Lourdes, of Fatima and whose name graces churches, cities, hospitals, schools and women worldwide. Catholic spirituality welcomes the vast number and variety of Saints as family members, people like us, examples of how to live and cope and pray to for needs great and small.

Catholic spirituality is communitarian. Catholics believe in the communion of saints, loving husbands or wives, mothers or fathers, dear friends in heaven who hear our prayers, share our struggles here 'below' and await us at our journey's end. Vatican II gave the church a new name, the people of God, the community united in faith and worship in liturgies of "full, conscious active participation."

Catholic spirituality is also positive and joyful. The prolific Catholic writer Hilaire Belloc captured Catholics' celebration of life in this delightful ditty.

Wherever the Catholic sun doth shine,
There's always laughter and good red wine,
At least I've always found it so,
Benedicamus Domino - Bless the Lord!

11. *A Multi-Cultural World Church*

The Catholic Church appeals to many today because she is *catholic,* that is, worldwide, present in every continent, embraces all cultures, welcomes people of all races, gender and sexual orientation, and is expert at bringing salvation to all. Her real name is Catholic; the title *Roman* Catholic distinguishes her from the other Christian churches, especially after the Protestant Reformation.

Through its missionaries, priests and sisters from many religious congregations, the church brings the good news of God's love and the salvation of Jesus to peoples of far-flung lands in every country and culture. These missionaries build churches to celebrate joyful Eucharists and sacraments as the cherished way of life for thousands; run schools and educational systems to help people emerge from poverty and create a future for themselves; staff clinics and hospitals to bring health care to heal deadly diseases like malaria, dengue fever and blindness that devastate whole peoples; and introduce farming techniques, construct wells and improve crop yields to combat malnutrition and famine.

Being multi-cultural, the Catholic Church works to preserve and promote peoples' culture and way of life and speaks out strongly when that culture is attacked and peoples' rights violated. Two examples: Bishop Pedro Casaldaliga and Sister Dorothy Stang for years fought for the rights of indigenous Amazon people in Brazil against wealthy landowners expropriating their land and destroying their way of life. Sr. Stang was murdered as a result. Jesuit missionaries living among the Lakota Sioux native Americans encourage the Lakota language and religious rituals like Sun Dance, Sweat Lodge, Vision Quest and the Pow-Wow festivals.

The Second Vatican Council praised and encouraged the practice of inculturation. (See Chapter 9) An early example of extraordinarily successful inculturation is the work of the famous Jesuit missionary to China, Mateo Ricci (1552-1610). He mastered the Chinese language, translated textbooks including Euclid's Geometry into Chinese, wrote popular treatises and became a renowned Confucian scholar. Impressed by his scholarship, his skill in mathematics, science and the maps of the world he made, the Emperor invited him to join his court. To make Christianity understandable and acceptable to the sophisticated Chinese, he wrote a catechism in Chinese, gave the Chinese name 'Lord of Heaven' to describe the Christian God, accepted Chinese religious rites of honoring ancestors as non-idolatrous, and even dressed in the silk robes and long beard of a scholar. To honor him, the Emperor permitted him to be buried in Beijing where his impressive tomb remains today. Catholic missionaries imitate Ricci's respect for native cultures and practice of inculturation.

12. *The Petrine Office*

Catholics believe one of the greatest strengths of the Catholic Church is the papacy, the office of the Apostle Peter as rock of unity held by the popes through two millennia.

Despite their human limitations, and in some periods of church history the scandalous lives of individual popes, the papacy or office of Peter has managed to keep intact the basic unity of the Catholic Church in belief, in worship and sacraments, and members with each other, thanks to Jesus' promise to be with his church through his Spirit until the end of the world. The papacy is thus a Christ-given value that Catholics can never relinquish. (See Chapter 7)

Major advances and changes have occurred in the church through the leadership of enlightened popes. Vatican II would not have happened without the spiritual vision and initiative of John XXIII. Leo XIII began the tradition of Catholic social teaching in 1891 by his encyclical *Rerum Novarum (Of New Things)*. Pius X dramatically changed Catholic practice of the Eucharist by admitting children to first Holy Communion at the age of reason. John Paul II's extensive pastoral visits to 100 countries highlighted by Masses attended by hundreds of thousands and subsequent trips by Benedict XVI, make vivid in people's minds that the successor of Peter is in fact a Holy Father and the visible symbol of the unity of over a billion Catholics.

The pope is also a unique value for the entire world. As head of Vatican City and leader of the worldwide Catholic Church, the pope receives world leaders for talks on peace, the needs of poor nations, and the rights of religion. John Paul II became a powerful voice for justice, for human rights and the cause of the poor through challenging encyclical letters and speeches from Rome and throughout the world. He is credited with contributing to the fall of communism and the Berlin Wall by his presence and speeches in Poland that led to the Solidarity movement and the eventual freedom of Eastern Europe. Pope Francis has become an example and voice for "a poor church for the poor."

13. *Religious Communities of Women and Men*

Throughout the world, more than 300 congregations of religious women numbering over 700,000 sisters and over 125 religious orders of men comprising over 200,000 members constitute an extraordinary value for the Catholic Church and the millions they serve. Chapter 8 lists the names of these communities, describes the amazing variety of their ministries and identifies their equally impressive roles as teachers, scholars, doctors, nurses and so forth.

These women and men and their religious communities are a phenomenon of the Catholic Church in their very existence, in their ancient and modern founding often by charismatic lay women and men, their presence in virtually every country, their heroic commitment, and their prodigious activity in building God's kingdom of love, justice and peace and planting and strengthening the church in far-flung lands.

These inspiring women and men religious see the face of Christ in the people they serve. "I was hungry and you gave me food, I was thirsty and you gave me something to drink, I was a stranger and you welcomed me, I was naked and you gave me clothing, I was sick and you took care of me, I was in prison and you visited me." (Matthew 25:31-46)

Their consecrated lives of poverty, chastity and obedience to their superiors make possible their availability for service worldwide and are a powerful contemporary witness to the human spirit, to Jesus Christ and gospel values, and to belief in an after-life with God.

Hundreds of informative biographies that capture the spirituality and explain the prodigious accomplishments of these women and men make fascinating and inspirational reading.

14. *Beauty, Timeless Aesthetic Treasures*

Today the Catholic Church is a veritable treasure house of artistic masterpieces that constitute an incomparable value for humanity both aesthetically and religiously. Soaring cathedrals with their hundreds of stone sculptures, colorful stained glass and dazzling mosaics; the profusion of religious paintings by Renaissance masters and more recent artists; the vast body of religious writings: novels, poems, spiritual treatises, biographies of Saints and of great Christian men and women; exquisitely wrought chalices, monstrances, and crucifixes; richly brocaded priestly vestments; the realistic polychrome wood-carved statues of Christ, Mary and the Saints, especially in Spain and Latin America: all these quicken the heart and raise mind and emotions to God and to religious values.

Cathedrals: Notre Dame, Rheims, Amiens (France); York, Durham, Salisbury, Lincoln (England); St. Peters, Mary Major, and John Lateran in Rome; the churches of Florence, Siena, Orvieto (Italy); of Toledo, Salamanca, Burgos, Gaudi's *Sagra Familia,* Barcelona (Spain).

Mosaics: the 4th and 5th century churches of Ravenna, Italy ; the church of Monreale near Palermo, Sicily; St. Mark's basilica, Venice; St. Louis Cathedral in the United States.

Stained Glass: Chartres Cathedral outside Paris, La Sainte Chapelle, Paris (France); Leon (Spain)

Sculpture: the stone statues on the exterior of Chartres Cathedral (France); Michaelangelo's marble Pieta and Moses in Rome and David in Florence (Italy); the thousands of life-size wood-carved painted Christs and Virgin Marys and Saints throughout Europe and Latin America.

Painting: thousands of Madonnas (Mary with child Jesus) of Renaissance Europe; rich Byzantine icons in Athens, Crete, Egypt; Michelangelo's incomparable Sistine Chapel ceiling and powerful Christ of the Last Judgment on the front wall; El Greco's dramatically elongated Christs and Mary and the Apostles; Giotto's giant frescos of the life of St. Francis of Assisi in the upper church in Assisi, Italy; the Book of Kells in Dublin and many other spectacular illuminated Gospels and Scriptures and manuscripts.

Literature: St. Augustine's *City of God* and *Confessions*; Dante's *Divine Comedy*; Chaucer's *Canterbury Tales*; St. John of the Cross' *Dark Night of the Soul* and St. Teresa of Avila's *The Interior Castle*; Newman's *Apologia* and *Idea of a University*; Bernanos' *Diary of a Country Priest*, hundreds more.

As repository of religious masterpieces of the human spirit, the Catholic Church has preserved and made available powerful means of experiencing the divine. The human family is immeasurably enriched.

15. *Immense Good for the Human Family*

Statistics. Expressions of the church's special option for the poor are Caritas International's 165 charities around the world and Cross

International Catholic Outreach assisting desperate families in feeding centers, orphanages, schools, job-training and home building programs. Catholic Charities USA in 2009 served 9.2 million people; its 171 agencies spent 4.28 billion dollars serving needy Americans; 637 non-profit Catholic hospitals serve one of every five Americans; Catholic schools educate 2.6 million U.S. students; the American Catholic Church sponsors 230 colleges and universities for 700,000 students. Worldwide the Catholic Church cares for 25% of HIV-AIDS patients. Religious communities through an extraordinary network of schools, hospitals, orphanages and leprosaria serve hundreds of thousands worldwide. 700,000 men and women members of the St. Vincent de Paul Society in 142 countries on five continents take care of the poor in the tradition of their founder and patron Blessed Frederic Ozanam. In 2010, the U.S. Vincentians served more than 14 million people in need, made 648,000 hone visits, and gave seven million service hours to those in need or living in poverty!

The Human Face: St. Peter Damien ministered to the lepers in Molokai, Hawaii and died there of leprosy; social justice activist and inspirer of Friendship Houses throughout the United States, Dorothy Day welcomed New York's hungry and homeless to her Friendship House while writing the Catholic Worker daily newspaper; Jean Vanier established homes for the severely disabled and the L'Arche homes he inspired in 40 countries.

Priests, sisters and lay men and women in the Jesuit Refugee Service work and live in refugee camps in 71 countries as teachers, doctors and nurses, counselors, resettlement facilitators and providers of medicines, food and clothing. Their presence in this immense human tragedy is their living witness to Christ's love for the lowest "stranger in our midst" and of the church's compassion, love and care for each human person regardless of race, religion, nationality.

Inspired by Vatican II, the community of St. Egidio consisting of young Catholics, single and married, took the gospel message of love for the poor seriously. They serve hot meals to 1500 men and women in Rome, provide psychological help to the Roman street people, teach poor students and tutor immigrants, minister to the elderly, handicapped and persons with AIDS. Now 55,000 members worldwide, they organize national meetings for peace and justice, inter-religious dialogues for world peace and have mediated wars between nations.

Benefits. By affirming the sacredness of marriage and life-long commitment, the unique dignity of each person and by encouraging personal friendship with Jesus, the Catholic Church establishes a high ideal for healthy, loving, life-giving *relationships.* In today's fast-paced competitive world with peoples' loneliness and diminished self-worth, the church provides experiences of supportive loving *community* in its numerous parishes and their weekly Eucharist celebrations. Though accused of rigidity and failure to be modern, yet the Catholic Church is praised for *integrity* and *consistency* in her doctrinal and moral teaching and for standing firm, often at considerable cost, in proclaiming human dignity, justice and the sacredness of human life.

In Their Own Words

At the beginning of each semester's class of 'The Church Today,' I asked my university students to list what they considered to be five values and gifts the church provides her members and society as a whole. Despite negative feelings many young people have about the church, their responses, surprisingly discerning and positive, are an apt description of the 'great soul' of the Catholic Church.

A moral conscience to guide us; a way to channel my faith in God; sanctuary from the world; God is alive in the church; diversity, not conformity; shows me how to love God; respect for justice;

receive God's forgiveness; a place to form community; love of neighbor; to come to know and love Jesus; respect the earth we live on; its teaching on marriage; compassion; is family-oriented; it takes marriage seriously; to serve the poor; sense of belonging; the Eucharist; recognize the signs of the times; moderating influence on materialism; teaches, challenges, supports Catholics; promotes morality and personal responsibility among its members; challenges us to conversion; protects human life; reminds me that God loves me; a guide in sexual matters; a great teacher of values, and so forth.

"The church leads me to God, fosters holiness, is the visible expression in history of humanity's new life in Christ."

"The church inspires high ideals and lifelong commitments in an age that experiences mostly opportunistic, transitory relationships."

"The church gives me the company of men and women who have lived the gospel in a secular, difficult world, challenged secular and religious leaders to reform and who have died for Christ."

"The church embraces the full diversity of humanity ..."

"Particularly since Vatican II the church is dedicated to the service of the poor and defense of their human rights."

Further Reading

Barron, Robert. *Catholicism, A Journey to the Heart of the Faith.* New York: Image Books, 2011. A personal tour of the many facets of the Catholic Church, drawing on Scripture, tradition, history, art, literature, the lives of the saints, *Catholicism* is a stunning achievement. A ten-episode DV-D brilliantly illustrates each chapter.

Groome, Thomas H. and Daley, Michael J. *Reclaiming Catholicism: Treasures Old and New.* Maryknoll, NY: Orbis Books, 2010. Organized according to perspectives, personalities, and practices, leading theologians and spiritual writers mine the treasury of pre-Vatican II American Catholicism to find spiritual resources for today. Their voices strike a chord that resonates with both pre- and post- Vatican II Catholics.

Groome, Thomas H. *What Makes us Catholic? Eight Gifts for Life.* NY: Harper-Collins Publisher, 2002. In vivid and engaging style grounded in the actual experiences of people, Thomas Groome portrays Catholicism as a rich, multi-faceted reality that meets the needs of Catholics of all kinds. He celebrates what is humorous, beautiful and lasting in the Catholic tradition.

Kelly, Matthew. *Rediscovering Catholicism, Journeying toward Our Spiritual North Star.* 2002. Written with enthusiasm tempered with realism, popular writer Matthew Kelly addresses the church's need for "life-giving change" today. He insists "we need to rediscover the abundant riches of Catholic spirituality" and "to articulate the relevance of Catholicism in the modern world in ways that are bold, brilliant, coherent, and inspiring." The challenge, "Am I willing to change?"

O'Malley, William. *Why Be Catholic?* New York: Crossroad, 1994. "A dazzlingly original and extraordinarily powerful summary of the Catholic heritage, free of catechetical gobblygook and theological gibberish" by a popular author "who injects new life into traditional Christian ideas and language."

Footnotes

1 Nicholas Kristof, "A Church Mary Can Love." *New York Times.* April 18, 2010, 11. He paid tribute to "the Catholic Church I immensely admire ... This is the church of the nuns and priests in the Congo toiling in obscurity to feed and educate children. This is the church of the Brazilian priest fighting AIDS ... of Maryknoll sisters in Central America and Cabrini sisters in Africa." He cited Sr. Cathy who trained 600 teachers in Southern Sudan and Fr. Mario Falconi who refused to leave Rwanda during the genocide and personally saved 3000 from being massacred.

2 Richard McBrien, ed. *Encyclopedia of Catholicism* (New York: Harper Collins, 1995), 499.

3 John Paul II. *The Ecological Crisis: A Common Responsibility* (1990). U.S. Catholic Bishops, *Renewing the Earth* (1992); Thomas Berry, *The Dream of the Earth* (San Francisco: Sierra Club Books, 1990).

4   Franz Jurgenstratter was an Austrian farmer who defied Hitler by refusing to join the Nazi army despite pleas from his pastor and family. He was imprisoned and executed for his convictions.

5   Edward P. DeBerri and James E Hug et alii. *Catholic Social Teaching: Our Best Kept Secret.* Fourth Edition. New York: Maryknoll, Orbis Press, 2003. 26-37.

6   Second General Conference of Latin American Bishops, *The Church in the Present-Day Transformation of Latin America in the Light of the Council.* Washington, D.C.: United States Catholic Conference, 1973. 25.

7   Irenaeus, Tertullian, Clement of Alexandria, Origen, Justin, Cyprian, Athanasius.

8   Yves Congar, Jean Danielou, Henri de Lubac, John Courtney Murray, John Henry Newman, Karl Rahner, Joseph Ratzinger,

9   Jacques Dupuis, Avery Dulles, Ignacio Ellacuria, Edward Schilleebeekx and Michael Buckley, David Coffey, Robert Doran, Bradford Hinze, Joseph Komonchek, Richard Lenan, Bruce Marshall, Jon Sobrino SJ, Lisa Cahill Soelle, John Thiel, Susan K. Wood, SCL. Elizabeth Johnson.

10   Raymond Brown, Joseph Fitzmeyer, Daniel Harrington, Luke Timothy Johnson, John Meier, Roland Murphy, Pheme Perkins, Sr.Sandra Schneiders, Elizabeth Schuessler-Fiorenza and others.

11   James Bretzke, Charles Curran, Klaus Demmer, Margaret Farley, Josef Fuchs, Germain Frisez, Richard Gula, James Keenan, Richard McCormick, Todd Salzman, William Spohn plus many "emerging" theologians.

12   In 2009, 7094 Catholic schools educated 2,119, 341 students: 5,889 elementary/ middle schools, 1,507,618 students; 1,205 secondary schools, 611,723 students. Minority enrollment is 632,590 or 29.8 %; non-Catholic 307,875 or 14.5 %. In Latin America the *Fe y Allegria (Faith and Happiness)* schools educate tens of thousands very poor students who can't afford traditional Catholic schools.

Chapter 18:
People of Hope

O ctober 11, 2012, marked the 50th anniversary of the beginning of the Second Vatican Council. Conferences and lectures and newly published books[1] celebrated this momentous event which John Paul II called the church's "sure compass," an event in the church of such "epic proportions" that it continues to reverberate in the lives of Catholics. Drew Christensen captures the impact of the council for the church today.

> For many years the renewal wrought by the council gave fresh hope to humanity. The Church itself was renewed with a new self-understanding. Its catholicity was enhanced with a stronger embrace of the Eastern [Catholic] churches, the fostering of Christian unity and the retrieval of a special relationship with Judaism. Abandoning centuries of intolerance, the Church committed itself to religious freedom. The liturgy was renewed in vernacular rites to promote congregational participation. Above all, the Church placed itself at the service of the world in pursuit of human rights, peace and just development[2]

Richard Gaillardetz emphasizes that celebrating the council John XXIII called to renew and update the Catholic Church carries special importance today "at a time in our church when much of the council's teaching is being minimized, dangerously re-interpreted, or altogether ignored, an authentic and informed understanding of the council is more important than ever.[3]

This book began by acknowledging that today's Catholic Church faces serious crises and finds herself at a crossroads calling for decisions in her pilgrim journey. Concerned lay Catholics, theologians, priests' associations from four countries, and individual bishops have publicly called for reform in specific areas.[44] Among the Cardinals assembled in Rome to elect the new pope, agreement surfaced in pre-conclave meetings and discussions for reform of church governance in the Roman Curia and the Vatican.[5]

Thus, the unprecedented vision of renewal and reform that 2400 bishops at the Second Vatican Council gave the Catholic Church remains unfinished and a work in progress. To further the reception of the council and incorporate the bishops' vision more fully in the life and structures of the church is, I believe, the major challenge facing the church and the promise of her bright future. Theologian and author Gerry O'Collins stated that "Vatican II's 16 documents mapped paths to follow in implementing the 'continual reformation to which Christ summons the Church in her inner life, relations with others, and service to the world." In commenting on the newly-elected Francis, he believes "The full implementation of the Second Vatican Council should be his highest priority."[6]

The Second Vatican Council, Path to the Church's Future

What then are some of the achievements of the council that present the Catholic Church today with the opportunity for renewal and reform that are a harbinger of hope for the future?

- *Collegiality, the 'great battle of the council.'* Genuine collegial relationships at all levels in the church holds great promise for today's renewal of the Catholic Church.

- *Liturgical Reform* by which Catholics experience the Eucharist and Jesus' paschal mystery as the center of their spiritual lives. Achieving the full power of the liturgy is the sure way to renew Catholic life.

- *Rediscovery of the Bible and the Word of God as the basis of liturgy, theology and the whole life of the church.* Catholics' prayer and worship and their spiritual lives, immeasurably enriched by knowledge and love of the Scriptures, inspire the conversion that leads to renewal.

- *Key Role of Baptism.* Vatican II affirmed the priesthood of all the baptized with rights in the church and called to ministry; to a great extent the future of the church depends on incorporating Catholic women and men more fully into the life of the church and utilizing their many gifts.

- *New Theology of the Church.* By re-imagining the church as the people of God made up of all the baptized and as the sacrament of salvation, the Catholic Church entered the ecumenical movement and addresses other Christians as fellow disciples and brothers and sisters in Christ, members of the Body of Christ the church.

- *"The Church exists to evangelize."* Vatican II's call to bring the good news of Christ and his church to all has the potential for newly-invigorated Catholic laywomen and men and younger Catholics to respond enthusiastically to the 'new evangelization.'

- *Church and World.* Vatican II's embrace of the world as the privileged place where the kingdom of God is to be established is the inspiration for Catholics' commitment to work for social justice, peace-making, war on poverty and hunger, and the ecological crisis.

- *Continual Reform.* Vatican II recovered the ancient truth that the church is always in need of reform, in members and leaders alike. Serious reform promises a new humility and gives hope for dispirited Catholics that the renewal envisioned by the council bishops can and will become reality.

- *Dialogue.* The experience of dialogue, meant to be the new lifestyle of the Church, shows Catholics the way toward healing the cancer of polarization within the church and of achieving renewal/reform.
- *Reality of Change.* That the bishops at Vatican II accepted the past reality of change and the development of doctrine thus proclaiming for the first time the Catholic Church's commitment to religious freedom, makes possible in the 'unchangeable' Catholic Church the change that appears urgent to Catholics today.
- *"An outpouring of the Holy Spirit"* occurred during the Second Vatican Council. Trust in the guidance and inspiration of the Spirit is the surest guarantee for a new springtime of the church.

Opportunities and Challenges

What initiatives might incarnate in the life of the church the great themes of Vatican II? What reform decisions might implement the renewal envisioned by the bishops at the council? What programs might animate and energize the Catholic Church for the New Evangelization in the Year of Faith?

I propose the following for the Universal Church and the church in the United States with the hope that these initiatives and programs may be helpful for both church leaders and the people of God.

The Universal Church

Among urgent needs and renewal challenges, the following have been cited by bishops, theologians and church scholars as demanding immediate attention. I suggest possible responses.

Governance and the Exercise of Authority. Prominent church leaders and scholars have called attention to this issue again and again; it emerged as a major concern of the Cardinals leading up to the papal conclave. Cardinal Walter Kasper acknowledged that "the right balance between the universal church and particular churches has been destroyed" since the council.[8] In referring to the Roman Curia's undermining "the collegial relationships between the bishops of the world and the pope," Archbishop John Quinn in his book on the papacy called for a reform of the Roman Curia. Bishops and theologians speak of the increasing centralization of power and decision-making in Rome that has made it difficult for bishops and bishops' conferences to raise issues important to their people. An obvious corrective is governing the church by genuine collegial action and decisions made by the college of bishops and the pope together and the exercise of authority by collegial relationships at all levels of the church. Examples are national bishops' conferences and the triennial Synod of Bishops having real authority.

Guaranteeing Eucharist and Sacraments. Because of the alarming shortage of priests in most parts of the Catholic world with dire consequences for Catholics and for preaching the Gospel and in response to repeated calls by bishops, the pope might call a special meeting of bishops representing national bishops' conferences to seek their pastoral counsel on the option of relaxing the discipline of celibacy in the Roman church. Such a major change would need a sensitive preparation for Catholics even though polls in the global North and areas of the South indicate increasing majorities of Catholics favor married priests. Precedent exists in Eastern Catholic churches, in married Anglican and Lutheran clergy who became Catholic priests, and in the present **Ordinariate** for Anglicans entering the Catholic Church.[9] Benefits for the church are many: potential increase in priestly vocations; a new vigor in the priesthood; improved homilies based on married experience; above all increased availability of Eucharist and sacraments for Catholics.

Catholic Women. With little meaningful voice or significant role in the Catholic Church today, Catholic women increasingly ask that the church take seriously their sense of exclusion and recognize and make available their many gifts for the good of the church. It is becoming more clear that the church must welcome their gifts, reverse their alienation and effectively confront the large numbers of women leaving the church over this one issue. One practical way, full of promise and possible for the church, is to recover the deaconate for women that existed in the first millennium of the church.

Among the many voices calling for the church to consider offering the deaconate to women, retired bishop Emil A. Wcela made a carefully-researched and stated case for expanding the permanent deaconate to include women.

Ordaining women as deacons who have the necessary personal, spiritual and pastoral qualities would give their indispensable role in the church a new degree of official recognition, both of their ministry and of their direct connection to their diocesan bishop for assignment and faculties. Besides surrounding such women with the grace of the sacrament, ordination would enable them to exercise deaconal service in the teaching, sanctifying and governing functions of the church.

That women deacons become a reality in the church's life, Bishop Wcela concluded "... it is up to episcopal conferences and bishops, to theologians and historians and concerned Catholics to raise the issue for wider and more public consideration."[10]

Imagine the enrichment of parish life by women giving homilies, baptizing, conducting funerals, counseling families and young mothers, and using their gifts in serving the poor in the spiritual and physical works of mercy!

Ecumenism. (See chapter 11*)* Jesus' prayer *That All Be One,* Vatican II's expressed commitment to Christian unity, and the urgency of a united Christianity in today's world place a special responsibility on the Catholic Church. Despite faith and theological agreements accomplished by years of official ecumenical dialogues, progress toward *actual* union appears to have ground to a halt. To the Orthodox sister churches and Protestant "ecclesial communities," the Catholic Church appears *in practice* to insist on a return to her before union can be achieved. Yet a Lutheran pastor insists: "Only Rome has the traditional, ecclesiological, and moral authority to work for the reunion of the Church."[11]

Several practical avenues hold much promise for the Catholic Church. To restore communion with the Orthodox after 1000-year estrangement, the bishop of Rome, following the suggestions of Pope Paul V1 and later Cardinal Ratzinger, embraces the relationship of the first six ecumenical councils when the five Patriarchs (Alexandria, Antioch, Constantinople, Jerusalem and Rome) were in communion with each other. Pope Francis, referring to himself as bishop of Rome, a fellow-bishop with Orthodox bishops, was noticed and appreciated by the Patriarch of Constantinople who attended Francis' inaugural Mass, a first. For achieving closer relationship with the Anglican Communion and Lutheran churches, the Catholic Church seriously explore mutual exercise of ministry and proclamation of the Gospel and the practice of limited Eucharistic sharing as fruitful steps toward the goal of union?[12] Formidable obstacles are resolvable with sensitivity, understanding, theological expertise, humility and prayer.

Regain Credibility. The Catholic Church is admired for her worldwide care for the poor, the sick, and victims of natural disasters and is recognized for her rich intellectual and cultural achievements and her moral authority. Yet these are often obscured and her message impeded by the tragic abuse scandals and her perceived inability to respond to the concerns and needs of her members in today's world. As church leaders more and more support the gifts of her competent lay women and men and the prophetic voices of her professional theologians and her priests, the church hierarchy will regain the attention and respect of her members and all people of good will.

The Church in the United States

The large number of educated and theologically knowledgeable American Catholic lay women and men are a tremendous resource for the Catholic Church in the United States. Those who recognize this reservoir of competent and devoted Catholic laity desirous of some part in the decision-making life of the church also call attention to their "immigrant disease" of submission to priests and bishops and their consequent slowness to take leadership. On their part, bishops are accused of excessive deference to Rome and of failing to exercise their pastoral responsibility to American Catholics in presenting the urgent needs of the American church to higher authority. What appears necessary is collaborative leadership between Catholic laity and bishops, a two-way street embracing the practice of collegiality and subsidiarity so emphasized by Vatican II.

Collaborative Leadership

Thanks to Vatican II's emphasis on the Catholic laity's baptismal rights and their call to holiness, Catholic lay women and men are increasingly exercising their vocation to transform their world by witnessing the Gospel in business and political life for justice and the poor. Presently, Catholic men and predominantly women serve as eucharistic ministers and lectors, catechists, directors of religious education, members of parish and diocesan councils and as professional theologians. With the shortage of priests, they increasingly serve as administrators of parishes and leaders of Sunday worship. By their many gifts, their love of the church and desire to be of service, and their determination to have greater say in the decisions of church leaders that intimately affect their lives and religious needs, they are a valuable force for change in tomorrow's church. Now it is up to Catholic lay men and women to take greater possession of their church in collaboration with their priests and bishops and become a powerful force for the renewal and transformation of the Catholic Church in America.[13]

For the health and future of the American church, this collaborative leadership might take the form of Catholic lay men and women stepping forward in a kind of "Catholic entrepreneurship" by working with their local diocesan bishop in addressing the concerns and needs of American Catholics. Rather than directly challenging bishops, Catholic men and women offer their professional skills to gain the confidence of both their pastors and bishops and to collaborate on carefully selected urgent challenges (see chapter 15). By the people of God thus exercising their baptismal call and responsibility for the church, the renewal mandated by the Second Vatican Council can become reality.

For their part, American bishops will be helped in their ministry by serious listening to the people of God. After years of pastoral experience, one American bishop expressed his conviction that the greatest need in the American church is for "bishops to begin to listen to the reasons for the discontent that exists today among Catholics and take them seriously." Likewise, Philippine Archbishop Luis Antonio Tagle of Manila, recently elevated to the College of Cardinals, told the 2012

Synod of Bishops: "The Church cannot and must not pretend to have easy answers to the dilemmas facing men and women today. Instead, it must be an attentive and listening Church ... a humble Church."[14] Catholics feel powerless with little or no voice in decisions and practices that intimately affect their lives. Were church leaders to hear and understand the depth and extent of frustration among Catholics and many priests, they might be empowered to take effective steps to bring about needed change, thereby recovering lost credibility.

Pastoral Programs

The comprehensive 2007 study of American Catholic beliefs, attitudes and practices[15] revealed five areas that most concerned both millennial and older American Catholics: 1. Shortage of priests. 2. Catholic young people. 3. The alarming number of Catholics who have left or are leaving the church. 4. Alienation of Catholic women. 5. Failure of church leaders, bishops and many priests, to listen seriously to the discontent of Catholics today, to their concerns and religious needs, and to their requests and calls for change and for input in decisions most intimately affecting them. By way of practical response to this study, American bishops, in collaboration with their priests and lay women and men today, might profitably take the following four promising initiatives.

The Lost Generation. It is critical for the future of the Catholic Church that a comprehensive outreach be made without delay to younger Catholics, the so-called "lost generation" of educated and involved adults under 40 with special emphasis on present high school and university students. Such a program is urgent in view of the graying of church goers, the prospect of future empty pews, and the influx of Hispanic youth vulnerable to the dominant secular culture and the attraction of missionary Pentecostals. With the backing of the Conference of Catholic Bishops, the bishop of each diocese might empower the Catholic laity, the church's great resource, to collaborate with their priests and bishop in this program of reaching out to today's younger generation. Such a collaborative program might energize the people of God with a new appreciation for their faith and for their priests and bishops and might to some degree heal the polarization within the Catholic Church.

It is interesting to speculate: what if the American bishops, in collaboration with their priests and laity, adopted a plan of outreach to Catholics, especially to young people, on the scale of their opposition to abortion and same sex marriage and their recent Religious Liberty program?

Parish Rejuvenation. The American church is blessed with many vibrant, welcoming parishes led by dedicated pastoral priests and effective and committed lay staff, 80% of whom are women. Such parishes are described by Paul Wilkes in *Excellent Parishes: Guide to the Best Places and Practices.*[16] Many bishops are personally involved in excellent spirituality programs for their people and for catechetical and school programs. Yet, many recognize the need for collaborative programs of parish renewal for those Catholics who seek more welcoming communities, challenging homilies and joyful worship and who leave to join other Christian churches. The challenges to parish life today are formidable: increasing lack of priests and parish closings and consolidations; the quality of homilies; the large number of foreign priests unfamiliar with American culture whose homilies often are difficult to understand; some recently ordained priests who emphasize a cultic rather than servant model of priesthood, thus creating faith obstacles to many parishioners and to collaboration with parish staff.

After carefully listening to the needs and suggestions of the people of God including their priests and in collaboration with them, the

United States Bishops' Conference might plan a broad program of parish revitalization as part of the year of faith and beyond. Such a program would embrace liturgy and homily evaluation, music, lectors, greeters, programs for the poor, on-going education, and spiritual formation including retreats and parish missions. Moribund parishes might thus be revived and successful parishes become even better, the quality of spiritual life deepened, and exodus from the church lessened. Since the parish is the foremost place where the life of the Catholic Church takes place, such a program would ensure the future of the American church.[17] For this to succeed, parish closings need to be conducted with great sensibility and with full collaboration of parish pastors and laity.

Latino/a Presence in the United States. The increasing number of Catholics of Latin origin has brought new vitality to the church in America, enriching her with strong family life, faithful Mass attendance at vibrant joyful liturgies, and devotion to the Virgin of Guadalupe. With 68% under 30, and half under 25, Latinos are projected to be the majority of Catholics in the United States by 2050. It will be a different church with great potential though with multiple challenges: the need for more Latino bishops and priests; full and welcoming acceptance of Latino families in worship and parish life by English-speaking Catholics; extensive programs for Latino youth to maintain their practice of the Catholic faith amid secularist American culture and aggressive Pentecostal action.[18]

The cover of *Time* magazine for April 15, 2013, "The Latino Reformation, Inside the New Hispanic Churches Transforming Religion in America," revealed a disturbing challenge to the American Catholic Church. Sixty-nine percent of first generation Latino Catholics in the United States dropped to 59% in second generation of Latino Catholics and to 40% in the third generation. Fr. Alejandro Aguileia-Titus of the U.S. Council of Catholic Bishops' office is quoted as saying "The challenge for the Catholic Church is to make the parish structure very flexible, very family oriented. To the degree we fail to do this . . . we will lose a significant number of Hispanic Catholics to other religious groups, mostly Pentecostals." The Pew Forum reports that nine of ten evangelicals say a spiritual search drove their conversion. "People are looking for a real experience with God . . . that comes from exploring the Bible."

The above programs for parish rejuvenation and to the lost generation must include both Latino/a adults and youth.

Outreach to Departed Catholics. "I just turned 50 and I can tell you that I am pretty much the teen-ager in my parish. Most of my friends have abandoned their faith . . . I wish the Vatican would listen."[19] One practical, guaranteed way for church pastoral leaders to understand and respond to why people are leaving the church is exit interviews with them. Enlisting Fr. William Byron's project of exit interviews, Bishop Daniel O'Connell of Trenton, New Jersey, has begun a program of asking people why they have left.[20]

This program - and the three above - might profitably lead to an examination of conscience along the lines of Pope John Paul II's call at the beginning of the church's third millennium for such an examination. To be most effective, this action might be undertaken by the United States Bishops' Conference after seeking input from individual dioceses. Such a collective act of humility might profitably consider three questions: (1) In addition to the priest-abuse tragedy, in what other ways have we fallen short of the hopes and concerns of our Catholic people? (2) What kind of church do the people of God yearn for? (3) How will we respond? Benefits to the church might be enormous. Lest this be dismissed as inopportune, impractical, and quixotic, might it rather be viewed as a humble act of faith in the guidance of the Holy Spirit and trust in the Catholic people at this period of crisis and opportunity in the American church? It might also present a fresh image of the church to Catholics and other Christians and the world at large.

The Risk of Change

The rich legacy of Vatican II and the challenges confronting the universal church and within the church in the United States offer the Catholic Church opportunity for renewal and for addressing major problems and challenges that involve change, always difficult and fraught with uncertainty. Change is the mark of a living church. Archbishop John Quinn prophetically told the priests and deacons of the church of San Francisco, "… a new church is struggling to be born. We cannot be content with the ways of the past. We have new challenges and we must be imaginative in meeting them; we must not be afraid to take risks. We must have vision, daring and more than a dash of courage."

Cardinal Carlo Martini, in the interview referred to in chapter 16, no. 12, expressed even more dramatically the church's challenge to change. "The Church is 200 years behind the times. Why does it not rouse itself?" The Cardinal asked. "Are we afraid? Afraid instead of being courageous?"[21]

How might change become reality in the church today? A few suggestions:

- By trusting the Spirit's guidance of the church as John XXIII did in entrusting the Second Vatican Council to the world's bishops and discerning the Spirit speaking through the people of God and the 'signs of the times.'
- By fully implementing the Spirit-inspired Second Vatican Council in the life of the church.
- By practicing collegiality at all levels of the church.
- By welcoming women and their gifts more fully in the church.
- By overcoming debilitating clericalism in the church.
- By dialoguing at all levels of the church, particularly with prophetical voices in the church.

- By pastoral bishops exercising their collegial episcopal leadership for the present and future needs of their people.
- By Catholic lay men and women taking the initiative in collaborating with their priests and bishop in the renewal of the church.

HOPE

Too many faithful Catholics are weary. Many have lost hope and left the church of their youth or adulthood. Yet reasons for hope far outweigh temptations to feelings of hopelessness.

A joyful reason for hope is the extraordinary growth and vigor of the Catholic Church in Africa.[22] The church increased from 1.9 million Catholics in 1900 to 137 million in 2000, a staggering 6,708% increase. The church is experiencing an abundance of vocations to the priesthood with seminaries full in Nigeria, Kenya and other African countries. African Catholicism manifests vitality and joy. That 43% of sub-Saharan Africa is under 14 years of age point to a church of the poor and the young. Pastoral African bishops realistically face the enormous social problems of tribal violence, aggressive Islamic fundamentalism, endemic corruption, poverty, trade wars, lack of education and health care, and the pandemic HIV-AIDS infection.

The Latin American Catholic Church has soared to 449 million Catholics today. Yet Pentecostalism, the fastest growing religious movement in the world with an estimated 600 million followers, has made huge inroads in predominantly Catholic Latin America. Brazil, once 95% Catholic, is now 67%. The New Evangelization is an enormous challenge yet hopeful opportunity for the Catholic Church in Latin America.

The following strengths of today's Catholic Church are further reasons for Catholics to be optimistic about their church.

- Vatican II's program of renewal/reform has already profoundly influenced the church.

- The Catholic Church is blessed with vast numbers of generous, holy, faith-filled laywomen and men devoted to the church and ready to serve. Pope Francis has called them "middle class saints!"
- Thousands of religious women and men in hundreds of religious communities are dedicated to education and health care and labor worldwide for the poor, the sick and the hungry and for justice and peace.
- Thousands of successful parishes worldwide are led by dedicated priests devoted to the people of God, the body of Christ.
- The hundreds of pastoral bishops in communion with Peter, the church's rock of unity, are the strength of the Catholic Church.
- Catholic social teaching is the church's universally recognized contribution to the political, economic and social world of today.

A Reflection

The Spirit whom Pope John XXIII prayed to come on the Catholic Church in a new Pentecost today guides the church, leaders and members alike, bringing us to a future yet unknown, but which, we may confidently hope, rich in promise. This Spirit founded the church at Pentecost, preserved her through crises and human sinfulness through 2000 years, inspired John XXIII and 2400 bishops to give us the Second Vatican Council, and is with the church as she faces her future. The Catholic Church lives by the presence and action of the Spirit who is the soul and very life of the church and of each member.

And so as people of *faith* we look with hope to the great *Catholica*: the church Vatican II proclaimed mystery of the presence of the risen Christ and his Spirit; the church that offers us Eucharist and the other sacraments, that guarantees Jesus' teaching of God's love and compassion and is the basis of our faith and hope; the church that stands before the world for justice, for the dignity of each person, and for the human rights of all; the church that embraces all the baptized. We rejoice in the faith conviction that our hope in the church and its future depends on the triune God whose grand enterprise it is.

The Pope of Hope[23]

In speaking about the newly-elected Francis I, a young Catholic wrote: "This pope is the right man for the times for the church. I think not since John XXIII has there been a man who will breathe new life and fresh air into the church. Hope is surely sky high for the church right now."

In talks to groups after his election, Francis always included a message of hope. To representatives of Orthodox churches, Protestant communities, Jews and Muslims and world religions, he pledged "to continue on the path of fraternal dialogue" and to embrace "all men and women who feel themselves to be in search of God's truth, goodness and beauty." To 5000 journalists in Rome for the conclave, he explained that the "church is essentially spiritual: the people of God who walk toward the encounter with Jesus Christ ... the center, the heart of the church ... which exists to communicate Truth, Goodness, and Beauty." In saying why he chose the name Francis, he confided "Oh, how I wish for a church that is poor and for the poor."

In his June 3, 2013 welcome address to pilgrims from Bergamo, Italy, on the 50th anniversary of the death of "good pope" John XXIII, Francis spoke of the Second Vatican Council as a "bright beacon for the path that lies ahead" for the Church.

Fifty years after his death the wise and fatherly guidance of Pope John, his love of the Church's tradition and his awareness of the constant need for renewal, his prophetic convocation of the Second Vatican Council and his offering his life for its success stand as milestones in the history of the Church in the 20th century and a bright beacon for the path that lies ahead.

At his "Inaugural Mass for the Petrine Ministry'" March 19, 2013, the feast of St. Joseph, protector of Jesus and Mary and patron of the universal church, Francis concluded his homily with this vision of hope for the Catholic Church today.

To protect the whole of creation, to protect every man and woman, especially the poorest, to look upon them with tenderness and love, is to open up a horizon of hope. . . this is the service the bishop of Rome is called to carry out, yet one to which all of us are called, so the star of hope will shine brightly.

Further Reading

Allen, John L. *A People of Hope, Archbishop Timothy Dolan in Conversation with John Allen.* New York: Image Books, 2012. In *People of Hope* Archbishop, now Cardinal, Dolan is at his best, capturing an upbeat, hopeful affirming Catholicism that is the untold story about the Catholic Church today. In a series of informative conversations on the present and future of the church, he shares his insightful, often humorous perspective on challenges facing the church.

Dietzen, John J. *Doors of Hope, Paths for Renewal in the Catholic Church.* Springfield, IL: Templegate Publishers, 2008. Drawing on years of experience, with pastoral sensitivity and sound theology, Fr. Dietzen shows how the church's positions on confession, ecumenism, priesthood, women, divorced and remarried need further study for possible reform.

Bernard Haring, C.Ss.R. *My Hope for the Church, Critical Encouragement for the Twenty-First Century.* Liguori, MO: Liguori/Triumph, 1997. In this forward-thinking book, Fr. Haring, the foremost Catholic moral theologian of the twentieth century, calls for changes in priestly celibacy, the role of women in the church, the pastoral care of divorced and remarried Catholics, and reform of over-centralization of church governance. Readable, scholarly, enlightening.

Muldoon, Tim. *Seeds of Hope: Young Catholics and the Catholic Church in the United States*. Mahwah, NJ: Paulist Press, 2008. Addressing the issues that often alienate young Catholics in America, the author argues that Catholic Social Teaching is a way to bridge the gap between spirituality and religious practice today. He proposes the practice of love with justice the basis of moral obligations.

O'Malley, William J. *Choosing to be Catholic For the First Time, or Once Again*. Allen, TX: Thomas More, 2001. "This is the perfect book for those who may have become disenchanted with the Church or perhaps even God." The author of over thirty books, Fr. O'Malley makes the Catholic faith and life come alive. Full of information, this book challenges the reader.

Footnotes

1   Massimo Faggioli, *Vatican II: the Battle for Meaning*. *(Mahwah, NJ: Paulist Press, 2012); Richard R. Gaillardetz and Catherine E. Clifford, Keys to the Council, Unlocking the Teaching of Vatican II* (Collegeville, MN: Liturgical Press, 201); Greg Tobin, *The Good Pope John XXIII and Vatican II: The Making of a Saint and the Remaking of the Church* (New York: Harper One., 2012). William Madges and Michael J. Daley, *Vatican II: Fifty Personal Stories* (Maryknoll, NY: Orbis Books, 2012); Margaret Lavin, *Vatican II: Fifty Years of Evolution and Revolution in the Catholic Church*, *(*St. Pauls Publications, 2012

2   Drew Christensen, S.J. "Of Many Things," *America* (Feb. 13, 2012): 13.

3   Gaillardetz and Clifford, *op. cit*, xvii.

4   The London *Tablet* editorialized "the most significant crisis in the church is the breakdown in *koinonia* – love, trust and fellowship – between the hierarchy and priests and people" that "demands a far-reaching reform of structure, including giving the laity the right to participate in church decision making. . . . The root of the profound crisis in church governance is structural. . . . The Second Vatican

Council wanted the church to be governed collegially, the formula expressed as 'never Peter without the Apostles, never the Apostles without Peter.'"

5   The Cardinals "sought a strong leader to reform the Roman Curia and promote the New Evangelization with vigor." They identified the "most pressing issues facing the church. Chief among them was the need to reform the Roman Curia ... over-centralization of the papacy and the Curia in recent decades ... and demanded greater collegiality. "Jorge Mario Bergoglio elected Pope," *The Tablet,* 16 March, 2013: 13.

6   Rev. Gerry O'Collins, S.J. "Still Far to Go," *The Tablet,* 9 February, 2013: 11

7   Joseph Ratzinger, a *peritus* theologian at Vatican II, stated that the aim of the council bishops was "to correct the one-sided functions of an overemphasized primacy by a new emphasis on the richness and variety in the church as represented by bishops." *Commonweal* (June 4, 2010) quote from his 1966 book *Theological Highlights of Vatican II.*

8   Cardinal Walter Kasper. "On the Church," *America* 184 (Apr. 23, 2011):10.

9   Benedict XVI's Apostolic Constitution, *Anglicorum Coetibus (To Groups of Anglicans)* on receiving Anglicans into full communion with the Catholic Church. Married Anglican bishops and priests may be ordained Catholic priests after a "process of discernment" and formation in the Catholic tradition. Rome, Nov. 4, 2009.

10   Bishop Emil A. Wcela, "Why Not Women? A bishop makes a case for expanding the diaconate." *America* (Oct. 1, 2012): 15-18. See Gary Macy, William T. Ditewig and Phyllis Zagano, *Women Deacons: Past, Present, Future.* (Mahwah, NJ: Paulist Press, 2012).

11   Mark Chapman. "Rome and the Future of Ecumenism: Rome as the Future of Ecumenism." *Ecumenical Trends* 23(1994): 8/40.

12   See the *Directory for the Application of Principles and Norms on Ecumenism,* numbers 104, 129, *159* for Eucharist sharing and 205-209 for proclamation of the Gospel. The Catholic position is that Eucharistic signifies and expresses the church; since separated churches and ecclesial communities are not in

communion with the Catholic Church, full eucharistic sharing is not yet possible though "intercommunion" by exception is possible on special occasions.

13 John Allen wisely observes, "to expect the hierarchy to be the primary 'change agent' in Catholicism, the chief source of its vision and new energy, is both unfair and unrealistic. Change in Catholicism typically percolates at the grassroots ... well before it is ever ratified and assimilated by the hierarchy." *Ibid.* Cardinal Peter Turkston, president of the Pontifical Council for Justice, agreed that "renewal in the church is often anticipated by the concrete actions of the faithful and this anticipates the official position of the hierarchy." *The Tablet.* Feb. 19, 2011: 31.

14 Philippa Hitchen, "Quiet Voice of Asia," *The Tablet* (Nov. 3, 2012).

15 William V. D'Antonio, Dean R. Hoge, James D Davidson, Mary L. Gautier, *American Catholics Today* (Lanham, MD: Rowman & Littlefield, 2007).

16 Paul Wilkes, *Excellent Catholic Parishes: Guide to Best Places and Practices.* (Mahwah, NJ: Paulist Press, 2001).

17 An excellent program, *Parish Assessment and Renewal,* by the Parish Evaluation Project, has for 30 years evaluated and helped parishes and staff in 225 parishes throughout the United States. (3195 S. Superior St., Milwaukee, WI 53207. TE: 414-483-7370)

18 John Allen, "The Horizontal Dimension," *National Catholic Reporter* (Oct. 30, 2009): 23.

19 Jerry Filteau, "Unusual study asks former Catholics why they left the Church," *National Catholic Reporter* (April 13-26, 2012): 9.

20 William J. Byron, S.J. "On Their Way Out: What Exit Interviews Could Teach Us." *America (Jan 3-, 2011): 17.*

21 "The Pope and the bishops should find 12 uncommitted people to take on leadership roles." *The Tablet* (Sept. 8, 2012).

22 John Allen, *The Future Church: How Ten Trends Are Revolutionizing the Catholic* Church (New York: Doubleday, 2009) 13-53.

23 "If this Francis, too, is a listener, there is hope for reconciliation, hope for healing, hope for development [change] of the church." Sr. Joan Chittister, "Who are the people waiting for?" *National Catholic Reporter,* March 14, 2013.

Epilogue

Can the Catholic Church move ahead resolutely with the renewal begun by the Second Vatican Council? Can it courageously confront crucial decisions no longer to be ignored? Can it create structures that make change possible? Can it respond to the ever-larger numbers of the faithful and their priests who seek a hearing and a voice in decisions affecting their lives?

This transition church is faced with difficult decisions. Should priestly celibacy be maintained when millions of Catholics are denied the Eucharist and idealistic young men forced to choose between marriage and a celibate priesthood? Can women be given a genuine role in church ministry and leadership? In the light of faith and theological agreements already achieved, what steps ought the Catholic Church take to restore the broken unity of Christ's church? What church structures need to be established to make the principles of collegiality and subsidiarity operative throughout the church? What development in sexual morality is possible today?

This book has endeavored to present the contemporary church as it exists today: renewed by Vatican II, rich in sacramental-liturgical life, alive with a thirst for justice and human rights, in the forefront of the ecumenical movement, unafraid to be countercultural in modern life, a strong voice for Christian values, human rights, and the preciousness of human life, increasingly the sacrament of Jesus Christ to its members and the world; yet a church wracked by inner tensions and divisions, burdened by its own limitations and sinfulness and in continuing need of renewal/conversion, at times rigid and insensitive to the religious needs of its members, resistant to change, too often jealous of its institutional prerogatives, authoritarian and overly insistent on obedience and punishment.

What will the Catholic Church be like in the future?

Many Catholics will likely remain in the church only if the church meets their religious needs and becomes more inclusive and respectful of freedom and democratic practices. The church will encounter growing opposition from the dominant culture. Questions abound. Will the scandal of divided Christianity become so intolerable that the Roman Catholic, Orthodox, Anglican and mainline Protestant churches take determined action to achieve a form of union respectful of each other's gifts and uniqueness? Will collegial relationships at all levels become the normal life of the Catholic Church? Will the papacy develop in its exercise of authority to ensure unity while protecting diversity? Will responsible pluralism become a mark of the church? Will affluent Catholics, especially those whose decisions affect the lives of so many, more fully live Gospel spirituality?

What is the Future of the Catholic Church?

Despite her many problems and seemingly un-resolvable internal divisions, the Catholic Church is in fact well-equipped for the future: highly-educated, committed lay Catholics ready to exercise their ministry in world and church; heroic Third-World Christians suffering and dying for justice and Christian love; intelligent, dedicated pastoral bishops exercising strong leadership; competent, holy recent popes like Blessed John XXIII, Paul VI, Blessed John Paul II and Benedict XVI. She is a church progressively purified through acknowledging her sinfulness and limitations and need for total reliance on her Lord and his guiding Spirit. She is a church of holiness, of saints and martyrs aplenty.

There is reason to foresee a bright future for the church. The renewal unleashed by the Second Vatican Council, with its vision for the church, is irreversible despite setbacks and pockets of opposition. Even when presenting the church's internal tensions and problems as well as values and gifts, a pervading spirit throughout this book is Christian optimism and hope. For tensions and problems are signs of life and inevitable in a church acknowledged by the council to be sinful and in need of continuing reformation. These are life giving, challenging the church to change and grow.

The new Pentecost is a continuing process with opportunities and surprises all along the way!

Bibliography

This list arranged according to each chapter supplements the books suggested for Further Reading at the end of each chapter, which are not repeated here. Current books are favored but older classics and important books are included. A separate section of prominent and popular Catholic periodicals, magazines and newspapers follows.

Part I: Foundations

Introduction

Eagan, Joseph F., S.J. *Restoration and Renewal: The Church in the Third Millennium.* Kansas City, MO: Sheed and Ward, 1994.

Ratzinger, Joseph. *The Ratzinger Report: An Exclusive Interview on the State of the Church.* San Francisco: Ignatius Press, 1985.

Chapter 1: Vatican II, Council of Change

Abbott, Walter. *The Documents of Vatican II.* New York: Guild Press, 1966.

Flannery, Austin, OP. *Vatican II: The Basic 16 Documents.* Northport, NY: Costello Publishing Co., 1995.

Alberigo, Giuseppe, Jean Pierre Jossua, Joseph Komonchak, eds. *The Reception of Vatican II.* Washington, DC : The Catholic University of America Press, 1987.

Clifford, Catherine E. and Gaillardetz, Richard, R. *Keeping the Council: Unlocking the Teaching of Vatican II.* Collegeville, MN: Liturgical Press, 2012.

Orsy, Ladislas. *Receiving the Council: Theological and Canonical Insights and Debates.* Collegeville, MN: Liturgical Press, 2009.

Ratzinger, Joseph. *Theological Highlights of Vatican II.* NY/Mahwah, NJ: Paulist Press, 1966.

Rynne, Xavier. *Vatican Council II.* Maryknoll, NY: Orbis Books, 1999.

Schillebeeckx, Edward. *The Real Achievement of Vatican II.* New York: Herder & Herder, 1992.

Stacpoole, Alberic, ed. *Vatican II: By Those Who Were There.* London: Geoffrey Chapman, 1986.

Sullivan, Maureen. *The Road to Vatican II: Key Changes in Theology.* New York: Paulist Press, *2007.*

Wiltgen, Ralph M. *The Rhine Flows into the Tiber.* New York: Hawthorne Books, 1967.

Chapter 2: Five Major Actors

Carey, Patrick. *Avery Cardinal Dulles, S.J.: A Model Theologian, 1918-2008.* New York: Paulist Press, 2010.

Gaillardetz, Richard R. ed. *When the Magisterium Intervenes: The Magisterium and Theologians in Today's Church.* Collegeville, MN: 2012.

Johnson, Paul. *A History of Christianity.* New York: Atheneum, 1985.

Sullivan, Francis. *Magisterium: Teaching Authority in the Catholic Church.* Mahwah, NJ: Paulist Press, 1983.

Part II: The Council's Vision: A Renewed Church

Chapter 3: Mystery-Pilgrim Church

Boff, Leonardo. *Ecclesiogenesis.* Maryknoll, NY: Orbis Books, 1986.

Dulles, Avery. *The Reshaping of Catholicism: Current Challenges in the Theology of the Church.* San Francisco: Harper & Row, 1988.

Fox, Thomas C. *Penecost in Asia: A New Way of Being Church.* Maryknoll, NY: Orbis Books, 2002.

Greeley, Andrew. *The Catholic Experience.* Chicago: University of Chicago Press, 1956.

_____ *The Catholic Myth:* The Behavior and Beliefs of American Catholics. New York: Scribner, 1990

Gula, Richard M. *The Call to Holiness: Embracing a Fully Christian Life.* New York: Paulist Press , 2003.

John Paul II. *Vocation and Mission of Lay Faithful in the Church and in the World.* Washington, DC: United States Catholic Conference, 1989.

Kaspar, Walter. *Theology of the Church.* New York: Crossroad, 1989.

Kung, Hans. *The Church.* Garden City, NY: Orbis Books, 1986.

Leahy, Brendan. *Ecclesial Movements and Communities, Origins, Significance and Issues.* New York:

New City Press, 2010.

Masters, Thomas and Uelman, Amy. *Foculare, Living a Spirituality of Unity in the United States.* New York: New City Press, 2011.

McBrien, Richard P. *Catholicism,* 2 vols. Minneapolis: Winston Press, 1980.

_____ *The Church: The Evolution of Catholicism.* New York, NY: HarperOne, 2008.

Rausch, Thomas. *Toward a Truly Catholic Church: an Ecclesiology for the Third Millennium.* Cellegeville, MN: Liturgical Press, 2005.

Sanks, T. Howland. *Salt, Leaven, and Light: The Community Called Church.* New York: Crossroad, 1992.

Tavard, George. *The Church, Community of Salvation: An Ecumencal Ecclesiology.* Collegeville, MN: The Liturgical Press, 1992.

Lay Ministry

Fox, Zeni, ed. *Lay Ecclesial Ministry: Pathways to the Future.* Lanham, MD: Rowman & Littlefield Publishers, 2010.

John Paul II. *Vocation and Mission of Lay Faithful in the Church and in the World.* Washington, DC: United States Catholic Conference, 1989.

Osborne, Kenan. *Ministry: Lay Ministry in the Roman Catholic Church.* New York: Paulist Press, 1993.

Chapter 4: Momentous Change: Liturgy & Sacraments

Bausch, William. *A New Look at Sacraments.* Mystic, CN: Twenty-Third Publications, 1983

Hellwig, Monica. *The Meaning of Sacraments.* Dayton: Pflaum-Standard, 1972.

Lawler, Michael G. *Symbol and Sacrament: A Contemporary Sacramental Theology.* Omaha, NE: Creighton University Press, 1995.

Marini, Piero. *A Challenging Reform: Realizing the Vision of the Liturgical Renewal, 1963-75.* Collegeville, MN: Liturgical Press, 2007.

Martos, Joseph. *The Catholic Sacraments.* Wilmington, DE: Michael Glazier, 1983.

Mitchell, Leonel. *The Meaning of Ritual.* New York: Paulist Press, 1977.

Chapter 5: New Life, Forgiveness, Friendship

Brunsman, Barry. *New Hope for Divorced Catholics: A Concerned Pastor Offers Alternatives to Annulment.* San Francisco: Harper & Row, 1985.

Coleman, Gerald. *Divorce and Remarriage in the Catholic Church.* New York: Paulist Press, 1988.

Hart, Kathleen and Thomas Hart. *The First Two Years of Marriage: Foundation for Life Together.* New York: Paulist Press, 1983.

Kavanagh, Aiden. *The Shape of Baptism: The Rite of Christian Initiation.* New York: Pueblo Publishing Co. 1978.

Kiefer, Robert. *Blessed and Broken: An Exploration of the Contemporary Experience of God in Eucharistic Celebration.* Wilmington, DE: Michael Glazier, 1982.

Lawler, Michael. *Secular Marriage, Christian Sacrament.* Mystic, CN: Twenty-Third Publications, 1985.

Osborne, Kenan. *The Christian Sacraments of Initiation: Baptism, Confirmation, Eucharist.* New York/Mahwah, NJ: Paulist Press, 1987.

Roberts, William. *Christian Marriage and Family: Contemporary Theological and Pastoral Perspectives.* Collegeville, MN: Order of St. Benedict, Inc., 1996.

Searle, Mark. *Christening, the Making of Christians.* Essex, Great Britain: Devin Mayhew Ltd., 1977.

Chapter 6: Jesus' Greatest Gift

Hellwig, Monica. *The Eucharist and the Hunger of the World.* New York: Paulist Press, 1976.

Jungman, Josef. *The Mass of the Roman Rite: Its Origins and Development.* New York: Benziger, 1951.

Brennan, Patrick. *Re-Imagining the Parish: Base Community, Adulthood and Family Consciousness.*

New York: Crossroad, 1990.

Forster, Patricia M. OSF and Sweetser, Thomas P., SJ. *Transforming the Parish, Models for the Future.* Franklin: WI: Sheed and Ward, 1993, 1999 revised.

Sweetser, Thomas P. SJ. *The Parish as Covenant, A Call to Pastoral Partnership,* Lanham, MD: Rowman & Littlefield Publishers, Inc., 2001.

Wilkes, Paul. *Excellent U.S. Parishes: The Guide to the Best Places and Practices.* Mahwah, NJ: Paulist Press, 2001.

Chapter 7: Church Leadership

Brockman, James. *Romero, A Life.* Maryknoll, NY: Orbis Books, 1989.

Brown, Raymond. *Priest and Bishop: Biblical Reflections.* New York: Paulist Press, 1990.

Hebblethwaite, Peter. *In the Vatican.* Bethesda, MD: Adler & Adler, 1986.

_____ *Pope John XXIII, Shepherd of the Modern World.* Garden City, NY: Doubleday, 1985.

_____ *Paul VI, the First Modern Pope.* New York: Paulist Press, 1993.

_____ *The Year of the Three Popes.* Cleveland, OH: Collins, 1978.

Rausch, Thomas. *Authority and Leadership in the Church. Past Directions and Future Possibililties.* Wilmington, DE: Michael Glazier, 1989.

_____. *Pope Benedict XVI: an Introduction to His Theological Vision.* New York: Paulist Press, 2009.

Reese, Thomas. *Archbishop: Inside the Power Structure of the American Catholic Church.* San Francisco: Harper & Row, 1989.

Rourke, Thomas R. *The Social and Political Thought of Benedict XVI.* Lanham, MD: Rowman & Littlefield Publishers, 2010.

Sobrino, Jon. *Archbishop Romero: Memories and Reflections.* Maryknoll, NY: Orbis Books, 1990.

Tang, Dominic. *How Inscrutable His Ways! Memoirs 1951-1981.* Hong Kong: Caritas Printing Centre, 1991, 2nd edition.

463

Thornton, John F. and Varenne, Susan B. *The Essential Pope Benedict XVI: His Central Writings and Speeches.* New York: HarperSanFrancisco, 2007.

Wilkes, Paul. *The Education of an Archbishop: Travels with Rembert Weakland.* Maryknoll, NY: Orbis Books, 1993.

Papacy

Brown, Raymond, Karl Donfried, and John Reuman, eds. *Peter in the new Testament.* Minneapolis: Augsburg Publishing House, 1973.

Empie, Paul and T. Murphy, eds. *Papal Primacy and the Universal Church.* Minneapolis: Augsburg Publishing House, 1974

Eno, Robert B, SS. *The Rise of the Papacy.* Wilmington, DE: Michael Glazier, Inc., 1990.

O'Malley, John W. *A History of the Popes: from Peter to the Present.* Lanham, MD: Sheed & Ward, 2010.

Robinson, Archbishop Geoffry. *Confronting Power and Sex in the Catholic Church: Reclaiming the Spirit of Jesus.* Mulgrave, Victoria, N.S.W.: John Garratt Publisher, 2007.

Schatz, Klaus. *Papal Primacy, from Its Origins to the Present.* Collegeville, MN: Liturgical Press, 1996.

Chapter 8: Trail Blazers: Men and Women Religious

Butler, Anne M. *Across God's Frontiers, Catholic Sisters in the America West, 1850-1920.* Charlotte, N.C.: The University of North Carolina Press, 2013.

Lernoux, Penny. *Hearts on Fire.* Maryknoll, NY: Orbis Books, 1992.

Martin, James. *In Good Company, the Fast Track from the Corporate World to Poverty, Chastity and Obedience.* Franklin, WI: Sheed & Ward, 2000.

_____. *A Jesuit Off-Broadway, Center Stage with Jesus, Judas, and Life's Big Questions.* Chicago: Loyola Press, 2007.

_____. *The Jesuit Guide to Almost Everything, A Spirituality for Real Life.* New York: HarperCollins, 2010.

Rogers, Carole G. *Habits of Change, An Oral History of American Nuns.* New York, NY: Oxford University Press, 2011.

Rupley, Elizabeth. *The Lord is Their Portion: The Story of the Religious Orders and How They Shaped Our World.* Grand Rapids, MI: Eerdmans, 2011.

Schneiders, Sandra, I.H.M. *Prophets in Their Own Country: Women Religious Bearing Witness to the Gospel in a Troubled Church.* Maryknoll, NY: Orbis Books, 2011.

Ware, Ann. *Midwives of the Future: American Sisters Tell Their Story.* Kansas City: MO: Leaven Press, 1985.

Part III: The Church's Mission

Chapter 9: The Great Commission

Beyerly, Timothy E. *The Great Commission: Models of Evangelization in American Catholicism.* NY: Paulist Press, 2008.

Fontana, Michela. *Matteo Ricci, A Jesuit in the Ming Court.* Lanham, MD: Rowman & Littlefield Publishers, 2011.

Griffiths, Bede. *The Marriage of East and West.* London: Fount Paperbacks, 1983.

Hillman, Eugene. *Many Paths: A Catholic Approach to Religious Pluralism.* New York: Orbis Books, 1989.

Phan, Peter C. *Christianity with an Asian Face: Asian American Theology in the Making.* Maryknoll, NY: Orbis Books, 2003.

Pope Paul VI, "Evangelization in the Modern World," in *The Pope Speaks, The Church Documents Quarterly* 21(#1, 1976): 4-51.

Schineller, Peter. *A Handbook on Inculturation.* New York/Maweh: Paulist Press, 1990.

Shorter, Aylward. *Toward a Theology of Inculturation.* London: Geoffrey Chapman, 1988.

United States Catholic Bishops, *Heritage and Hope, Evangelization in the United States.* Washington, DC: U.S. Catholic Conference, 1991.

Chapter 10: Spirituality & Spiritualities

Barry, William. *Spiritual Direction & the Encounter with God.* New York/Mahwah,NJ: Paulist Press, 1992.

Conn, Joan. *Spirituality and Personal Maturity.* Mahwah, NJ: Paulist Press, 1989.

Cunninghamn, Lawrence, *The Meaning of Saints.* San Francisco: Harper & Row, 1980.

Egan, Harvey. *What Are They Saying About Mysticism.* New York: Paulist Press,1982.

Gonzalez, Michelle A. *Embracing Latina Spirituality: A Woman's Perspective.* Cincinnati, OH:L St. Anthony Messenger Press, 2009.

Groeschel, Benedict J. and Kevin Perrotta. *The Journey Towards God: In the Footsteps of the Great Spiritual Writers, Catholic, Orthodox and Protestant.* Ann Arbor, MI: Charis Books, 2002.

Merton, Thomas. *New Seeds of Contemplation.* Norfolk, CN: New Directions, 1961.

Nouwen, Henri. *Making All Things New: An Invitation to the Spiritual Life.* San Francisco: Harper & Row, 1981.

Pennington, Basil, OCSA. *Centering Prayer.* Garden City, NY: Doubleday, 1980.

Part IV: A World Church

Chapter 11: "That All May Be One"

Baptism, Eucharist & Ministry 1982-1990, Report on the Process and Responses. Geneva: WCC Publications, 1990.

Congar, Yves. *Diversity and Communion.* Mystic, CN: Twenty-Third Publications, 1985.

Dessaux, Jacques. *Twenty Centuries of Ecumenism.* New York/Ramsey, NJ: Paulist Press, 1984.

DeVille, Adam J. *Orthodoxy and the Roman Papacy, Ut Unum Sint and the Prospects of East-West Unity.* Notre Dame, IN: University of Notre Dame Press, 2011.

Dupuis, Jacques. *Toward a Christian Theology of Religious Pluralism.* Maryknoll, NY: Orbis Books, 1997.

The Final Report, Anglican-Roman Catholic International Commission. Washington, DC: U.S. Catholic Conference, 1982.

Flannery, Edward. *The Anguish of the Jews: Twenty-Three Centuries of Anti-Semitism.* New York: Macmillan, 1965.

Fries, H. and Karl Rahner, *Unity of the Churches, an Actual Possibility.* Philadelphia: Fortress Press, 1985.

Groupe des Dombes. *For the Conversion of the Churches.* Geneva: World Council of Churches, 1993.

Hughes, John Jay. *Absolutely Null and Void: An Account of the 1896 Papal Condemnation of Anglican Orders.* Washington, DC: Corpus Books, 1968.

Kaspar, Walter, ed. *The Petrine Ministry, Catholics and Orthodox in Dialogue.* Mahwah,NJ: The Newman Press (Paulist Press), 2006.

Kilcourse, George. *Double Belonging, Interchurch Families and Christian Unity.* New York/Mahwah, NJ: Paulist Press, 1992.

Nilson, Jon. *Nothing Beyond the Necessary: Roman Catholicism and the Ecumenical Future.* Mahwah, NJ: Continuum Publishing Group. 2009.

Panikkar, Raymundo. *The Intra-Religious Dialogue.* Mahwah, NJ: Paulist Press, 1978.

Tavard, George. *A Review of Anglican Orders, The Problem and the Solution.* Collegeville, MN: The Liturgical Press, 1990.

Ware, Timothy. *The Orthodox Church* . New York: Penguin Books, 1983.

Chapter 12: Best Kept Secret

Coleman, John, ed. *One Hundred Years of Catholic Social Thought.* Maryknoll, NY: Orbis Books, 1991.

Dorr, Donal. *The Social Justice Agenda: Justice, Ecology, Power and the Church,* Maryknoll, NY: Orbis Books, 1991.

John Paul II. *Centesimus Annus (On the Hundredth Anniversary of Rerum Novarum).* Washington, DC: U.S. Catholic Conference, 1991.

_____ *Laborem Exercens (On Human Work).* Washington, DC: U.S. Catholic Conference, 1981.

_____ *Sollicitudo Rei Socialis (On Social Concern).* Washington, DC: U.S. Catholic Conference, 1988.

Lappe, Francis, and Joseph Collins. *World Hunger: Twelve Myths.* New York: Grove Press, 1986.

Massaro, Thomas. *Living Justice: Catholic Social Teaching in Action.* Lanham, MD: Rowman & Littlefield Publishers, 2008.

Paul VI. *Populorum Progressio (The Development of Peoples)*. Washingon, DC: U.S. Catholic Conference, 1967.

U.S. Catholic Bishops. *The Challenge of Peace*. Washington, DC: U.S. Catholic conference, 1983.

_____ *Economic Justice for All*. Washington, DC: U.S. Catholic Conference, 1986.

Chapter 13: Liberation Theologies

Alvarado, Elvia, and Medea Benjamin, ed. *Don't Be Afraid, Gringo, A Honduran Woman Speaks from the Heart*. San Francisco: Institute for Food and Development Policy, 1987.

Boff, Leonardo. *Church, Charism and Power*. New York: Crossroad, 1985.

Casaldaliga, Pedro. *I Believe in Justice and Hope*. Notre Dame, IN. Fides/Claretian, 1978.

Ferm, Deane. *Profiles in Liberation: Portraits of Third World Theologians*. Mystic, CN: Twenty-Third Publications, 1988.

_____ Ford, John, and Darlis Swan. *Twelve Tales Untold: A Study Guide for Ecumenical Reception*. Grand Rapids, MI: William Eerdmans Publishing Co., 1993.

Gutierrez, Gustavo. *A Theology of Liberation*. Maryknoll, NY: Orbis, 1990.

Kita, Bernice. *What Prize Awaits Us: Letters from Guatemala*. Maryknoll, NY: Orbis, 1988.

Lernoux, Penny. *Cry of the People*. Garden City, NY: Doubleday, 1980.

McGovern, Arthur. *Liberation Theology and Its Critics*. Maryknoll, NY: Orbis, 1989.

Medellin Conference of Latin American Bishops. *The Church in the Present-Day Transformation of Latin America in the Light of the Council*. Washington, DC: U.S. Catholic Conference, 1973.

Schlesinger, Stephen and Kinzer, Stephen. *Bitter Fruit: the Untold Story of the Coup in Guatemala*. Garden City, NJ: Doubleday, 1982.

Tamez, Elsa, ed. *Through Her Eyes, Women's Theology from Latin America*. Maryknoll, NY: Orbis,

Chapter 14: Living Ethically

Cahill, Lisa Soelle., Garvey, John, and Kennedy, Frank T. editors. *Sexuality in the U.S. Catholic Church: Crisis and Renewal.* Herder & Herder Book/Crossoad Publishing Company, 2006.

Curran, Charles. *The Living Tradition of Catholic Moral Theology.* Notre Dame, IN: University of Notre Dame Press, 1992.

_____. *Catholic Moral Theology in the United States, a History.* Washington, D.C.: Georgetown University Press, 2008.

Dwyer, John. *Human Sexuality: A Christian View.* Kansas City, MO: Sheed & Ward, 1987.

Ferder, Fran and Heagle, John. *Tender Fires, The Spiritual Premise of Sexuality.* New York: Crossroad P Publishing Co. 2002.

Gula, Richard. *Reason Informed by Faith, Foundations of Catholic Morality.* New York: Paulist Press, 1989.

Hanigan, James. *As I Have Loved You: the Challenge of Christian Ethics.* Mahwah, NJ: Paulist Press, 1986.

_____ *Homosexuality: The Test Case for Christian Social Ethics.* New York: Paulist Press, 1988.

MacNamara, Vincent. *Love, Law and Christian Life: Basic Attitudes of Christian Morality.* Wilmington, DE: Michael Glazier, 1988.

Mahoney, John. *The Making of Moral Theology.* New York: Clarendon Press, 1990.

Noonan, John T. *A Church That Can and Cannot Change: The Development of Catholic Moral Theology for the 21st Century.* Notre Dame, IN: University of Notre Dame Press, 2005.

U.S. Bishops. *Human Sexuality: A Catholic Perspective for Education and Lifelong Learning.* Washington, DC: U.S. Catholic Conference, 1990.

Part V: A Church for the Future

Chapters 15 and 16: Urgent Challenges

Beaudoin, Tom. *Virtual Faith: The Irreverent Spiritual Quest of Generation X.* Jossey-Boss Publisher, 2000.

Carr, Anne. *Transforming Grace: Christian Tradition and Women's Experience*. San Francisco: Harper & Row, 1988.

Chittister, Joan. *Winds of Change: Women Challenge the Church*. Kansas City: Sheed & Ward, 1986.

Congar, Yves. *True and False Reform in the Catholic Church*. Collegeville, MN: Liturgical Press, 2011.

Cozzens, Donald B. *Freeing Celibacy*. Collegeville, MN: The Liturgical Press, 2006.

_____. *The Changing Face of the Priesthood, A Reflection on the Crisis of the Priest's Soul*.
Collegeville, MN: The Liturgical Press, 2000.

_____ *Sacred Silence: Denial and the Crisis in the Church*. Collegeville, MN: Liturgical Press, 2002.

Daigler, Mary Jeremy. *Incompatible with God's Design: A History of Women's Ordination Movement in the United States Roman Catholic Church*. Scarecrow Press, 2013.

Hoge, Dean; Dinges, William; Johnson, Mary; Gonzalez, Joan Jr. *Young Adult Catholics: Religion in the Culture of Choice*. Notre Dame, IN: University of Notre Dame Press, 2001.

Lacey, Michael J. and Oakley, Francis. *The Crisis of Authority in Catholic Modernity*. New York: Oxford University Press, 2011.

Macy, Gary; Diteway, William T. and Zagano, Phyllis. *Women Deacons, Past, Present, Future*. Mahwah, NJ: Paulist Press, 2002.

Macy, Gary. *The Hidden History of Women's Ordination: Female Clergy in the Medieval West*. New York: Oxford University Press, 2008.

Manuel, Gerdnio Sonny. *Living Celibacy: Healthy Pathways for Priests*. New York: Paulist Press, 2013.

Mannion, Gerard. *Ecclesiology and Postmodernity: Questions for the Church of Our Time*. Collegeville, MN: Liturgical Press, 2007.

Oakley, Francis and Russett, Bruce. *Governance, Accountability, and the Future of the Catholic Church*. New York: Continuum, 2004.

O'Callaghan, Joseph F. *Electing Our Bishops, How the Catholic Church Should Choose Its Leaders:* Lanham, MD: Rowman & Littlefield Publishers, 2007.

O'Mahony, T.P. *Why the Catholic Church Needs Vatican III.* Dublin: Columbia Press, 2010.

Pruseck, Bernard. *The Church Unfinished: Ecclesiology through the Centuries.* New York: Paulist Press, *2004.*

Swidler, Leonard. *Making the Church Our Own: How We Can Reform the Catholic Church from the Ground Up.* Franklin, WI: Sheed & Ward, 2005.

Unsworth, Tim. *The Last Priests in America: Conversations with Remarkable Men.* New York: Crossroad, 1991.

U.S. Bishops. *Partners in the Mystery of Redemption: A Pastoral Response to Women's Concerns for Church and Society.* Washington, DC: U.S. Catholic Conference, 1988.

Zagono, Phyllis. *Holy Saturday: An Argument for the Restoration of the Female Deaconate in the Catholic Church.* New York: Crossroad Publishing. 2000.

_____ *Women & Catholicism: Gender, Communion and Authority.* New York: Palgrave Macmillan, 2011.

Chapter 17: Core Values

Dulles, Avery. *A Church to Believe In: Discipleship and the Dynamics of Freedom.* New York: Crossroad, 1982.

Groome, Thomas H. *Will There Be Faith?* New York: HarperOne, 2011.

Kelly, Matthew. *Rediscovering Catholicism: Journeying toward Our Spiritual North Star.* Cincinnati, OH: Beacon Publishing, 2002.

Leach, Michael. *Why Stay Catholic? Unexpected Answers to a Life-changing Question.* Chicago: Loyola Press, 2011.

O'Malley, William J. *The WOW Factor, Bringing Catholic Faith to Life.* Maryknoll, NY: Orbis Books, 2011.

Osborne, Kenan. *Priesthood: A History of Ordained Ministry in the Roman Catholic Church.* Mahwah, NJ: Paulist Press, 1988.

O'Toole, James M. *The Faithful, A History of Catholics in America.* Cambridge, MA: Belknap Press, in Harvard University Press, 2008.

Rohr, Richard and Martos, Joseph. *Why Be Catholic? Understanding Our Experience and Tradition.* Cincinnati, OH: St. Anthony Press, 1989.

Chapter 18: Hope-Filled Future

Allen, John. *The Future Church: How Ten Trends are Revolutionizing the Church.* New York: Doubleday, 2009.

Buhlmann, Walbert. *The Church of the Future: A Model for the Year 2001.* Maryknoll, NY: Orbis, 1986.

Cahill, Brian. "Why I Stay in the Church." *National Catholic Reporter.* May 27, 2011.

Carroll, Colleen. *The New Faithful: Why Young Catholics are Embracing Christian Orthodoxy.* Chicago: Loyola Press, 2002.

Dulles, Avery. *The Resilient Church: The Necessity and Limits of Adaptation.* Garden City, NY: Doubleday, 1977.

Haring, Bernard, CSSR. *My Hope for the Church. Critical Encouragement for the Twenty-First Century.* Liguori, MO: Liguori-Triumph, 1997.

O'Murchu, Diarmuid. *Adult Faith: Growing in Wisdom and Understanding.* Maryknoll, NY: Orbis Books, 2010.

Roberts, Tom. *The Emerging Catholic Church, A Community's Search for Itself.* Maryknoll, NY: Orbis Books, 2011.

Glossary

These glossary entries are printed in bold in their first appearance in the text. The following references were helpful in composing the explanation given below: Gerald O'Collins and Edward Farragia, *A Concise Dictionary of Theology* (New York/Mahwah, NJ: Paulist Press, 1991); John Hardon, *Modern Catholic Dictionary,* (Garden City, NY: Doubleday, 1980).

Acts of the Apostles. The 28-chapter account attributed to the evangelist Luke of the church's origin and growth from Jesus' Resurrection to Paul's imprisonment in Rome. Peter and the Jerusalem community dominate the first half; Paul's mission to the Gentiles in his travels throughout Asia Minor founding churches compose the second half.

Agape. (Greek, love) The New Testament term to designate the love of God or Christ for us; the common meal every Christian held in connection with the Eucharist.

Advent: Four week period of preparation for Christmas which begins the liturgical year.

Anglican Communion: Various national churches which arose from the English Reformation of Henry VIII in the sixteenth century which recognize the honorary leadership of the Archbishop of Canterbury.

Annulment: Official declaration after thorough investigation by a church court that a marriage did not in fact exist because of a pre-existing impediment to a valid sacramental marriage.

Apostolic See (Latin, *sedes* or seat): The governing and spiritual authority of the pope over the Catholic Church symbolized by his chair (seat) as bishop of Rome. Another term is Holy See. Both terms include the various offices of the curia that assist the pope in church government.

Apostolic succession: The office given by Christ to the 12 Apostles continues in the church today in properly ordained bishops. In a broader sense, the unbroken continuity in essential belief and practice between the church today and the church Christ founded on the Apostles; this continuity is expressed in bishops being the successors of the Apostles.

Assumption: the dogma defined by Pope Pius XII stating that at the end of her earthly life Mary, the mother of Jesus, was taken up body and soul into eternal glory. From the fifth century, eastern Christians celebrated the "dormition" (falling asleep) of Mary.

Baptist: Numerous evangelical churches that trace their origin to the seventeenth century when they broke with the Anglican Church of England. Only believers who make a conscious profession of faith in Christ are baptized. Each local congregation is relatively autonomous.

Biblical criticism: The scientific study and analysis of the human elements in the writing of the Bible. Called the historical-critical method, it includes textual, historical, form, tradition, redaction and literary criticism. It does not deny the divine inspiration of the Scriptures as the inspired word of God.

Cardinal: The honorary title conferred by the pope to archbishops of major dioceses throughout the world. The College of Cardinals act as advisers to the pope. Their major office is to elect the pope.

Carmelites: The contemplative Discalced (shoeless) Carmelites founded by St. Teresa of Avila in 1563 live enclosed lives of poverty, abstinence from meat, prayer and manual labor. The Carmelite order for men was founded in the twelfth century, taking its name from Mt. Carmel in Palestine.

Catholic Worker: The newspaper of the Catholic Worker Movement founded by Dorothy Day (1897-1980) to promote concern for the poor and oppressed, for social justice, and pacifist non-violence against war.

Catechumenate. The lengthy period of preparation for baptism in the early church culminating in the scrutinies and prayers of healing on the third, fourth and fifth Sundays of Lent and baptism during the Easter Vigil. Catechumens were those preparing for baptism.

Celibacy: The renunciation of marriage. In the Latin tradition of the Roman Catholic Church celibacy is required of candidates for the priesthood; permanent deacons are not permitted to marry after their ordination. Eastern Catholics have a married clergy. Orthodox priests and deacons are generally married but bishops must be celibate.

Charism, (Greek, gift or talent): St. Paul's term for special gifts given Christians by the Holy Spirit. The **charismatic renewal** is a movement within the Catholic Church since Vatican II of persons (**charismatics**) who experience the gifts of the Holy Spirit, especially joy in prayer and sometimes healing and speaking in tongues.

Collegiality: Reponsibility for the whole church shared by the bishops in communion among themselves and with the head of the college of bishops, the pope. Collegiality is most fully exercised in an ecumenical council but also through episcopal conferences and synods of bishops. It was a major emphasis of Vatican II.

Communion (together with): Multiple usage in this book: to express how the Catholic Church is united worldwide through bishops and their people being "**in communion with**" the successor of Peter the pope (Vatican II thus described the worldwide church as a **communion of local churches** to describe the Council's favored **communion model** of future church union -- churches re-establishing communion with each other and the bishop of Rome; the **communion of saints** is the spiritual union between Christ and all Christians, whether already in heaven (or purgatory) or still living on earth.

Concordat: Formal agreement between the Vatican state and various nations to protect the spiritual and temporal interests of the Catholic Church and the rights of its members in those countries.

Conscience: The ability to judge and choose a course of action in accordance with the law God has "written" in every human person (Rom 2:12-16).

Conscientization (raising awareness): The effort in liberation theology to cause native peoples, oppressed for centuries, to realize their human and Christian dignity and rights and the causes of their oppression in order to rise above their condition and fashion their own destiny.

Contemplation: Form of silent prayer in which the mind and imagination are less active and the person "contemplates" or looks at and rests in the love of God and the divine mysteries.

Convergence: The term used to express drawing closer in common understanding rather than full theological and faith agreement resulting from the dialogues between the Catholic Church and the various Christian churches since Vatican II.

Conversion Complete change of heart or turning away from sin, selfishness, attachment to worldly values toward God, spiritual values, and living for God and others. Biblical word is *metanoia* (Greek, change of mind).

Counter-Reformation: Movement of Catholic reform that began in reaction to the Protestant Reformation, was legislated for in the Council of Trent (1545-63), and carried out in succeeding centuries especially in Europe.

Covenant: Special formal friendship-love agreement or compact between God and the Jewish people; between Jesus and Christians through his blood on the cross; between a Christian man and woman in a sacramental marriage.

Curia, Roman or Vatican: The large organization in Rome of administrative and judicial offices, especially the nine curial congregations, that help the pope govern and lead the universal Catholic Church.

Devotions: Non-liturgical prayers and practices like the way of the cross or the rosary that nourish Catholics' spiritual lives and deepen their faith and love of God.

Dialogues, theological: Scholarly discussions between theologians from the divided Christian churches to clarify differences, discover common faith, and reach theological agreement where possible. Vatican II encouraged Catholics to dialogue also with members of non-Christian religions (interreligious dialogue) and with the world at large.

Dissent: Disagreement with official non-infallible teaching of the church. Private dissent as a conscience matter is permissible; the tension today concerns public dissent. Dissent has played a major role in both the development of doctrine and change in church discipline throughout the centuries.

Doctrine: Official church teaching in its many forms. Not to be confused with dogma, a divinely-revealed truth proclaimed infallibly by the church and binding permanently on all Catholics. **Development of doctrine** (1) is growth in the church's understanding of the truths of divine revelation since the age of the Apostles. The substantial truth of revealed mystery remains unchanged; the church's understanding with the help of the Holy Spirit and confronted with historical events can change or "develop." Such "new" teaching cannot contradict the original revealed "deposit of faith." Theologians are indispensable in the development of doctrine.

Dulles, Avery: Jesuit theologian recognized as perhaps the leading American ecclesiologist owing to his broad scholarship, balance, and clear writing. Convert to the Catholic faith and son of former Secretary of State John Foster Dulles.

Encyclical :(Greek, circular letter): A bishop's letter intended for wide circulation. Since the eighteenth century a letter addressed by the pope to the whole Catholic Church; such papal encyclicals are not infallible but are authoritative statements of the ordinary magisterium.

Enlightenment, Age of: Movement starting in seventeenth-century Europe that resisted authority and tradition, defended freedom and human rights, stressed empirical methods in scientific research and the use of reason. Many of its followers rejected divine revelation and miracles, strongly opposed Christianity, and supported biblical criticism. It contributed a healthy respect for human reason and religious freedom.

Episcopacy (Greek, overseer, hence bishop): Church government by bishops. The world's bishops make up the **episcopate** as **episcopal college** they are successors of the apostolic college. An episcopal conference is the assembly of bishops of a certain country or region that meet regularly.

Euthanasia (Greek, mercy killing): Use of direct, intentional means to bring about a suffering person's death or the failure to use reasonable ordinary means to keep a person alive.

Evangelicals (Greek, good news or gospel): Term for Protestant Christians who stress justification by faith and the supreme authority of the Bible.

Evangelization: The proclamation to all peoples (Matt. 28:19-20) and to all cultures the good news about Jesus Christ.

Excommunication : (Latin, exclusion from communion): Church penalty for specific serious moral acts or faith denial that excludes from receiving the sacraments and being part of the church community.

Faith and Order: Unit within the World Council of Churches in Geneva, Switzerland, devoted to studying theological problems dealing with faith belief and church ordinations in order to achieve the unity of the separated Christian churches.

Fatalism: The belief among native peoples of Latin America that their poverty and oppressed condition was God's will and therefore to be accepted as their cross in life in the hope of a better eternal life. Liberation theology seeks to destroy this attitude.

Fathers of the Church: Title given to the great Christian thinkers and writers (mostly bishops) beginning with St. Clement of Rome (d. 97 AD) and ending in the west with St. Isidore of Seville (d. 636) and in the east with St. John of Damascus (d. 749). Because of their outstanding teaching and holiness, their unanimous consent became a norm of orthodox doctrine in theological controversies.

Fundamental option (basic choice): The radical orientation of one's life toward or away from God by a personal, serious decision that determines one's essential moral and religious life situation for good or evil. A person's destiny is determined by this basic choice rather than by individual actions. This theory developed in reaction to a legalism that considered moral actions in isolation from the whole context of one's life and personal growth.

Fundamentalism: Movement in twentieth-century Protestantism., especially in the U.S., which interprets the Bible literally without considering its historical formation, literary forms and original meaning -- thus opposing the historical-critical method of biblical criticism.

Glossolalia (Greek, speaking in tongues): A gift of the Holy Spirit by which persons speak in unintelligible words or in foreign languages. The early Christians in the time of St. Paul spoke in tongues; today's charismatics often do the same. Individuals gifted with prophetic inspiration are sometimes able to interpret these utterances to others.

Gustavo Gutierrez: Peruvian priest-scholar who launched liberation theology with his book *A Theology of Liberation* in 1971. Though he continues to publish and lecture, his chosen work is with the poor as pastor in Lima.

Heresy: A false teaching which denies an essential doctrine of the Catholic faith. A **heretic** is a baptized person who deliberately and persistently denies orthodox doctrines of faith.

Hierarchy (Latin, holy authority or order): The ordained ministers in the church, bishops, priests and deacons. By reason of jurisdiction, the hierarchy is made up of pope and bishops. Thus in popular usage the term refers to the pope and bishops. The concept of a hierarchy of bishops-priests-deacons deriving their authority from the sacrament of orders and not from the consent of the people distinguishes the Roman Catholic and Orthodox tradition from Protestant churches.

Hierarchy of truths: The principle enunciated by Vatican II (UR 11) for interpreting the truths of faith by their nearness to the central mystery of faith: the revelation of the Trinity; the Incarnation of the Son; the divinity of Jesus and his saving death and resurrection; and the role of the Holy Spirit. Such "classifying" of truths according to their relative importance can eliminate false emphases and facilitate ecumenical dialogue.

Holy Office. Name applied to the Roman Curia Congregation for the Doctrine of the Faith.

Holy Spirit: The third person of the Trinity, adored and glorified together with the Father and the Son as one in nature and equal in personal dignity with the Father and Son. The work of sanctification is attributed to the Spirit through the Spirit's many gifts. The Spirit came upon the Apostles on Pentecost Sunday to begin the church.

Holy Week: The most solemn and important week in the church's liturgical year that celebrates Jesus' saving death and resurrection. It begins with the blessing and procession with palms on Palm Sunday, recalls Jesus' institution of the Eucharist on Holy Thursday and his passion and death on Good Friday and culminates in the Easter Vigil on Holy Saturday night. In the eastern churches it is known as "The Week of Salvation" or "The Great Week" by the Greek Orthodox.

Icon (Greek, image): A sacred image painted on wood or formed by a mosaic, highly revered by the Orthodox and eastern churches. Icons of Christ, Mary, angels and the Saints present them symbolically rather than realistically. Icons are noted for brilliant colors and spiritual quality and often are valuable works of art.

Immaculate Conception: The dogma defined in 1854 by Pope Pius IX that Mary was free of all sin including original sin from the moment of her conception through the merits of her Son. Her special privilege is celebrated by the western Roman Church on Dec. 8.

Incarnation (Latin, enfleshment): The event of the eternal Son of God, while remaining fully divine, becoming truly and fully human in Jesus of Nazareth by taking on human flesh.

Inculturation: Contemporary term to express how the Christian message and life must be incarnated in the various cultures and peoples of the world.

Indigenous: Refers to peoples originally native to a country as the Mayans in Guatemala, native Americans in the United States. "Indians" as a term for indigenous peoples is inaccurate and resented by them as too often a debasing title.

Institutionalized violence: The moral and physical suffering done to the oppressed peoples of Latin America when the very institutions of society -- health care, education, legal system, police and military, etc. -- far from helping, are deliberately used to oppress poor indigenous peoples in order to keep them in subjection. Liberation theologians call it structural sin.

Jurisdiction (Latin, judgment on what is lawful): The right and duty (legal authority) the pope and bishops possess to govern the church. In practice, bishops get jurisdiction in some matters from the pope, priests from their bishops. Vatican I stated that the pope has full jurisdiction over the whole church.

Kingdom of God : The reign or rule of God in the world at large, especially in the minds and hearts of people. As a *process* of establishing respect-love-obedience for God and justice-love-peace in human affairs, it is called the reign of God; as the *future goal* of this effort it is often referred to as the eschatological or perfect kingdom of God at the end of the world. Jesus' and the church's main mission is to establish and work for the reign and kingdom of God; the church, however, is not to be identified with God's kingdom, which can and does exist outside the church and its members.

Koinonia (Greek, "fellowship," "communion"): Rich ecclesial term used by St. Paul in the early church to refer to the bond of love with Christ and among Christians and between Paul's various churches. Popular term today to express the union which already exists and should further exist between Christians and their separated churches.

Laity (Greek, *laos* or people): The faithful who have been fully incorporated into the church through baptism, confirmation and Eucharist but who have not received holy orders and become clerics. Vatican II sought to restore lay persons in the church to their proper importance and rights.

Lent: The forty-day period beginning with Ash Wednesday of prayer, fasting, almsgiving, penance and conversion to prepare Christians for Easter, the greatest feast of the liturgical year. In the early church Lent was the special time for catechumens to prepare for baptism.

Liturgy (Greek, "public service"): Official community worship, especially the eucharist or Mass.

Local church: The Christian community in union with its bishop, hence the geographical "diocese" made up of one bishop (the Ordinary), his priests and the baptized believing lay members. The universal or worldwide church presided over by the pope as center of unity is, in Vatican II's term, a "communion of local churches." Vatican II restored the importance of the local church and its bishop.

Lutheran: Those churches that follow the basic teachings of Martin Luther, the initiator of the German Reformation: *sola fides* or justification by faith alone, not by good works; *sola gratia* or justification through God's grace alone; and *sola Scriptura* or the Bible, not human traditions, as the only authoritative rule of faith. Lutherans emphasize Christ's cross and human bondage to sin.

Magisterium (Latin, "office of teacher"): The official teaching office of the Catholic Church composed of pope as successor of Peter and all the bishops as successors of the 12 Apostles. The *ordinary*, day-by-day non-infallible magisterium is exercised by the pope and by individual bishops; the *extraordinary* magisterium is exercised when the pope or all bishops in an ecumenical council proclaim a revealed truth to be believed absolutely. In the middle ages theologians and theological faculties exercised a certain kind of magisterium. Despite today's tension between theologians and the ordinary magisterium, theologians and Scripture scholars are an essential aid to the church's teaching office.

Manualist: The name given to the authors of theological manuals or textbooks in the late 17th and 18th centuries that organized and explained Catholic doctrine. Textbooks on moral theology were used in seminaries up to Vatican II to train priests hear confession. They fell into disuse for being too legalistic and lacking Scripture basis.

Martyr (Greek, "witness"): A person who witnesses Christ through his or her freely offered suffering and death rather than deny their faith in Christ and the truths of the Christian faith. Martyrdom is the supreme act of love. The church liturgical calendar is full of Saint-martyrs.

Mass (perhaps from the Latin *ite missa est,* go the mass is ended): Popular term before Vatican II for the full eucharistic liturgy. The terms Eucharist or "THE liturgy" are supplanting "Mass" since Vatican II.

Ministry (Latin, service): Sharing in Christ's roles as prophet, priest and king by all Christians through their baptism and confirmation and the clergy in a special way through the sacrament of orders. Since Vatican II the ministry of the laity has been stressed resulting in a proliferation of lay ministries.

Moral theology: That branch of theology which studies God's revelation in the Scriptures and church teaching, in philosophic reasoning and human experience, and in various sciences to show how Christians ought to live and to determine the rightness or wrongness of human action. **Moral theologians** (17) are professionally trained to practice moral theology for the benefit of the church. acts.

Mysticism: A special, deep experience of union with and knowledge of God freely given as gift by God. Mystical experiences are often accompanied by ecstasy, visions and other phenomena. Genuine **mystics** (7) are dedicated to prayer, sensitive to God's presence in their lives, and show great love of God and other people.

Natural law: The universal, moral law given by God in the very act of creating human beings and able to be known by human reason. Or simply put, God's plan or will for humans "written" into the physical and human natures God created. The Catholic Church has for many centuries followd natural law philosophy in its moral judgments. Moral theologians before and especially since Vatican II have criticized a narrow, rigid understanding of the natural law, developing a more nuanced, complete explanation.

New Evangelization. The effort begun by Pope John Paul II and championed by Benedict XVI to bring the gospel of salvation to the world and particularly to once Christian countries where the practice of the Catholic faith has become minimal.

John Henry Newman: (1801-1890) An Anglican priest, preacher, author, leader of the Oxford movement, he became a Catholic in 1845, was named a Cardinal in 1879, and declared Blessed by Benedict XVI in 2010. His most famous books are *Parochial and Plain Sermons (1833-41), Essay on the Development of Christian Doctrine (1845)* that greatly influenced Vatican II, *Idea of a University (1854) , On Consulting the Faithful in Matters of Doctrine (1859), Apologia pro Vita Sua (1864), Grammar of Assent (1870)..*

Nicene-Constantinopolitan Creed: The creed or statement of Christian belief about God, the divinity and nature of the eternal Son and Jesus, and the divinity of the Holy Spirit. It was formulated at the first ecumenical council at Nicaea (modern Turkey) in 325 and completed at the second council at Constantinople (current Istanbul) in 381. This creed is accepted by all Christians and recited every Sunday at Catholic Eucharists.

Nuncio (Latin, messenger): The pope's representative in a country that has diplomatic relations with the Vatican. The nuncio has the status of ambassador representing the Vatican state. He is always a bishop. In a country not having diplomatic relations with the Vatican, the pope's representative is called an apostolic delegate, as was the case in the United States until recently.

Ordinary: The bishop of a diocese (local ordinary) who has jurisdiction and chief responsibility for his local church. In larger dioceses or archdioceses, the Ordinary is aided by "auxiliary" bishops who do not exercise jurisdiction over the diocese.

Orthodox (Greek, "right belief"): Those eastern churches, generally national churches like the Greek Orthodox (8) and **Russian Orthodox** (1), ruled by a patriarch, which are not in communion with the bishop of Rome as a result of the schism or break finalized in 1054 between the eastern and western portions of Christianity.

Parish (Greek, "neighborhood"): Catholic people living within a specific area of the diocese with their own priest as pastor and their own church building, generally named after a Saint or title of Christ or Mary (Sacred Heart parish, St. Anselm, Holy Redeemer, Star of the Sea -- the titles are ingenious in their variety).

Paschal Mystery. The redemption effected by Christ through his death, resurrection and ascension in which Christians participate through baptism, the eucharist, the other sacraments and their whole life.

Patriarch (Greek, "father who rules"): Since the sixth century the title given to the bishops of Rome, Constantinople, Alexandria, Antioch and Jerusalem, each of whom exercised wide authority within their own area. A title of the pope today is patriarch of the western church. Ecumenical patriarch is the title of the patriarch of Constantinople. Patriarch is the usual title of that bishop with major authority in Orthodox churches today who heads a **patriarchate** (8) made up of Orthodox Christians in a given country or area.

Patriarchy: The mentality and institutionalization of male dominance over women in society and in the church with men holding power and denying it to women. In the Catholic Church today women complain they are excluded from decision-making that affects their lives, the major exclusion being ordination to the priesthood.

Paul: A Jewish Pharisee who severely persecuted Christians until knocked off his horse on the road to Damascus by a vision of the risen Christ. This changed his life; he became the great Apostle to the Gentiles through indefatigably preaching the risen Christ and founding churches all over Asia Minor. His letters to these churches contain profound theology centered on the resurrection of the crucified Jesus.

Pentecost: Originally a major Jewish feast, the Christian feast of Pentecost recalls the day the Holy Spirit descended on Jesus' disciples, Peter preached to the people, and three thousand accepted his

message and were baptized, thus beginning the Christian Church.
Pentecostal (1) churches stress baptism in the Spirit, special gifts like healing and prophecy, and convert-making through aggressive preaching and missionary programs, especially in Latin America.

Poor Clares. Women contemplative religious congregation founded by St. Clare, sister of St. Francis of Assisi.

Popular religiosity: Very personal devotion of indigenous peoples, especially in Latin America, to Saints, Mary and the suffering Christ, expressed in elaborate feast-day celebrations, processions, acting out the suffering and death of Jesus by whole villages on Good Friday, etc. Because "pagan" elements and superstition were intermixed, the church had criticized this popular religion; now it is appreciated and respected as nourishing the faith life of people oppressed for centuries and as helping them cope with their hardships and suffering.

Primacy (Latin "the first seat") of **honor and jurisdiction**: The office of the leading bishop or *primate* in a church and the respect due his rank. The pope is considered by Orthodox and a growing number of Anglicans and some Protestants as the first bishop of the world in terms of *honor* because the Apostle Peter was martyred in Rome. Only Catholics recognize the bishop of Rome's pre-eminent *jurisdiction* or spiritual and teaching authority over the whole church.

Purgatory (Latin, "purification"): A process of purification for those who die in God's friendship and are thus assured of heaven but who need to be purified from the effects of personal sin and to grow spiritually before enjoying the presence of God in heaven. Scripture does not "prove" the existence of purgatory; but the ancient tradition of the church indicates that Christians prayed and offered the Eucharist for their dead loved ones since the second and third centuries. Martin Luther rejected the value of indulgences for the dead and the existence of purgatory. Vatican

II briefly endorsed Catholic teaching on purgatory made by the councils of Florence (1438-45) and Trent (1545-63).

RCIA (Rite of Christian Initiation of Adults): Based on the ancient catechumenate, this ritual introduced after Vatican II in 1972 is a year-long course preparing adults for baptism and entrance into the Catholic Church. They receive the sacraments of Christian initiation -- baptism, confirmation and first Eucharist -- at the Easter Vigil Mass.

Reception: Technical term denoting the process by which official church teachings and decisions are accepted, assimilated and interpreted by the whole church. The "reception" of the papal encyclical *Humanae Vitae* by the entire Catholic Church has been problematic.

Reformation: Though the cry for "reform in head and members" existed in the church at least since the Council of Vienne (1311-12), Reformation popularly refers to the Protestant reform begun by Martin Luther and carried on by John Calvin, Ulrich Zwingli and others in the first part of the sixteenth century. Vatican II acknowledged the need for "continued reformation" in the Catholic Church (UR 6).

Reformed: Term applied to Christians following the teachings of John Calvin in Geneva, Holland and France and John Knox in Scotland. In the United States Presbyterians and the United Churches of Christ formed from various Congregational churches are in the Calvinist-Reformed tradition.

The Restoration: Term used by Cardinal Ratzinger, head of the curial Congregation for the Doctrine of the Faith, to describe the current effort in the Catholic Church to restore traditional values, teachings and discipline alleged to have been lost or distorted since the Second Vatican Council.

Resurrection (Latin, "rising," "being raised"): Not a mere return to earthly life but the passage of Jesus through death to his transformed glorified life. Jesus' resurrection guarantees the resurrection of human beings as the creed states ("resurrection of the body"). The Resurrection is the central truth of Christianity and was the heart of the Apostles' early preaching of the good news.

Revelation (Latin, "taking away the veil"): God's self-communication through creation, historical events, prophets, and especially Jesus Christ in his life, death, resurrection and sending of the Spirit. Thanks to Vatican II, theology understands that God's revelation is on-going today.

Rubric (Latin, "red"): Directives printed in red alongside the main text in black that guide bishops, priests and deacons while celebrating Mass, administering sacraments and preaching. Because of over-emphasis on external actions and minute practices, rubricism came to be looked down on as distracting from the deeper meaning of liturgy.

Sacrament: Any visible sign of God's invisible presence. The **sacraments** (5) of the church are ritual signs through which the church manifests its faith and gives the grace of Christ present in the church and in the signs themselves. Catholics, Orthodox and Anglicans accept seven sacraments; Protestants generally accept only baptism and the Lord's Supper.

Scriptures: The sacred writings inspired by God and expressing the Jewish and Christian faith in a way that is normative for all time. Other terms are the Bible, the Old and New Testaments. Today Hebrew and Christian Scriptures is the more appropriate designation.

Sense of the Faith or of the Faithful (Sensus fidei* or *sensus fidelium): That instinctive sense in matters of the Christian faith possessed by the whole body of Christian believers because guided by the Holy Spirit. Cardinal John Henry Newman (1801-90) developed this theological concept. Since Vatican II theologians have called attention to the importance of the agreement of the faithful rising from their sense of what constitutes Christian faith and practice.

Jon Sobrino: Prominent liberation theologian who teaches theology at the Jesuit Central American University in El Salvador. An extensive writer, his best known works are *Christology at the Crossroads, The True Church and the Poor, Jesus in Latin America, Spirituality of Liberation, Archbishop Romero, Memories and Reflections.*

Social Teaching: Comprehensive body of teaching beginning with Pope Leo XIII in 1891 concerning the rights and obligations of different members of society in their relationship to the common good, both national and international. **Social** deals with the basic rights and corresponding obligations of individuals in society.

Spirituality: Systematic practice of and reflection on a prayerful, devout and disciplined Christian life. Schools or styles of spirituality have often followed the charisms of various religious orders and their founders.

Subsidiarity (Latin, "assistance"): A principle of the social teaching of the church by which decisions and activities that belong to a lower level should not be taken to a higher level. In social and civil life and in the church since Vatican II, this means that central organs of authority should not intervene at the local level which often acts equally as well or better than the higher level.

Syllabus of Errors: A list of 80 errors attached to Pope Pius IX's encyclical *Quanta Cura* in 1864 and expressed in propositions that are strongly condemned.

Synod (Greek, "council"): An official meeting of bishops and other church leaders to determine matters of church doctrine, discipline and worship. These meetings can occur at the international, regional, national or diocesan level. The **Synod of Bishops** mandated by Vatican II, meets every three years in Rome during the Fall to advise the pope in matters of faith, morality and church discipline.

Tradition (Latin, "transmission" or "handing on"): *The* tradition refers to the entire "church in her doctrine, life and worship" (DV 8), that is, the full Christian belief and life. It is to be distinguished from traditions in the plural which refer to particular practices that have accumulated in the church through the centuries. Tradition also refers to the *process* or many ways by which Catholic teaching and life is passed on to succeeding generations.

Trappists: Popular name for Cistercian monks forming a contemplative religious group of men who stress prayer, physical work and penance. Thomas Merton, author of the best seller *Many Storied Mountain* and many books on contemplation and prayer, was the best known American Trappist.

Council of Trent (1545-63): The nineteenth ecumenical council held in the northern Italian city of Trent to meet the grave need for reform in the Catholic Church and respond to the Protestant Reformation. It met for three periods, clarified church doctrine and renewed discipline. Its comprehensive decrees initiated the Catholic Counter-Reformation and resulted in a remarkable revitalization of Catholic life in succeeding centuries.

Ultramontanism (Latin, "beyond the mountains"): A negative term applied to European Catholics after the French Revolution who exaggerated papal authority and looked for all solutions "beyond the Alps" to the authority of Rome. The ultramontane movement culminated in the definition of papal infallibility at Vatican I in 1870.

Universal church: Emphasis on the worldwide Catholic Church and its central authority in the pope and in its organizational structures in Vatican City. The post-Vatican II Catholic Church is experiencing difficulty in balancing emphases between the universal church and the local churches of the Catholic world.

Validity (Latin, "strong" or efficacious"): A term describing the conditions necessary for an action (a sacrament) to be efficacious or really existing, as a valid sacramental marriage. An invalid act or sacrament is one that is null or void. Validity has special ecumenical significance in evaluating Anglican Orders and Protestant sacraments, ministers and ministries.

Made in the USA
Charleston, SC
06 January 2014